T0342279

# ENGLAND'S CROSS OF GOLD

A VOLUME IN THE SERIES

*Cornell Studies in Money*
Edited by Eric Helleiner and Jonathan Kirshner

A list of titles in this series is available at cornellpress.cornell.edu

# ENGLAND'S CROSS OF GOLD

## KEYNES, CHURCHILL, AND THE GOVERNANCE OF ECONOMIC BELIEFS

JAMES ASHLEY MORRISON

CORNELL UNIVERSITY PRESS

*Ithaca and London*

First published 2021 by Cornell University Press

Library of Congress Cataloging-in-Publication Data

Names: Morrison, James Ashley, 1980– author.
Title: England's cross of gold : Keynes, Churchill, and the governance of economic beliefs / James Ashley Morrison.
Description: Ithaca [New York] : Cornell University Press, 2021. | Series: Cornell studies in money | Includes bibliographical references and index.
Identifiers: LCCN 2020046850 (print) | LCCN 2020046851 (ebook) | ISBN 9781501758423 (hardcover) | ISBN 9781501758447 (pdf) | ISBN 9781501758430 (epub)
Subjects: LCSH: Gold standard—England—History— 20th century. | Monetary policy—England—History— 20th century. | Great Britain—Economic policy— 1918–1945.
Classification: LCC HG950.E54 M85 2021 (print) | LCC HG950.E54 (ebook) | DDC 332.4/222094109042—dc23
LC record available at https://lccn.loc.gov/2020046850
LC ebook record available at https://lccn.loc.gov/2020046851

*To Maggie*

# CONTENTS

# Acknowledgments

Two decades ago, Richard Boyd prompted me to consider the political consequences of John Locke's particular understanding of money. Pursuing this simple question has proved more engaging and enriching than I could have imagined. It has begot a family of related questions across several fields. First, theoretically, what is the role of "the invention of money" in liberal accounts of the origins and purpose of political society? Next, historically, how did Locke's rendering of currency as a contract between individuals and between individuals and their sovereign shape the Glorious Revolution, the birth of the Bank of England, and the Great Recoinage? In the field of International Political Economy, did the anointing of the metallic pound necessitate the mercantilism it engendered—the ineluctable imperial struggle for precious metals and the draconian controls at home? Normatively, were the benefits of an inflexible gold sovereign worth the austere, arbitrary, and asinine policies that often followed? Last, in economics, is it possible to bind the sovereign to a different mast—to a different metric of macroeconomic stability beyond just the price of gold in London? Any one of these questions could drive a lifetime of scholarship.

As a first step, this book addresses Richard's original question from the opposite direction. It asks, *What does it take to evolve beyond Locke's monetary legacy?* It takes us to that moment one century ago in which the old orthodoxy faced unprecedented challenges, mounted a heroic (although tragic) response, and ultimately collapsed. It retraces the first crucial steps by which Keynes's revolutionary understanding of money—as a social-political-economic construct with a variable relationship to all material objects—became the new orthodoxy. For now, it must remain to explore the full complement of the consequences of Mr. Keynes.

These past years, the gold standard has been my daily bread. And there are few in my life who have not helped to advance the pursuit of it. I cannot fully express my gratitude in printed words, but I will try to specify the many ways in which others have made this book far better than it would have otherwise been.

It began with Richard Boyd, and happily it continues. He remains a patient mentor and dear friend, challenging my story with equal parts vigor and encouragement. At the University of Chicago, Bill Novak and Steve Pincus modeled the historian's craft of unmasking mythologies; and Allen Sanderson taught me how to think like an economist. At Cambridge University, Mark Goldie shared the incomparable vision that comes from ascending to the shoulders of giants. At Stanford University, Jack Rakove underscored this with a complementary perspective from the American context. Barry Weingast brought me to the nexus of my puzzles: how changing understandings of money have driven the evolution of international order across the last several centuries. Judy Goldstein taught me more ideas—and more about ideas—than anyone. One could not ask for a better supervisor: as devoted as she is demanding. Jerry Cohen and Josh Cohen shared invaluable wisdom as I pushed this analysis into unfamiliar territory.

My colleagues and students at Middlebury College helped me translate these esoteric pursuits into the fodder for this book. Erik Bleich, Allison Stanger, and Sarah Stroup pressed, and helped, me to take my Locke-Smith-Keynes material into conversation with contemporary social science. Zach Mollengarden, Colin Taylor, Avery White, and Spencer Wright did the same with respect to thoughtful nonexperts. My time as a fellow at the Niehaus Center for Globalization and Governance at Princeton University gave me a kind of second graduate education. In particular, John Ikenberry, Harold James, and Bob Keohane offered incisive feedback and innumerable insights into the interwar gold standard.

Many colleagues and friends have contributed to this project in ways that are clear to me but that might not be obvious to them. This book emulates J. T. Lobert's discussion of those obscure committees that define the ideas that rule the day, grapples with Yair Mintzker's account of Inquisitorial power, and follows J. P. Herzog's contention that religious ideas might still be the linchpin of social, political, and even economic order. Tarak Barkawi, George Lawson, and Ayşe Zarakol introduced me to the indispensable tools of history and international relations theory used throughout this book. Ben Ansell, Tom Hale, and Duncan Snidal welcomed me in Oxfordshire and helped me sharpen my understanding of Churchill's decision in particular. I am similarly indebted to friends in and around the Political Economy Round Table: Jeff Colgan, Adam Dean, Julia Gray, Raymond Hicks, Ashley Jester, Maggie Peters, Molly Roberts, David Skarbek, Emily Skarbek, David Steinberg, Felicity Vabulas, and Rachel Wellhausen.

I have presented elements of this book at numerous conferences and various institutions over the last decade. There is a long list of discussants, participants, and hosts who have sped me along and, as necessary, back to the archives. Among them are Andrew Baker, Michael Bordo, Bill Clark, Alexandre Mendes Cunha, Robert Dimand, Barry Eichengreen, Christoph Gelbhaar, Eric Grynaviski, Marina Henke, Ed Mansfield, Nathan Marcus, Kate McNamara, Steve Meardon, Donald Moggridge, Stephen Nelson, Tom Pepinsky, Jon Pevehouse, Andrew Phillips, Paul Poast, Ariel Ron, Aditi Sahasrabuddhe, Claudio Sardoni, Erin Snider, Carlos Eduardo Suprinyak, Adam Tooze, Mat Watson, Stefanie Walter, and Jessica Weeks.

I gained distance, external perspective, and some extra time to write from several stays at Korea University, the Singapore Institute of Management, and Le Centre de Recherches Internationales (CERI) at Sciences Po. I am particularly grateful to Jérôme Sgard for his several reviews of this material and to Ewa Kulesza for helping me to see the British interwar context through new eyes. No experience has proved more inspiring or heartening than my visits to the Duke Center for the History of Political Economy. In addition to offering specific feedback, Bruce Caldwell, Craufurd Goodwin, and Kevin Hoover deepened and broadened my understanding of the intellectual contexts from which Keynes emerged.

This book was helped immeasurably by the opportunity to live and work in England. The London School of Economics itself has been quite generous, particularly in granting the year of leave necessary to bring this book to fruition. The US Centre at the LSE provided extensive support and research assistance across several years. The International Relations Department also sponsored a book workshop in which Olivier Accominotti, Nicole Baerg, Jeff Chwieroth, Jeff Frieden, Doug Irwin, Cova Meseguer, and Natacha Postel-Vinay read an early draft of the manuscript and, together, steered it onto a more promising trajectory. Being near the archives has enabled a deeper, more ambitious historical enterprise. This book depends on the diligent and important work done by the archivists at the Bank of England, the UK National Archives, Churchill College (Cambridge), and the Federal Reserve Bank of New York. It has also depended on the efforts of a small army of research assistants who have helped me to wrangle the many thousands of pages of material I have collected over years: Katherine Bennett, Anna Cooper, Cher Griffith, Olivia Horn, Amalia Kane, Aleksi Lahikainen, Maitrai Lapalikar, Oksana Levkovych, Will Loubier, Keshya Rana, and Conrad Trimbath. Last, I am also grateful to Roger Cunliffe, third Baron Cunliffe, for sharing insights into his grandfather, Walter Cunliffe, and for granting access to the Cunliffe family's personal papers.

More broadly, a thousand conversations around Houghton Street brought me into English political economy in the place where Westminster abuts the City of London. In addition to my many colleagues already listed, I am particularly grateful to Milli Lake, Kate Millar, Mary Morgan, Waltraud Schelkle, Cheryl Schonhardt-Bailey, David Woodruff, and Steve Woolcock. I am most indebted to Peter Trubowitz, whose guidance and feedback kept the project advancing at every difficult turn. If the argument is intelligible, it is because he and Jon Herzog helped me make it so.

I thank the editors at Cornell University Press—Roger Haydon, Jonathan Kirshner, and Eric Helleiner—who had faith in this project and in me. I am immensely grateful to the two anonymous reviewers who provided the most detailed feedback I have ever received. Their guidance helped to excavate the story told here from the far-less-wieldy manuscript that I submitted to them. I regret that this book cannot more fully reflect their many great suggestions for improvement.

Closer to home, my parents set me on this path. My father encouraged my iconoclasm, and my mother nurtured my faith. My daughter Hadley arrived as I finished the first draft of my analysis of Keynes and Churchill. Since then, she has become my most committed—and meticulous—research assistant. Samantha and Penelope have followed, providing welcome diversion and unfaltering moral support. They follow the best examples of their mother, my wife. In our house, "Daddy's book" has been too much like the return to gold it recounts: perennially promised but, seemingly, only ever in the offing. That it should now be made material reality is due to my girls' generosity and to Maggie's magnanimity. I dedicate this book to her, she who has carried this with me on all of our journeys, near and far.

# Note on Transcription

The spellings within all quoted material have been Americanized, and some punctuation and capitalization have been adjusted for the sake of readability.

# PART ONE

## *Introductory*

Belief in the gold standard was the faith of the age. . . .
The war between heaven and hell ignored the money
issue, leaving capitalists and socialists miraculously
united. (Polanyi, *The Great Transformation*)

# CHAPTER 1

# Genesis and Exodus

## The Tragedy of England's Return to Gold

In the spring of 1925, Winston Churchill settled upon a plan to make Britain great again: he would restore the gold standard. This was Churchill's first significant policy initiative since becoming the chancellor of the exchequer in the new Conservative government. It was a quintessential "conservative" policy. For one thing, it advanced the interests of the Conservatives' key constituents. It similarly aligned with the Conservatives' economic ideology. And it fit with tradition. After all, the gold standard traced it roots back to the era of the Glorious Revolution, when the Bank of England was founded and when John Locke convinced Parliament to permanently fix the metallic value of the pound.[1] Since then, the metallic convertibility of the pound had almost never been suspended. The most conspicuous exception was during the French Revolutionary and Napoleonic Wars. Crucially, however, the pound's prewar gold value was restored shortly after the wars ended. Churchill thus faced a strong precedent. For all of these reasons, it seemed fated that he would make the 1920s follow the 1820s by similarly resurrecting the gold standard.

Yet, it was anything but an easy decision. In the wake of the First World War, Parliament extended the UK's wartime capital controls. This gave the monetary authorities some time in which to prepare for the return. But it also created an opportunity for the revered economist—and feared polemicist—John Maynard Keynes to wage an aggressive, highly visible campaign against this very course of action. Driving up the value of the pound, Keynes explained, really meant driving down prices and wages—and, thus, exacerbating national unemployment. With more than a million Britons already out of work, Churchill could scarcely afford to ignore these warnings. Indeed, he did not. He took them more seriously than did most of his colleagues in the Treasury, in the Bank of England, and in the Conservative Party.

Yet after much consternation, Churchill resolved to maintain the long continuity of this institution, whatever the cost.[2] Parliament's capital controls were not due to expire until the end of 1925, but on the afternoon of April 28, Churchill informed the House of Commons, "We have . . . decided . . . that a general license will be given . . . for the export of gold bullion from today. We thus resume our international position as a gold standard country from the moment of [this] declaration."[3] With that, the United Kingdom was "back on gold."

It was a disaster. The UK began to hemorrhage reserves immediately, losing nearly two million pounds' worth of gold in as many weeks.[4] In the months that followed, the overvalued pound hammered the UK's export industries; but, committed to the gold parity, the Bank of England refused to cut interest rates. Unemployment swelled to 1.75 million.[5] The following spring, the Trades Union Congress organized a national general strike. It brought Britain to the brink of revolution. Several million workers downed tools and walked out. Prime Minister Stanley Baldwin denounced the action as "a challenge to Parliament and . . . the road to anarchy and ruin."[6] Rather than seeking absolution, Churchill took to the offensive in a massive media blitz. "It is a very much more difficult task to feed the nation than it is to wreck it," he told one skeptical editor.[7] There were surprisingly few physical assaults. But saboteurs derailed trains and cut the power to the London docks, imperiling the capital's food supply. When mobs began burning public buses, the Conservative government deputized "auxiliary constables," deployed tanks on the streets, and dispatched warships to the UK's industrial north.[8]

These were only the immediate, local results. The long-run and systemic consequences were vastly worse. Churchill's announcement set the tone—and the standard—for the other countries of the world: despite the wartime inflation, the UK would do whatever it took to drive the pound back to its prewar gold parity.[9] The effects were as lamentable as the motivations were laudable. "Far from being synonymous with stability," Eichengreen has shown, "the gold standard itself was the principal threat to financial stability and economic prosperity, between the wars." It became "a central factor in the worldwide [Great] Depression," and "[economic] recovery proved possible . . . only after abandoning the gold standard."[10] The implications for international relations were worse still. "So far from currency *laissez-faire* having promoted the international division of labor," Keynes subsequently observed, ". . . it has been a fruitful source of all those clumsy hindrances to trade which suffering communities have devised in their perplexity as being better than nothing in protecting them from the intolerable burdens flowing from currency disorders."[11] And as trade war led to real war across the 1930s, Keynes exclaimed, "Never in history was there a method devised of such efficacy for setting each country's advantage at variance with its neighbors' as the international gold (or, formerly, silver) standard. For it made domestic prosperity directly dependent on a competitive pursuit of markets and a competitive appetite for the precious metals."[12] Thus, the return to gold in the 1920s—the very paragon of classical liberal political economy in action—both sowed the seeds of the Great Depression and propelled beggar-thy-neighbor international relations.

Why did Churchill drive the world down this road? Why was Keynes unable to change this calamitous course? Why, as William Jennings Bryan had famously lamented, must humanity be crucified upon this cross of gold?

The passage of time has only underscored the significance of this essential puzzle. There are the ceaselessly fascinating historical and counterfactual questions of whether the calamities of the 1930s and 1940s could have been avoided had the UK chosen a more attainable, less ambitious course. Perhaps for this reason, debates about the interwar gold standard have become central to the study of international political and economic relations. Thus, since Polanyi's landmark *Great Transformation*, several generations of scholars have analyzed the structures—material and ideational, system level and subsystem level— that led the UK, and the world, down this perilous path.

And yet the gold standard is back. It is back in spirit in currency unions like the Eurozone, in the competitive undervaluation of China's renminbi, and in the global propagation of financial crises. In Europe, the orthodoxy once again reigns supreme as the commitment to limit inflation everywhere ensures that changes in the money supply are not optimal anywhere. For surplus countries like Germany, only careful labor market management prevents wage-price spirals. For deficit countries like Greece, all other policy goals are subordinated to retain the euro—the supply of which they do not control, the destabilizing flows from which they cannot block, and the austerity for which they must abide.[13] China, too, has discovered the benefits of being a surplus country. Its foreign economic policy can only be described as neomercantilism. Of course, the People's Bank amasses reserves so as to retain export markets rather than promoting exports so as to acquire reserves, but the trade war this instigates is indistinguishable from those engendered by the gold standard a century ago.[14] For now, our global economy remains as deeply integrated as ever before—for better and for worse. The good goes in every direction, and so too does the bad. With a level of capital market integration that rivals that brought by the gold standard system, it is hardly surprising that the latest financial crisis became a global one—and that it swept us into a Great Recession to rival the Great Depression. Of course, gold plays no formal role in any of these instances, and yet the international dynamics are precisely those brought—imposed—by the gold standard itself.

At the same time, a growing number of pivotal policymakers have spoken *explicitly* with fondness about the gold standard era. The last several presidential elections have seen increasing support among Republicans for another return to gold. Senator Ted Cruz was emphatic: "Instead of adjusting monetary policy according to whims and getting it wrong over and over again and causing booms and busts, what the Fed should be doing is . . . keeping our money tied to a stable level of gold."[15] The experience of the 1920s taught Keynes and Churchill the dangers of prioritizing a strong currency over the preservation of free trade, but then-candidate Donald Trump declared, "We have fallen into the Chinese trap. We are now destroying the dollar in order to try and compete. . . . We should be keeping the dollar strong and stable and we should tax Chinese products." True to his word, President Trump launched his promised trade war and sought to appoint avowed gold bugs to the Federal Reserve Board.[16]

The 1930s show us where 1920s-style policies lead. As "the people" around the world march against the liberal postwar order that Keynes and Churchill themselves helped to create, we must again probe the relationship between unfettered economic integration and political radicalism. All of this raises the transcendent, timeless question of whether the ascent of liberal internationalism inevitably generates its own antithesis: national socialism.

This book grapples with these crucial questions. It directly challenges the conventional wisdom that the course advanced by Churchill in 1925 was inevitable given the UK's position in the international system, the design of the UK's policymaking institutions, and the dominance of financial and trade interests in British politics at the time. Instead, it argues that the UK's particular path back onto gold in the 1920s followed directly, although not inevitably, from a combination of three things: a zealous and widespread faith in "orthodox" political economy; the reality that such beliefs were less an "orthodoxy" than a mythology; and the theocracy to which this gave rise.

The gold standard is meant to be the simplest and the most materialistic of all monetary systems. After all, is not the gold standard simply the reality that money is either gold itself or costlessly convertible into gold? In fact, this has never been true anywhere. This book shows that "the gold standard" was a highly complex intellectual abstraction.[17] As such, on the path "back to gold," ideas proved decisive at every turn. From political and economic elites in London to ordinary people at the fringes of the British Isles, conceptions of the gold standard defined these actors' perceptions of themselves and of their interests. Their beliefs about how the gold standard worked—and that it had worked—defined the policies Britons believed to be viable and delimited those that they accepted as appropriate given the UK's extraordinary identity as the center of the international gold standard system. Their understanding of the practical operation of the gold standard constructed—and reconstructed— the political and economic institutions that defined England's imperial order.

Yet the gold standard itself was less a political or economic institution than it was a religion born of the capitalist age. As money seeped into ever more relations, ordinary people increasingly felt monetary power working in their lives; but they could not fathom its depths, anticipate its droughts and deluges, or control its ebbs and flows. Just as the earliest people conjured the supernatural as the superintendents of the seasons, so too have modern people created economic religions to ascribe some meaning, purpose, and direction to the forces that govern our lives. This is the abiding allure of the gold standard to the public: it appears to be a simple, concrete way of encasing mammon, of curbing the caprice of those deities whose whims rule our world. In reality, however, our central banks are not tombs but temples, and our central bankers their high priests.

Most social scientific treatments of central banking examine the structures— the institutions, the social context, and the political climate—that select particular individuals and advance specific monetary policies. This book shows, however, that the elites orchestrating the UK's return to gold did far more to define the government than the government did to govern the Bank of England's governors.[18] It suggests that to understand sorcery, we must seriously study the sorcerers. To understand monetary policy, we must seriously study the governors of the Bank of England and England's chancellors of the exchequer. Compared with the usual social scientific studies, this book thus offers an altogether different approach to the study of money: it acknowledges that money is, in the first instance, a metaphysical abstraction; and it then analyzes the individual actors who define money and its all-encompassing structures. It thus studies the gold standard orthodoxy as the religion that it was.

This book also shines a new light on the broader politics of *restorationism*. Whether it be to "return to gold," to "take back control," or to "make America great again," the promise to roll back the clock is a proven path to power. This is nowhere truer than in "declining" powers, where the past excels the future. But the appeal is far wider and deeper than that. Restorationism plays on the pangs of nostalgia, invokes the apparent wisdom of the tried and true, and harnesses the hostility toward loss aversion. And when the costs begin to mount and the prospects appear ever bleaker, the restorationists remind us of our antecedents' sovereign nobility—and their consequent accretion of nobles and sovereigns.[19] After all, what can progressives do in the face of such conservatism? To criticize the rosy view of history or to question the viability of its promises is "unpatriotic"—as liberals like Keynes learned in the 1920s. Nevertheless, this book endeavors to do just that.

The remainder of this introduction develops this argument more fully. But first, it presents the traditional explanations of the return to gold and the limitations of those explanations.

## Previous Explanations

As soon as the calamitous political and economic consequences of Churchill's return to gold became clear, Keynes pounced with a vituperative attack. Keynes's I-told-you-so tract served both as personal vindication and as fodder for explaining the decision in the first place. "Why did [Mr. Churchill] do such a silly thing?" Keynes asked. He was merciless in answering the rhetorical question: "Partly, perhaps, because [Mr. Churchill] has no instinctive judgment to prevent him from making mistakes; partly because, lacking this instinctive judgment, he was deafened by the clamorous voices of conventional finance; and, most of all, because he was gravely misled by his experts."[20] The momentous decision, in other words, turned on the bad ideas embraced by this immensely small cadre of English elites: the top bankers in the City of London, a handful of mandarins in HM Treasury, and Chancellor Churchill himself.

Keynes was essentially right in his explanation, but he was deeply unfair in his exposition, as Moggridge has shown.[21] So far from ignoring Keynes's warnings, Churchill was intimately familiar with them. Indeed, he spent the first several months of his chancellorship debating the return with his subordinates in the Treasury and his colleagues at the Bank of England. Again and again, Churchill took Keynes's very arguments to them, demanding written refutations of each of the essential points. The "experts" were indignant, sometimes even insolent. But Churchill refused to acquiesce until they had persuaded him that every one of Keynes's prophesies would prove false.

This is the stuff of legends. What could be more compelling than the clash between these two titans—"the Last Lion" and "the Savior"—over this, one of the most important decisions in the history of the global financial system?[22]

Yet while historians have reveled in the rich complexity of this drama, modern social science deprecates such personalist narratives.[23] Keynes's treatment of Churchill is too *ad hominem* and his explanation of the consequences too *de hominem*. Typically, the former is bracketed as the vengeful rant of a spurned suitor. It is thus forgiven—although also plundered—for its literary excesses. The latter, however, is the greatest imaginable affront to social *science*. Keynes assumed that the UK's restoration of the prewar gold standard is only intelligible in terms of the idiosyncrasies of the individuals involved. By definition, such explanations are not systematic. They cannot be generalized. They are mere *stories* rather than "science."[24]

Moreover, social scientists ask, what could these individuals have possibly done in the face of overwhelming structural forces? Circumstances selected them, conditioned their approaches, and determined the consequences of their actions. The individuals themselves were the actors who tended—or, perhaps, only attended—the processes. But they did not have "agency" in any meaningful sense.

This structuralist and materialist approach was advanced most powerfully by Polanyi in his 1944 classic, *The Great Transformation*.[25] For him, the gold standard was bigger than any individual or any group of individuals. "The essentiality of the gold standard to the functioning of the international economic system of the time," Polanyi argued, "was the one and only tenet common to men of all nations and all classes, religious denominations, and social philosophies." He continued: "It was the invisible reality to which the will to live could cling," and it was thus inevitable that "mankind" would attempt to restore it. "[That] effort, which failed, was the most comprehensive the world had ever seen."[26] Polanyi admitted that his thesis "appears extreme, if not shocking in its crass materialism." Nevertheless, he insisted, "the peculiarity of the civilization the collapse of which we have witnessed was precisely that it rested on economic foundations."[27]

The structuralist-materialist approach to foreign economic policy reached new heights in the "hegemonic stability theories" of the 1970s. Kindleberger, for instance, was at pains to emphasize that the "puerile central bank quarrels" were mostly "the product of . . . imagination" and mattered only "in small part" in comparison with the deep structural forces at play. So while it was foolish to return to gold, it took a decade for contemporaries to update their preconceptions. By 1931, though, it was finally "clear that Britain could not provide the leadership" required to "stabilize the world economic system."[28] In such accounts, the interwar period is the story of the international system beating self-aggrandized individuals into acceding to the dictates of structure.[29]

It is hardly surprising that international-system-level explanations eschew emphasis on leading individuals. But even analyses of "the domestic sources of foreign economic policy during the interwar years" fixate on the design of institutions and the advance of economic interests through political parties. Simmons, for instance, defines the puzzle as explaining "why individual states chose either to break or to abide by the prevailing norms of internationally accepted economic policy."[30] For her, the key actors are *individual entities* rather than *individuals* as such. Within those states, we hear much about *central banks* but rather less about *central bankers.* Thus, the likes of Churchill and Keynes play virtually no role in her account at all.[31]

Even in those accounts that explicitly consider the leading figures, we are informed that they nevertheless hardly mattered. Eichengreen acknowledges that Churchill seriously considered the objections launched by Keynes and several others, but he reports that Churchill "found their arguments unconvincing." Instead, the return to gold was driven by broader factors such as "blind faith, the popular association of the prewar parity with Britain's status as a global power, the special benefits accruing to the City," combined with the paramount—if not also amorphous—commitment to maintain the monetary authority's credibility.[32] Simply put, the story of the international monetary system is a story of "path dependence."[33] For Frieden, the decision to return to gold was another in the long history of interest groups trumping intellectuals' ideas: "Hard-money supporters of the gold standard regarded a government commitment to gold as tantamount to a government promise to secure the value of their property. Gold protected investors, and gold guarded against inflation; devaluation was expropriation. Keynes's arguments had little power in the battle with such entrenched interests."[34]

Against this materialism, a small group of scholars have emphasized the role of ideational variables in shaping the course of events. Some of the most influential such accounts, however, merely suggest that ideas be added as additional variables.[35] Some even treat the "political power of economic ideas" as dependent upon "the orientation of the governing party."[36] Ideas do play a larger role here, but most such constructivist accounts treat ideas as *structural* variables, as the circumstances that condition and constrain leading individuals.[37] Such characterizations have been affirmed by historians, who similarly downplay Keynes's influence between the wars.[38] One Pulitzer Prize–winning account even goes so far as to reverse causality, arguing that Keynes's prominence may have been due to his having "simply wrap[ped] the mantle of academic theory around the practical dictates of instinct and necessity."[39] Ultimately, there are virtually no accounts of these shifts that stress the importance of leading individuals' particular ideas—that emphasize both agency *and* ideas.[40]

Thus, despite their conspicuous points of difference, the various perspectives can be synthesized into a sweeping account of "the great transformation" that differs little from the structuralist-materialist account given by Polanyi seventy-five years ago. England, a hegemon in decline, was willing to lead but no longer capable of doing so.[41] The Great War had transformed the international system—and England's position within it.[42] Just as it was becoming more difficult for the UK to make the international gold standard system effective, a host of domestic changes limited the ability of the monetary authorities in London to impose these costs on Britain and the rest of the empire. In the "conservative twenties," powerful interest groups took to the battlements of the old institutions to defend their position. But the "great transformation" was already underway. "The breakdown of the international gold standard," Polanyi argued, "was the invisible link between the disintegration of world economy since the turn of the century and the transformation of a whole civilization in the thirties."[43]

## The End of England's Order?

But was the English global order really finished by 1919? The Great War saw England's enemies defeated, its rivals chastened, and its empire expanded to an unprecedented extent. France and Italy were "disordered" and dependent.[44] Russia had fallen into the throes of revolutionary madness and civil war. Japan could press the British Empire at its periphery but never at its core. The United States had the international capacity, but not the domestic political will, to challenge the British order.

While the disorder that followed was bound to create challenges, it is striking that all of this came at relatively low cost. The casualty rate of the British Empire was lower than that of its major allies and far lower than that of its principal enemies. Within the empire, England's casualty rate was hardly the highest. True, the UK owed the United States nearly £900 million, but the European allies owed the UK almost four times as much.[45] At home, the public debt was now enormous, but Prime Minister David Lloyd George had a plan: the defeated Central Powers would pay those bills on the UK's behalf. Unbelievably—and contrary to virtually all discussions of this period–the English monetary authorities actually held *more* gold at the end of the war than they did at the beginning.[46] If wars could pay, no power had ever been in a better position to ensure that this one did.

Why then did the return to gold prove so disastrous?

Those at the helm blamed the war. From Polanyi to Eichengreen, scholars have accepted this conclusion. Eichengreen's classic account asserts that the Great War "shattered" "the central elements"—the key structures—of the gold standard system. Following the war, there was less central bank cooperation and less credibility to the commitment to maintain the gold standard. He explains, "More than a decade was required to complete their reconstruction. Quickly it became evident that the reconstructed gold standard was less resilient than its prewar predecessor."[47]

It could be true that the gold standard's foundations themselves were irreparably damaged by the time we reached the 1930s. But this would not explain how we arrived there in the first place. Put another way, to describe the "reconstructed" structures of politics and economics is not to explain how or why they were reconstructed. Following the abandonment of the gold standard in 1931, markets wisely questioned the ability and willingness of the UK to return to the gold standard once again. But what of the first return, in the 1920s? As Churchill emphasized in 1925, virtually every expert was in agreement; and every government—including Liberal and Labour governments—had done the utmost to follow that expert advice. Moreover, the Bank of England and the Treasury worked closely together and with other central banks, borrowing and lending as necessary to rejuvenate the integral interdependencies. Why—if it were not—was the commitment to return to gold in 1925 not credible? Why—if it were so—was the level of international cooperation inadequate in this decade? Structural theories take for granted that these crucial conditions changed, but they cannot explain why. To explain the change, we must look to that handful of agents most responsible for charting the UK's return to gold.

The account that emerges will resonate with anyone who has followed the Brexit process. It is a story of leading figures with a mandate—a dictate—to do the impossible: to restore an imagined past, to return to a world that never existed.[48]

In the wake of the First World War, preeminent policymakers made England's "return to the gold standard" into the sine qua non of the restoration of global peace and prosperity. Specific individuals in the Bank of England and the UK Treasury came to define the gold standard in particular ways. They set a timetable for achieving this return that was largely arbitrary and altogether too tight. And then several of those same individuals repeatedly chose *not* to implement the policies and practices required to achieve this restoration. Their erratic approach spared Britons little pain but granted these leading individuals considerable personal political (and perhaps economic) gain.

The price was not simply England's failure to sustain the gold standard. The UK's failure to pass this impossible examination in the 1920s brought into question, in the 1930s, the whole principle of liberal international order.

But it did not have to be this way. The elite figures in the Bank of England and the UK Treasury could have defined the gold standard—or, to avoid the solecism, responsible monetary policy—in a more sensible way. The leaders in London could have heeded the sage perspectives of their colleagues in rural England, in Scotland, and in Ireland. They could have set achievable objectives. They could have done the hard bureaucratic work to make adequate provision to realize these objectives. And they could have managed—tempered—the expectations of policymakers, Britons, and the world. Simply put, Britons "failed" to save that global order not because they were unwilling or incapable but because their leaders operationalized its defense in a quixotic way.[49] Thus, this book shows, the calamities of the 1920s, the 1930s, and the 1940s were not inevitable, as Polanyi and so many others have insisted.

## Explaining England's Cross of Gold

In England, a gold standard orthodoxy ruled policymaking at least into the 1930s. This orthodoxy, however, was a false religion, rooted in a mythologized history. When it came to the gold standard, most of the stories Britons told others, and themselves, about this history simply were not true. This became increasingly clear as elites debated the gold standard. How much gold did the UK have before the war? Estimates varied by a factor of more than two. How much gold would the UK need to maintain the gold standard given the wartime inflation? This was not only unknown; it was unknowable. So much had changed—from the position of the UK in the global economy to everyday practices involving the use of notes, checks, and currency—that these policymakers faced Knightian uncertainty. More to the point, even history could not be a guide. The golden calf was not just "dead as mutton," as Keynes put it.[50] That idol—the gold standard ideal—had never drawn a breath.

The indeterminacy of "the gold standard" left gaps that could only be filled with faith. But as with all religions, no two individuals held precisely the same beliefs or drew the same conclusions.[51] In this case, there was deep disagreement about the three critical questions that would define England's return to gold: What are the essential properties of the gold standard? What is the best path back onto gold? What is the role of the Bank of England in effecting this return? The proffered answers varied widely, even within the confines of "the gold standard" orthodoxy, and promised profoundly different consequences.

In 1925, the gold standard was restored in England, for England. As such, the English were its first victims, but they were hardly its last. This system was simultaneously inflicted upon England's "co-equal" kingdoms, its empire and its commonwealth, and the world. This was done without serious investigation of the consequences that would follow. Perhaps more disappointing, it was done without any thoughtful grappling with the insights that the victims at home and abroad had already discovered.

All this was done in England's name, but it was not done by England. To speak of "England"—or any national entity—as if it were a real entity is to fall prey to the tribalist ontology, to grant that the world is comprised of peoples rather than of people. Of course, it is not. But even "London" is not small enough. It was not either the City of London or the Bank of England. Neither was it Westminster nor Whitehall. They are all still too collective, too subsuming. Such formulations bely the incredible variation in the views advanced from each such quarter. Such metonyms personify institutions when this was really a struggle between individuals to institutionalize their personalities. As we seek to understand the causes of things, we too often ask "What?" when we ought to ask "Who?" This book takes the latter approach. It is a story of how the words and deeds of a few key individuals at a critical juncture bound humanity to a cross of gold.

England's last crusade was led by four men at the very top of the political-economic establishment: a joint permanent secretary to the Treasury (John Bradbury) and three governors of the Bank of England (Walter Cunliffe, Brien Cokayne, and Montagu Norman). Each was pivotally placed, decidedly devout, and awesomely ambitious. And, so, each was equally determined to enshrine his own distinctive gold standard dogma. Their battles determined the route to Calvary, the pace of travel, and the particulars of the crucifixion itself.

But as those four men drove the global economy toward judgment, two men took up positions that may have altered the course of history. In 1923, Keynes launched his crusade to free England from the unholy gold standard. The next year, Churchill was anointed chancellor of the exchequer. As chancellor, Churchill proved to be far less hard-headed and far more soft-hearted than most accounts have appreciated.[52] Recognizing the suffering that would follow from the planned return to gold, he challenged the orthodoxy using Keynes's very arguments. But as the preordained date of return approached, there was still no Barabbas option available for Churchill to choose. Keynes had articulated the barbarousness and the barbarity of the gold standard, but it would take him two more decades to develop an unambiguously superior alternative to it. Thus, the doubt-filled Churchill placed his wager as Pascal advised: he swallowed the orthodox elixir, mouthed its creed, and steeled himself for the worst.

Churchill and Keynes were right. The worst did come. But why? We will not know the answer to this question until we grapple with the stories of the likes of these figures.

## The Stories

These rich tales are recounted here, each with new details and new conclusions. Some of the major characters in this book, such as Walter Cunliffe and John Bradbury, have scarcely had their stories told before. Others, such as Montagu Norman, have had their accounts told many times but always with crucial details missing. And two legendary figures—Keynes and Churchill—now stand so tall that we too often neglect the essential context from which they emerged. Taken together, an altogether new account of England's cross of gold emerges.

This book is divided into five parts. The balance of this first part explicates the theory and mode of analysis used throughout.

Part II explores the complexity, confusion, and contradictions at the core of the gold standard *orthodoxy*. It takes on the conventional view that there was a single, monolithic "gold standard" either in practice or in theory. In particular, these chapters show that there were profound dogmatic disagreements among the top civil servants, leading bankers, and preeminent scholars. Not a single one of these figures ever suggested abandoning the gold standard. It was just that each of these men had his own beliefs about what, precisely, it meant to be "on the gold standard." These chapters show that this was true of those actors—financiers and traders—who would benefit the most from the return to gold. But they also show that this was equally true for those actors—the UK's producers and exporters—who would be harmed the most. In order to systematically reconstruct those positions, these chapters draw on primary source material that has been almost entirely missed in previous accounts.

Part III deconstructs the *mythology* that has surrounded the gold standard. It challenges the conventional narrative—constructed in the 1920s and repeated to this day—that the UK implemented the recommendations of the Cunliffe Currency Committee following the First World War. Soon after hostilities ceased, HM Treasury began to liberalize the wartime capital controls, just as the Cunliffe Committee had recommended emphatically. Bank Governor Montagu Norman, however, resisted this liberalization. He also ignored the

Cunliffe Committee's directives on the use of interest rate adjustments to appreciate the pound and speed the restoration. At the end of 1920, a small group of Conservatives forced through new legislation extending the wartime capital controls for another five years. This move was not only substantively significant, but it also cuts directly against the predictions of social scientific theory: both the party closest to finance and the highly independent central bank rejected the demands of their key constituents and the dictates of orthodox theory.

Part III also shows that the position of the working class similarly defies our expectations. Following the First World War, the Trades Union Congress conducted debates on, and extensive research into, the inflation brought by the war. Its largely neglected reports contain sophisticated analysis of the rise in the cost of living. Fearing that price growth would continue to outpace wage growth, the working class embraced the return to gold as a tool to restart global trade and to protect their real wages. Their approach was thus nuanced and deeply informed—more so than the simple models that predict that they would have clamored for a devaluation.

This part also recounts Keynes's *apostasy* from one of the wartime saviors of the gold standard to its preeminent critic. At its most ambitious, it challenges the conventional view of Keynes's effect on economic theory and practice. It contends that his great contribution was not in convincing policymakers that they *should* engage in countercyclical macroeconomic policy but in showing how they *could* do so. This transformation only came about gradually, in editorials, lectures, and private conversations with policymakers. These were the laboratories in which Keynes picked apart the myths of the gold standard orthodoxy and constructed a revolutionary understanding of the actual operation of the gold standard in the 1920s. This critique culminated in Keynes's masterful *Tract on Monetary Reform*, published at the end of 1923.

Part IV explores the ways in which these forces combined to transform the UK's monetary *theocracy* and the gold standard that it implemented. It challenges the century-old narrative of the "Norman Conquest of $4.86"—the contention that Bank Governor Norman defeated Keynes, captured the policy apparatus, and imposed a restoration of the old order on an unwitting Churchill. It shows, first, that Norman embraced Keynes's vision of the Bank of England as a modern central bank, one that was active, insulated from market and political pressures, and internationalist. It then examines the extensive meetings and discussions of the successor to the Cunliffe Committee—the Chamberlain-Bradbury Committee. It shows that even while Keynes failed to fully persuade these policymakers to abandon the orthodoxy, he nevertheless significantly reshaped their approach to the restoration of the gold standard.

This part then examines Keynes's extensive influence on Churchill and Churchill's deep grappling with Keynes's criticism. It highlights the many ways in which the "new gold standard" established by Churchill and Norman constituted a decisive step away from the antiquated prewar system and toward the modern approach to central banking that persists today. Last, it examines the causes and the effects of Keynes's failure to persuade Churchill to avert the resumption of the gold standard entirely. Simply put, the return both affirmed Keynes's critique and galvanized him to more fully develop his theory of unemployment in equilibrium.

Telling these stories sheds new light on the past, offers insights into the present, and provides lessons for the future. The concluding part reconsiders the past as it happened and, counterfactually, how it may have been. It then applies the insights from this book to three of today's most pressing topics: Brexit, the growing movement to return to the gold standard (yet again), and the role of belief in political economy.

CHAPTER 2

# The Road to Calvary

## From Orthodoxy to Theocracy

"Probably there are countries where you can predict a man's opinions from his income," Orwell reflected following his journey to the Wigan coalface in 1936. "But it is never quite safe to do so in England; you have always got to take his traditions into consideration as well."[1] Orwell's instruction proves indispensable in understanding England's return to gold. However well structural-materialist accounts fit other contexts, to understand the choices that emanate from England, we must grapple with tradition, which reigns here.

This chapter does just that. It elaborates the framework used to explain England's return to gold in 1925. It reconstructs the narratives that Britons told themselves about the place of the gold standard within the British Empire and the position of the United Kingdom within the international gold standard system. It shows that the cataclysm of the First World War, particularly the introduction of (largely) unbacked pound notes, materially challenged these ancient myths, ripening conditions for a "critical juncture."[2] It summarizes the essential features of the contending gold standard dogmas that then emerged among the monetary authorities. It also extends recent scholarship on uncertainty and story-telling in political economy to illuminate the use of such constructed narratives. Last, this chapter shows the usefulness of the metaphor of religion in explaining the ascent of belief in "the return to gold" and of that small group of men anointed to bring it about.

## Orthodoxy

England's gold standard "orthodoxy" built upon two critical assumptions. First, "sound money" was the sine qua non of a functioning economy. Second, the gold standard was the only way to ensure that the monetary system was "sound."

These beliefs were paramount. Policy in every other area was made in light of its expected effects on the Bank of England's ability to maintain the gold standard. And in a number of areas—from trade and fiscal policy to decisions about the international lines of alliance and enmity—policy was driven by gold standard imperatives.

These ideas were deeply rooted. They dated back to the 1690s—to the creation of the Bank of England itself. For more than two centuries, the monetary authorities in London maintained their commitment to the metallic standard. In the handful of crises in which convertibility was suspended, the suspensions were lifted once the danger had passed, and, crucially, the gold value of the currency was fully restored.

And these ideas were widely held. Of course, the elites and their Conservative representatives in government clung to old-fashioned ways. But so too did the newfangled Labour Party. So too did the labor unions themselves. So too did virtually all of the monetary "innovators" and "radicals" at the time. The academic consensus today that there was any kind of party, class, or sectoral divide on this question is simply wrong—as this book shows in exquisite detail. Thus, faith in the gold standard was the most durable, prevalent, and influential set of ideas in British policymaking from the late seventeenth to the early twentieth centuries.[3] To understand the "vast and consistent logical superstructure" erected by this orthodoxy, we must briefly excavate its foundations.[4]

The English gold standard traced its roots all the way back to the "financial revolution" that attended the Glorious Revolution and the creation of the modern English state in the 1690s.[5] The creation of the Bank of England in 1694 was followed by "the Great Recoinage," in which the English silver and gold currency was almost entirely reminted using the latest technology and according to the most exacting standards. Crucially, John Locke convinced Parliament *not* to reduce the quantity of gold and silver minted into the new coins. Parliament did this despite that "restoring" the coins to their prior "parity" would come at enormous public expense. More significant, combining the many worn and clipped coins into new, heavier, "full-bodied" coins would measurably reduce the quantity of pounds in circulation, thus generating deflation and dislocation. For such reasons, the Treasury secretary himself (William Lowndes) argued, "devaluations" had been commonplace across English history.[6] Yet Locke prevailed, the precedent was set, and England's commitment to the unalterable metallic (first silver, then gold) standard was born.

Over the next two centuries, there was virtually no meaningful deviation from this fixed exchange rate regime. The Napoleonic Wars and several banking crises prompted *temporary* suspensions of the ability to "convert" between the currency—increasingly composed of gold-backed paper Bank of England notes—and the precious metals themselves. But in every case, the pound was returned to its prior metallic parity once the turmoil had abated. Thus the holders of sterling might, in a serious crisis, face some inconvenience. But they never lost a single ounce of the gold in their pounds. This became the first tenet of the gold standard orthodoxy: responsible monetary policy means that one pound sterling should always and everywhere be worth precisely the same quantity of precious metal. The second of the two tenets followed naturally: policymakers must allow the "natural" equilibrating forces of the market to operate. Among other things, this meant that countries on the gold standard could not use "capital controls" to restrict gold inflows and outflows.

Across the same period, most countries struggled just to establish monetary sovereignty within their own borders.[7] But by the dawn of the twentieth century, the pound was held to be as good as gold the world over. Virtually no country beyond England and virtually no bank beyond the Bank of England could match this standard—the gold standard. Thus, England's predominance was the oldest, largest, and (seemingly) most durable in the realm of finance.

Before the Great War, Keynes later reflected, "the influence of London on credit conditions throughout the world was so predominant that the Bank of England could almost have claimed to be the conductor of the international orchestra."[8] It was not always costless, and it was seldom easy. Indeed, this pursuit often dictated both the UK's monetary and fiscal policies as well as Britain's relationship with its empire. But the international gold standard system brought considerable advantages, to London in particular.[9]

The war threatened both the centrality of the pound in Britain's global monetary order and the centrality of the Bank within the British Empire. The arrival of an armistice, however, would bring its own challenges. When the fighting ceased, so too would that most effective form of de facto capital control: unrestricted submarine warfare.[10] The resumption of international gold exports would leave the inflation-racked UK exposed to the threat of capital flight—and thus to a collapse in the exchange rate. The reputation earned over centuries could be lost in a moment.

In the autumn of 1917, the Ministry of Reconstruction, the main body responsible for the UK's postwar planning, created a Committee on Currency and Foreign Exchanges tasked with addressing this issue. It was a most serious group. The governor of the Bank of England, Walter Cunliffe, served as chair, making it forever known as "the Cunliffe Committee." John Bradbury joined as the senior Treasury official. Among others, the committee also included Arthur Cecil Pigou, the Professor of Political Economy at Cambridge. And these men took their work most seriously. They met regularly for over a year, interviewed more than a dozen witnesses, and drafted extensive memoranda. Ultimately, the Cunliffe Committee stressed unanimity—both in terms of its members and of the witnesses who appeared before it.[11]

Several years later, Churchill stressed the same point—consensus—in his 1925 announcement to Parliament. On this point, Churchill was not exaggerating. Of course, the British-led international trading system, and the inexorable expansion of the British Empire, generated incomparable demand for pounds sterling across the globe. This sterling hegemony abroad cultivated—and empowered—hard money interests at home. But the zeal to defend the pound was both more expansive and more deeply rooted than simple materialism can explain.

Throughout this period, British labor remained fully committed to the gold standard orthodoxy. So far from challenging the gold standard, the Labour Party saw the return to gold as the means to aid the working class. This position was given its clearest expression by Labour's first chancellor of the exchequer: Philip Snowden. As chancellor in 1924, Snowden strictly adhered to the gold standard dictates of fiscal prudence and sound finance. In early February 1925, he joined the chorus of financial experts calling for Churchill, the new Conservative chancellor, to formalize the return "imminent[ly]," meaning upwards of a year early.[12]

The UK's labor unions echoed these views. In this period, they hardly discussed the gold standard; and they never questioned it. Indeed, the Trades Union Congress (TUC) broadly endorsed the major recommendations of the Cunliffe Committee's *First Interim Report* at its annual congress in 1918.[13] To alleviate the pressure of deflation, the TUC simply resolved that every effort should be made to grow the real economy to match the nominal price level. When its proto-Stakhanovism failed and austerity became de rigueur, the TUC proposed a levy, a tax, on capital. Must the gold standard be re-erected entirely on the backs of labor, they asked? Despite this apparent boldness, the TUC nevertheless explicated its proposal using orthodox models of the "automatic" adjustment brought by the gold standard.

Why did labor support the gold standard so earnestly? The answer is simple: they did not imagine that there was any better alternative. Their lives (they believed) had improved markedly over the last several centuries, and the gold standard (they concluded) was the cornerstone of this development. Moreover, they saw the gold standard as curbing increases in the cost of living. They were convinced that inflation allowed "profiteering," that prices tended to rise faster than wages. Indeed, the disastrous experience in Central Europe following the war provided fresh evidence (they perceived) of the collapse that would inevitably follow any deviation from the tried-and-true gold standard system.

Thus, this gold standard orthodoxy was broadly embraced and deeply held.[14] There was virtually no disagreement within or between the different parties, sectors, and regions of the UK. They all shared the axiom that the pound sterling must be freely convertible into gold at the prewar exchange rate. Following the First World War, this was a top priority—often *the* top priority—for virtually every social segment in the UK. These views were held as broadly as they were held unequivocally, and yet these beliefs were less an orthodoxy than they were a *mythology*.

## Mythology

By carefully tracing the words and the deeds of the actors who led the return to gold, this book lays bare the defects of the gold standard orthodoxy: its underspecification, its contradictions, and its unrealistic assumptions. Simply put, there was no such thing as "the gold standard."[15] This is true in two important respects. First, there was no single monetary standard across time or space. This was obviously true across the several centuries in which the gold standard operated. But even at its highpoint, there was no single British gold standard. Indeed, "the gold standard" was essentially a different thing even within the different parts of England, let alone the UK, let alone the empire. Second, most of the economic interchanges in the UK (even before the war) were conducted using money that was not comprised of actual gold.[16] In other words, the relationship between "money" and gold specie was specious. Yet this mythology persisted because both the high priests preaching it, and the people worshiping it, could hardly imagine themselves persisting without it.

"Before the war," the Cunliffe Committee declared, "the country possessed a complete and effective gold standard."[17] In fact, before the First World War, there were at least four distinct versions of "the gold standard" that operated across the British Isles. Scotland and Ireland each had their own distinctive laws regulating the emission and convertibility of currency. Similarly, there was considerable variation in the norms and practices in London and those that prevailed elsewhere around England and in Wales. At their extremes, these monetary systems were virtually incommensurable, and yet ordinary

Britons almost always referred to *the* gold standard as if there were only one way to "be on gold."

Perhaps more important, there was not even a single gold standard *ideal*. What was the gold standard meant to be? Does being on the gold standard mean that a society uses gold coins exclusively as its currency? This has never been true anywhere. Even the center of the gold standard system, London, had always minted coins from other "lesser" metals alongside those minted from gold. And what of paper notes? The Bank of England had issued banknotes since its founding; and for several centuries before that, goldsmiths issued their own notes. The governors of the Bank of England could—and did—debate just what share of the circulating medium ought to be comprised of gold for a country to qualify as being "on the gold standard." But no one thought that gold should—or could—entirely displace other forms of currency. So the elites in London had a powerful mandate to "return to gold," but no two authorities had the same notion of what this actually meant.

The Cunliffe Committee defined "the essence" of the gold standard thus: "Notes must always stand at absolute parity with gold coins of equivalent face value, and . . . both notes and gold coins stand at absolute parity with gold bullion."[18] In other words, the (nominal) market price of gold ought never to change. Since Locke's victory in the Great Recoinage debate, this had been London's policy. Since Newton's overvaluation of the gold guinea (relative to the silver shilling) in 1717, the mint's official gold price had stood at £3 17s. 10½d. (£3.894) per troy ounce of standard gold. Over the ensuing centuries, the monetary authorities pursued gold price stability with incomparable zeal. From 1819 to 1914, the London gold price did not rise more than 1% above that parity, even during the Bank of England's three emergency suspensions of convertibility.[19]

For goldbugs, this was the natural, "automatic" result of simply allowing the market to freely create and destroy currency by monetizing and demonetizing gold. But simplicity in theory gives way to complicated reality wherever there is currency that is not itself specie—minted precious-metal coins. In addition to the notes issued by banks and goldsmiths, monetary authorities are bedeviled by the "big problem of small change."[20]

If there are multiple metallic and nonmetallic forms of currency, how will we know if the sovereign has succeeded in the Sisyphean task of maintaining a stable metallic value of the money? From Locke and Newton to the present, even just defining the meaning of "the metallic value of the pound" is fraught with confusion and misunderstanding.[21] Moreover, how stable must this price remain, and over what period of time? Never mind the extraordinary issue that the original purpose of the metallic standards was to increase overall price stability, and yet its very nature was to ensure volatility of non-gold prices.[22] There were always costs to converting into and out of gold. These costs created "specie bands" in which the market price of gold could fluctuate before gold conversion became profitable. It was one thing to prescribe that the monetary authority not deliberately increase these costs—through capital controls, restrictions, and so forth—but what effort and expense must be expended to minimize these costs? Even with a 100% gold backing, there would still be costs. The real cost of redeeming a Bank of England note was quite different for those in Land's End—let alone in Scotland and Ireland—than it was on Threadneedle Street. Must the Bank of England establish branches in every community, standing ready to convert its notes whenever, wherever, and to whatever extent "the market" demands?

That was only half the problem. The Scots and the Irish were quite clear that they had little use for the gold-backed Bank of *England* notes. Dating back centuries, each had their own laws and norms governing their respective monetary systems. Their banks issued their own notes. Indeed, Bank of England notes themselves expressly were *not* legal tender in Scotland and Ireland.[23] The Scots and the Irish were equally committed to the gold standard. But like everyone else, they just defined it in their own terms. Yet here were the monetary authorities in London painting over these key intra-UK distinctions. It would not be the first or the last time that English beliefs overruled Celtic practices.

Even in London, how low must be the cost of converting into gold in order to say that there was a gold standard? As Adam Smith described, even a delay in converting "is equivalent to a small duty" that dissociates the market value of the pound from its gold value.[24] How many hours per day and days per week must the gold window remain open? How many staff must stand ready to convert notes into gold on demand? How short must be the queue outside of the Bank for it to achieve "the gold standard"?

Those authorities tasked with implementing "the gold standard" faced all of these questions—and a thousand more, as we shall see.[25] But the very existence of all these practical questions begs another, much larger one: If there is no single, certain metric, can we call the gold standard a "standard" at all?

At stake is nothing less than the set of rules we use to code our dependent variable. Or, in humanistic terms, the way we define "the gold standard" determines how we understand the meaning and significance of particular actions and changes with regard to that "standard." Naturally, to say that England "returned to gold" is to say that England left gold and came back to it. But what did it mean to leave the gold standard? What did it mean to come back to it? Before we can address the *why* questions, we must answer the *when* and *how* questions. Finding those answers is far less straightforward than has been assumed.

Did England leave the gold standard on August 1, 1914, when the chancellor of the exchequer and the prime minister, following the conventional practice, formally authorized the Bank of England to ignore it statutory obligations under the 1844 Bank Act? Or was it, as the Cunliffe Committee argued, that England left as—and because—the Treasury printed millions of paper currency notes that were formally legal tender but effectively unbacked by gold? Was the gold standard still operational in the summer of 1917, as Bank Governor Cokayne argued, because it was still technically legal to export gold bullion (even as virtually every other form of capital flow was formally regulated)? Was the gold standard "abandoned," as Howson argues, in the spring of 1919 when the UK government ceased propping up the sterling dollar exchange rate? Or was this the first critical step back toward gold, as the Cunliffe Committee had prescribed? Was the gold standard working again in the summer of 1924, when the gold reserve ratio was the highest it had been in years, when the dollar and gold values of the pound were close to their prewar values, and when the Treasury was steadily reducing the supply of the wartime currency notes? Or was it "dead as mutton," as Keynes argued, because all of this occurred behind the shield of formal capital controls and informal monetary manipulation by the Bank and the Treasury, together with the US Federal Reserve? Can we really say, as Churchill and Bank Governor Norman did, that the UK returned to gold in 1925 when the export restrictions were removed but the convertibility of notes into (and out of) specie was permanently suspended? Or was the gold standard not really restored until 1928, when the Treasury's currency notes were finally, fully retired and the Bank was given singular authority over monetary policy?

There is no obviously right answer to these questions. Each is an eminently reasonable understanding of the gold standard, even as each would organize—and explain—the course of events in an entirely different way. To insist upon any single understanding of the gold standard would be akin to crafting a narrative of the religious wars around one particular conception of the Eucharist. Instead, we must excavate the varied understandings buried in that past and reconstruct those debates that raged among the monetary authorities themselves. Doing so offers not just a richer but also a more accurate picture of England's trek to Calvary.

## From Uncertainty, Faith

What of markets? Did not financiers define, at least conventionally, the standard according to which policymakers were judged?

The policymakers considered in this book faced much looser "market" constraints than is often assumed. For instance, to say that "financial markets" demanded an "adequate" reserve is hardly to say just what form that reserve ought to have been. Or that "financial markets" agreed on what would be "adequate."[26] Or that demanding a larger reserve would not just prompt the Bank of England to plunder the private banks' own reserves—either through forced loans, as during the war, or by collecting all private gold into a "centralized" gold reserve, as was proposed by several of the Bank's governors. In every case, there would be less than a 100 percent gold backing of the pound notes, and thus a run on the pound of sufficient size could break the Bank. The question that kept these policymakers awake at night was this: What reserve would be large enough to deter (and if necessary defeat) such an attack?

So markets might have collectively agreed that the Bank was wrong. But if, as often happened, markets did not agree on whether the Bank's actions were too loose or too tight, who could say what effect it would have? Who could say the direction in which the "animal spirits" would drive the herd?[27] Thus, looking to markets to "discipline" the monetary authorities is akin to looking to the flock to steer the shepherd.

The answers to these questions were unknowable ex ante—unknowable by the governors of the Bank of England and unknowable by any individual actor in financial markets. These information problems went beyond mere risk. Markets and policymakers faced what Frank Knight called "uncertainty"—a situation in which probabilities cannot be measured.[28]

In recent years, a number of scholars have reintroduced Knightian uncertainty into economics. As Beckert and Bronk put it, "The radical uncertainty implied by innovation and novelty constitutes a major problem for economic actors: how are they to make decisions, and coordinate their actions with others, if they cannot know what future will follow?" In a word, "imagination" becomes "one of [the] principle tools for coping with [uncertain futures]."[29] This is at the core of Beckert's concept of fictional expectations: "If we take uncertainty seriously instead of conflating it with risk, it becomes evident that expectations cannot be probabilist assessments of the future states of the world. Under genuine uncertainty, expectations become interpretative frames that structure situations through imaginaries of future states of the world and of causal relations. Expectations become determinate only through the imaginaries actors develop."[30]

Similarly, Morgan shows how economic models (more generally) are made and used as a technique to simplify the overwhelming complexity of the world.[31] Returning to the fertile tradition of constructivism, Nelson and Katzenstein applied this framework to the 2008 Global Financial Crisis. They argue that "market players and policymakers must often rely on social conventions that help stabilize uncertain environments."[32]

In all such approaches, narrative becomes essential. With their models, Morgan exclaims, economists "tell stories! Or more exactly: They ask questions, use the resources of the model to demonstrate something, and tell stories in the process."[33] "In economic practice," Beckert explains, "fictional expectations take a narrative form, and become articulated as stories that tell . . . how the economy will unfold into the future from the current state of affairs."[34] The upshot is that we cannot understand the past without grappling with the stories that actors themselves believed about their own past, present, and future. Nelson and Katzenstein, for instance, show that the Global Financial Crisis was rooted in the promulgation of a "new 'story'" about the past and future trajectory of average home prices in the United States.[35] Blyth similarly shows how just-so stories told about austerity—including by the UK Treasury in the interwar period—perpetuated this "dangerous idea."[36] Such thinking underpins Shiller's embrace of "narrative economics." "It seemed to me," he explains, "that the trajectory of the stock market and the economy, as well as the onset of the Great Depression, must have been tied to the stories, misperceptions, and broader narratives of the period."[37]

Shiller is not wrong. When faced with the endemic uncertainty of exchange rate politics, "markets" in the interwar UK drew on social conventions, models, and imaginaries—what Blyth calls "instruction sheets"—to clarify their objectives and guide their paths. Specifically, they looked to the gold standard to provide their marching orders.

Thus, to use the language of science, the specifics of the gold standard were under-determined, but Britons' commitment to the gold standard was over-determined. Monetary theory is abstract, and monetary policy is complex. The gold standard always appears simple and concrete: money is gold, and gold is money. But Britons were also governed by their perception of history, the stories they told to themselves and others about who they were as a people. They believed that the gold standard had brought peace, prosperity, and power to the UK. More than that, this was the thing that had set them furthest apart from their rivals.[38] The strength and salience of this identity only grew in the interwar years, as one rival after another debased its currency and suffered hyperinflation. As the Fabian socialist paper *The New Statesman* put it, "to what depths . . . depreciation may go is being demonstrated by Russia to a world which has forgotten the assignats."[39] The reference to the assignats—the debased currency of the French Revolution—was deliberate. It invoked Britons' political and economic triumphs a century prior—their restoration of the Bourbon Monarchy in France and the gold sovereign in England.

More generally, the seeming sensibleness of restorationism only increases its seductiveness. Even if they are not fully conscious of the uncertainty they face, people know to be suspicious of politicians' promises of progress. Their sense and sensibility, however, is softened when the proposal is simply to conserve, to preserve, or to restore the old order of things. This substitutes the (supposedly) known for the unknown. Thus, Churchill's mandate to "return to gold"—like Trump's to "Make America Great Again" and Johnson's to "take back control"—appears less vague, convoluted, and fungible than it was in actuality.

Beckert and Bronk analogize these "fictional expectations" to the "imaginaries" of romantic literature.[40] Certainly, seeing Trump's wall or feeling that the UK is back in control requires some imagination, just as one had to imagine the beautiful gold bars that "backed" the pound notes after Churchill "returned to gold" without resuming the circulation of gold coins. But there is another powerful term to describe "visions (of the future) that go beyond observable truths."[41] That term is *faith*. This is how Karl Polanyi conceptualized these dynamics: "Belief in the gold standard was the faith of the age. With some it was a naive, with some a critical, with others a satanistic creed implying acceptance in the flesh and rejection in the spirit. Yet the belief itself was the same, namely, that bank notes have value because they represent gold."[42] Keynes, too, discovered that the zeal to return to gold defied our vocabularies of political economy. Only the language of organized religion captures the place of gold in England.[43] To play on Wittgenstein, this was the Word that dictated the deeds.

Britons' religious commitment to a "strong" pound—combined with the unavoidable underspecification of what it means to "be on gold"—exalted England's monetary authorities. As the restoration of the gold standard became the highest cause, so too did the monetary priests become the highest authority. The simplification of monetary policy into a series of anodyne platitudes meant that this authority went essentially unquestioned. It was not a question of central bank independence, dependence, or "interdependence."[44] It went well beyond even the "unelected power" that we see today.[45] Before the war, the gold standard conquered the United Kingdom "as completely as the Holy Inquisition conquered Spain."[46] After the war, the desire to resurrect the gold standard proved so zealous that a theocracy was anointed to save this church of England's.

Under the gold standard orthodoxy, the Bank of England became Britain's Holy See. The Bank's Court of Directors became its Roman Curia. The Bank's governor became its pope. Ultimately, the gold standard orthodoxy constrained the governor of the Bank of England just as Catholicism limits the power of the bishop of Rome. For one who believes the dogma, the supreme pontiffs never had less autonomy than when they spoke ex cathedra. For one who questions it, they never had more.

Here, as in all religions, well-meaning, thoughtful people disagreed about essential questions—everything from axioms to everyday practices. Indeed, there were as many "gold standard" faiths as there were figures pontificating upon it—just as there are as many ways to be Jewish as there are Jews, just as there are as many ways to be Christian as there are Christians, just as there are as many ways to be Muslim as there are Muslims. In every heart lives the fervent conviction that this particular idiosyncratic bundle of notions constitutes the true faith. Many, of course, prove tolerant, even catholic. But the inevitable binary lurks: on gold or off gold—chosen or not, saved or damned, forgiven or condemned.

## Dogma

It is true that the Cunliffe Committee was unanimous in its reports. And there was never any disagreement among the authorities on the objective specified: restoring the prewar gold standard. But within the Bank of England, within HM Treasury, and between the two, there was perennial, bitter, and ultimately irreconcilable conflict over not just the means but also the very meaning of restoring the gold standard. Specifically, the dogmatic disputes among England's monetary authorities played out along three key dimensions: the nature of the gold standard itself, the responsibility for effecting the return, and the right path back onto gold.

What was the nature of the gold standard? More specifically, how tightly must paper notes be coupled to gold itself? This deceptively simple question actually subsumed a number of subsidiary ones: Was it necessary to circulate gold coins at all? Who had the right to issue paper notes? What was the appropriate ratio between those notes and the gold reserves? Who should hold those reserves? What were acceptable forms of reserve: gold, foreign currency, and/or government debt? Each might answer these questions in his or her own way.

These disagreements were not minor, and they were not between minor figures. For instance, one Bank of England governor demanded that England increase its total reserve to £200 million worth of gold. His predecessor, however, insisted that England only needed half that amount to operate an effective gold standard. One Bank of England governor wanted to monetize the national debt. Most of his colleagues viewed such a scheme as anathema. Another

Bank governor went to the other extreme. He defined the gold standard so strictly that the return would not be effected until gold coins themselves were circulating once again. He nearly pulled down the Bank's façade by proposing that the public be *encouraged* to cash in their paper notes for gold. Simply put, these were all questions about how "hard" the authorities should make the standard. How large a role would gold itself play in the nation's money?

Second, what was the role of the Bank in effecting the return to gold? At first blush, the answer to this question seems obvious: as the UK's central bank, its role under the gold standard was to ensure the stable gold value of the pound. This is how we understand things now, but this was hardly the starting point. The Bank was chartered as a private institution. It was governed by its Court of Directors (comprised of shareholders), who appointed the executive staff: the governor; the deputy governor; and the Committee of Treasury, the Bank's principal policymaking body. The government had no formal role in making these appointments, and in the case of those governors discussed in this book, there was little or no consultation of the government in the governors' appointment, renewal, or termination.

Thus, to speak of the degree of "central bank independence" in England in the 1920s is not simply ahistorical. It is putting the matter largely backward. The real question is about the degree to which *the government* was independent of the Bank. This is clearest in the approach taken to the millions of pounds worth of Treasury notes printed during the war. The question was always whether the Bank would agree to take on these liabilities and on what terms. In the end, Montagu Norman browbeat Winston Churchill into transferring all of the Treasury's gold to the Bank three years before the Bank took over responsibility for retiring the Treasury's paper notes. This was a sore point, one which Churchill sneaked through Parliament with rhetorical subterfuge.[47]

But this was not the only option. Norman's predecessors worked closely with the Treasury during and after the war to coordinate interest rate adjustments and to facilitate government borrowing. During the darkest days of the war, Governor Cunliffe proposed refunding the enormous commission it charged the government for managing the ballooning public debt. Ultimately, it returned merely tens of thousands of pounds to the government—from the more than £1.5 million it had collected. Instead, it used its profits to issue a dividend to shareholders. This was the gold standard at war: not gathering reserves in the national vaults, but transferring private wealth from taxpayers to shareholders by way of Threadneedle Street. And this was English democracy under the gold standard. It was hardly enough for Britons to commit their sons and daughters to Flanders. They would also have to pay the boatman who ferried them to the killing fields.[48] Only the divine right of a theocracy could moralize such ritual sacrifice. Or if we must put it into the language of social science: war made the state, the state made war, the state then made the Bank, and the Bank then made the money.[49]

In the years following the war, the Bank hardly consulted the government on its monetary policy, its foreign borrowing, or its foreign lending—including to major rivals and sometime enemies. The gold standard created the imperatives that governed, and the morality that justified, the interwar monetary order. After all, the evil twins of war debts and reparations were "settled . . . as a problem of theology," to use Keynes's apt formulation.[50] And so it was left to synods of monetary authorities to "cloth[e] with the flesh of life" the conditions of the armistice and the demands of the treaty.[51] It was not a coincidence that the UK's reparations demands were largely defined by Cunliffe himself. Nor was it a coincidence that these demands were revised by Bradbury, the single most influential member on the government's several gold standard committees. And it was only as Bank governor that Norman could recast Europe's lines of comity and enmity, reconstructing France as the rival and Germany as the ally. Thus did these pontiffs prescribe the path to Europe's salvation.

Last, what was the appropriate path back onto gold? The textbook approach was to simply restore convertibility and then to defend the exchange rate by raising interest rates—both the Bank's discount rate and the rate offered by the government on public debt. This was the approach endorsed explicitly by the principle authors of the Cunliffe Committee—Cunliffe, Bradbury, and Pigou. It was also advanced by sometime Bank governor Brien Cokayne and most of the establishment, including a young John Maynard Keynes.

Yet, this approach was frequently internationally uncooperative. After all, there was a (relatively) finite pool of gold in the world. Interest rate hikes might stimulate mining and the conversion of nonmonetary into monetary gold in the long run; but in the short run, unilaterally raising interest rates meant drawing gold from other countries. In times of gold scarcity, such as during the war and in the 1920s, such a "self-help" approach could lead to a vicious circle of retaliation abroad as each country struggled to protect its share of the limited global gold pool. Such an approach could even become self-defeating if policymakers abroad restored to other tools, like retaliatory tariffs.[52]

It could—and did—get far worse than that. In several cases, nations' gold reserves were pillaged. Scotland's gold was sent to London in 1920, a fate that Ireland only narrowly escaped.[53] And it was at the core of the war debts and reparations issues in the 1920s. Not for nothing, Keynes came to abhor these gold-standard dynamics.[54]

But Keynes did not begin with this position. In fact, the Englishman most committed to the "internationalist" approach appears to have been Montagu

Norman. Certainly, he was deeply connected to the international network of leading central bankers.[55] In this period, he appears to have deprecated the use of high interest rates and routinely made adjustments that ran directly contrary to the dictates of the Cunliffe Committee's reports. He was also perhaps the leading advocate of capital controls and may have even been personally responsible for their imposition in 1920. In a further rebuke of Cunliffe, Norman personally arranged a massive gold loan to support Germany's return to gold in 1924. The loan itself was highly irregular and attracted derision, and suspicion, from people like Bradbury.

These were more than just interpersonal squabbles. They were dogmatic disagreements along these three dimensions between the four major architects of the return to gold: Cunliffe, Cokayne, Bradbury, and Norman.

## Dogmatists

### Walter Cunliffe

When the UK began discussing the postwar return to gold, Cunliffe was the incumbent and enjoyed incomparable opportunities to define the UK's monetary trajectory. He was governor of the Bank of England from 1913 to 1918—the first governor in history to serve more than three years at the helm. Throughout the war, he endeavored to harmonize Bank policy with the Treasury. He was well ahead of his time in stressing the Bank's public responsibilities and acknowledging its accountability to Parliament. He went so far as to propose fully refunding the £1.5 million in profit that the Bank had made managing the government's debt during the war.

Following these efforts, the chancellor appointed him to head up the committee responsible for defining England's postwar monetary policy—the Cunliffe Committee. Cunliffe was committed to doing whatever it took to save the gold standard, but he was terrified that the UK simply did not have the reserves to do so. As the committee chairman, he proposed to (essentially) monetize the national debt by allowing banks to issue banknotes against government securities. This would have significantly reduced the need for deflation, but it also would have severely reduced the gold value of the pound—materially softening England's gold standard.

After the committee rejected the bold scheme, Cunliffe went to the Paris Peace Conference as the UK's representative on reparations determined to amass gold for England. So far from internationally cooperative, Cunliffe's ploy to save England's gold standard was a most egregious form of self-help. Initially, he proposed imposing on Germany a total obligation of £25 billion—a "monstrous" figure, by his own admission.[56]

## Brien Cokayne

At the Bank, Cunliffe was succeeded by Sir Brien Ibrican Cokayne in 1918. Cokayne was—and remains—the least recognizable of these four pivotal dogmatists.[57] Unlike Cunliffe and Norman, he only served one term as Bank governor (which had been the norm prior to Cunliffe), from 1918 to 1920. But he led the Bank in the critical period during the transition to peace, and as governor he defined the Bank's official position in his testimony before the Cunliffe Committee.

Cokayne was committed to the very hardest imaginable standard. All of the other figures considered here agreed that it was best to discourage the circulation of gold, but Cokayne was emphatic in the other direction. He was so determined to see gold coins once again "in the pockets of the people" that he argued for encouraging the public to trade in their notes for specie even before the excessive wartime note issues had been stamped out. This, Cokayne seems to have thought, would force the Treasury to implement the austerity he so earnestly desired.

This speaks to Cokayne's traditionalist notions about the role of the Bank. He bragged that the Bank had maintained its reserves even as it maintained (technically) gold convertibility throughout the war. As Cokayne saw it, the problems emanated from the Treasury's irresponsible printing of the (largely unbacked) pound notes. He denounced those notes, even suggesting that the Treasury's pound notes were worth less than the Bank's own pound notes. This flew against the conventional experience that the market treated all the different types of "pounds" as equivalent. When the Cunliffe Committee challenged him, Cokayne was only able to allude to anecdotal evidence of a supposed "premium" attached to Bank notes abroad. He then fell back to insisting that markets *would* begin to discount the Treasury notes if they were continued. This was a prediction rather than a fact. But it reflected, and advanced, the view that the underbacked Treasury notes were not the Bank's responsibility.

Yet Cokayne was not entirely averse to cooperating with the Treasury. Like Cunliffe and Bradbury, he embraced the self-help approach, believing that the gold standard must be defended using interest rate hikes (rather than capital controls and/or international loans). Throughout his two years as governor, he continuously pressed to raise Bank rate from the wartime level of 5 percent.

He was checked only by his desire to coordinate these moves with the Treasury, which he did consistently. In the end, he saw interest rates raised a full 1 percent.

## John Bradbury

Sir John Bradbury was a career civil servant who climbed to the heights of power across the first several decades of the twentieth century. In 1913, he was appointed as one of the two permanent secretaries to the Treasury and thus one of the government's principal economic advisers. Chancellors came and went, but the stalwart Bradbury remained. Through a combination of patience, perspicacity, and personableness, he drove much of the monetary agenda.

Bradbury was the man who, at the outbreak of the war, resolved the impending liquidity crisis by pumping the economy full of the (largely unbacked) paper Treasury notes. Much to Bradbury's chagrin, the issuance of so-called "Bradburys" became the principal source of wartime inflation. Whereas Cunliffe sought to back these notes with government securities, Bradbury spent the next decade endeavoring to stamp them out. He wielded the most influential voice on the Cunliffe Committee, leading the charge to overrule Cunliffe's proposed reforms and to harden the standard.[58]

Hailing from the Treasury, Bradbury welcomed Cunliffe's efforts to build bridges between the Treasury and the Bank. Both men believed that the Bank's public functions ought to be coordinated with the government. They also agreed that interest rate adjustments were the principal mechanism for securing the gold standard.

But Bradbury did not go nearly so far in the direction of international self-help. As the principal British delegate to the reparation commission, he whittled down by half the £12 billion sum that Cunliffe and others had agreed to impose on Germany. Then, in 1924, Bradbury worked assiduously to help craft the Dawes Plan, the international agreement in which the United States offered fresh loans to Germany, France quit the (occupied) Ruhr, and Germany's payment schedule was extended. Bradbury's approach was thus a hybrid of self-help and international cooperation.

## Montagu Norman

Norman is typically seen as the victor in these struggles. Governor of the Bank of England for more than two decades (1920–1944), he was certainly the last man standing. It is true that the particulars of England's return are unthinkable without reference to Norman. But his success was hardly inevitable. Indeed, he was initially outranked and frequently outnumbered. But through a combination of ruthless perseverance and good luck, he did come to bend England's gold standard to his will.

Norman broadly rejected the path back to gold specified in the Cunliffe Committee reports. Most conspicuously, he resisted efforts to resume gold convertibility. In 1920, he successfully saw capital controls imposed, reversing Bradbury's steady postwar liberalization. In 1924, he fought to have those controls extended by several more years, but this time Bradbury prevailed. As governor, Norman also took a different approach to monetary policy. Whereas Cunliffe, Cokayne, and Bradbury embraced interest rate hikes as the first line of defense, Norman generally kept interest rates low. When he did adjust rates, it often did not follow the logic specified by the Cunliffe Committee or employed by his predecessors.

Instead of relying on "self-help," Norman dedicated himself to forging international collaboration between leading central bankers.[59] Whereas Cunliffe had sought to rob Germany of its gold, Norman personally arranged a massive (highly unconventional) loan to Germany in 1924. As a chair of the follow-up to the Cunliffe Committee, Bradbury himself dressed down Norman for imperiling the UK's gold reserves in this way, but Norman remained defiant. He only embraced Bradbury's timetable for returning to gold after he had secured a special loan from the US Federal Reserve and cajoled Churchill to accept his particular dogma for the "new" post-1925 gold standard.

Throughout, Norman fought vigorously to preserve the Bank's role as a private institution. When approached by the Treasury, he was often recalcitrant. Indeed, when Cunliffe proposed refunding the Bank's wartime profits, Norman personally torpedoed the plan by unilaterally obtaining a legal opinion that the money belonged to the Bank's shareholders. Later, when he appeared before the successor to the Cunliffe Committee—chaired first by the former chancellor Austen Chamberlain and then by Bradbury—his behavior bordered on obstructionism. When he was called to account for his unconventional approach, he was indignant.

Of course, Norman never contemplated anything so radical as Cunliffe's scheme to monetize the debt. But his version of the gold standard was certainly "softer" than those versions advanced by Bradbury and Cokayne. Indeed, the gold standard that Norman advanced in this period—protected by periodic capital controls and managed through international cooperation—bears a striking resemblance to the Bretton Woods gold standard forged by Keynes and White two decades later.

As they discussed the return to gold, England's monetary authorities became increasingly aware of these damning problems. For these high priests

*Table 1*   Gold Standard Dogmas

|          | STANDARD | MANAGEMENT | PATH | BANK'S ROLE |
|----------|----------|------------|------|-------------|
| Cunliffe | medium | automatic | self-help | public |
| Cokayne | hardest | automatic | self-help | mixed |
| Bradbury | hard | automatic | mixed | public |
| Norman | soft | managed | internationalist | private |
| Keynes | softest | managed | internationalist | public |

of money, such disagreements about the essence of money had all the gravitas, and irreconcilability, of debates about the substantiation of the Eucharist. The stakes became even higher when policymakers attempted to rebuild the international order upon these schismed foundations.

## Theocracy: Councils, Curia, and Conclaves

To say that (Knightian) uncertainty forces policymakers and markets to rely on "social conventions," "models," and "imaginaries" is not to explain which such "instruction sheets" ascend. To say that the UK would become a theocracy is not to say which dogma—which particular version of the gold standard—it would embrace. It does not, as Beckert puts it, answer the essential question: "What narratives become credible?"[60]

Thus far, the social scientific literature has been unable to resolve this puzzle. In fact, some leading scholars contend that doing so may even be impossible.[61] Of course, there are some "factors that play a role in this," as Beckert suggests. These narratives must circulate broadly, they must prove (rhetorically) convincing, and they must resonate with the "cultural and institutional background" of the audience.[62]

Such factors are necessary but manifestly insufficient. They might narrow the range of "instruction sheets" under consideration, but they do not themselves dictate which is adopted. In the case of the gold standard, all of the four dogmatists' different versions of "returning to gold" enjoyed these features. Each of the different paths back to gold was ideologically robust and politically viable. Each was recognizable as a return to gold. Each would have served the mandate delivered by the people of the British Isles.[63] Each was crafted by an immensely powerful actor with impeccable credentials. What brave soul would impugn the governor of the Bank of England for saying that he would return to gold by raising interest rates and seizing Germany's reserves? What brave soul would impugn his successor for saying that he would return to gold by, instead, limiting speculative capital flows, supporting Germany's economic recovery, and borrowing extra gold from the US Federal Reserve? Moreover, the mere fact that these approaches appeared to be different did not itself undermine either (or both) of them. For the faithful, there is no fundamental contradiction between the Gospels of Matthew, Mark, Luke, and John. So too with the teachings of Montagu, Walter, Brien, and John. But for the skeptical, the question remains: Why did Norman's dogma triumph over the others?

In the face of such a puzzle, social scientists might seek refuge among the titans of the timeless metaphysical debate of materialism versus idealism.[64] For Marx, the intellectual superstructure is erected by (materially) powerful actors pursuing their interests.[65] For Foucault, that superstructure—what he called "power-knowledge"—both defines actors' interests and those means by which they pursue them.[66]

Neither perspective, however, fully explains England's cross of gold. This book shows that the dogmatists at the top dictated to the most powerful interest groups–from elite City of London bankers to the empire's leading gold producers to the general secretaries of the Trades Union Congress.[67] It also shows that these dogmatists themselves defined the paradigm, the episteme in which "truth" was "revealed."[68] What of the elites themselves? The small cadre that drove this history was determined to both forge material reality and to define its meaning and significance. They did not believe they needed to prioritize the one or the other, or that doing so was even possible. Ultimately, it hardly matters which segment of that virtuous circle glistened more in their eyes as their hands grasped the golden ring.

Here again, the metaphor with religion proves indispensable. Because the gold standard was a matter of religious faith, all expected that adherence to it would require material sacrifice. And so the bankers, the employers, and the workers alike accepted their prescribed penance as righteous punishment for England's wanton wartime wickedness.[69] Because the gold standard was a matter of religious faith, all expected that adherence to it would defy logic and rationality. It was thus only as a religion that the gold standard orthodoxy could opiate the blissful, ignorant masses and the blissful, ignorant elites.[70]

Instead, the binary that really mattered was inside versus outside the councils, the curia, and the conclaves of this church. The struggles of the Cunliffe Committee to define the orthodox creed is reminiscent of the history of the Council of Nicaea. The attacks on Keynes's apostasy echo the Roman Inquisition. And the ascent of Norman parallels the rise of Rodrigo Borgia, Pope Alexander VI. Just as the adherents to a given religion often believe that the hand of God guides our holy controversies on earth, so too did the faithful believe that the high priests of the gold standard orthodoxy were so directed. But for those who do not so believe, the story of England's cross of gold reads more like the history of an earthly, profane institution. That history turned on the interpersonal struggles between a small group of fervent, but flawed, men.

In the struggle to control England's monetary policy, the stakes could not have been higher. Incomparable expectations were placed upon the authorities' shoulders, and unprecedented power was transferred into their hands as a result. Throughout this period, betrayals, recriminations, and lies became the currency of internal politics among this unhappy band of monetary monks. The disputes were often deeply principled but, just as often, profoundly unprincipled. Indeed, governors of the Bank of England repeatedly accused one another of manipulating the monetary order for their own personal political and financial gain. They actively "intrigued"—to quote one such governor's accusation—against one another as they lusted after power.[71] At numerous points, several of these men (and all of them were men) nearly came to blows.

The vituperations that echoed through the corridors of power beggar belief. Rather, they *would* beggar belief were we not forced daily to witness the same such gory scenes in Trump's White House and Brexit's Westminster. But in an age before Tweets, WikiLeaks, and "memoirs" that tell all even before the stories themselves have run their course, respectable policymakers kept the shambles hidden behind the curtain.[72] Indeed, this group of men did more than anyone else to construct and advance the gold standard mythology. This is partly because each was sure that his version of the gold standard was the true one. But each also recognized that the ability to make the order work depended upon preserving that mythology—the source of their collective authority. The wars for control raged with fire and fury—but within, far from public view.

# PART TWO

# *Orthodoxy*

We do not destroy the heretic because he resists us: so long as he resists us we never destroy him. We convert him, we capture his inner mind, we reshape him. . . . We make him one of ourselves. (George Orwell, *Nineteen Eighty-Four*)

# CHAPTER 3

# The Cunliffe "Consensus"

The efforts to restore the prewar gold standard began even before the First World War had ended. In late 1917, HM Treasury created the Committee on Currency and Foreign Exchanges to address "the various problems which will arise in connection with currency and the foreign exchanges during the period of reconstruction and report upon the steps required to bring about the restoration of normal conditions in due course."[1] It brought together banking heavyweights representing interests from across the United Kingdom. Among them, F. Gaspard Farrer came from Baring and Company; Rupert Beckett and Herbert Gibbs came from their families' respective eponymous banks; Sir Charles Addis, who later served as a director of the Bank of England, derived from the Hong Kong and Shanghai Banking Corporation; and Harry Goschen spoke as the chairman of the Clearing Bankers' Committee. They were joined by William Wallace from the Royal Bank of Scotland; G. C. Cassells from the Bank of Montreal; R. W. Jeans from the Bank of Australasia; and G. F. Stewart, the former governor of the Bank of Ireland. Lord Inchcape was among the greatest shipping magnates in the British Empire and a sometime president of the Chamber of Shipping. He was also a regular adviser to the government and, at one point, had nearly been made the viceroy of India.[2]

All ten of these men, however, said almost nothing compared to the three remaining members of the committee. Arthur Cecil Pigou, the Professor of

Political Economy at Cambridge, was a commanding presence. Sir John Bradbury, one of the two joint permanent secretaries to the Treasury, virtually
never missed a meeting. He threw himself into the work, and the volume of
his contributions was matched only by those of the committee chairman: Walter Cunliffe, the governor of the Bank of England.[3]

The Cunliffe Committee's infamous *First Interim Report* stressed the consensus of opinion, both within the committee itself and between the committee and the witnesses it interviewed. As the war drew to a close, the
committee had only interviewed the first half of its outside experts. Nevertheless, the report announced, "there was no difference of opinion among [their]
witnesses . . . as to the vital importance of these matters."[4] The committee
continued meeting for another year, consulting another dozen witnesses and
finally—for the first time—considering the operation of the rather distinct
Scottish and Irish financial systems. None of this seems to have affected their
conclusions. A mere two pages long, the committee's *Final Report* simply restated the principal conclusions presented in the *Interim Report*. "We have
reviewed the criticisms which have been made upon . . . our Report," the
committee claimed, "but we see no reason to modify our opinion. We have
found nothing in the experiences of the war to falsify the lessons of previous
experience that the adoption of a currency not convertible at will into gold or
other exportable coin is likely in practice to lead to over-issue and to destroy
the measure of exchangeable value and cause a general rise in all prices and
an adverse movement in the foreign exchanges."[5] It was all so simple and clear,
the committee averred. Who could possibly disagree?

The practical significance of the Cunliffe Committee's *First Interim Report*,
and the consensus it supposedly expressed, was not lost on contemporaries.[6]
Scholars similarly point to the report as setting the agenda for the international
monetary order in the decade that followed.[7] Yet there has been rather little
exploration of the origins of this report. The Cunliffe Committee kept good
records, and much of its discussion has survived in hundreds of pages of minutes, testimony, and memoranda.[8] Among the many scholars to analyze the
interwar gold standard, however, a mere three have drawn on these collections.[9] As a result, the perception of a clear Cunliffe consensus remains the
conventional wisdom.[10]

But was this true?

The next several chapters offer a systematic analysis of the Cunliffe Committee's extensive archival papers—the first ever conducted—and then reex-
amines the committee's published reports in light of these prior, confidential
discussions. The next chapter examines the several months of internal discussion that transpired in the first half of 1918. The following chapter explores

the committee's examination of witnesses, commencing in the summer of 1918. The last chapter in this part documents the reception of the Cunliffe Committee's recommendations among policymakers, the broader public, and, crucially, the UK's labor unions. These chapters show that, to a person, every single individual recorded in these papers was committed to returning to the gold standard. This was equally true for the labor movement, as its extensive, broad-based discussions conclusively show.[11] The return to gold was affirmed explicitly at every turn. There was never a question of the commitment to that ideal.

These chapters also show, however, that there was persistent, deep, and ultimately irreconcilable conflict about precisely how to achieve that objective. The experts who sat on and appeared before the Cunliffe Committee could not agree on the steps to take to return to gold, when to begin taking these steps, or even how to keep the UK on the gold standard once it had arrived there. It went further than that. At numerous points, there was even disagreement about what that ideal meant, both in theory and in practice.

The Cunliffe Committee and its witnesses—including the governor of the Bank of England—disagreed about basic, practical questions. What quantity of gold would be required to maintain the pound at the prewar parity? How much gold was in the UK already? Should—or could—the Royal Mint circulate gold coins? Or were paper notes and checks a suitable—or perhaps superior—substitute form of currency? What were—and what should be—the forms of currency in England, in Scotland, and in Ireland?

They disagreed about a simple but crucial question: When should the UK return to gold? Should the return occur immediately upon an armistice, or should there be a transition period, as there had been after the Napoleonic Wars? The Cunliffe Committee recommended an immediate return, only to be overruled by parliamentary decree.

They disagreed about the distance to be traveled. Everyone recognized that, in real terms, the pound bought less of everything, including gold, than it did before the war. But how much purchasing power had the pound lost since then? How should this be measured? Could this be calculated using relative price indices? If so, how ought they to be constructed? These questions led to a most acrimonious debate between a Cambridge professor, who had published several such studies, and a governor of the Bank of England, who insisted that they were nonsense.

They disagreed about the relevant benchmarks. Under a traditional gold standard, the London gold price (in pounds sterling) would serve as the measure of the pound's market value. But reserve adjustments at home and abroad could obscure this relationship. For instance, the UK could raise the gold value of the pound by selling its gold reserves, but this alone would not be enough to bring it back to the prewar parity. As gold accretions would have to come from abroad, some commentators suggested that it was better to directly target the exchange rate. But which exchange rate? And what if the gold value of that other country's currency itself changed?

They disagreed about the sequencing of the steps to be taken back onto gold. When the committee began meeting, the market exchange rate was below the official parity, the Bank discouraged the conversion of notes into gold specie, and gold exports were practically limited by submarine warfare. Thus, the question of *when* was also a question of *how*. Should convertibility be restored first, leaving the exchange rate to float freely at a depreciated rate until its value could be driven back up to the prewar parity? Or should the monetary authorities delay the official return—by formally limiting convertibility and/or gold exports—until they had driven the market value of the pound back to the prewar parity? The former promised de jure adherence at the cost of a de facto devaluation. The latter promised de facto adherence at the cost of a de jure devaluation. Thus, the Pharisees debated: Was it permissible to break the law to fulfill its spirit?

They disagreed about the tactics to be used to defend the gold standard once it was restored. When the currency became overvalued, what should be the Bank of England's first line of defense? Should it raise interest rates to attract speculative capital? Or should it liquidate its reserves to directly affect the gold price and/or the exchange rate? Under what conditions, if any, should the Bank of England suspend gold convertibility? Some thought this was a permissible palliative, while others held it as a last resort.

They disagreed about strategy. What were the most effective means to organize and mobilize the country's reserves? Should all of the country's gold be gathered into a central reserve, so as to maximize its usefulness? Or should it be left distributed in private hands, so as to increase the "total reserve" the UK might acquire? By claiming such eminent domain, the Bank would increase its resources for defending the exchange rate; but it would also dissuade inward capital flows in the first place, thus creating downward pressure on the exchange rate. Which effect would prove greater? What should be the rate of compensation, if any, paid to the private parties whose gold was thus "centralized"? Even several sometime governors of the Bank of England disagreed about these questions.

They disagreed about the relationship between monetary and trade policy. Prior to the war, the story went, the stable exchange rate and Britain's healthy foreign trade were mutually reinforcing. But which was the dog, and which was the tail? Now that both factors had been upended, there was the critical question of sequencing, if not also priorities. Could trade be resumed before stabilizing the exchange rate? Could the exchange rate be stabilized, and defended, without gaining control over the swelling trade deficit? When one good thing bred another, the chicken-and-egg question of healthy trade and stable exchange rates was academic. But in the downward spiral of a vicious circle, there was no room for mistakes. The experts felt this pressure, and it heightened the tensions that attended all of their discussions.

They disagreed about political economy. These discussions reopened basic questions: What was the purpose of the Bank of England? Was it to facilitate government borrowing? This had been the original purpose in creating the Bank in 1694. Of course, the government's gargantuan wartime borrowing and now its unprecedented need for debt management brought this founding purpose to the minds of many commentators. Or was the purpose of the Bank of England to preserve monetary stability? This aspiration underpinned the 1844 Bank Charter Act, the most frequently cited charter in these discussions. Yet the Bank was still a *private* institution. None of the commentators in this period put the case as prosaically as did Milton and Rose Friedman.[12] But many on Threadneedle Street did raise the question of protecting profits and of maximizing shareholder return. It was well and good if, as before the war, all three of these endeavors were generally compatible. But in this postwar context where the trade-offs were conspicuous, which ought to take precedence? The Cunliffe Committee saw advocacy of each position.

They disagreed about the many political questions that related to monetary policy and the financial order. What ought to be the governing structure of the Bank of England? To whom was this, the world's most central bank, accountable? To the shareholders? To the UK Treasury? To the British public? To the international community?

They disagreed about essential questions of financial regulation. The 1844 Bank Charter Act gave the Bank of England a virtual monopoly on emitting banknotes in England. Even in England, however, this was not exclusive, and in Scotland and Ireland most of the currency took the form of private banknotes. Should those old rights be respected? If so, how ought the emission of notes be regulated? Ought the Bank of England to regulate these banks, given that it was, in effect, the lender of last resort? Or should the authority remain with the government? There is no surprise that there were deep cleavages on these questions. After all, real money was at stake for the wealthiest institutions in the country.

But these apostles of the gold standard also divided over far more profound questions. They debated the purpose and nature of money itself. They debated the role that gold played within the gold standard. Was it meant to ease international exchange? Was it meant to protect the market from governments'—and banks'—debasement of the currency? Was it simply a sop to special interests like the empire's gold miners? Or was it, as Keynes later said, just a "barbarous relic"? These discussions became surreal at points, such as when the Cunliffe Committee literally asked, "What is a bank?"[13]

Perhaps the biggest disagreement within the Cunliffe Committee stemmed from its return to the old debate about the relationship between public credit and currency. The most traditional commentators maintained that the public debt was the sap of national wealth. Yet Cunliffe himself vigorously questioned this; in doing so, he posed the greatest challenge to this aspect of the orthodoxy. He did *not* suggest that "public debts are public blessings," as some accused Alexander Hamilton of having done. But, like Hamilton, Cunliffe thought that a portion of the money supply could be backed by government bonds.[14] For most, this was pure heresy: only *gold* can give value to paper, they effectively argued. It was a bizarre claim, one that Cunliffe did not explicitly question. But, Cunliffe might have thought, if a fig tree is to produce olives, why could not a vine produce figs?[15] In this case, gold itself produces nothing, but public debt is a claim on the bounty of the public's endeavors. Moreover, Cunliffe must have thought, if debt-backed currency passes in the market, who are we to judge the takers of these notes?

With authority firmly invested in the Cunliffe Committee, England's theologians would get down to the business of defining the Word. It was easy enough to proclaim, "Restore the gold standard," just as it is easy to declare, "Follow the Torah," "Believe in Christ," or "Submit to Allah." But beyond that, what must one believe? Moreover, how does one practice this faith? The directive "return to gold" was clear, but the path back to gold and the nature of the destination were not. As ever, there was a long and varied journey from a few articles of faith to an entire religion.

Even with several chapters dedicated to the Cunliffe Committee, it is still not possible to cover the full range of disagreements, constructive ambiguities, and contradictions that comprise the "orthodoxy" advanced by that committee. This part does convey, however, the overwhelming impression that there were usually more questions than answers—and many more axes of disagreement than commentators. Indeed, the Cunliffe Committee counted thirteen members who had the opinions of a dozen expert witnesses. In the end, there were at least two dozen distinct understandings of the gold standard. None was held by John Maynard Keynes, although Cunliffe's came closest, as we shall see later.[16]

# CHAPTER 4

# Atop Sinai

## More Heat Than Light

At the turn of the twentieth century, London was the world's preeminent financier of international trade. This hegemon had evolved the sterling bill of exchange as an almost idyllic instrument for resolving the age-old problem of moving capital across space and time. The standard sterling bill was a fixed-date, short-term (typically three-month) obligation. Endorsed—that is, guaranteed—by London banks, these bills were accepted the world over, enabling merchants from the UK and well beyond to make purchases abroad. Over the decades, a number of London merchant banks—often called "accepting houses" or, metonymically after their traditional locale, "Lombard Street"—had come to specialize in guaranteeing these bills for a small percentage (usually 0.25 percent) of the bill's face value. The accepting houses often resold these bills on a secondary market, via discounting houses, comprised largely of banks that would then hold these bills as a liquid reserve. This allowed the accepting houses to endorse as much as six times the volume of their own capital. Before the First World War, between £400 and £500 million of bills might have been endorsed at a given time. In 1873, Walter Bagehot had characterized this as "by far the greatest combination of economical power and economical delicacy that the world has ever seen."[1]

In fact, the system proved even more powerful—and less delicate—than Bagehot imagined. Lombard Street thrived across another four decades, weathering one financial crisis after another. Contemporaries estimated that before the war, half of world trade and virtually all of British trade were financed by these sterling bills.[2] Indeed, the prewar system of commercial and financial interdependence fared so well that many liberals came to hope that it would prove powerful enough and valuable enough to avert a general war between the world's major empires. Certainly, the City did its best to avert the catastrophe that came in the summer of 1914.[3] Tragically, interdependence did not cool the world's tempers; but the conflict did fan the flames of international contagion.

Indeed, the intricate webs of the global economy began to unravel even before war was declared. The threat of hostilities confounded the shipment of goods. It became even more difficult to move gold itself. That summer, Keynes subsequently reflected, "the insurance rates for the transit of gold across the Atlantic were becoming almost prohibitive."[4] As Austria-Hungary prepared, and then issued, its infamous ultimatum to Serbia, markets went into a tailspin.[5] Within a few days of the first declarations of war, virtually all of the world's major stock exchanges had been closed. At the same time, other countries began imposing moratoria on debt payments. Taken together, this constituted a "complete breakdown of the system of foreign remittance." "The banks," Keynes explained, "are depending on the accepting houses and on the discount houses; the discount houses are depending on the accepting houses; and the accepting houses are depending on foreign clients who are unable to remit."[6]

The problems did not end there. The UK's joint stock banks often issued their loans against collateral in the form of shares. The stock market crises had sent the value of those assets plunging. The closure of the exchanges did stop the situation from getting worse (on paper, at least), but it also left the banks with weakened balance sheets and little recourse to recover from non-performing loans.[7]

Almost overnight, the City of London had been rendered veritably insolvent. Foreign debtors could not (or would not) service their obligations in London. Domestic debtors were protected by a new moratorium. And the value of London's loans' collateral either sank or was unrealizable. As Edward Holden, chairman of the UK's largest bank, explained to the chancellor on August 4, "You have the Stock Exchange frozen up; you have the bill brokers frozen up and you have ordinary bills frozen up. You cannot go to your farmer and get money from him. While you have frozen up that side of the balance sheet, turn your attention to the other side. . . . Anybody can come and demand money from the banks."[8] London needed a serious cash infusion—and fast.

Unfortunately, the 1914 financial crisis interacted negatively with a long-standing shortcoming of the UK monetary system: there was too little "small change."[9] At this time, half of the UK's currency took the form of minted coins. These could not be increased without obtaining more metal, and even the process of minting took time. What of banknotes? There was a handful of private "banks of issue" that printed legal tender notes, but contemporaries estimated that they issued less than 5 percent of the money supply, and most of these banks were in Scotland and Ireland.[10] This left the venerable notes of the Bank of England. But the Bank's smallest denomination banknote was £5. Equivalent to roughly £550 in 2020 pounds, it was far too large to be useful for ordinary transactions.[11] Even these were in short supply. By August 1, the Bank's governor complained that he had run out.[12]

The obvious solution was to print more banknotes, particularly in smaller denominations. The Bank tried to do so, but its in-house printing facilities were woefully inadequate.[13] Meanwhile, without consulting the Bank, the Treasury contracted with a commercial printer to produce £1 and 10 shilling (worth half a pound) notes at the scale required. Hastily printed on postage paper at an unusually small size and with a simple design, the notes were clearly not physical substitutes for the Bank of England notes. But the Treasury notes explicitly declared that they "are Legal Tender for the payment of any amount" and bore, in large size, the signature of Joint Permanent Secretary to the Treasury John Bradbury as their vouchsafe.[14] The UK's banks came to accept the notes in lieu of gold, and few questioned whether they would remain as good as gold in the future. The public also took to using the notes—and to calling them "Bradburys."

At first blush, it appears that the Treasury's unilateral move removed the governor limiting currency production. It would not have been the first time a government curtailed central bank independence in the name of wartime, inflationary finance. But recent historical scholarship shows that just the opposite was true. On August 1, the prime minister and the chancellor signed a letter authorizing Bank Governor Cunliffe to suspend the gold convertibility of the Bank's notes. Cunliffe had sought this letter and was prepared to use it, but ultimately he never did.

The explanation why is fit for the silver screen. In the first few days of August, the Treasury notes proved sufficient to satisfy the UK's immediate, internal demands for cash. At the same time, Bradbury mobilized a clique of like-minded Treasury officials and external advisers, working almost ceaselessly, to make the intellectual case against suspending the gold standard. The foremost among them was John Maynard Keynes. He was called to London from Cambridge in the heat of the crisis early on Sunday, August 2. Not wanting to wait for the next train, he enlisted his brother-in-law to drive him directly to Westminster in the sidecar of a motorcycle. Over the next few days,

Keynes produced his brilliant "Memorandum against the Suspension of Gold." It proved so powerful, Keynes was told, that it converted Chancellor David Lloyd George to the Bradbury camp.[15] A few days later, Lloyd George announced the triumph to Parliament: "We had already taken steps in anticipation of a possible emergency to suspend the Bank Act, in order to enable the bankers to secure an adequate supply of notes. We came to the conclusion . . . with the unanimous assent of every interest . . . that it was not necessary to suspend specie payments."[16] Keynes had saved the gold standard—for now, at least.

While Bradbury had hoped to keep the emission of Bradburys under his watchful eye—and thus under control—he was up against the ineluctable needs of wartime finance. What began as a short-term public convenience soon became a long-term national nuisance as the Treasury found that (essentially) printing notes was a convenient way to run the economy hot and, indirectly, to fund the war. By the end of 1914, there were £38 million worth of Bradburys in circulation, rivaling the quantity of the Bank's own notes.[17] Over the next three years, this number quintupled. By 1918, there were £184 million Bradburys circulating. Against this issue, the Treasury held just £28.5 million of gold in reserve, providing a paltry 15 percent gold reserve rate. The Bank, too, increased its note issue, from £57 million to £75.6 million, during the war; but it also increased its gold reserves from £38.5 million to £57.1 million. Thus, the Bank of England actually *increased* its gold reserve rate from 68 percent to 76 percent.[18]

While the Bank's governors looked upon this distinction with no small amount of pride, it made little difference as a practical matter. For one thing, the injection of Bradburys to meet wartime demands is what enabled the Bank to limit the emission of its own notes. Without these Treasury notes, where else would the public get the cash with which to buy all of those war bonds? More important, the two currencies would rise or fall together. After all, pounds were pounds, and the two were treated interchangeably both in law and in practice.[19] Unless the UK's monetary authorities were to formally distinguish the different forms of money—a contingency they did not seriously contemplate—the comparison that ultimately mattered was between the total quantity of gold available to the monetary authorities and all of the "pound" notes in circulation. As the war dragged on, the ratio became ever less. How long before the pound became worthless?

Thus, the ad hoc, "temporary" expedient of multiplying the "pounds" in circulation was becoming an existential threat—to the gold standard at least. Certainly the material reality sat increasingly at odds with the all-important narrative that a pound was "as good as gold." This was "original sin," in more ways than one.[20] But whether this would prove damning depended on whether this situation were constructed as a crisis.[21] Before we can explore that, however, we must first reconstruct the orthodoxy that prevailed at the time.

## Cunliffe's Proposed Reformation

The Cunliffe Committee began meeting in the middle of February 1918. From the start, a cleavage developed between Cunliffe and Bradbury. Cunliffe "thought that the first question to consider would be that of any necessary alterations in the Banking Laws." He proposed inviting experts to give evidence on this. Bradbury tried to contain Cunliffe's initiative. Speaking for HM Treasury—and invoking the chancellor's authority—Bradbury suggested that taking witnesses would be unnecessary, as the committee members "themselves would for the most part possess the necessary information."[22] Rather than reforming banking regulation—and the charter of the Bank of England—Bradbury argued that the committee ought to focus on simply rolling back the wartime issuance of paper currency. "The question of the exchanges," he argued, "would largely depend on placing the currency on a satisfactory basis."

Cunliffe shared the objective. But how to accomplish that? Supported by Pigou, he pointed to the importance of the balance of trade. Bradbury, though, highlighted the choice between allowing "the exchanges . . . to go" and "borrowing abroad . . . to keep them up."[23] Cunliffe thought that this ignored the deeper issue. Certain that more drastic reform was necessary, he insisted that, as Bank governor, he "had tried to keep the exchanges up" but to no avail. Favoring the pursuit of international loans, he insisted that "generally adverse exchanges would be harmful to us." Bradbury was not convinced, and he resisted rethinking the approach before trying the existing framework. But what could he do? Here was the (outgoing) governor of the Bank of England and the committee chair insisting that the Bank was due for a rethink. This echoed the long-standing calls for reform led by Holden, the UK's largest banker. Perhaps, Bradbury proposed, they ought to start there. Cunliffe agreed to this, but the committee also acquiesced to his insistence that it consider the Bank's charter as well.

At the next meeting, Cunliffe declared Holden's traditional approach to be wholly inadequate "in present circumstances." "The Bank Charter Act dealt with small figures which we had outgrown," he argued. Furthermore, it was not "in the power of anyone to reduce the currency note issue at present." "It must continue for many years," he insisted. There simply was not enough gold, and times had changed. Because it would be "very expensive" to "compel [banks] to hold a large percentage of gold," Cunliffe proposed that they be allowed to hold "a given percentage of their liabilities in . . . Government securities." Cunliffe even suggested allowing banks to borrow from the Bank of England against these reserves.[24]

Bradbury was stunned. The banknotes issued on this basis "would be an uncovered addition to currency." The only way to limit their emission would be to charge the banks a "penal" rate of interest. In effect, "the scheme would serve the same purpose as a suspension of the Bank Act." He admitted that "the Government and the Bank were at present perhaps too unwilling to suspend the Bank Act." But Cunliffe's de facto suspension "would be more readily available"—and would thus occur regularly.[25]

At the third meeting, Bradbury opened with a salvo. He proposed a "gradual" but steady reduction in the wartime currency notes. Cunliffe, however, was unequivocal. The "Currency Notes had come to stay and . . . gold should be reserved for external use." He proposed continuing to use foreign credits (loans), as they had during the war. To husband the country's meager gold supplies, he also proposed creating a central reserve pool that "could be drawn upon for external requirements without its being generally known." Ignoring Bradbury's stated objections, Cunliffe resolved that "the Committee were agreed . . . [that] all Banks trading in the United Kingdom should be called upon to hold considerable reserves in some form of interest-bearing security." Of course, the committee did not agree, and Bradbury and Pigou protested. Citing the £200 million of notes already in circulation, Bradbury warned, "The continued increase of Currency Notes would mean a cumulative rise of prices and an eventual breakdown of the exchanges." Whereas Cunliffe was content to use Bank rate to limit the issuance of notes, Bradbury insisted that "some restriction would be immediately required."[26]

Facing resistance from the committee, Cunliffe tried his luck at the Bank. He did not fare any better. As Montagu Norman tells the story, Cunliffe demanded that his Bank colleagues support his agenda. When they refused, he made a "violent display . . . like a spoiled child." It was a "clear case of megalomania." While the account seems (at least) slightly exaggerated, it is clear that Cunliffe was being stymied.[27]

When the Cunliffe Committee met on March 4, its chairman faced attacks on multiple fronts. Even with a "penal rate of interest," Gibbs "doubted if this rule . . . checked speculation before a crisis; and it tended to intensify the crisis when it came." Bradbury had more faith in the power of interest rates: "There was little danger in the issue of currency provided that money rates were sufficiently stringent." But Pigou speculated that banks could sidestep borrowing at the penal rate by calling in loans and issuing "checks on their balances with the Bank of England." Cunliffe surrendered some ground. He admitted that the Bank of England "could find it difficult to put up rates sufficiently." "As things were," he conceded, "the Bank was sometimes too slow in putting up rates."[28]

Cunliffe also compromised on his proposed reforms to the Bank's reserve holdings. Fighting off the financial panic in 1914 had taught him two things: "that larger reserves were necessary and that all gold should be held by the central institution." Others did not object to centralizing the gold holdings, and they agreed that more reserves were better. But they questioned the feasibility of increasing those reserves. Cunliffe acquiesced here as well, and the Bank's reserve level was not changed.[29]

The committee agreed that capital controls should be avoided.[30] Instead, it would have to determine the root causes of gold flows. But members were divided over this issue as well. Cunliffe blamed cheap money: "The only way to reduce inflation was for the Government to restrict the creation of credits which led to a demand for currency to pay wages, etc." Bradbury disagreed. The real issue was profligate fiscal policy: "[The Government] had raised money by borrowing in one form or another, and the credits created in consequence by the banks involved as a necessary condition an unlimited issue of currency." "The first essential," he argued, "was to reduce Government expenditure . . . within revenue and at a very early stage . . . to pay off debt." But "unless credit or currency were checked or contracted," he warned, "prices would rise indefinitely and the exchanges could not be restored." When Pigou seconded these concerns, Cunliffe invited the two to draft memoranda laying out their analyses.[31]

Yet Cunliffe proved unwilling to turn the matter over to them entirely. At the fifth meeting, he proposed that a subcommittee draft a memorandum of its own, outlining provisional conclusions. Cunliffe talked in terms of a fixed ratio between the gold reserve (assumed to be £150 million) and the total monetary circulation (of about £300 million). But Bradbury challenged this approach—and, more important, the steep reduction of the gold-to-note ratio to just 50 percent. While "[t]he country would probably be satisfied with a gold reserve of £150 millions . . . the actual amount [of fiduciary issue] could only be fixed by experiment and it would be determined . . . by the level of world-prices after the war." The good news was that Bradbury expected global prices to rise, reducing the amount of deflation that Britain would need to swallow. But as Beckett pointed out, Britain would have to remit its gold to service its overseas debts. As before, Cunliffe had faith in the combination of high interest rates at home (to attract foreign capital) and continued borrowing abroad. Highlighting the limits of the latter, Bradbury once again insisted that most of the work would have to be done by the former. "Until it was clear that we could keep £150 millions of gold," Bradbury cautioned, "we must have higher money rates here and no increase of the present fiduciary issue."[32]

But how much higher, and for how long? More broadly, how much gold would be required to maintain the gold standard at the prewar parity? Bradbury used the figure of £150 million, but as yet there had been little discussion to justify this quantity as the appropriate national reserve. Beyond this, there was another critical question that was yet to be considered: Just how much gold did the UK already have in 1918? The reality is that nobody knew.

## The Committee's First—and Only—Monetary Estimates

Over the next week, Bradbury made the committee's first estimates of the UK money supply. These were highly preliminary, as Bradbury himself admitted. He does not seem to have solicited information from any of the private banks. He also had little basis for estimating the quantity of gold held by private subjects. Ultimately, Bradbury's figures clashed markedly with the accounts subsequently submitted by the Scottish and Irish banks. But these original estimates were never properly updated or seriously questioned. As we shall see, they remained the basis for all subsequent discussion.

Before the war, Bradbury calculated, the UK had a total of £189 million pounds in circulation. Of these, £161.5 million were gold or were notes covered by gold, leaving £27.9 million uncovered. By the end of 1917, the total money supply had risen to £377.7 million. Yet, he suggested, Britain's total gold stock was less—perhaps much less—than £165 million. With the war still raging, Britain's cover ratio had already fallen from 85 percent to 44 percent.[33]

That was the bad news: the gold cover rate had fallen by half. But the good news was that the UK had actually *increased* its total stock of gold 2.5% over the course of the war, from £161.5 to £165.6 million pounds.

This result is surprising, to say the least. It flew in the face of the orthodox view that the wartime sins of public borrowing must have cost the UK its golden soul. It pointed to the viability of a managed currency, insulated from market forces by capital controls.

But all of this was unfathomable to Bradbury. And so he simply did not believe his own calculations. He had estimated private banks' gold holdings at £40 million. He remarked that the gold held by Britons themselves "is quite unknown. It may be as much as £40,000,000 but it is in all probability very much less."[34]

*Table 2*    Bradbury Estimates of the UK Money Supply

|  | CURRENCY TYPE | JUNE 30, 1914 | DECEMBER 31, 1917 |
|---|---|---|---|
| Bank of England Fiduciary Issue | Unbacked | 18.45 | 18.45 |
| Non–Bank of England Fiduciary Issue | Unbacked | 9.43 | 9.37 |
| Bank of England Notes | Backed | 38.48 | 57.13 |
| Privately Held Gold | Gold | 123.00 | 80.00 |
| Treasury Fiduciary Issue | Unbacked | – | 184.23 |
| Treasury Notes | Backed | – | 28.50 |
|  | *Totals* |  |  |
|  | Unbacked | 27.88 | 212.05 |
|  | Backed and Gold | 161.48 | 165.63 |
|  | All Currency | 189.36 | 377.68 |
|  | UK Gold Coverage Rate | 85% | 44% |

Millions of Pounds. Excludes silver and bronze coin. Source: NA T 185/2, Bradbury, "Future Dimensions of the Fiduciary Issue," March 9, 1918.

Bradbury's amendment begs the question: Where would the public have taken their gold sovereigns? For ordinary citizens, export became increasingly difficult due to submarine warfare. Perhaps they preferred the more convenient denominations of the Bradbury notes. But Bradbury expected that the coins in private banks and private hands fell from £123 million to "much less" than £80.[35] With the benefit of hindsight, it seems that the coins were being hoarded by the British public and particularly by the private banks. Subsequent calculations show that the latter increased their "cash" two and a half times across the war, from £128 million to £319 million.[36] Yet what the banks counted as "cash" varied. Many included different types of notes, along with gold coin, which makes it impossible to determine the all-important ratio of notes to gold.[37] While we cannot be sure just how much gold remained in the UK, it is clear that Bradbury and his colleagues on the Cunliffe Committee erred on the side of (perhaps excessive) pessimism. They did this on the basis of virtually no evidence.

In the face of a diminished gold-backing of pound notes, there were three options. The most straightforward was devaluation: simply altering the official gold price to match the new ratio of pounds in circulation to the gold in reserve. Across time and space, this had always been the last refuge—if not the first recourse—for embattled policymakers. But not in England. In 1914, the official price for gold was still that price set by Newton two centuries prior.

To restore convertibility at the prewar parity, conventional economic theory dictated that the UK drive its gold-to-pound ratio back toward the prewar rate. This could be done by removing pounds from circulation and/or by increasing the quantity of gold in the UK. The former meant deflation. The latter meant mercantilism. The former meant problems at home. The latter meant problems abroad. There were no good options.

Bradbury danced around this difficult question. Following "the restoration of an effective gold standard," he explained, "the amount of unlimited legal tender which can be kept in circulation will determine itself *automatically*, since if the currency becomes redundant, notes will be presented for exchange for gold for export and . . . [if] the supply of currency falls below current requirements gold will be imported and new notes taken out in exchange for it." It then became a question of which—the money supply or the quantity of reserves—was targeted and which was left to adjust in response. Crucially, Bradbury prioritized the stability of reserve holdings over the stability of overall prices:

> If we attempt to prescribe now a fixed amount for the fiduciary issue the amount of the gold reserve at which stable equilibrium will ultimately be established would be left in entire uncertainty. . . . It therefore seems desirable to approach the problem from the other end, and attempt to fix . . . the amount . . . in gold in the central reserve and leave the ultimate dimensions of the fiduciary issue to be settled as . . . the amount of fiduciary notes which can be kept in circulation without causing the central reserve to fall appreciably below the amount so fixed.[38]

What then should be the minimum reserve? Bradbury followed Cunliffe's suggestion that they pool the existing gold stock into a "central reserve," allowing them to stretch it further.[39] And he admitted that the public might be happy to accept a greater supply of unbacked currency at the same prewar exchange rate with gold. But this would only allow the UK to shave, at the most, £12 million pounds from its total prewar stock of gold, which Bradbury estimated at £162 million. Bradbury thus concluded, "The normal minimum limit of the central gold reserve should be £150,000,000."

Simply put, Bradbury opted for deflation in a two-step process. First, the UK would set its minimum reserve at £150 million. Then it would reduce its money supply to whatever level this reserve could accommodate at the prewar long-run London gold price.

Yet such a course meant deflation and, with it, economic strife. Recognizing this, Bradbury advised, "It will be necessary to apply this policy with extreme caution and without undue rigidity. And it may even be necessary from time to time instead of reducing the fiduciary issue to permit a temporary expansion." But the proposal was one of steady pressure—a virtually unabated tightening of the deflationary screw: "If . . . these steps . . . create unduly high money rates . . . a temporary increase of the fiduciary issue should then be permitted but on conditions calculated to ensure its re-absorption within a strictly limited period of time."[40]

## Pigou's Plan

Like Bradbury, Pigou considered Cunliffe's reformism to be heresy. Instead, he offered his own variety of orthodoxy in several of his own memoranda. In the first, he expounded his critique of Cunliffe's proposal to allow banks to issue currency backed by government securities. The upshot was damning: Allowing banks to issue notes against government securities would encourage them "to treat their holding of securities . . . as equivalent to their reserves in gold. . . . This would have the effect of raising prices and driving gold abroad." Whereas Cunliffe had hoped to simply avoid having to increase the gold supply, Pigou insisted that this scheme would positively reduce it.[41]

In another memorandum, Pigou tried to redefine the agenda by specifying the two essential sets of questions taken up by the committee. First, how ought the UK to arrange its economic policy so as to bring the monetary system back into equilibrium at the prewar levels—meaning the exchange rate back "within the specie points and [UK] price levels in equilibrium with countries whose currency is at par with its nominal gold value"? Second, how ought the gold standard to operate in normal times—"after equilibrium has been restored"?[42] Pigou systematically considered the leading approaches to achieving equilibrium in the first "phase." Whereas Cunliffe had sought to moderate reliance on interest rate hikes, Pigou insisted that all alternative mechanisms were fraught. "Ultimately, unless we are prepared to lose all our gold and go upon a pure paper currency," he argued, "discount rates here will have to be raised sufficiently to stop the tendency of gold to be drained abroad." He welcomed the deflationary effects—"a contraction of credits, a fall of prices, and an inflow of notes from the circulation into the reserves." This was the classic depiction of the gold standard's automatic operation. In the end, Pigou explained, "equilibrium will be established with a discount rate and a level of prices more or less equivalent to the world gold level."[43]

This result was inevitable. The deflation "can be postponed," as Cunliffe had hoped, "by a continuation of loans abroad and the restriction of gold export." But, Pigou argued, "clearly . . . we cannot go on borrowing abroad forever. When we either choose, or are compelled to stop doing this, the embargo on gold exports will have to be removed and either discount rates here raised to the foreign level or all our gold drained abroad." Moreover, this was really borrowing trouble: "The more discounts are lowered and credits and note circulation expanded . . . the greater the wrench will have to be in raising discounts and contracting credit when the temporary expedients . . . are brought to an end." Instead, he continued, "it will . . . be desirable . . . not to add to 'inflation' but rather to begin the process of deflation, bringing up the discount rate and bringing down credits and circulation towards the level they will have to assume when gold exports are released and equilibrium restored." Pigou blithely concluded, "It may well happen that this policy will prove less difficult than is often supposed."[44]

Pigou's excessive optimism similarly underpins his discussions of the gold standard in "ordinary times." He set the reserve target at £200 million. He surmised, "In view of high price levels and great danger of foreign drains, this obviously wants increasing. Say that it should be doubled."[45]

Sure, just *double* the supply of reserves. Of course, getting pounds and pounds of gold *would be* a silver bullet. But how to do so? And at what cost? What villainy and vengeance would be inflicted abroad? After all, the gold would have to come from somewhere. And until those ships came in, what would Britons' sufferance be? What dislocation and humiliation must they swallow? However Pigou might better the instruction, it would go hard. If the inflation had been less than supposed, doubling the stock of reserves would have imposed an unnecessary contraction of the British economy. If the inflation had been worse than feared, such a doubling would have failed to defend the exchange rate despite untold deflation.

Yet Pigou showed even less concern for getting the numbers right than did Bradbury. For him, all that mattered was that the Bank stood ready to "put the discount rate high enough to turn the exchanges when it falls below this figure."[46] Such was Pigou's orthodox faith: follow these commandments and God will provide.

Prior to the war, the Bank of England had separate reserves for its banking and issuing departments. The former averaged £35 million of gold, and the latter held about £50 million of gold. Cunliffe had proposed reforming the Bank's charter as part of his efforts to centralize and stretch the UK's limited gold supply. Pigou acknowledged the effects of pooling the reserves: "100 millions centralized is stronger than 120 millions scattered."[47] But he rejected this proposal precisely because it would allow the UK to get by with less gold: "If people think that the same reserve as before . . . is still sufficient in the Banking Department, the large addition to that reserve made by the introduction of the gold will obviously cause a great fall in discount rate. Equilibrium will ultimately be established with a Banking Reserve only a little exceeding the gold Banking Reserve. . . . Meanwhile we shall have lost abroad the main part of the gold that used to be in the Issue Department."[48]

The view echoes the goldbug-ery of the seventeenth-century mercantilists. But Pigou was not a simple bullionist. He did not seek excessive reserves because he had fallen prey to the old Midas fallacy—because he had a deontological commitment to acquiring gold. Instead, he was thinking in terms of the balance-of-payments constraint. With excess reserves, it was possible to lose gold without necessarily contracting the money supply. "Before," Pigou explained, "if 10 millions of gold were wanted for export, it was got by withdrawing 10 millions of notes either from circulation . . . or from the Banking Reserve. . . . The fiduciary issue of notes was left unchanged." By eliminating all excess reserves, gold outflows would necessarily constitute changes in the domestic money supply. After Cunliffe's planned amalgamation, "the 10 millions wanted for export will be taken direct from the Banking Department." In order to maintain "the rule of a fixed fiduciary issue," the Bank must follow "the peculiar rule . . . of destroying notes whenever gold is exported." In modern terms, Pigou argued that without surplus reserves, the UK would lose its monetary policy autonomy any time its balance of payments turned negative. Yet Pigou does not appear to have considered the loss of autonomy that would attend driving the exchange rate back to the prewar level, let alone going beyond that to make this massive acquisition in the first place. As Cunliffe had surmised—and as Pigou would eventually recognize—just returning to the prewar equilibrium could only be achieved with years of painful deflation.[49]

The Bradbury and Pigou analyses had virtually no effect on Cunliffe's approach. When the committee met again the following week, he "thanked Professor Pigou for the memorandum" but then bracketed all of its arguments. "So far as it dealt with the Foreign exchange," Cunliffe explained, "the memorandum went rather beyond the point which the Committee had so far reached." Of course, this was not true. The questions of whether and how to preserve the gold standard were at the core of the committee's considerations. But Cunliffe simply ignored the concerns that had been raised by Pigou and Bradbury: "When the time came, we should either have to ship gold to restore an adverse exchange or to borrow abroad." He returned to his own reserve figure of £150 million—£50 million less than Pigou's recommended minimum—and "postponed" "the fixing of the fiduciary issue . . . for consideration later." Instead, Cunliffe returned to his mantra. "The development of the check system had altered the position under Peel's [1844 Bank Charter] Act," he insisted. Again, he proposed, "banks should keep reserves in some form of interest bearing government security on which emergency currency might be issued at suitable rates."[50]

Bradbury and Pigou must have been surprised to see their memoranda summarily dismissed. It was only on the next day that they swung back against Cunliffe. Pigou "asked whether there was any danger that the emergency currency scheme would induce banks to weaken their cash reserves." Cunliffe placed his faith in the pressure markets would apply to banks by their "publication of monthly accounts." Bradbury was not convinced that this alone would dissuade profligacy, particularly in crisis moments. "The emergency currency privilege," he insisted, "must be made sufficiently unattractive to prevent any weakening of the first line of defense." Cunliffe conceded that loans "would have to be for fixed periods with a sliding scale of rates as the issue increased." Bradbury demanded more specificity. The scale itself "would need very careful consideration." Pigou pressed Cunliffe to put "the scheme . . . into draft form for the consideration of the Committee."[51]

As these tensions mounted, Gibbs drafted a memorandum that worked to reconcile the two perspectives. He followed Cunliffe in holding that the introduction of the modern check system had changed the operation of the gold standard. He also agreed with the proposal to centralize reserves. "It is abundantly clear," he stated, "that the actual and moral effect of gold in the Bank of England is much greater than when the gold is scattered." But he rejected Cunliffe's scheme to allow banks to use government securities as reserves. Like Bradbury and Pigou, Gibbs deprecated that implicit violation of the gold standard. This was too much reform. Instead, he said, "we should hold to tried methods so far as possible." "Any emergency issue should be on the lines of the Chancellor's letter" providing an explicit, one-off suspension. Gibbs, too, was overly optimistic about Britain's likely postwar position. "After the war," he surmised, "the demand for currency notes will probably fluctuate, probably no doubt with a general tendency to contraction." As such, "there should be power in someone's hands to issue . . . notes." Nevertheless, this power was to be "more sparingly exercised and would be continually checked by a rising rate of discount."[52]

Last, Gibbs broached "the effect abroad . . . of increasing the Capital of the Bank." Up to this point, the committee had ignored this crucial question. But if Britain were to increase its reserves, it would have to attract gold from somewhere. If it pulled gold from foreign markets, this would impose adjustment burdens abroad. Even if it simply monopolized new emissions from the imperial mines, this would create opportunity costs for all other gold standard countries. Gibbs could only broach these intricate considerations. It would be some time before the committee grappled with them in all their political complexity.[53]

## Cunliffe Attempts a Coup

The coalescence of the opposition within the committee threatened to derail Cunliffe's plans. As Cunliffe saw it, Bradbury, Pigou, and Gibbs did not appreciate Britain's dire economic straits. If his ad hoc committee would not address this issue, perhaps Cunliffe could resolve it himself as governor of the Bank of England. He was *still* the governor, after all, if only for a few more weeks. He would need more time. To get it, he would have to revise the Bank's very charter. Cunliffe could dither no longer.

Cunliffe forced this issue at the Cunliffe Committee's next meeting. "There was nothing in the Charter applicable to present day conditions," he declared, as he had many times previously. But this time, he brought a list of specific reforms. First, the "the election of the directorate . . . was too much a close borough. . . . Their election should be on the lines followed by a public Company and . . . a certain number of directors should retire regularly."[54]

Bradbury and his allies stopped Cunliffe there. Jeans suggested, "The question was one primarily for the [Bank's] shareholders." In support of Cunliffe, Goschen proclaimed that "the Bank was a national institution," and Cassels "agreed that, before placing increased powers in the Bank's hands, the Committee ought to satisfy themselves as to its constitution." Yet Bradbury was unflinching: "The Committee might be criticized for going beyond their terms of reference." "If they wished to go into detail," he warned, "it would be better to ask for an extension of the terms of reference" for the committee. He signaled that the chancellor was likely to grant this extension, but he resolved that it was better to ask for permission than for forgiveness.[55]

With the question of the Bank's charter bracketed for now, Cunliffe turned to Bradbury's earlier memorandum.[56] Bradbury again championed increasing the UK's gold reserve. Increasing the gold reserve would allow for a greater volume of fiduciary notes—and currency more generally—which "would postpone the need for recourse to the emergency expedient," namely, suspending gold convertibility. For Bradbury this was axiomatic: "It was very important that emergency rights should not be an excuse for the weakening of normal reserves." The debate then played out just as it had done many times before. Cunliffe argued that the money supply should be determined first, with the quantity of reserves determined as a result. Gibbs underscored the benefits of stretching a smaller supply of gold. But Bradbury "was strongly opposed to having less gold in the country than before the war." As expected, Pigou seconded Bradbury's objections. Cunliffe once again placed his faith in high interest rates and foreign borrowing. Bradbury and Pigou again stressed the "severe limitations to the policy of continued borrowing abroad." The schism remained.[57]

Cunliffe returned the next day with the chancellor's blessing to "examine the constitution of the Bank of England." He immediately launched back into his list of desired reforms. He proposed mandatory retirement for the directors at the age of seventy. He similarly rejected suggestions that the governor should be appointed for life. At this point, however, Bradbury interrupted him again. "The Committee ought to hear the official views of the Bank," he interjected. This must have stung. Cunliffe had not yet stepped down as governor, but here was Bradbury insinuating that Cunliffe could not speak for it. He quickly agreed to consult the Bank, and he just as quickly returned to his list of reforms. Implying that some of the Bank's directors were redundant, Cunliffe proposed paring down the directorate to a smaller number who "were active." One wonders precisely which directors Cunliffe thought could be removed.[58]

With a shake-up of the Bank of England's directorate in play, the private bankers on the Cunliffe Committee sought to carve out a few seats to formally represent their own interests. The others, however, closed ranks, and even Cunliffe and Bradbury found common cause on this front. As the latter put it, "The Bank had to hold the balance between bankers and [l]enders . . . There were serious objections to the representation of definite interests. This might lead to pressure for Government representation which would affect the character of the Bank as an independent institution."[59]

Cunliffe steered the conversation back to his proposed reforms. He wanted to "widen" the "circle of choice of directors" and to raise their compensation to "£800 or £1000 a year." He rejected a proposal to lengthen the governor's term, as "a longer period might give a Governor too much power." But then came the reveal: the former governor proposed that "an ex-Governor might be eligible for re-election after an interval."[60]

Uncomfortable with the plot for a coup d'état apparently unfolding before his eyes, Bradbury intervened. He "thought that the precedent of the American President was the right one, an unwritten rule against re-election for more than 2 terms"—just the quantity that Cunliffe himself had served. More important, he was "unfavorable to recall after an interval, though there should be no actual rule against it."[61]

Blocked again by Bradbury, Cunliffe would have to relent. The best agreement he could secure from the committee was hardly far-reaching. The Court of Directors should be reduced from twenty-six members to twenty. Each would serve for four years, with one-quarter retiring annually. That would bring fresh blood onto the board, but it would also prevent any individual from packing it with supporters.[62]

The following day, Cunliffe took this thin mandate to the Bank's Committee of Treasury. Things did not go well. Rather than supporting Cunliffe's agenda, the committee instead embraced a scheme advanced by Deputy Governor Cokayne to reform the election of the Committee of Treasury. Evidently, the committee preferred to follow the lead of the incoming governor rather than the demands of the lame duck.[63] Norman reported, "Nothing doing beyond receipt of letter fr[om] C[hancellor] of [the] E[xchequer] whitewashing" Cunliffe's crisis interventions in 1914–1915. Norman evidently disapproved of Cunliffe's approach, and he was growing weary of the governor's self-justification.[64]

But Cunliffe still did not surrender. The next day, he took his case directly to the Bank's Court of Directors. In an attempt to preempt this, the court moved to thank Cunliffe for his service "during the unprecedented period of five years." The court's official record did not minute what happened next.[65]

A "very hot" Montagu Norman, however, painted a disturbing scene in his diary. Cunliffe, Norman suggested, used the vote of thanks as a chance to read "a longish speech—of wh[ich] the D[eputy] Gov[ernor] and Directors knew nothing." He asked for a "free hand for . . . [the] time being." When this was not granted, he issued "an underhanded" and "very bitter" "hit at" a predecessor for irresponsibly leaking the Bank's financial weakness. Norman summarized the rant as "i. eulogizing the Bankers," "ii. bum-sucking the press," and, astoundingly, "iii. promising, as chairman of [the] Currency Com[mittee], changes by statute in [the Bank] Charter Act of 1844." Cunliffe, Norman said, had become a "a dangerous and insane colleague."[66]

Norman and his colleagues were right to worry. Cunliffe's gambit was nothing less than a threat to conquer the Bank from without. If Norman is to be believed, it laid bare the ambitions that had animated Cunliffe's direction of the (Cunliffe) Currency Committee from the start. And it charted the direction in which Cunliffe hoped to steer it going forward.[67]

For now, however, the plot went nowhere. Ambushing the Bank's court was obviously a bad strategy. They did not take kindly to Cunliffe's explicit threats.

A cowed Cunliffe returned to his committee the following day. He circulated some (loosely related) research on foreign note issues. He broached a few straightforward points, on which there was wide agreement. And he proposed unremarkable—and uncontentious—changes to the Bank's internal organization. With that, he proposed that the Cunliffe Committee begin to take witnesses. Perhaps *they* would see things Cunliffe's way. It was his last hope of saving the gold standard through reform. After drawing up a list of names, the committee agreed to resume a fortnight hence. This was its first serious break since it had convened in mid-February.[68]

# CHAPTER 5

# The Golden Calf
## The Public Idolize Gold

By the spring of 1918, there really had been only one major policymaker to seriously reconsider the gold standard orthodoxy: Bank Governor Walter Cunliffe. But his scheme was less an attack on the gold standard than a tempering—a reforming—of it. He believed that modern financial innovations (such as checks), better management of the financial system (using centralized reserves), and capital diversification (holding bonds as well as gold) could allow the UK to circulate a larger quantity of money *without* sacrificing the currency's convertibility into gold at the prewar rate. It was no more (or less) heretical than had been the introduction of fractional reserve banking in the first place, centuries before. In both cases, a one-to-one gold backing was diluted in favor of a monetary system that functionally achieved the same practical effects as a gold standard: reliable convertibility at the established rate.

Had Cunliffe put the case in these terms, he might have persuaded his colleagues that his proposed innovations were different in degree (rather than in type) from those that they themselves celebrated. But he did not. After several months of heated disagreement, it had become painfully clear to Cunliffe that his colleagues on the so-called Cunliffe Committee were no more imaginative than had been his subordinates in the Bank of England. Outnumbered on both fronts, Cunliffe sought support from leading figures beyond the policymaking establishment. They too proved immensely disappointing.

Indeed, the committee was truthful when it reported that nobody questioned the preeminence of making the gold standard operational once again. All the parties concerned assumed that this was the sine qua non for whatever else they might hope to achieve. Thus, there was far less tension between the City of London, the government, and the rest of the British economy than the conventional Polanyian accounts predict.

Historians have traditionally framed the Cunliffe Committee as a kind of bankers' swindle. As Boyce puts it, "The Committee, chaired by . . . [the] governor of the Bank of England, and composed overwhelmingly of City financiers, heard several dozen like-minded City men and economists advocate the early return to the gold standard at the prewar parity of £1 = \$4.86. The sole expression of industrial opinion came from the [Federation of British Industries]."[1]

But this view does not do the Cunliffe Committee justice. Over its eighteen months of work, its members interviewed more than a dozen expert witnesses and discussed memoranda from a number more. They grappled with everything from banking regulations in Ireland to the cost structures of gold mining in the Rand. The range of perspectives they considered was truly broad. So far from simply reciting the incantations of the gold standard orthodoxy, these witnesses brought varied understandings of the practical operation of the monetary system in their domains of expertise: retail banking, manufacturing, and trading. Unshackled by formal training, these men (every one of them a man) felt free to think creatively about Britain's likely postwar struggles. Many, including the elite City financiers, even questioned the assumptions that underpinned orthodox theory, although they did so only inadvertently and only until the orthodox committee members maneuvered them into doing otherwise.

And this was the problem for any who might hope for a radical rethinking of the British monetary order. The witnesses were both too creative and not creative enough to do much good for Cunliffe. There was no consensus about the many questions required to effect the "return to gold." Each was convinced that his was the authentic orthodoxy. In the discussions, however, they—and Cunliffe included—were all too easily steered back to those particular assumptions, invocations, and prescriptions favored by the Cunliffe Committee's dominant members. Throughout, Bradbury and Pigou exposed their trespasses and took their confessions.

# The City of God: The Bankers Bear Witness

## Sir Edward Holden, London City and Midland Bank

Predictably, Sir Edward Holden was the first witness heard by the Cunliffe Committee. Holden had built the London City and Midland Bank into the UK's most powerful clearing bank. Having displaced the Rothschild dynasty during the war, Midland was now arguably the largest bank in the world.[2] Even before the war, the rather orthodox Holden had pressed for inquiries into the adequacy of the Bank of England's reserves. A sometime potential chancellor himself, Holden's persistent calls for "reforming" the Bank had partly inspired Chancellor Bonar Law to convene the Cunliffe Committee in the first place.[3]

Holden's appearance before the committee in April 1918 was a display of unambiguous bullionism. He insisted that all notes be backed one-to-one by gold.[4] Moreover, he wanted secondary and tertiary reserves in the Bank of England and in the joint stock banks. He proclaimed, "The more gold I could get in the aggregate, the better it would be for the country."[5] His solution to financial crises was "Keeping bigger reserves." Cunliffe asked for clarification: "Simply keeping bigger reserves?" "Yes," Holden replied.[6]

Gibbs calculated that Holden's proposals would require a total gold reserve of £185 million.[7] Cunliffe pressed him on how Britain could acquire so much gold. Holden "quite admit[ted] that difficulty."[8] And he even deprecated Bank rate adjustments, which have little effect on the balance of payments.[9] In true mercantilist fashion, he fixated instead on the balance of trade: "The exchanges are depreciated now because exports have been diminished and imports have been increased. . . . We want to combat that condition by increasing the exports." More than anything, he feared gold outflows. Following the war, he said, "if you are not careful you are going to lose your gold, but instead . . . I would get stocks ready to increase exports, and I would send out exports in the place of gold."[10]

Insofar as Holden accepted the influence of interest rates on Britain's economic position, he had little concern for the deflationary effects of his proposals. Cunliffe warned that this "plan would be a very wasteful one . . . which would mean a very high rate of interest for a very long number of years . . . and consequently a bar to a great deal of the trade of the country." But Holden simply returned to his first principles: "We have to hold our reserves."[11]

## Felix Schuster, National Provincial and Union Bank

Felix Schuster was the only banker whose reputation and influence could compare to that of Edward Holden. He thus appeared before the committee the next day. Like Holden, Schuster had built his family's banking enterprise, through mergers, across the previous decades into one of the largest clearing banks in the world.[12]

Schuster followed Holden's bullionist strand of the monetary orthodoxy. "The only way of correcting our exchange," he declared, was "to increase production and reduce imports."[13] He agreed with the proposals to centralize Britain's reserves in the Bank of England.[14] But he thought that further international borrowing would be both unnecessary and counterproductive.[15] He admitted the need for the Bank to retain the power to issue currency against government securities—but only "in times of emergency, and not as a normal everyday thing."[16]

Schuster was more bullish than Holden on the power of interest rate adjustments. He was more bullish still on London's potential to remain the global financial center.[17] With enough austerity, Schuster speculated, "after the War . . . it seems quite conceivable to me that you may have a very sudden movement of the Foreign Exchanges in favor of this country. I think that is the most likely thing to happen."[18] He even envisioned the government "step[ing] at once [to] take advantage of the Foreign Exchanges to wipe out all our foreign debt, and get rid of it immediately after the war."[19]

## Robert Benson, the Merchants Trust

Robert Benson came as a representative of the Merchants Trust. He read a prepared memorandum with a proposal that was designed to avoid the deflation that all knew was coming. He explained, "There is 'good money' and 'bad money'; but the worst money is that which is liable to be suddenly, or capriciously, withdrawn."[20] Benson proposed various institutional reforms, but the key was that the British monetary authority should lend money at different rates of interest at home and abroad. Benson explained, "I hope very much that it may lead to cheaper and cheaper money, and that we may end in refunding our debt at a very much lower rate of interest."[21] He insisted that the paper currency would only depreciate if "means are not provided to utilize, and liquefy, the capital locked up in War Loans."[22] Continued cheap money would keep the economy growing—in real terms—allowing Britain to increase production and trade enough to meet this new volume of money. In the meantime, Benson acknowledged that this would require the imposition of capital controls and, possibly, continued foreign borrowing.[23]

The committee pushed back rather hard against him. The very title of Benson's proposal must have appealed to Cunliffe. After all, Cunliffe had similarly sought "to Provide Means for After-War Development by enabling Holders of Government Securities to borrow thereon."[24] But the committee suspected that Benson's scheme was inflationism in another guise. Even Cunliffe was incredulous. The capital controls could not last forever, he reminded Benson, and the money borrowed at low interest at home would be sent abroad as soon as "the restrictions are taken off."[25]

The real battle began when Pigou took over the questioning. He could hardly believe what he was hearing. He returned to first principles, asking Benson to explain "the sense in which [he was] using 'capital' here." When Benson seemed to conflate money with capital, Pigou made the orthodox argument that simply increasing currency will not increase "real capital"—"the labor and material" in Britain. To him, it was obvious that Benson's scheme would invariably lead to inflation. "Given that the discount rate is to be low and that a lot of money is to be lo[s]t for reconstruction purposes," he queried, "that presumably would tend to make prices higher than they would have been otherwise; would that not be so?"[26]

Benson was outmatched. In hindsight, he must have believed that prices had already risen during the war. He simply intended to avoid deflation rather than to encourage additional inflation. He would have favored what Keynes later called "stabilization" at the current price level. But in the spring of 1918, Benson lacked the vocabulary and conceptual understanding required to defend himself against Pigou. He simply replied, "That is theoretically true, but you would have a number of other forces working in the other direction. . . . I wonder what percentage of tendency—I ask you as an economist. Perhaps it might be a negligible percentage."[27]

Pigou redirected the discussion to the balance of trade. "The point is quite simple," Pigou explained. "Given that we are importing more than we are exporting, how would you propose to meet the difference? If you do not allow gold to go, must you not necessarily go on continually borrowing from abroad?"[28] Benson was far more sanguine than others had been about the prospect of getting "foreign credits." In his prepared remarks, he had predicted that the United States would roll over the British debt rather than demand gold. He saw the interests of "the Anglo Saxon race" as intertwined, going so far as to propose that the United States and the United Kingdom "join in pooling stocks and production of gold in order to stabilize the dollar to the pound and avoid shipping gold to and fro."[29]

Of course, Pigou was not satisfied with this. Eventually the borrowing would have to cease. He questioned Benson's commitment to the gold standard itself: "Would you be prepared that the rate of discount should go up if there appeared to be a risk of our gold going away or of our having to borrow extensively from abroad?" But Benson evaded the question: "I should leave it to the directors of the Central Institution in conjunction with the Bank of England to regulate the rate."[30]

When Bradbury pressed him, Benson expressed almost inconceivable optimism about Britain's likely postwar international position. He argued that Britain was likely to have a positive balance of trade with the neutral powers: "I think we may find after the War that the British Empire, in conjunction with the United States, will have the best of the neutrals." He also bet on depreciation of the US dollar: "The marriage of the dollar with the pound has depreciated the dollar in neutral countries." As a result, "we shall have the whip hand of the foreigner when Peace comes." The committee found this prediction to be incredible, and no one came to Benson's defense. To get this on the record, Bradbury similarly questioned Benson's commitment to the gold standard: "In your opinion it would be better to let the exchanges go for a time rather than to penalize industry by high rates?" But once again Benson evaded the question: "I should not like to say that until I was confronted with the situation." Thus, Benson refused to deprioritize the gold standard.[31]

Benson's proposal combined perspicacious realism about the impending deflation with excessive optimism about Britain's postwar international position. He thus thought that a leap away from the gold standard was both more viable and more necessary than even Cunliffe had proposed. He and the committee had agreed to disagree in their predictions about the postwar conditions. No one could know just what those empirical realities would be. But Benson needed to make a strong theoretical case for the possibility of leaving the gold standard. He needed to convince the committee that the wartime price level was a viable equilibrium and that the costs of remaining there were likely lower than those of moving back to the prewar equilibrium. He needed to make a principled defense of low interest rate policy following the war. Yet Benson proved incapable and unwilling to try.

## Christopher Nugent, Head of the Discount Market

When Christopher Nugent, the head of the discount market, testified, the committee must have been pleased to see him align with many of its agreed-upon proposals.[32] He favored the pooling of gold reserves in the hands of the Bank of England.[33] He agreed that it would be impossible to maintain dual interest rates, as some had proposed, without imposing capital controls.[34] And he "consider[ed] gold in circulation [to be] a waste of gold. Gold should be used exclusively as a basis for credit."[35]

But little could have prepared the committee for the zeal with which he sought "to provide an abundant and cheap supply of money, so that anybody with ability and energy can get it."[36] Nor could they have expected such a vast rejection of the essentials of orthodox theory. When asked about the expansion of the money supply, he distinguished between what he called "the credit inflation" and price inflation.[37] Moreover, he said, "the currency expansion can pass away as easily as it has arisen. In the meantime it is discharging a very useful purpose. The London Money Market can work freely knowing that under present circumstances it can easily obtain all the money it requires. . . . This inflation . . . will gradually be reduced by a natural process and that it will not be necessary to take any particular steps to contract it any more than you have taken any particular steps to expand it."[38]

Nugent argued that Britain cannot—and should not plan to—rely upon attracting capital with high interest rates. This will have fewer positive effects than it did in the past, and it will slow trade. Instead, he insisted, "fairly cheap and abundant money is [in] our interest in order to develop our trade and commerce." He thus concluded, "Everything that would unnecessarily raise the value of money should be deprecated."[39]

At the same time, Nugent postulated that Britain needed to acquire a gold supply of upwards of £300 million—twice as much as Bradbury himself had set.[40] In the short run, Britain should borrow from its "rich friends . . . like the United States."[41] It was much better to "get this gold by negotiation rather than to attract it by a high rate of interest and a great fall in prices here to start with."[42] Ultimately, though, "the only cause which would affect the Bank of England reserve of gold would be foreign trade."[43] As such, it was vital to secure a positive balance of trade: "We must do nothing that will check exports. We must stimulate exports and discourage imports."[44] Cheap money—to stimulate industry—was vital toward that end. Nugent explained, "You do not want to have your rate of discount higher than other countries; you want to have it lower—you want to be the cheapest market."[45]

All this was heresy. But it quickly became clear that Nugent was not as much radical as he was confused—and not especially committed to his heretical views in any case.

Nugent informed the committee that "a rise in the rate of interest generally accompanies a demand for gold for export."[46] This, of course, cut against the most basic assumptions of the gold standard orthodoxy, namely, that capital chases high real interest rates. In the face of this, Pigou questioned Nugent's commitment to the gold standard. "But you would not take the view that the rate of discount ought to be kept very low to encourage our home trade . . . irrespective of the foreign market?" he asked, bewildered.[47] Despite the manifest self-contradiction, Nugent acquiesced: "No. I do not think that would be wise, because if you do that, you may lose a large amount of gold and threaten your international position. I feel that you must maintain that."[48]

Bradbury hammered Nugent on the current account. He questioned whether it were so obvious that Britain would become a debtor country. "I do not want to put it too high," Bradbury explained, "because I think if the War comes to an end within a reasonable time we shall have a certain number of debtors abroad as well as creditors."[49] He challenged Nugent's theory more aggressively. Nugent had favored reducing imports and obtaining foreign loans, but Bradbury reminded him that these are only "temporary expedients."[50] Nugent did not go so far as to deny the Lerner symmetry theorem—"that if you do not buy from abroad you cannot sell to abroad"—but he came close to doing so.[51] Rather than reducing internal purchasing power, Nugent hoped that Britain could bring its output into line with the money supply using "increased cleverness in production."[52] But here too there were limits. One expects many foreign competitors sought to increase their "cleverness" as well.

Bradbury simply did not see how the UK could compete abroad without either depreciating the exchange rate or reducing domestic prices.[53] The former was unconscionable, as Nugent himself admitted. "I think every stimulus should be given to our means of earning money," he explained. But he also averred, "The maintenance of confidence in England's ability to meet her engagements abroad in gold has been of very great use in establishing our international position, and we should do all we can to maintain it—I do not wish to abrogate it in any shape or way."[54]

This left only one option: deflation. Bradbury's challenge to Nugent on this point is telling. He argued, "If the price of commodities generally has to drop, I take it there could be considerable difficulty in reducing wages."[55] Evidently, Bradbury believed that reducing the money supply would not necessarily press prices and wages downward. Nugent did not know well enough to argue that British prices and wages had already risen.

## Walter Leaf, the London and Westminster Bank

Walter Leaf was a tour de force. He inherited a position in the mercantile world of silk and ribbon-making. This was never his passion, but he nevertheless thrived. He cofounded the London Chamber of Commerce in 1882. A decade later, he was made a director of the London and Westminster Bank. Like the others, Leaf grew his bank into one of the five largest in the UK.[56]

But Leaf was different in some remarkable ways. His heart lay in antiquity. His success at Trinity College, Cambridge—where his attendance overlapped with Cunliffe's—became a prelude to a lifetime of academic work. Even while he prospered in the world of commerce and finance, he produced a steady stream of classical scholarship. This included, among several other books, the standard English-language translation of the *Iliad*. His was a serious, thoughtful mind.[57]

Leaf posed an interesting challenge for the Cunliffe Committee when he appeared before it in late May 1918. On the one hand, he boldly rejected the need for the currency to have a gold backing. But on the other hand, he knew better than to debate the economics of the quantity theory of money with the likes of Pigou.

Almost from the start, Leaf stipulated as much. He agreed that "the only means by which you can cancel Currency Notes" is for "Government borrowing [to] cease at the earliest possible moment."[58] Fearing the effect of high interest rates on trade, he supported the proposals to maintain different rates of interest on domestic versus foreign investment.[59] But he also conceded that this would prove impossible without extensive capital controls. Leaf insisted upon the importance of the balance of trade: "Nothing can put the foreign exchanges right except sending merchandise in one form or another—whether gold or otherwise, but preferably otherwise—to pay our debts abroad."[60] But to do this, he continued, "we may even have to increase credits . . . until we have got sufficient raw material to enable us to increase our exports."[61]

Leaf's radicalism came in his rejection of bullionism. "The holding of gold is uneconomical and undesirable in itself," he declared.[62] He "regard[ed] the gold reserve as . . . a concession to human weakness. . . . All credit is a psychological question, and the only reason for keeping a gold reserve is what people will stand without taking fright."[63] As such, a mere one-to-three gold-to-note ratio "would probably be considered ample by public opinion . . . [and] would be sufficient to stop panics—which is the only thing one has to consider."[64] On the basis of his calculations, this worked out to a reserve of £110 million. This was, by far, the lowest estimate anyone proposed to the committee.[65]

But he did not stop there. Leaf objected to the farce in which "things are to go on all very well while they are quiet," but "the moment there is an emergency the law has to be broken."[66] He "should prefer to see some method by which the expansion of currency in times of emergency should be made automatic."[67] He thought that "currency notes should be issued against a certain proportion of gold and securities."[68]

Wittingly or unwittingly, Leaf had stumbled into championing Cunliffe's precise proposals. He explained, "If there is to be a Bank [of England] statement [detailing its reserves] at all, it should be one which is more or less intelligible. If you want to conceal, as you very properly and very justly may want to do . . . it would be almost better not to have a Bank return."[69] Cunliffe replied that he himself was the one who stopped circulating the Bank's return during the war.[70] The result, Leaf explained, is that "we have naturally all of us been in the dark as to the destination of the between 3 and 3.5 millions monthly, which has been produced in South Africa during the War. . . . That, properly, is within the knowledge of the Government and the Bank of England only. We presume that the greater part of it has gone to the United States or elsewhere. Whether any of it may have come into this country we are quite in the dark."[71]

Here, finally, was a reasonable defense of Cunliffe's intuition. Cunliffe welcomed the targeted criticism of the orthodox fixation on gold holdings. He dominated the questioning, giving Leaf plenty of space to expound his perspective.

The orthodox members launched their attack only as time was running short. Addis fired the first shot, pressing Leaf on his incredibly low one-to-three gold-to-note ratio. He clarified that Leaf meant "30% against the total note issue, and in addition to that such gold as might be required by ordinary human wisdom for external trade abroad."[72] Leaf assented, but he stressed that this was in the "Utopia" in which "our currency circulated in other countries," such as "all our Colonies."[73]

Then Pigou started in on the witness. He criticized the plan to issue the currency as a multiple of the gold reserve, particularly following gold outflows. The gold standard ideal of a 100 percent backing "reduces [the note volume] at one to one," but "if you had your . . . rule it would reduce it at three to one, which would make it very sudden and violent?"[74] Leaf responded that the current equilibrium was a good one: "We know we have got practically an inconvertible currency. On the whole it is working well, and we have got to feel our way back to get to a more or less convertible currency. How it is to be done I cannot altogether say, because I do not know how it has been made inconvertible."[75] But Pigou mocked this suggested paradox: "Your idea would be to make it formally convertible, and yet as a matter of fact to make it inconvertible?"[76]

Pigou had just begun to attack Leaf on the export-led strategy when time ran out. So when Leaf returned the next day, Bradbury started in on him straight away. "Whereas a reserve of one-third might be adequate in the legal-tender-using country," Bradbury insisted, "it might be inadequate in a country like this where a large part of the currency is a check currency?"[77]

But Leaf was defiant. He insisted, "The gold reserve we have held has been small and quite useless for keeping up the exchanges, as compared on the one hand to what has been done by the export of securities, and the other by obtaining credits abroad."[78] He pointed to the examples of France and Russia, which were "two of the largest gold-holding countries at the beginning of the war . . . [but] neither of them [were] able to keep up their exchanges even as well as we were."[79]

The committee tried to pin Leaf down on the practical operation of the financial system absent the gold backing. And Cunliffe tried to steer him toward some "automatic means" of avoiding the old system in which crises prompted Bank rate hikes (to 10 percent) and an emergency suspension of the gold standard. Of course, Leaf shared this aspiration with Cunliffe. But he refused to commit to any specifics: "I do not profess to have worked out a scheme, or to have any theory of my own. I have only suggested on the very broadest lines what seemed to me the main weaknesses in our present system."[80]

For Cunliffe, this was as good as it would get. Here was a prominent City financier recognizing the challenges of a simple return to the prewar system. But simply seeing the dangers was a far cry from developing viable alternatives, as Leaf himself admitted. Of course, Cunliffe had a plan: monetize the government's debt. But with such tentative external support, could he push it past his skeptical colleagues?

## Concluding Provisionally

After completing its interviews of the London bankers, the committee turned to the "provisional conclusions" crafted by Cunliffe's subcommittee. There was plenty on which the members agreed. They began with their central axiom: "The first condition of the restoration of a sound currency and of the exchanges is the restoration of an effective gold standard."[81] Pursuant to that, "government borrowings should cease at the earliest possible moment." There would be no capital controls: gold would be imported and exported freely. Instead, the Bank should aggressively raise interest rates to protect the exchange rate. There was "no necessity for the resumption of the internal circulation of gold," but the Bank "should be under obligation to supply sovereigns (or bullion by arrangement) for export." The Bank would also monopolize all note issue across the UK.[82] As before, the committee agreed that the country's reserves should be concentrated in the Bank of England, but members debated the adequacy of a £150 million reserve. Pigou conciliated both sides with wily words: the central reserve should be "not less than £150 million."[83]

The real argument arose over Cunliffe's plan to require banks to hold government securities in reserve. Even members of the subcommittee that had drafted the provisional conclusions "did not altogether agree with the proposal." Others suggested that it would be "a serious departure" from past practice and went beyond the committee's purview. Yet Cunliffe insisted that the first concern was funding the public's wartime debt, particularly "short-dated Government securities." Allowing banks to hold this debt as an asset—and allowing the Bank of England to issue currency against these holdings— would both alleviate the public funding problem and reduce the need for deflationary pressure. He saw this as a response to the "prevailing compulsion to hold larger reserves than formerly."[84]

But Bradbury simply did not see government debt as a substitute form of reserve. For him, government securities were merely more liabilities rather than assets. "If [the banks] claimed repayment of these, how could the Government repay except by borrowing from the banks' deposits and reducing deposits, proportionately?" he asked. "Deposits could only be reduced by the destruction of credit or the export of gold. In one form or another the banks would have to find the money to pay off the Treasury Bills," he argued. In effect, the banks were lending money to the government rather than to their customers. Public borrowing would thus crowd out private borrowing: "That money could not be made available for financing trade." Thus, Bradbury's object was to contain and *reduce* government borrowing rather than to *facilitate* it, as Cunliffe sought to do. "Unless Government borrowing from the banks were tied up in some way," he concluded, "the currency problem would be much more difficult." The competition for funds would drive up interest rates. "Rather than face this," Cunliffe's scheme would grant the government "recourse to the vicious expedient of borrowing from the Bank of England and increasing the credit inflation." Bradbury saw Cunliffe's proposal for what it was: an attempt to reduce the gold backing of the pound. But "if credit was to be created after the war in the same proportion to paper as it bore to gold before the war," he admonished Cunliffe, "disaster would follow."[85]

In early June, the committee revisited the draft "provisional conclusions." Again, the discussion centered on Cunliffe's proposal to issue notes against government securities held in reserve. Goschen threw his weight behind Cunliffe's original proposal. But Bradbury was insistent: "It must be made clear that the issue was to be an emergency one only and not an easy method of inflation and safeguards must be provided to ensure the withdrawal of the issue after the crisis. With this proviso he was willing that responsibility for the issue should in future rest with the Bank of England."[86]

As before, Gibbs proposed language to bridge the everlasting divide between Cunliffe and Bradbury. He used some of Cunliffe's key formulations. He noted that "the check is the main currency of the country," and he mentioned

Cunliffe's objective of "rendering the currency system more elastic." But the substance hailed from the Bradbury camp. Cunliffe had "required" "all banks . . . to hold an amount equal to 25% of their deposits in short-dated government securities." Gibbs raised the proportion to 40 percent, but in addition to government securities this also included "cash in hand and at the Bank of England." He also "objected . . . to the proposal . . . to impose a legal obligation on the Banks and he wished to leave the actual working of any arrangements to the discretion of the Bank of England."[87] Losing heart, Cunliffe said that he "did not think that the points of difference at issue were really material." In fact, the debate was far from over.[88]

## The View beyond the City of London

Sir James Hope Simpson hailed from a large, prominent family in Liverpool. His father (of the same name) had capitalized on the growth of the northern mercantile and manufacturing sectors to make the Bank of Liverpool one of the largest banks in the UK. The younger Simpson first spent several decades rising through the Indian Civil Service. When he took over the Bank of Liverpool following his father's death, he spent several years pursuing a favorable merger with one of London's elite clearing banks. This diligence paid off. By the end of 1918, the Bank of Liverpool had been joined with Martins of Lombard Street. Thus, Simpson came to the committee as an able banker with an international perspective and ambitions to expand. But his fortunes nevertheless depended, in the first instance, on the strength of northern English trade and commerce.[89]

Simpson submitted a memorandum to the committee in late May and testified on June 3. He placed great hope in receiving American support: "The American Exchange is the key of the position today, and will probably remain the key when Peace comes. If the problem of restoring American Exchange can be solved, the rest of the problem, while difficult, should not be insoluble."[90] He proposed simply that the Americans "cancel our debt to the United States in exchange for Allied debt to us."[91] He noted with delight that this would restore Britain as "creditors of the States as holders of Dollar Securities, as Ocean Carriers and as Exporters of manufactured goods, and our credits would be used for the purchase of Foodstuffs, Cotton and other indispensable imports from the States."[92] Of course, this "would involve a tremendous sacrifice on the part of the United States."[93] But this was conceivable given the American "attitude of remorse . . . that they have not come into the War before."[94]

The committee members knew that this was beyond the pale. They had doubts about whether the United States would be willing to allow the UK just to refinance its existing debt. The prospect of outright cancellation—particularly if it allowed the UK to retake its position of financial leadership—was downright preposterous. "I wish our problem was as simple as you make it," Cunliffe stated.[95] Simpson replied, "I do feel that America with its enormous mass of gold, if she will come to the rescue, is the real source of help for all the Allies in the matter of exchange."[96] Cunliffe was blunt: "We have had it put to us here, and I think we rather agree with it, that we may not look for gold from the States."[97]

In light of this, perhaps Simpson could be won over to Cunliffe's scheme to back notes with a mix of gold and securities. But Simpson would not bite. He wanted a 100 percent gold-backed currency. To achieve this, he estimated that the Bank of England alone would need £120 million and Britain should acquire enough gold to keep £80 million to £100 million of gold in circulation as an additional reserve.[98] This additional reserve, he stated, "was invaluable to us at the beginning of the War."[99] All told, Simpson's reserve of £200 million to £220 million was upwards of 50 percent higher than the committee had specified and even higher than Pigou's highest suggestion. Simpson issued the orthodox defense: "The extraordinary difficulty of regulating an issue of Notes which is purely, or mainly, fiduciary has been repeatedly shown in Economic History. . . . Notes, the value of which can be affected, as they were recently in Ireland, by rumor, however ill-founded, are not a proper Currency for a great Commercial Nation."[100]

At this point, it was important for "our Government to buy Gold, and to continue buying Gold, on a considerable scale, and to hold it until the stock became large enough to justify the announcement that the Notes will be exchanged for Gold at any time and no further Notes issued."[101] "Fortunate[ly]," he noted, ". . . three-fourths of the Gold production of the World come from Mines in the British Empire and we ought to . . . [arrange to] have the right of preemption over Gold produced in the Empire."[102] Simpson suggested that the government acquire gold even if it meant paying above market rates and above the statutory price to do so.[103] Despite that the costs of such policies "would be very great," he said, "I think it is worth it."[104]

The good news was that "there has [not] been any serious inflation of the Currency." And the postwar adjustment will be almost automatic. As "wages fall, and the spending power of the population is reduced," he said, "we may have redundancy which may affect prices."[105] How blithely he referred to the "redundancy" of production—and producers.

All this was too bullionist for even the most orthodox members of the committee. Some of it was pure nonsense and thus easily dispatched. Bradbury, for instance, pointed out that having the Bank selling gold cheaper than it bought it would mean "buying the same gold over and over again in the very shortest period of time"—an objection to which Simpson immediately conceded.[106] More important, Bradbury pressed Simpson on the rate at which the paper currency could be reduced. When Simpson explained that "by 'gradual' [he] would suggest two or three years," Bradbury quipped, "He would be sanguine who hoped it could be done in that time."[107] An angry Goschen objected to "all the waste that the internal circulation of gold entails."[108] He defended the record of the willingness and ability of the governors of the Bank of England—including Cunliffe—to use Bank rate to protect the gold reserve. Here too Simpson conceded.[109]

Ultimately, rather few of Simpson's proposals survived the interrogation. He subsequently sent a series of amendments to his memorandum and testimony. He agreed that there could be no simple, automatic mechanism for emitting and retiring unbacked notes. Most important, he agreed that his timing was far too aggressive. He concluded, "However desirable it is for us to get back to a Gold basis by providing full cover for our Currency Note Issue and then withdrawing the issue, thus restoring the Gold Currency, it would take so long to accomplish this that one must assume that the Currency Note Issue will have to continue."[110]

## Ivory Tower Ultraorthodoxy

In the spring of 1918, the Cunliffe Committee solicited the opinions of several prominent academics. The responses were brief but also highly orthodox. One might say they plumbed the depths of extreme gold standard orthodoxy. Perhaps for this reason, the committee did not discuss them at length or invite their authors for interviews. Nevertheless, it is worth presenting a representative example here, as it shows the climate of contemporary academic opinion.

Joseph Shield Nicholson was among the most respected economists of the day. By this point, he had been the chair of political economy at the University of Edinburgh for nearly forty years. His illustrious accomplishments included an unparalleled knowledge of Scottish economic history and *Principles of Political Economy*, which he spent fourteen years crafting. His reply to the Cunliffe Committee was considerably shorter but no less powerful.[111]

In most of the world, Nicholson argued, the gold standard had been more of a fiction than a reality. "In most cases," he lamented, "the use of gold in international payments was more or less managed by the Government." More broadly, "gold had come to be regarded as of secondary importance for internal national currency." "India," he noted, "was said to have the gold standard without gold."[112]

Prewar Britain, however, was a shining counterexample: "Gold showed no diminution in use for internal currency, and all the notes were absolutely convertible in the strictest sense. For International payments also London was described as the only free market for gold, and the bill on London was regarded as international currency."[113] He praised the 1844 Bank Charter Act, both its beauty in theory and its strong record in practice. "Its failings lean to virtue's side—to an over-emphasis of the observance of the requirements of the gold standard."[114] The wartime "departure from the principles of the Bank Act has assisted materially in the general and in the specific depreciation of the pound sterling."[115] The solution, of course, was to make the gold standard fully operational once again. This meant "(1) absolute convertibility of the notes, (2) the normal parity of the foreign exchanges, and (3) the normal price of gold for non-monetary uses."[116]

But how to achieve this?

Nicholson was even more conservative than were Bradbury and Pigou. He argued that a higher relative interest rate is "properly only a temporary expedient." After all, this would mean higher interest payments on the public debt, many of which would go abroad. Also, insofar as higher interest rates did attract foreign capital, Nicholson feared that this could exacerbate inflation. He was highly traditional on the use of gold as currency. He conceded that "the restoration of the full gold circulation in England to prewar conditions would not be practicable for some time." But "considering the importance of the maintenance of the gold standard in the most effective form the . . . full gold circulation as before the war might be recommended as a most effective support of convertibility." After all, "the free market implies convertibility in the strictest sense. Economy after a point means limitation of convertibility just when it may be most needed."[117]

The real source of danger lay in the considerable "credit inflation." Up to this point, price inflation had generally been "checked" by "the extension of control prices." But things would be different after the war. The removal of price controls would unleash the pressure that had been building for years. So Nicholson advocated the "stoppage of further Issues and the gradual reduction in the outstanding amount" of inconvertible currency notes. Moreover, he insisted that "the process of deflation ought to be begun as soon as peace is restored." Pursuant to that, Nicholson called for "absolute *immediate* convertibility" of notes into gold.[118]

Nicholson warned that following this path would require "considerable effort and sacrifice," meaning austerity.[119] It would be "very difficult with falling prices and reduction of war profits to make the revenue cover expenditure."[120] At the same time, "the demands for keeping up government departments will be great and the demands for financing new schemes for reconstruction will be greater. It will be very difficult to reduce the war bonuses of labor and the excess profits of capital. In other words it will be very difficult to begin the process of deflation." But the alternatives would be even worse: "A continuance of the easy finance of the war period can only lead to greater inflation, instead of deflation and the inevitable reaction will be more disastrous."[121] Nicholson was so worried about inflation that he wanted to *increase* Britain's gold reserves well above their prewar levels. "For some time before the war," he claimed, "it was generally maintained that our gold reserves were too small."[122] Britain had no excuse for this: "With so wealthy a country as this and with so much dependent on the stability of its credit, undue economy of gold is the most dangerous of all economies."[123] For him, "a surplus of gold beyond ordinary requirements is a cheap form of insurance for the stability of credit, and for the maintenance of London as a free market for gold."[124]

That might well have been true. But Nicholson did not consider the enormous costs of acquiring that reserve in the first place. These costs must have proved particularly—perhaps prohibitively—high when considering the international dimensions of the postwar gold standard. There was "credit inflation" the world over. As wartime price controls were removed, prices would rise far higher still. This meant that few, if any, countries could return to their prewar gold exchange rates without significantly increasing their gold reserves, imposing deflation, or some of both. Insofar as countries attempted to increase their gold reserves, this would create an international scramble for gold.

Nicholson gave some passing thought to this, noting, "The endeavor to restore the gold standard in other countries after the war may give rise to exceptional demands for gold." But given that few countries fully adhered to the gold standard before the war—by Nicholson's own depiction—and that the challenges of maintaining it were about to rise substantially, he ought to have considered just whether and how the postwar gold standard would operate. Instead, he simply "presumed that other nations will as soon as possible wish to re-establish convertibility."[125] He did not explain this presumption, and because these responses were submitted in writing, the committee could not press him on it.

Thus, the academic perspective was orthodox in the extreme. It was *ultraorthodox*. But it was also familiar to Pigou and the others. So there was little point for the Cunliffe Committee to invite these clerics to criticize their comparatively moderate orthodoxy.

## The Producers' Inquisition

The opinions of Britain's merchants and manufacturers broadly echoed those expressed by its financiers, investors, and academics. Not surprisingly, they lobbied for more direct representation of their interests.[126] On this point, the producers were united. So too were they united in the faith they placed in the gold standard. But like everyone else, each witness had his own view of just what it meant to return to gold.

### Lord Harris, Gold Fields of South Africa

The industry most directly concerned with the return to the gold standard was that which was geographically farthest from London: the imperial gold mines. This was also, perhaps, the industry left most precarious by the war. Of course, the limitations on gold shipment curtailed the mine owners' opportunities to bring the gold to the market. This says nothing of the miners pulled deep (literally) into the trenches and tunnels that ran through and under the Western Front. How much had these workers suffered disproportionately in the war (and as usual)?

More broadly, the wartime monetary policy and the gold standard orthodoxy were a particularly costly combination for the gold producers. The printing of paper money had raised prices and thus triggered demands for higher wages. This increased the gold producers' costs. At the same time, however, the monetary orthodoxy maintained that the price of gold was the one price that would not—must not—change. This lowered the relative value of gold. The orthodoxy's postwar prescription of deflation would *eventually* restore gold's real value by lowering the nominal prices of everything else. But in the meantime, how many gold mines would close?

Thus the interest of the gold producers was quite clear, and the policy recommendation ought to have followed directly. Conventional models of political economy predict that the gold producers would have lobbied the Cunliffe

Committee to depreciate the pound so as to raise the price of gold.[127] But the gold producers did not do this. In fact, it does not seem they ever contemplated it. This became clear when the Cunliffe Committee interviewed the gold producers' representative in June 1918, George Robert Canning Harris, fourth Baron Harris.

Lord Harris was a man who was pleased to be known more for his having captained the English cricket team than for his success in business and colonial management.[128] He was a man who had the right name, the right swing, and the right tickets. That proved to be enough. After his first-class athletic career finished, his service in the Anglo-Boer Wars won him a place among Africa's colonizers. He then followed the gold road to the top of the imperial hierarchy. By 1899, he was the chairman of the Gold Fields of South Africa Group, the company that Cecil Rhodes and his partners had founded twelve years earlier.[129]

How did this blessed son use the opportunity to lobby the Cunliffe Committee? Not well. From the start, he made clear that he would "not attempt to deal with the intricate subject of the relations of gold to currency and to commerce." Why did he bracket this essential question, the place where there was clear overlap between the gold producers' economic interests and the mandate of the committee? The answer is simple: Harris, and evidently those other gold producers for whom he spoke, believed in the gold standard deeply but understood it only superficially. As he admitted, "I do not profess to give any opinion about the exchanges, or about currency, or about credit, or about any of those more abstruse difficulties." Instead, he approached the issue strictly in terms of producing a commodity. He spoke at length about the rising costs of operating mines. Colonizing for profit is not always profitable, apparently.[130] And so he made that most banal of all imaginable requests: a government subsidy for the failing mines. Without it, he warned the committee, "they must anticipate a heavy reduction in the output of gold in the next 20 years."[131]

This struck a nerve with Cunliffe, who was already deeply concerned about the shortage of gold reserves. Without a second thought, he answered, "We will do anything we can to help the industry, because of the importance it is that we should get every ounce of gold in the Empire that we possibly can." Speaking "on behalf of the Committee," he assured Harris, "I am sure we are all of one mind in regard to that."[132]

In fact, they were not. "I think it is a matter of degree," Bradbury interjected. "Particularly, gold at any price," Addis added.[133]

The scheme of committing gold to bring gold home might have worked for the conquistadors. But in the age of total war, it was a preposterous proposal, the kind that could emanate only from mouths that knew little but the silver spoon. To think of the blood and treasure that had been sunk already in Africa's gold fields. To think that the British public ought to pay yet more—in the midst of the Great War and unprecedented government borrowing—to support these private companies' for-profit colonial "adventures." To think of the gold standard—the cornerstone of laissez-faire liberalism—held up by the visible largesse of government handouts.

The far more potent move would have been to lobby the government to allow the price of gold to rise (via devaluation) in time to match the rest of the price level. Here was the group with the most to gain from a devaluation. Here was the group with control over the lifeblood of the international gold standard system. Here was this group at the very center of that system, with a private audience before the government's all-important currency committee. Yet in its moment of greatest need and maximum leverage, this most powerful interest group deliberately deferred to the experts on all monetary matters. The gold producers did not "demand devaluation" because they did not know that they could, or understand that they should, do so.[134] And so what good are power, interest, and position when confronted by, as Harris put it, the "abstruse difficulties" of "the exchanges"?

Of course, Harris was a unique specimen. It is not surprising that conventional models of exchange rate politics break down when interest groups send cavaliers, chancers, and cricketers to lobby on their behalf. But do they work any better when the capitalists speak for themselves?

## Alexander MacIndoe, the Glasgow Stock Exchange

Alexander MacIndoe was a former chairman of the Glasgow Stock Exchange. He submitted a memorandum to the committee and appeared before it in June. Claiming some expertise on economic history, he hailed the 1810 Bullion Committee report as "the most authoritative and valuable document available on the subject of Currency."[135] He thus redeployed the very recommendations made then: "The only practical remedy is to restore the convertibility of the note issue."[136] He held the UK's monetary system as "infinitely superior to that of any other nation."[137] And he decried "tinkering with the essential provisions of the [1844] Bank Act."[138] These views were widely held, he insisted. The "general commercial opinions in . . . Glasgow" harbored "no desire for any change in the essential provisions of the [1844] Bank Act."[139]

The committee pressed him, but MacIndoe resisted their proposed modifications. Pigou asked about making the currency elastic in times of emergency, but MacIndoe "object[ed] very much to the Issue Department being elastic to any extent."[140] Bradbury broached the possibility of an internationally coordinated stabilization of the new standards at the inflated price level.[141] MacIndoe responded that "the country which first tries to return to a gold standard will have the easiest task, seeing that for a long time, many other countries will not be able to do so."[142] Of course, restoring the gold standard was necessary to "secure the trading and Banking prosperity of London."[143] But this was "in the interests of all concerned . . . rich and poor alike." "At the present moment," MacIndoe cried, ". . . the standard of value is lost . . . totally." And "the standard of value is a matter of such vast importance that that should be undertaken in preference to anything else."[144]

Yet MacIndoe questioned whether the Cunliffe Committee would have the courage to follow the example of the Bullion Committee. After all, much of the current situation was the fault of the committee's own members. He criticized Cunliffe for failing to raise interest rates as governor: "If the bank rate had been kept higher, you would not have had such a demand for these [unbacked] Treasury notes."[145] Cunliffe deployed his mantra that "the only remedy for us is to live within our income." But even this was not good enough for MacIndoe: "I also would like to see the continued issue of paper money . . . stopped."[146] Continued reluctance to do so would make the monetary situation "hopeless."[147]

At points, the committee members became defensive. MacIndoe's criticisms, in person and in print, moved Bradbury to renounce the unbacked "Bradbury" notes: "Though my name has been closely associated with the so-called inflation of the currency . . . there is very little . . . in what you have said . . . with which I do not find myself entirely in agreement."[148]

From our perspective, the attacks were entirely unexpected. Conventional theory suggests that stock-jobbers—from the industrial Clyde Valley, no less—would much prefer inflation to deflation. Most directly, cheap money drives up share prices (along with everything else), but it also reduces the real burden of the private sector's debt, diverts savings into consumption and investment, and drives up profits. Yet here was a major stockbroker demanding deflation. Here was the former head of the Glasgow Stock Exchange lecturing the Cunliffe Committee on the virtues of austerity—and indicting specific committee members for failing to keep the orthodox faith during the war. He who had kept borrowing costs low (Cunliffe) and he who juiced the money supply (Bradbury) confessed their sins and recited the orthodox creed. Here then was one more commitment by the Cunliffe Committee—this one to the commercial community—to restore the prewar gold standard.

## Hugh Bell, a Middlesbrough Manufacturer

Within England, the most geographically distant perspective was also the least conventional. In early July, the committee interviewed Hugh Bell, a manufacturer from Middlesbrough in Northeast England—250 miles from London. Bell was either untutored in orthodox monetary theory or his experience had taught him to be skeptical of it. In any case, he was content to think for himself, come what may.

In some respects, Bell was years ahead of his contemporaries. He insisted that there was little benefit in the domestic use of gold from the standpoint of industry. He only cared about having the "physical power of paying . . . wages."[149] The workers themselves, Bell pointed out, actually preferred the convenience of lower denomination—and even token—coins. "I do not doubt," he declared, "that everybody in my employment would rather be paid in silver than in any other sort of currency merely for the convenience of user."[150]

In other respects, however, Bell embraced the most simplistic of the "classical" assumptions: zero adjustment costs. Even David Hume had recognized that it was possible for monetary policy to have real effects before nominal factors were able to adjust. But for Bell, wages were perfectly elastic in response to changes in prices—and vice versa. The "sliding" wage scale, among other things, ensured that prices and wages moved in lockstep, he maintained.[151]

Just what drives the changes in prices and wages? Bell intuited that "the ultimate cause" of the current price-wage spiral was the "extravagant expenditure" attending the war. Of course, the Cunliffe Committee agreed with this. But Bell must have shocked the committee when he questioned whether the growing money supply was the proximate cause—and whether reducing the money supply would generate deflation. Addis could hardly believe this. He asked, "Neither . . . raising the rate of interest nor the contraction of the currency . . . would have the effect of lowering the prices?" Bell was clear: "I am not quite sure that they have any causal connection."[152] Thus Bell cast aside the quantity theory of money in a single breath.

Bell carried these assumptions into the domain of international trade. He questioned the a priori commitment to "maintaining the exchanges," as the committee put it. He argued that exchange rate shifts would affect imports and exports to the same extent. And the UK's industrial exports relied upon imported raw material.[153] The nominal prices and the exchange rates might shift, but in the end, the real prices would remain largely the same.

This was true abroad as well as at home. He picked a fight with Addis, questioning the assumption "that the prices here are higher relatively than they are in other countries. . . . It may be that the inflation is world-wide."[154] Rather than taking the bait, Addis maneuvered him into accepting the orthodox solution of restoring convertibility and reducing the money supply, provided that inflation were worse in the UK.[155]

Bell and the committee alike recognized the challenges of "reduc[ing] the present credit inflation." Cunliffe assumed the manufacturer would agree that the reduction ought "to be very gradual and done with great consideration and watchfulness, or there would be clearly dissatisfaction amongst the operatives and wage earners?" Bell replied, "Yes. If . . . there is going to be a very great fall in wages after the war . . . we shall run very serious risks indeed."[156] In the face of this, the committee assumed that Bell might hope to avert this, "the greatest danger." But he was emphatic to the contrary: "What I want to do is *not* to check the reduction [of prices and wages]; I want to see the reduction take place."[157]

It would not be easy, particularly since "the great mass of people are better off than they have ever been in their lives." Nevertheless, Bell had faith that "the working classes of this country will be persuaded of the advisability of accepting reduction in prices, and consequently in wages." They "must be content to live in a much simpler way." "I do not want them to work any longer," Bell explained, "but I want them to do their work . . . better." They "must be more industrious . . . [and] more earnest in their work."[158] Or, as Nugent had advised, at least more "clever."

Thus, Bell was convinced that price and wage levels were highly responsive to underlying economic factors. He was not certain just what comprised these factors, but he was positive that the money supply was not among them. He seriously doubted that there had been any more inflation in the UK than elsewhere, and given the flexibility of prices and wages, dis-inflation was hardly necessary on macroeconomic grounds. But on moral grounds, austerity was good for the soul. Britons never had it so good. The time had come to reduce their "extravagance." Bell thus welcomed deflation as the penance necessary to atone for wartime indulgences. So for all of his overt questioning of the gold standard articles of faith, Bell preached gold standard ethics. It was for labor to suffer and for capital to help the laborers see the virtue in their suffering.

## The Manchester Chamber of Commerce

Manchester is fifty miles closer to London than is Middlesbrough. And its chamber of commerce was at least that much closer to the gold standard orthodoxy.

The Manchester chamber broadly accepted the proposals that the Cunliffe Committee had shared with them. They agreed that the Bank of England needed the authority to issue unbacked currency in emergencies—but only in consultation with HM Treasury. But the chamber "[does] not think that the other conditions viz., that there should be a 10% Bank rate, and that the Foreign Exchanges should be in our favor, are necessary or desirable—they have proved to be impracticable."[159] Beyond this, however, the chamber did not specify whether the Bank ought to make defensive hikes in such contexts and, if so, to what rate.

The chamber welcomed Cunliffe's initiative to allow banks to diversify their reserve holdings beyond just gold. Yet it did not see why government debt should be given this exclusive privilege. Why should not firms' shares and bonds be valued as they are in the market? Besides, this (inflationary) policy would only encourage the government to borrow more. Instead, these business owners proposed including bills of exchange "and/or First Class Securities."[160]

But this was not a revolt of industry against finance. Indeed, the chamber was actually *more conservative* than was the committee's own chairman. However the non-gold reserves were comprised, they demanded a 40 percent gold reserve, casting Cunliffe's proposed "one-third as hardly sufficient."[161] It is hard to believe that just one month earlier, Cunliffe had proposed a reserve rate of just 25 percent.[162]

## Arthur Michael Samuel, Norwich Chamber of Commerce

The chamber of commerce for Norwich—120 miles from London—was closer still to the orthodoxy. In a memorandum submitted in April, the Norwich chamber generally accepted the suggestions made by the committee. Its members were happy to see the gold concentrated in a central pool in London. And they even embraced the emission of notes on a one-to-three gold backing.[163] Their representative, Arthur Michael Samuel, appeared before the committee in June.

While he effusively praised the Bank, Samuel pressed it to exercise greater oversight over City lending practices. But as he insisted repeatedly, he did *not* seek easy lending or cheap money. This was really just a call for more nationalism in Britain's monetary policy. Currently, he complained, British banks were lending cheaply abroad, which "allowed those foreigners to manufacture foreign goods to compete with British goods actually produced by British depositors like ourselves."[164] Things would be worse after the war, as Germany would use an undervalued currency to promote exports and build its reserves.[165] The Bank should prevent this.

But Samuel had trouble explaining precisely how the Bank could do this. He did not want to limit foreign borrowing: "It is a very lucrative business for Britain that we should lend money to foreigners."[166] Instead, he sought to harm German industry by limiting the holdings of German banks in Britain. But, Cunliffe emphasized, having the German capital "tend[s] to make money rates easier" in the UK. Samuel conceded this but offered that "the advantage will be counter-balanced by the disadvantage of supporting the shoe-maker in Dussel-dorf who is working against us when I send my boots out to Shanghai."[167]

Samuel was thus a mercantilist of the economic nationalist sort. And like the Yorkshire representative, he struggled with the finer points of orthodox economic theory. As he misstepped, he deferred to those formulations offered and approved by the committee. He happily, emphatically, recited the gold standard creed: "I am not a banker, and I know nothing about banking. But I know this . . . whatever happens, even if we manufacturers suffer . . . a £5 note of the Bank of England, must . . . be capable of fetching £5 in gold on demand at any moment. That is paramount. . . . The credit of the country, even if we have to starve, must be kept up. That is the proper view for even us manufac-turers to take."[168]

## Ferdinand Faithful Begg, the London Chamber of Commerce

One could not get closer to the Bank of England than the London Chamber of Commerce, which had been founded in 1881 at Mansion House across the street from the Bank. Since then it had become a major voice for British trade and industry within the British financial system. In fact, it counted 158 peers and 103 MPs among its members.[169] Across June and July, its representative— Ferdinand Faithful Begg—met several times with the Cunliffe Committee, and Begg submitted detailed statements of its position on the currency question.

The official position of the London chamber was only as progressive as that of Cunliffe, and its representative strongly intimated that much of the asso-ciation was even more conservative still. The chamber lent formal support to Cunliffe's proposal to issue notes backed by government securities with just a 20 to 25 percent gold cover.[170] Predictably, Bradbury found it "rather startling to suggest that a central gold reserve of 50 millions . . . is an adequate reserve against a note issue of 180 millions."[171] Begg replied that this was a bare mini-mum and that he, personally, expected the Bank to "be normally . . . working on 50%."[172] Indeed, he deprecated "the lavish way in which the notes are be-ing issued now without cover in gold."[173] Begg's limits on the emission of emergency notes took Cunliffe aback. "Is that not rather drastic?" Cunliffe interjected. "What are people to do for money?"[174]

Cunliffe did not appreciate just how exercised Begg had become about the Treasury notes. In an initial draft of the chamber's submission to the committee, Begg had argued "that these notes have been issued in excess of requirements, are now redundant, and in fact at a discount."[175] This draft went on to praise the orthodoxy enshrined in the Bullion Committee of 1810. It especially praised that committee's specifications of what counts as gold-backed currency and then used those standards to denounce the unbacked Treasury notes as "redundant and depreciated."[176] It was a stinging indictment. These several pages were dropped from the printed version, although it appears that Begg gave the Cunliffe Committee the earlier draft in any case.

In his two appearances before the committee, Begg explained that the chamber was not yet fully resolved on how, or even whether, the Treasury notes could be put onto a sound basis.[177] But he was also sensitive to the market effects of attacking these notes with the vigor he thought warranted. When Cunliffe asked, "You are very much sterner with the Government than you are with the Bank?" Begg replied, "If I gave the answer I should desire to give, you might wish that it should not be put on the Minutes."[178] This was saying something, given that the chamber's printed statement itself said that it was "of the highest importance that every step possible should be taken to minimize the rise in prices."[179]

These representatives of British industry were indistinguishable from Britain's most traditional bankers: if the British economy needed more money, then Britain must get and keep more gold. Begg confirmed to Bradbury that his "view, and the view of the Chamber of Commerce, is that the gold reserves in this country were dangerously small before the War."[180] Goschen pushed back, questioning why even private banks must suffer the expense of acquiring gold if they "never use it."[181] "We are fundamentally at variance on the principle," Begg simply replied.[182]

The chamber's hunger for gold was partly predicated on a belief that a larger gold reserve would minimize interest rate adjustments.[183] Gibbs was at pains to show that a fluctuating interest rate was less significant than the chamber assumed.[184] Begg granted him that; but rather than rethinking the objective, he subsequently returned with a different justification. The private banks had a "moral duty" to help the public move into and out of gold, he argued.[185]

All of this was much too conservative for Cunliffe. He objected that the chamber's proposals would make it "all the more difficult for the Directors and the Governor of the Bank to accumulate a sufficient stock of gold." Begg invoked the orthodoxy: "They would do it by the discount rate." "But it is very difficult," Cunliffe exclaimed. There would be the "outcry." "Why you are raising your rate, and yet you have far more gold than you are compelled to have by law against your note issue," the public would complain.

But Begg was unfazed: "That criticism would be made, no doubt."[186] The "public interest," the Chamber of Commerce representative explained to the Bank of England governor, demanded that "the burden should be distributed. I do not think the central institution should be called upon to bear the whole strain of the demands of commerce."[187] In other words, it was wrong of Cunliffe to suggest that "the burden" should be lessened. The solution was simply to call upon the whole commercial community—Begg's colleagues and chamber members—to share that burden more widely.

The chamber explained that all British industry depended upon British financial stability—and global centrality. In its printed memorandum, the chamber declared, "To whatever extent we may have lost temporarily the financial supremacy of the world owing to the [war] . . . the Bank of England's name still stands second to none throughout the financial centers of the world. And it is therefore in the highest degree necessary not to . . . disturb the basis of our financial system."[188] Begg concluded his appearances with a homily: "I am clear . . . and so is the Chamber that it is . . . in the public interest . . . [and] that it is better for the commercial community that the bankers should all be strong, and all should have their reserves in gold, than that they should always be falling back on the Bank of England, and throwing strain on the central institution. It is a commercial view I am advocating all the time—what the commercial community expects of its bankers."[189] Whatever the challenges, whatever the costs, the British commercial community expected nothing less than a restoration of the world-leading, gold-backed pound sterling.

## British Industry

The Federation of British Industries (FBI)—founded in the Midlands but headquartered in the City of London—was the de facto spokesperson for British industrial interests. It boasted 20,000 member firms and 190 affiliated trade associations. It was, as Boyce put it, "the voice of British industry." And it spoke, unequivocally, for the gold standard.[190]

In a memorandum submitted to the Cunliffe Committee in July, the FBI aligned directly with the committee's approach to the economy. Like the committee, the FBI advocated continued foreign borrowing but recognized that "such arrangements are . . . purely artificial expedients and should be removed as soon as possible."[191] "The only real and lasting remedy for an unfavorable

Exchange," the FBI pronounced, "is the 'natural' one. That is to create a favorable 'Trade Balance.'"[192] "For these purposes," the FBI argued, "Industry and Agriculture should be encouraged to the fullest extent by the Government, who should recognize the supreme national importance of redressing the balance of the Exchange."[193] The FBI thus advocated all manner of restrictions on imports. While the committee might have quibbled with the means—legislated protection rather than abstemious self-denial—the priorities and the project were precisely aligned.

Most important, the FBI explained why manufacturers were so committed to restoring the gold standard. Simply put, it saw the empire's financial and trade interests as interdependent. "The position of London as the world's financial market," the FBI wrote, "has in the past been one of our great sources of revenue, and one of the great factors in putting the exchanges in our favor." Just as Samuel had explained, it did not want to allow "the use of British financial resources for the promotion of the trade of foreign countries . . . to [the] prejudice [of] British trade." But it wanted exchange rate fixity within the empire as quickly as possible, as a precursor to fixed exchange rates beyond. And right in line with the committee's own conclusions, the FBI advised that "there should be no immediate drastic change from the note issue until there is a lesser demand for currency," which depended upon repaying the public debt. Far from challenging the orthodoxy, the FBI resolved that "the restoration of London's financial position should be as complete as possible."[194]

This view was stressed repeatedly by the representatives of British industry. Alongside the Cunliffe Committee, the UK's Ministry of Reconstruction also convened the Committee on Financial Facilities specifically "to consider . . . whether . . . the provisions of financial facilities for trade by means of existing banking and other financial institutions will be adequate to meet the needs of British industry" following the war. The Committee on Financial Facilities was comprised of leading industrialists, along with several bankers and a handful of government experts. It was chaired by Sir Richard Vassar-Smith of Lloyd's Bank, and, crucially, it included Bradbury. Like the Cunliffe Committee, this was a serious group of leading individuals. They met seventeen times, interviewed eleven witnesses, and "considered a large amount of documentary evidence."[195]

What was their conclusion? It was simple and eerily familiar. "In order to achieve the reconstitution of Industry on sound financial and economic lines," the Committee resolved "(1) To re-establish a sound financial basis by means of an effective gold standard; (2) To check any undue expansion of credit which can only be reflected by a further rise in prices; (3) To take steps to reduce to more normal proportions the inflation of credit due to the war."[196]

The correlation is striking, but any who followed the workings of the Cunliffe Committee would not have been surprised. With the principles broadly shared, Bradbury must have been happy to furnish those same formulations he had brought to the fore in the Cunliffe Committee.[197] To what extent did Bradbury lead these industrial interests? To what extent was he led by them? It is impossible to know. In any case, at the end of the day the shepherd was with his flock. British industry, and the bankers who financed them, asked the government to lower prices and to contract credit. They sought deflation as a penitent seeks penance. They wanted to be right with Gold again.[198]

## Conclusion: Paradise Lost

The Cunliffe Committee spent months interviewing the UK's leading bankers as well as its major traders and producers.[199] Additionally, Bradbury confirmed these opinions in his work with the mercantile and industrial representatives on the Committee on Financial Facilities. Those consulted comprised a broad group, but they had only a narrow range of opinions. True, each of the spokesmen brought his own particular notions about the essence of the gold standard, its practical operation, and the best tactics to effect the return. Interestingly, the further one journeyed from the Bank of England, the more imaginative these notions. But the faith itself was never questioned. The priests who administered England's Church of Gold *were* occasionally challenged, but in every one of those few instances they were challenged for being *too avant-garde, too cavalier, too unorthodox.*

We know now that this was wrong. We know now that these well-placed interest groups should have resisted the return to gold, and so we project that position onto them.

So to the modern mind, these discussions are shocking. Here was the sometime governor of the Bank of England and a joint permanent secretary to the Treasury defending their (comparatively) "easy money" policies against the assaults of those powerful actors who had gained by far the most from those non-strictly-orthodox approaches. Here were the high priests of the orthodoxy warning those actors who demanded a return to orthodoxy—or even ultraorthodoxy. Here they were arguing that such a return would inflict excessive—and unnecessary—pain on the UK's financial system, its trade, and its commerce. Capital would suffer from the contraction; and, of course, so too would labor. But here was this congregation of businessmen and bankers demanding less money, lower prices, and higher borrowing costs.

Never mind that all of these interest groups had been the great beneficiaries of the cash infusion brought by the Bradbury notes. Never mind that all of these interest groups would have been better served to have welcomed Cunliffe's far less puritanical version of the gold standard. Never mind that there was relevant experience across time and space—beyond each individual's idiosyncratic beliefs—that might have proved instructive. These groups *demanded* policies that we know, in hindsight, were mortifying.

How can we possibly explain this? The only type of explanation that fits is, simply, religious faith. The principle article of faith in the gold standard orthodoxy was that all of British civilization rested upon a foundation of gold. Everything depended upon the stability of the currency, the sanctity of the pound. Of course, every industrialist, every worker, and every merchant was tempted by the allure of easy money. But all believed that such a path could only lead to chaos, ruin, and eternal damnation. What would it profit England, this orthodoxy asked, to gain the whole world but to lose its soul? And what kingdom awaits those who keep the faith?

This perspective might be shocking, but it is not absurd. The UK's bankers, manufacturers, and traders saw a direct correlation between their global ascent and the ascent of the gold standard in England. Was this not proof enough? Moreover, this interpretation had an eminently reasonable rationale: fidelity will be rewarded in the final judgment. Across history, there have only been a handful of such ascents, and there are more variables than we can count, let alone test. We might know now that the gold standard was the consequence rather than the cause of that ascent, but can we fault these chambers of commerce, these bankers, these industrialists for not being prophetic?

And yet materialism can still explain even the self-flagellation of British industry. For those fearing their mortal death, a decade of austere virtue was well worth another century of heavenly rewards. Or, more simply put, those who were to suffer the most under the gold standard orthodoxy zealously embraced it because they believed that this sanctification—and only this—would save them from death. The pieces might still fit together.

But, as social scientists, we still inquire after the nature of the conversion. For Saint Paul on the road to Damascus, there can be no question. The causes were fully material. But for every Pauline conversion since, the question remains: If a sinner should be "saved" at the hand of, say, Hieronymus Bosch, ought we still term that a "materialist" transformation? For in the case of British industry, it was blinded only metaphorically, not literally. It was not moved physically but cognitively. British industry could only *imagine* the torments of an existence after gold.

And it preferred not to do so.

# CHAPTER 6

# Commandments
## Defining the Law

For the monetary authorities, the widespread consensus that the UK must "return to gold" was both a blessing and a curse. It was a blessing because it provided an unrivaled mandate to do whatever necessary to effect the return. It was a curse because no two figures agreed on the all-important specifics of returning to gold. Simply put, the authorities did not lack the will or the means, but the understanding. More precisely, they wanted a shared understanding of what it meant to be "on gold." And because they disagreed about the nature of this promised salvation, they inevitably disagreed about the means to achieve it.

Here the devil was in the details. Should the UK concentrate its reserves and cease the circulation of gold coin to stabilize the gold price as quickly as possible? Or should it defer the return until it had done the penitent work of stamping out the wartime inflation and had sufficient reserves to render unto note-holders the gold that was theirs to demand? Both were credible returns to gold, but each was a vastly different path. But to those charged with charting the course, the differences had all the import—and all the irreconcilability—of the Christian debate over faith and good works. Thus, the return to gold became, in the first instance, a battle to specify the orthodoxy in all of its particulars.

Within that struggle, there was only one set of actors who had the information, position, and ambition to contend against the Cunliffe Committee: the governors of the Bank of England. The Bank had centuries of experience and data related to the operation of the gold standard. The Cunliffe Committee, by contrast, had Bradbury's rough estimates of the money supply across a few years. At home and abroad, the Bank had an unparalleled reputation for safeguarding the gold standard. By contrast, the Treasury, and Bradbury especially, was associated with the shoddy wartime paper currency. There was no question whose voice commanded more public authority. Just as important, the Bank was practically a veto player. Short of a government takeover, the Cunliffe Committee would have to depend upon the Bank to implement whatever policies it prescribed. Last, the governors of the Bank of England knew all these things. They expected the Bank to endure another two hundred years. They knew the Cunliffe Committee would not be around in so many days. These men saw themselves as the guardians, the proprietors, the masters of the gold standard.

Three men served as governor of the Bank of England from the start of the First World War until the last phase of the Second World War. Cunliffe's first term began in 1913. When it was due to expire in 1915, the Bank's Court of Directors renewed his appointment in recognition of his success in handling the 1914 crisis and to avoid changing leaders in the midst of the war. Cunliffe tried invoking this same imperative again in 1918 but to no avail. That spring, Brien Cokayne was appointed as his replacement, with Montagu Norman as the deputy governor. Two years later, Norman succeeded Cokayne to the governorship. Norman retained the position until 1944.

More than anyone else, these three men constructed the Bank of England's vision of the gold standard in this period. As governor during the First World War and as the head of the Cunliffe Committee, Cunliffe had the opportunity to define the starting points. Cokayne oversaw the transition to peace and could thus set the postwar trajectory. Norman was the last man standing, and his would be the final word on the matter.

The conventional view emphasizes the consensus among the Bank's governors and between the Bank and the Cunliffe Committee.[1] Of course, there *was* zealous agreement about the objective and its priority. But there was endemic conflict between these authorities over the translation of faith into practice, of ideals into institutions, of the word into the law. Thus, the commandments that defined the UK's return to gold were hammered out in the arguments within and between the Cunliffe Committee and the Bank of England. The doctrine that emerged was riddled with contradictory assumptions, logical missteps, and underspecified prescriptions. Despite this—perhaps because of this—the Cunliffe Committee's landmark first report garnered support from every corner.

## *Fidei defensores*: Norman, Cokayne, and Cunliffe

It is telling that the Cunliffe Committee did not solicit the Bank's official opinion on the postwar currency plans until after it had formulated its provisional conclusions. When the invitation did finally arrive—months after Cokayne had replaced Cunliffe—it included a series of leading questions, many of which began, "Would you agree that . . ."[2] It appears that Norman, the new deputy governor, drafted the Bank's replies to the committee's queries.[3] As Cunliffe must have anticipated, this brought yet another version of the orthodoxy.

The Cunliffe Committee might have been alarmed at seeing "The first action should be the arrangement of the debt which the Government has contracted with foreign countries."[4] Many, including Cunliffe himself initially, assumed that savvy foreign borrowing might reduce the need for painful interest rate hikes. But Bradbury and Pigou deprecated this as merely a temporary palliative. Yet Cokayne still favored it, and Norman held it as a first recourse.

The position on gold exports was even more arresting. The Bank's reply stated, "The Government should retain power to prohibit and control [gold exports] during the reconstruction period."[5] Norman himself would have gone further, adding trade restrictions and "the prevention of export of capital and foreign loans" more generally.[6] The Cunliffe Committee had unanimously, adamantly condemned such capital controls.

These replies were approved by the Bank's Court of Directors and sent on to Cunliffe.[7] Interestingly, Cunliffe did not circulate them to the rest of his committee. In fact, when Cokayne appeared before a poorly attended meeting of the Cunliffe Committee in early July, he did not feel at all bound to the plan Norman had prepared. Crucially, he went to the opposite extreme of Norman's position on the movement of gold and capital.[8]

Cokayne's doctrine is best described as ultraorthodox, veritably bullionist. Even after the gold standard was fully operational, he thought the UK ought to continue amassing gold. Cunliffe was incredulous. "It is very easy to say we must have so much gold," the former governor said to the new governor, "but you and I know how very difficult it is to get gold and keep it." "Exactly," Cokayne replied. "But that of course does not apply to the gold in the pockets of the people. . . . It has . . . been immensely useful in this war to have all that hidden reserve."[9]

With that, Cokayne rolled back economic theology by several centuries. This was precisely the logic offered by John Locke and other mercantilists: reserves prove invaluable in times of war.[10] This requires securing a positive balance of trade, as both Cokayne and the committee agreed.[11] But it also means eschewing paper money to force the circulation of gold as currency.

Dethroning such thinking was a principal objective of *The Wealth of Nations*. For Smith, "Money is neither a material to work upon, nor a tool to work with; and . . . the workman['s] . . . real revenue . . . consists . . . not in the metal pieces, but in what can be got for them." Thus, "the gold and silver money which circulates in any country may very properly be compared to a highway, which, while it circulates and carries to market all the grass and corn of the country, produces itself not a single pile of either." By using bank notes, however, "gold and silver . . . will be sent abroad," and "the quantity of the materials, tools, and maintenance . . . may be increased by the whole value of gold and silver which used to be employed in purchasing them." This rejection of the "Midas fallacy" was the cornerstone of Smith's laissez-faire liberalism. But here was Cokayne recasting the wealth of nations.[12]

Yet the church of the gold standard was a large one, accommodating bullionists, mercantilists, and liberals alike. So Cunliffe advanced the Smithian proposal to economize the country's supply of precious metals. Day to day, the UK enjoyed little credit for "this gold in the pockets of the people," he insisted.[13] "If we held all the gold in one central place," however, "we should compare more favorably with France and Germany and those countries where they only have one store."[14] Moreover, Cunliffe argued, the Bank of England would have to adjust rates based on its own gold holdings, not the total "reserve" scattered throughout the country. Thus, movements in the bank's gold holdings would drive frequent, sizable shifts in interest rates.

But for Cokayne, this went to the heart of whether the currency were "really absolutely convertible." "If [people] are to be discouraged from cashing their notes, you can hardly call them gold warrants, can you?" he gibed.[15] He went to the extreme, suggesting it was "desirable to encourage the public to seek to exchange their notes for gold." "The surest way to make them happy with their notes," he insisted, "is to tell them to come and get gold for them."[16]

This was too much for the committee. Cunliffe insisted that it would be hard enough just to make the gold standard operational with paper notes backed by gold at a high ratio. Encouraging the circulation of gold coins in addition to this "would be an extravagance and a luxury."[17]

But for Cokayne, this was not a distant ideal to be pursued. He "looked forward to . . . there coming a time *during* the reconstruction period when you could allow the use of gold internally."[18] He announced with great pride that the Bank of England never stopped exchanging gold for its notes. Even with the war still raging, "anybody can get it." Given the difficulties of exporting, though, due diligence required that "we . . . make it our business to find out why he wants it." This did "discourage without prohibition." But this was just a wartime exigency. After the war, "it would be a great mistake to prohibit the export of gold." In fact, Cokayne assured the committee, "it does not seem certain that it will be necessary to prohibit it at all."[19]

But when it came to the importation of gold, Cokayne was a good deal less committed to the free market. He sought to have all gold imports run through the Bank of England, giving it the first chance to purchase gold. At best, this was proprietary favoritism of the Bank's own interests. At worst, it was the kind of contradiction that can only be reconciled within the theology of bullionism. Cunliffe thus countered with laissez-faire in response: "The Committee is very anxious that there should be no appearance of restriction on dealings in gold."[20]

It came as little surprise that Cokayne was determined to reduce the supply of unbacked currency quickly and—crucially—automatically. Precisely because "it is bound to be a very painful process [to commerce and industry]," Cokayne argued, "it would be very difficult to effect sufficient reduction unless there were a law to make it compulsory."[21] Bradbury feared that Cokayne was being too aggressive. Reduction was necessary, but "the reduction step in the first instance is a more drastic remedy than the patient is likely to be able to stand."[22] Moreover, judgment was required, as Cokayne acknowledged: "You cannot be wise before the event and say exactly by how much it should be reduced."[23] Cunliffe interjected: "Now Mr. Governor, if you feel you are not competent to suggest what reduction is possible, could you expect this Committee to do so?"[24]

At points, the simmering tensions came to a head. Bradbury was clearly insulted by Cokayne's pains to prevent the Bank's notes from becoming "sullied" by the Treasury's "Bradburys."[25] Bradbury defended the emission, reminding Cokayne that both types of pound notes "are of value, and the only difference . . . would arise if one of the issues was inconvertible." Cokayne agreed with the economic theory here, but he asked, "Do you think . . . Parliament is likely to sanction the Government going on printing its own notes in times of peace?" "What do you think, Sir John?" he taunted. "I am here rather to ask questions than to answer them," Bradbury snapped back. Cokayne backed down, and Cunliffe redirected the questioning.[26]

Traditionally, Cunliffe has been castigated as the "bully," while Cokayne has been celebrated as the "brilliant mediator between angry giants."[27] On this occasion at least, the characters played opposite roles. From the start, Cunliffe welcomed Cokayne as "one of the most important witnesses."[28] "If you can allow us," he said deferentially, "we should like to consult you, not as a witness giving evidence, but really in consultation now and again before our work is terminated."[29] Cunliffe mouthed such graciousness throughout the discussion. One could almost forget the Bank's internecine conflict of the past year.

But Cunliffe was only being polite—likely, just politic. As the meeting closed, he mentioned Cokayne's possible reappearance before the committee. Cokayne was keen: "Do you mean next week or some other day this week?" Cunliffe was less so: "I should not think it would not be for some weeks."[30] That invitation, however, never materialized.

In fact, the committee dispatched with Cokayne's proposals the day after his appearance. Bradbury's characterization of one was typical: "sound in theory but . . . too drastic in practice." The committee also deprecated (Norman's proposal of) prohibiting gold exports. "The maintenance of adequate [interest] rates," the committee held, "should be sufficient." With that agreed, the committee returned to drafting its report.[31]

But while the proposals from Cokayne and Norman were stymied, the Bank's intervention did affect the Cunliffe Committee's approach. Specifically, it shifted the terms of contention within the committee. Moderate by comparison, Bradbury's position was now the compromise between Cokayne's ultraorthodoxy and Cunliffe's reformism. Moreover, it made clear that Cunliffe was a spent force within the Bank. No longer could he threaten to play the Bank against his committee's majority. At the same time, Cunliffe recognized that protecting the church required preserving its façade. He could not attack either the Bank or his own committee without shaking the edifice he hoped to save.

So as the committee formulated its conclusions, Cunliffe's bold scheme of using government securities alongside gold in reserve was trimmed back to nothing.[32] Within a month, the Cunliffe Committee had finished its *First Interim Report*. It aligned most directly with the Bradbury-Pigou position. But that is not to say that it was internally consistent or coherent.


## The Infamous Interim Report

The Cunliffe Committee's *First Interim Report* is remembered for its simple diagnosis and prescription. "Before the war," it declared, "the country possessed a complete and effective gold standard." "During the war," however, "the conditions necessary to the maintenance of that standard have ceased to exist" due to the "unlimited issue of Currency Notes."[33] The conclusion thus followed: to restore the gold standard, it was as simple as removing those excess notes from circulation. But there was much more to this report than just this simple dictate.[34]

## Toward a Balance-of-Payments Model

The *First Interim Report* went beyond the textbook price-specie-flow model, first developed by David Hume in the mid-eighteenth century.[35] Since then, the Bank of England had interposed itself as the manager of the gold standard. The report stressed the centrality of interest rates, but it contradicted itself on the direction of causation.

At several points, the report espoused mercantilist economics. "When the exchanges were favorable," it explained, "gold flowed freely into this country. . . . When the balance of trade was unfavorable and the exchanges were adverse, it became profitable to export gold."[36] In turn, these changes in the money supply drove changes in the interest rate: "The amount of legal tender currency . . . which can be kept in circulation . . . will determine itself automatically, since, if the currency becomes redundant, the rate of discount will fall, and prices will rise; notes will be presented in exchange for gold for export, and the volume of the currency will be reduced *pro tanto*. If, on the other hand, the supply of currency falls below current requirements, the rate of discount will rise, prices will fall, gold will be imported and new notes taken out in exchange for it."[37] This thinking followed from primeval assumptions: unbacked paper money has no long-run market value, the quantity of gold determines the money supply, the balance of trade is the primary determinant of the country's gold supply, and the market rate of interest follows changes in the quantity of money in the economy.

Yet the report also took significant steps into the modern age. It recognized the power of the Bank of England to set interest rates and the effects of interest rates on both international capital flows and domestic macroeconomic conditions. As gold flowed outward, the Bank learned to make defensive interest rate hikes. This had two effects. First, "the raising of the discount rate had the immediate effect of retaining money here which would otherwise have been remitted abroad and of attracting remittances from abroad to take advantage of the higher rate, thus checking the outflow of gold."[38] Of course, to compete internationally for funds, "it is essential that the rate of discount in this country should be raised relatively to the rates ruling in other countries."[39] Second, it contracted credit, generated unemployment, reduced inflationary pressure, and strengthened the balance of trade. The report blithely explained how "the consequent slackening of employment . . . diminished the demand for consumable goods." This generated the needed domestic price deflation, "which, by checking imports and stimulating exports, corrected the adverse trade balance which was the primary cause of the difficulty."[40] Thus, causality was reversed; here the report held that changes in the interest rate drove the balance of trade.

The report's rendering of the balance of payments was underdeveloped in other ways as well. Beyond the outsized importance of the balance of trade, it offered no serious consideration of the capital account beyond movements chasing high interest rates. There was no serious consideration of investment—either foreign direct investment or speculative flows. For those looking to invest, loose monetary policy and/or expansionary fiscal policy might *attract* capital as both stimulate the economy. In such cases, investors must determine whether they think the gains will outpace the (real) losses due to inflation. But the report considered none of this. It also ignored the earnings on prior investments—the so-called invisibles. Whether these earnings are returned home depends upon the exchange rate, investment prospects, and tax rates at home and broad, among other things. In the British case, this share of the capital account came to play an outsized role in the balance of payments throughout the 1920s.[41] Yet it hardly entered into the considerations of the Cunliffe Committee, and it certainly did not appear in that committee's *First Interim Report*.

Last, the report was inconsistent on the position of reserve adjustment in achieving balance within the balance of payments. On the one hand, it talked as though gold inflows "automatically" increase the money supply. But on the other hand, it also prescribed that Britain grow its reserves. How could this be done other than by "sterilizing" gold inflows? The implication for international economic relations is significant: If the UK could (and should!) bend these "rules of the gold standard game," what hope was there that other countries will not do the same? And if every country were to pursue gold inflows, what hope was there of avoiding mercantilist trade war?

## Economics Meets Politics

While the report gave little thought to the ways that the gold standard could underpin international conflict, it did not hesitate to highlight the ways in which the Great War had undermined the gold standard. The war had "brought influences into play in consequence of which the gold standard has ceased to be effective."[42] The report put it delicately: "The need of the Government . . . to finance the war in excess of the amounts raised by taxation and by loans from the public has made necessary the creation of credits in their favor with the Bank of England." In plain terms, HM Treasury had printed money.

Normally, "this large issue of new notes, associated, as it is, with abnormally high prices and unfavorable exchanges," would have been cashed in for gold. This would have depleted Britain's gold reserves and prompted the Bank to take defensive action. "But," the report notes, "[wartime] conditions have not been normal. The public are content to employ currency notes for internal purposes, and . . . war conditions interpose effective practical obstacles against the export of gold."[43] This has "severed the link which formerly existed between the values of coin and of uncoined gold." The result was at least "some depreciation" in the pound.[44]

These were general statements about the working of the gold standard in broad terms. Yet the report stressed that these lessons applied even more strictly to the UK "by reason of the vital importance of its position in international finance." The UK was exceptional. Other countries "have not in practice maintained the absolutely-free gold market which this country . . . is bound to do."[45]

But this was *not* a case of monetary stability taking priority over other macroeconomic goals—of finance trumping industry or of capital dominating labor. Indeed, restoring the gold standard was in the interest of all Britons. "The uncertainty of the monetary situation," the report warned, "will handicap our industry, our position as an international financial center will suffer and our general commercial status in the eyes of the world will be lowered."[46] Simply put, there was no trade-off between postwar adjustment and the restoration of the gold standard. Quite the contrary: "Nothing can contribute more to a speedy recovery from the effects of the war, and to the rehabilitation of the foreign exchanges, than the re-establishment of the currency upon a sound basis."[47]

## Proscription as the Prescription

But how to restore the prewar monetary order? The short answer was austerity. "If a sound monetary position is to be re-established and the gold standard to be effectively maintained," the report declared, "it is . . . essential that Government borrowings should cease at the earliest possible moment after the war."[48] There could be no shortcuts: "The shortage of real capital must be made good by genuine savings. It cannot be met by the creation of fresh purchasing power in the form of bank advances to the Government or to manufacturers under Government guarantee or otherwise, and any resort to such expedients can only aggravate the evil and retard . . . the recovery of the country from the losses sustained during the war."[49] This included capital controls and foreign support. Following Pigou's memorandum, the report warned, "This result may be postponed for a time by restrictions on the export of gold and by borrowing abroad. But the continuance of such a policy after the war can only render the remedial measures which would ultimately be inevitable more painful and protracted."[50]

Instead, the UK's gold supply would be economized just as the Cunliffe Committee had agreed. "All banks should transfer any gold now held by them to the Bank of England."[51] And most boldly, the report insisted that it was neither "necessary for the maintenance of an effective gold standard, nor . . . desirable, that there should be an early resumption of the internal circulation of gold coin."[52]

What of Cunliffe's reformist scheme? Throughout, he had repeatedly stated that "the development of the check system had altered the position under Peel's [1844 Bank] Act." As such, gold had become less central to the financial system. On this basis, Cunliffe had proposed that "banks should keep reserves in some form of interest-bearing government security on which emergency currency might be issued at suitable rates."[53] The report used Cunliffe's language to describe this as a positive matter but condemned this trend as noxious. "During the transitional period," it insisted, ". . . new notes should be issued, not against Government securities, but against Bank of England Notes."[54]

What of the unbacked notes already circulating? The report was clear: "To ensure that . . . the gold standard [is not] . . . endangered, it is . . . imperative that the issue of fiduciary [unbacked] notes shall be . . . once more limited by law."[55] But rather than setting a maximum fiduciary issue or proposing a strict ratio between the reserves and the fiduciary issue, the report followed Bradbury's recommended minimum of £150 million held in a centralized reserve. It also embraced Bradbury's precise approach: "Until this amount has been reached and maintained concurrently with a satisfactory foreign exchange position for a period of at least a year, the policy of reducing the uncovered note issue as and when opportunity offers should be consistently followed." The reductions would work like a ratchet: "When reductions have taken place, the actual maximum fiduciary circulation in any year should become the legal maximum for the following year." In emergency contexts, the Bank (in consultation with HM Treasury) could temporarily increase the fiduciary issue. In such instances, however, "Bank rate should be raised to, and maintained at, a figure sufficiently high to secure the earliest possible retirement of the excess issue."[56]

Just how excessive had these issues been?

## Enough Gold?

In mid-July, the Bankers' Clearing House in London sent Bradbury estimates of the reserve holdings of banks across the UK. The most important figure—the estimate that banks held £40 million in gold reserves—was close to Bradbury's previous estimate. Unfortunately, the figures were wrong—dreadfully wrong in the case of the Scottish and Irish banks.[57] Bradbury would have realized this if only he had asked those bankers directly. In fact, he never updated his estimates even after they pressed their figures upon him a year later. His initial estimates fit with his priors, and neither he nor his colleagues cared much about how the gold standard actually operated, in practice, in Scotland and Ireland.[58] For Bradbury and the Cunliffe Committee, this would remain a story about the gold in London.

Throughout the course of the war, the Bank of England and HM Treasury somehow trebled their gold holdings, from £36 million in 1913 to £113 million by 1919. At the same time, the UK's share of the world's official gold reserves rose from 3.4 percent to 10.4 percent. The year 1920 alone saw the Bank's and HM Treasury's combined reserves swell by another £31 million. Some portion of this came when London seized the gold held by the Scottish banks. Some came from South Africa.[59] The magnitude of this shift, however, underscores the paucity of Bradbury's gold estimates.[60]

What does all of this matter? Who cares how much actual gold the UK had in 1918? The answer is plain: anyone and everyone who would have to live under the doctrine handed down from the Cunliffe Committee. That is to say, everyone in the UK; everyone in a country that would have to compete with London to maintain its own share of the world's finite gold supply; and everyone in those locales—from Belfast to Berlin, from the Gold Coast to the Gold Fields—that might face gold predation in the wake of the Great War.

In time, the world would learn that there are other (less zero-sum) ways to organize the international monetary order. Some had already learned there are even other ways to operate a "gold standard." Indeed, Cunliffe himself had advanced numerous such plans, all of them designed to loosen the coupling between the UK's gold supply and its money supply. But Bradbury, together with Pigou and Governor Cokayne, were emphatic: anything that tempered the central role of gold was anathema to the gold standard system itself. It was a heresy that would lead inevitably to a deluge of valueless paper pounds. Nothing less than a reserve of £150 million of actual gold could prevent this. Even according to their own principles, this figure could have been larger, thus requiring more gold accumulation and less currency note deflation. Or it could have been smaller, thus requiring less gold accumulation and more currency note deflation. But they ultimately agreed on the nice round figure of £150 million. We saw earlier that this figure was derived a priori, more through hunches and intra-committee compromises than through any serious empirical analysis of the UK's prior monetary history. We see now that about the same low level of rigor was employed to gauge the UK's present monetary circumstances. Suffice it to say, these were the most important figures in the London-led global monetary order, and none of the monetary authorities did

*Table 3*  Cunliffe Committee's Reported June 1914 UK Money Supply

| CATEGORY | CURRENCY TYPE | BRADBURY ESTIMATE | CUNLIFFE COMMITTEE INTERIM REPORT |
|---|---|---|---|
| Bank of England Fiduciary Issue | Unbacked | 18.45 | 18.45 |
| Non–Bank of England Fiduciary Issue | Unbacked | 9.433 | not listed |
| Bank of England Notes | Backed | 38.476 | 38.476 |
| Privately Held Gold | Gold | 123 | 123 |
| | *Totals* | | |
| | Unbacked | 27.883 | 18.45 |
| | Backed and Gold | 161.476 | 161.476 |
| | All Currency | 189.359 | 179.926 |
| | UK Gold Coverage Rate | 85.28% | 89.75% |

Millions of Pounds. Source: NA T 185/2, Bradbury, "Future Dimensions of the Fiduciary Issue," March 9, 1918; Cunliffe Committee, *First Interim Report.*

*Table 4*  Cunliffe Committee's Reported 1917/1918 UK Money Supply

| CATEGORY | CURRENCY TYPE | BRADBURY ESTIMATE DECEMBER 31, 1917 | CUNLIFFE COMMITTEE INTERIM REPORT JULY 10, 1918 |
|---|---|---|---|
| Bank of England Fiduciary Issue | Unbacked | 18.45 | 18.45 |
| Non–Bank of England Fiduciary Issue | Unbacked | 9.366 | 5 |
| Treasury Fiduciary Issue | Unbacked | 184.232 | 230.412 |
| Bank of England Notes | Backed | 57.131 | 65.368 |
| Treasury Notes | Backed | 28.5 | 28.5 |
| Private Banks' Gold | Gold | 40 | 40 |
| Private Individuals' Gold | Gold | 40 | "unknown" |
| | *Totals* | | |
| | Unbacked | 212.048 | 253.862 |
| | Backed and Gold | 165.631 | 133.868 |
| | All Currency | 377.68 | 387.73 |
| | UK Gold Coverage Rate | 43.85% | 34.53% |

Millions of Pounds. The sums in the Cunliffe Committee report are reputed to be from July 10, 1918, but most are precisely the same as those that Bradbury estimated the previous March. Source: NA T 185/2, Bradbury, "Future Dimensions of the Fiduciary Issue," March 9, 1918; Cunliffe Committee, *First Interim Report.*

much to derive them. As Foucault put it, there was no "exteriority" "between [their] techniques of knowledge and strategies of power." What really mattered were "the relations that obtain between penitents and confessors, or the faithful and their directors of conscience."[61] Conveniently for them—but horrifyingly for us—the Cunliffe Committee members' back-of-the-envelope calculations all aligned with the priors of those individuals who made them.

The most important conclusion, albeit implicit in the report, was that England was ready to begin restoring the gold standard straight away. The report's figures listed the UK's 1918 gold supply at nearly £134 million. But it noted, "There is also a certain amount of gold coin still in the hands of the public which ought to be added to the last-mentioned figure." Bradbury had previously estimated this at upwards of £40 million, but the report simply stated, "[This] amount is unknown."[62]

This was a brilliant bit of subterfuge. The headline figure of "£134 million" was nice and large. So it was good news to any who assumed that England was destitute. But ostensibly, the figure was well below the crucial £150 million threshold. Of course, the informed, careful reader would have included private gold holdings in his or her calculations. After all, as Cokayne had explained, the pound's gold value was buoyed by the gold it could draw from the private market. Given that every estimate of the gold held privately would have greatly exceeded £16 million, it was easy enough to follow the report to its logical conclusion: the time for austerity was nigh. But for now, the report seemed to offer some breathing space for the politicians. Those who embraced it would be obliged but not compelled.

## Conclusion: After the Interim Report

The Cunliffe Committee's *First Interim Report* was shared with the Cabinet in the late summer of 1918.[63] It was published that autumn.[64] As the report circulated, it was widely hailed in the City of London. Meredith & Company, one of the City's financial houses, praised the committee's "courage" in laying bare "the real causes underlying . . . inflation in this country, and its corollary, the practical breakdown of the Gold standard."[65] The report was forthright: "The firm determination to get back as quickly as possible to the unimpeachable Gold basis of our Currency necessitates drastic measures."[66] The bankers were clear that this cut against their short-term interests. The alternative of cheap money would stimulate their lending and inflate their profits, "but to supply [capital] by a dilution of our Money would, in the end, be suicidal."[67] "In times of difficulty," the bankers explained, "we want a Money

Dictator . . . and he can only be supplied by the Bank of England."[68] The report promised this. And as a result, it was "destined to become a classic in our financial literature ranking side by side with . . . the report of the Bullion Committee of 1810."[69]

At the same time, Cokayne led the Bank in drafting a formal position on the postwar currency arrangements. Ostensibly, this memorandum built upon the formal replies Norman had led in drafting for the Cunliffe Committee the previous June. Yet Norman was either uninvolved in this new paper, or he objected to its conclusions. In either case, this deputy governor's name was conspicuously missing from the memorandum's signatories.[70] Instead, it was a fulsome restatement of the views that Cokayne deployed during his testimony, including his ambition to see gold coin circulating again.

Crucially, Cokayne's position on capital controls was the most important departure from the Norman draft. In contrast to Norman's gold embargo, the Cokayne paper "intentionally avoided recommending that exports . . . of gold should be prohibited." Just as Cokayne had testified, the Bank sought "the complete re-establishment as soon as possible of our free market for gold."[71] Thus did Cokayne fashion the Bank's position along his own lines. On this vital issue, the Bank was aligned with the Cunliffe Committee—for now. But Norman had only begun to fight.

# PART THREE

# *Mythology*

The mind is its own place, and in it self
Can make a Heav'n of Hell, a Hell of Heav'n.
(Milton, *Paradise Lost*)

# CHAPTER 7

# Myths

## Theirs and Ours

As a practical matter, "returning to the international gold standard" in 1925 was really an abandonment of capital controls.[1] It was effected by Churchill in his announcement to Parliament that "a general license will be given . . . for the export of gold bullion from today."[2] Under the 1920 Gold and Silver (Export Control, &c.) Act, gold export required authorization from the Treasury.[3] This was the latest mechanism by which the government controlled international capital movements.

But for all of the (well-warranted) discussion of the abandonment of these capital controls, there has been almost no analysis of their introduction in the first place. Most of the historical accounts we do have are brief and unsatisfying.[4] Typically, the 1920 legislation is treated as a continuation of the capital controls introduced during the war. Sayers, for instance, casts them as an "inevitability." In the spring of 1919, he explains, the authorities accepted "the Bank's view—that the gold standard should be restored and that the Bank should protect the exchanges by unrestricted manipulation of Bank rate." The only issue was the "question of timing." "Nobody," we are told, regarded an "early" return to gold as "immediately practicable." So Lloyd George's War Cabinet used its authority to create an embargo as a "technical" fix to the problem. Then the following year, when the government's wartime powers were due to expire, Parliament simply passed the Gold and Silver (Export Control, &c.) Act to provide "a new statutory basis for the gold export embargo."[5]

This account, however, overstates the continuity of the UK's monetary policy in this period. Across 1919, one of the Cunliffe Committee's leading members, Bradbury, brought this mandate to the center of the government's postwar planning and transition. That spring, he persuaded Lloyd George to largely eliminate the extensive wartime controls. In the summer, Bradbury reconvened the Cunliffe Committee and pushed through its *Final Report* to entrench his version of the orthodox dogma in general and to continue the liberalization of the capital controls in particular. He was remarkably successful at this stage. Indeed, by the start of 1920, Keynes later reflected, "all controls had been abandoned."[6]

At that time, Keynes still followed Bradbury as a major exponent of precisely this version of the orthodoxy. Instead, Bradbury faced stalwart opposition from the most unlikely of quarters: the rising figure within the Bank of England, Montagu Norman. Norman shared Bradbury's commitment to return to the gold standard, but he deeply disagreed with the strategy laid out in the Cunliffe Committee's reports. From the start of 1919, Norman made clear his priority to strictly regulate international capital movements. So as Bradbury and Governor Cokayne worked to roll back the wartime capital controls, Norman offered only tepid support at best. As deputy governor, Norman undermined efforts to restart the global gold trade at several points. He even appears to have thwarted Bradbury's efforts to unify the UK's bankers into a coalition lobbying for this capital account liberalization.

When he became governor in 1920, Norman set an entirely new course for the Bank and its return to gold. He deprecated the cooperative arrangements established between the Treasury and his predecessors at the Bank. At the same time, he ceased using interest rate adjustments in the "self-help" manner prescribed by the Cunliffe Committee's reports and deployed by his predecessors. In fact, the highest interest rate that Norman imposed in his twenty-four years as governor came in the first month of his tenure. It was just 7 percent, and this was really the fulfillment of the plans charted by the outgoing governor (Cokayne) at the time.

Instead, Norman focused on cultivating cooperative relationships with like-minded central bankers abroad. In time, this would become his favorite tool of monetary policy. Crucially, he appears to have been instrumental in encouraging the Conservative government to create the Gold and Silver (Export Control, &c.) Act at the end of 1920, essentially reversing Bradbury's trend toward liberalization. He then vigorously defended capital controls until the very end of 1924, against Bradbury's vocal objections. He only relented after he had arranged the terms of a return in conjunction with the United States and secured a commitment from the Treasury to restore the gold standard on the terms he set. Norman was indeed zealous, but his was a different dogma.

This radical change in approach—this reformation of the faith—has gone largely unnoticed. Just as important, when it does come into view, it appears positively mystifying. It simply cannot be explained using social scientific—particularly, structural—theories of the interests and institutions of the UK in the 1920s.

Scholars have long recognized that foreign economic policy carries with it huge distributional implications. Whether interest groups are defined in terms of class or in terms of economic sector, we know that different policies dole out the pain and the gain in different directions. Over the years, economists have become quite adept at predicting the economic effects of various policies. The field of political economy goes one step further. It has been built upon the premise that political cleavages form as actors lobby for those foreign economic policies that best serve their own particular interests.[7]

Such interest-group models of social science ought to have little trouble explaining restrictions on capital flows simply because the distributive implications are so clear. Insofar as they are effective, they hold capital captive, allowing the authorities to run more lax monetary and fiscal policies.[8] This tends to shift the burden of adjustment from labor to capital. Indeed, the conventional model is simple: "Leftist governments, who are more likely to pursue expansionary monetary policies, are more likely to rely on capital controls than rightist governments."[9] If we were to apply the conventional model to the UK in 1920, we would expect the Conservatives and right-wing Liberals to support the removal of the capital controls, and the Labourites and left-wing Liberals to support their extension and expansion.

But any who might hope for a simple mapping of economic interests onto policy preferences will be disappointed by the findings in this book. In fact, the Conservatives were the ones who pushed the gold export embargo through Parliament. Indeed, the very man who introduced the legislation in 1920, Stanley Baldwin, was the prime minister who presided over the controls' removal by Churchill in 1925.[10] At the same time, the Labour Party *and* the labor unions vigorously criticized the controls on the grounds that they introduced inflation and thus reduced real wages. In fact, concerns about the rising cost of living made workers and their union leaders some of the most zealous advocates of a deflationary return to gold, as these next several chapters will show.

Last, there is the potential explanatory power of institutions. "One of the strongest and most interesting findings" of the classic account of "the political economy of capital controls" "is that independent Central Banks are less likely to impose capital controls than more dependent ones," observe Alesina, Grilli, and Milesi-Ferrett.[11] Of course, the Bank of England was hugely independent, and its governor faced few checks either within or without. This became even truer as Norman deprecated the deferential disposition of his predecessors. Yet Norman was the monetary authority who did the most to preserve and extend the UK's capital controls in this period. He used his position within the Bank not to force the government to liberalize the capital account but to stop the Treasury from continuing on its course doing so.

Thus, this part of the book shows that we have this crucial story largely backwards. The ideas that defined the introduction of capital controls directly violated the intellectual consensus at the time. The interests that were advanced were not those of the party that imposed the controls, while the very actors who could have benefited the most from them—that is, the working class—vigorously opposed them. And the institutions that granted the Bank of England unprecedented autonomy were actually used by its governor to foist these controls upon the government.

The trouble, of course, is that those setting policy seldom behave as our structural models predict—or prescribe. To understand why and how the UK embraced capital controls after the First World War, we must grapple with the words and deeds of the actors themselves.

# CHAPTER 8

# Liberalization

## Implementing the Orthodoxy

We are inured to thinking that the First World War "ended" at the eleventh hour of the eleventh day of the eleventh month of 1918. But this was merely the date at which the armistice began, at which hostilities were suspended. The war itself was not over, as Parliament shortly made clear in the Termination of the Present War (Definition) Act. The act granted "His Majesty in Council" the authority to "declare what date is to be treated as the date of the termination of the present war." It continued: "The date so declared shall be as nearly as may be the date of the exchange or deposit of ratifications of the treaty or treaties of peace."[1] Thus, as far as the UK was concerned, the "state of war" would continue until the last peace treaty was ratified.

This had enormous practical implications. Abroad, this enabled the British Empire to keep its soldiers mobilized, effectively shifting the balance of power—and thus bargaining power—across the belligerents. At home, it granted the government the authority to continue its wartime economic management policies. Discretionary authority thus remained in the hands of the prime minister (Lloyd George) and his ministers in the "War Cabinet."

Originally formed by the Ministry of Reconstruction, the Cunliffe Committee had crafted a plan for peacetime, for a return to gold after the war had finished. But the committee never considered that the "state of war" might be maintained as a political and economic matter long after military hostilities had ceased. This, Bradbury rightly came to fear, might create an effective fiction that reduced the pressure on the government to effect the committee's prescribed polices immediately. He was determined that this would not become a space in which the Cunliffe Committee doctrine was exalted but not implemented.

It was always going to be difficult to convince Lloyd George and his cabinet to voluntarily surrender their control over capital markets. These were ministers accustomed to authority and control. But Bradbury's mission was all the more difficult because the Cunliffe Committee's orthodox resolutions prescribed austerity for the postwar period. Few victorious governments would have welcomed the sudden economic shock of quickly shifting from wartime (expansionary) fiscal policy to gold standard orthodoxy. And Lloyd George in particular hoped to return to his longstanding social mission and thus to extending the period of expansionary policy.

Bradbury's approach to, and management of, the government can only be described as masterful. He encouraged the Conservative members of the cabinet as they reigned in Lloyd George's spending plans. For the more progressive members, he made the implementation of the Cunliffe Committee's recommendations (in general) and the liberalization of capital controls (in particular) seem not just desirable but unavoidable.

This variegated history cuts against the potted accounts of this transitional period. Ahamed's Pulitzer prize-winning account, for instance, casts Norman as "the most orthodox" among "the purists within the Bank of England." "In 1918," we are told, he "had wanted to return to gold the moment the guns stopped firing." Yet, there is no evidence to support this supposition; and there is little discussion of the other major figures within the Bank. At the same time, Ahamed glosses over the deep, increasingly important divide between Norman at the Bank and Bradbury at the Treasury.[2]

It is not just that the history is more complicated than we have appreciated. The received wisdom gets this history largely backwards. As this chapter shows, Bradbury fought successfully to see the capital controls steadily liberalized across the two years following the armistice. He did this even as Norman emerged as a major advocate of *increasing* those restrictions and *delaying* the restoration. Bradbury did this even as Norman's influence over, and resistance from, the Bank grew. Carefully tracing the shifting terms of debate and policies embraced by these figures reveals the roots of the titanic clash between competing versions of the gold standard that erupted several years later. It also provides additional evidence disconfirming the prediction of social scientific theories about the policy preferences of treasuries and independent central banks.

## Toward Peace—and Orthodoxy

Famously, Parliament first abandoned capital controls in 1663.[3] England's tradition of free capital movement was thus even older—by a generation—than the Bank of England itself.[4] So it was with great pride that Governor Cokayne reminded the Cunliffe Committee that, even in the darkest days of the war, the export of gold itself "never [had] been prohibited."[5] This was technically true, but it was a broken reed. As contemporaries from the Cunliffe Committee to Keynes noted, maritime hostilities made the cost of insuring gold shipments prohibitively expensive. And, Cokayne admitted, even the promise to convert notes into gold was diluted by the substantial disapprobation the Bank served to every customer who came to make the conversion.

More important, just about every other form of capital movement was restricted during the war. Using the blanket powers granted by the Defence of the Realm Act (1914), the cabinet began by limiting overseas investments and loans.[6] Over the next several years, these controls were steadily expanded. At the start of 1917, Regulations 7D and 7E restricted UK residents' rights to dispose of foreign securities and even granted the Treasury the authority to seize them as necessary. November then brought Regulation 41D, "the grandfather of codified exchange control in the United Kingdom."[7] It essentially eliminated all rights to remit money abroad.

These were more than just "rudimentary" controls.[8] They went well beyond moral suasion—"discourage[ment] without prohibition," as the Cunliffe Committee had put it. And they proved quite unpopular. Beyond the departure from the centuries-old norm, the wartime restrictions, Bradbury later explained to the cabinet, "depended for their enforcement on the postal and cable censorships." And enforce them the government did. Bradbury was emphatic: "There can be no doubt that . . . until quite lately these prohibitions have been made sufficiently effective to secure the main purposes which we had in view."[9]

These were only some of the costs of continuing the state of war. Even by the spring of 1919, the daily expenditure on war services was only about £1 million less than it had been prior to the armistice.[10] Taking the economy off of a wartime footing would save tremendous expense, but bringing home millions of soldiers—now workers—and reconfiguring the "war economy" could bring significant economic shocks.

Lloyd George was determined to prevent such a crisis at home. Fearing a repeat of the dislocation following the Napoleonic Wars, he set the Board of Trade to work in February 1919.[11] He demanded to know why the "trade in the country was more or less at a standstill."[12]

The collective response was simple: uncertainty—"(1) Uncertainty as to Government action; (2) Uncertainty as to prices and materials; (3) Uncertainty as to labor."[13] The academic economist and civil servant Sydney John Chapman particularly emphasized the uncertainty of prices. "The policy of the Government," he insisted, "should be to remove as far as possible the obstacles which stood in the way of the attaining of a new natural level of prices." "If this could be obtained," he stated, following the gold standard orthodoxy, "trade would restart itself."[14]

All agreed with these principles. And both Lloyd George's Liberals and his Conservative rivals relished the chance to roll back government intrusion into the economy, albeit for different reasons. Lloyd George thus directed Auckland Geddes, the minister in charge of reconstruction, to draft plans for as much liberalization of the wartime controls as possible.[15]

Lloyd George wanted more than just laissez-faire, however. Fearing "Bolshevism," he laid out ambitious plans for social reform, particularly house building. "I am assuming there is great unemployment, and that you have to spend in order to keep things going," he explained.[16]

But continued public spending ran directly contrary to the dictates of economic orthodoxy, as Geddes and his fellow Conservatives made clear. Geddes reminded the prime minister that the orthodoxy had "been very strongly pressed at many meetings by representatives, that the main interest of the country at the present time was to get back to the gold standard, and to stop every possible form of Government expenditure." He invoked what later became known as the "Treasury View": "If we are to have this great development of social amenities in the country a very great deal of national capital is going to be locked up," which "will . . . be unavailable for trade purposes."[17] When Lloyd George insisted that the UK could afford the programs nevertheless, the Conservatives used the gold standard as a cudgel. "Are we, or are we not, going to try and get back rapidly to the gold standard basis?" asked the exasperated Geddes.

The discussion then followed the same stages, and arrived at the same conclusions, as had the conversations of the Cunliffe Committee. There was the knee-jerk denial of the problem. "Inflation must be kept up," Bonar Law declared. This was followed by the realization that this would imperil the exchange rate. As Chancellor of the Exchequer Austen Chamberlain pointed out, the devaluation would alleviate the imbalance of trade; but, he also noted, "of course gold will be shipped."[18]

They tried bargaining with themselves. Perhaps they could borrow abroad to support the exchange rate? But, like the Cunliffe Committee, Chamberlain reminded them that the Americans' willingness to lend would soon be exhausted, if it were not so already.[19]

Finally, they arrived at the familiar, orthodox conclusion. There was only one solution to saving the pound, ensuring stability, and alleviating unemployment: achieving a positive balance of trade. "We cannot live by taking in one another's washing," Chamberlain explained. "What we want to do is to get a healthy trade started," he insisted. "That is far more important than stocking a great lot of expensive relief work."[20] Indeed, for these Conservatives, public spending projects were "rather distinct from the immediate question of unemployment."[21]

How then ought the UK to promote its exports? Here again, the orthodoxy pointed the way forward: restore peace, remove government intrusion into the market, and remove the uncertainty. With these principles, the cabinet ministers were agreed in their optimism: "The needs of the world [are] so great that somebody would have to supply them, and ourselves and America must do it."[22]

By the middle of March, Geddes had compiled a 180-page report entitled "Unemployment and the State of Trade."[23] It specified the (orthodox) ideal, explained why the war confounded the pursuit of that ideal, and charted the postwar course to achieve it. "If the Treasury were in a position to cease borrowing to meet its residuary war expenditure and had not to find money for reconstruction," Geddes wrote, "it could, with advantage, end its control of internal capital issues, though it would still require to maintain its control over the emigration of capital." For now, though, "the control must continue, but equally that control must be highly intelligent, rapid in decision, and of such a character that it is not suspect by commercial men."[24] The wording here is important. It suggests that Geddes wanted the government to satisfy most requests for capital movement.

Like the Cunliffe Committee, Geddes concluded that "it is impossible immediately to get rid of inflation" and that "rapid deflation would . . . be disastrous." So, following the plan first proposed to the Cunliffe Committee by Bradbury, Geddes proposed removing the inflation in stages, perhaps even with temporary reversals if necessary.[25]

The Geddes report was especially forceful on the question of the exchange rate. It cast "the artificial support . . . given to the Foreign Exchanges . . . [as] a temporary expedient devised to meet exceptional conditions." "The real decision to be taken is not whether it should be continued," he insisted, "but for how long." Geddes reported that the group discussing the matter "were unanimously of the opinion . . . that from the purely commercial point of view it has ceased to be sound in so far as it is now undoubtedly delaying the recovery of normal trade." In a direct challenge to Lloyd George's hopes for social expenditure, he pressed for "an early decision from the Cabinet whether . . . advantages of the policy of supporting Foreign Exchanges outweigh its manifest commercial disadvantages."[26]

Lloyd George answered the call. Over the coming weeks, his government began implementing each of Geddes's recommendations on monetary policy. This included extensive decontrolling of markets. Crucially, on March 20, the government ceased supporting the pound-dollar exchange rate.[27] From the government's perspective, this was not "abandon[ing] the gold standard" but taking the crucial first step on the road back to gold.[28] Of course, the exchange rate fell—from $4.76 to $4.58 by the end of the month. But it was necessary to allow the "automatic" machinery of the gold standard to begin working again. Without that, Bradbury and the Cunliffe Committee had insisted, it would be impossible to determine what quantity of currency can be kept in circulation without allowing the UK's gold supply to fall below that recommended minimum of £150 million.[29]

The same is true of the new regulations on capital flows. Defence of the Realm Regulation 30F (enacted March 28, 1919) required licenses (granted at the discretion of the Treasury) for foreign loans and investments.[30] On its face, it has the look of a draconian capital control. But seen in this broader context, it was clearly a significant reduction of the wartime restrictions that preceded it. After all, the governing principle was to "allow the greatest possible amount of capital to be devoted to business development consistently [sic] with meeting the essential expenses of the State."[31] With that, the UK took its first significant steps towards Bradbury's version of the gold standard.

Lloyd George's cabinet included several titans of industry, so this was not simply the promise of Panglossian politicians. But what of the financial community? How did the bankers approach the return to gold in this transitional phase?

## The Norman Resistance

Montagu Norman began 1919 with a plan. He was only nine months into his term—and still only the deputy governor at that. But he knew just what he sought to accomplish. The first page of his diary includes a long list of objectives. Throughout the year, Norman returned to this list, updating the disposition of each endeavor.[32]

The list is a testament to Norman's vision and particular bent of mind. Some items were pedestrian: "Simplify terms of borrowing from customers." Some were routine: "Fill 2 vacancies on Court." Some were surprising: "Erect [a gold] refinery." Others were peculiar: "Always discount for Bankers below m[ar]k[e]t rates"—as if a deputy governor would not already know this. Others were problematic: "Lobby for next years [*sic*] C[ommittee of] T[reasury]," the Bank's most powerful committee and the one that would choose the next governor.

The most important items concerned shifts in macroeconomic policy. Most simply, Norman demanded the decontrol of private banks' interest rates: "unrestricted money-rates now." One might have expected this was a prelude to higher interest rates generally. But this list contained no such clear advocacy of rate hikes. Instead, Norman wanted the Treasury to consolidate its short-term borrowing into lower-interest, long-term debt. This was prudence over austerity.

Easily, the most significant item was Norman's statement that it was "essential to maintain [the] prohib[itio]n ag[ain]st Export of Cap[ita]l." Norman specifically cited Regulation 41D, the most extensive iteration of the wartime controls. Cokayne and the Cunliffe Committee had already agreed that these restrictions ought to be eliminated as quickly as possible. It would not be easy to resist the liberalizing tide, but Norman remained determined to do so.[33]

As the government moved toward decontrolling the exchange rate in March 1919, the Bank consulted private bankers on the "limit on uses of Gold after peace."[34] As usual, Norman's opinions were strong, but his reasoning was elusive. An initial meeting led by Cokayne was, in Norman's words, "generally unsatisfactory."[35] Norman does not explain precisely what about it proved "unsatisfactory." More internal discussions followed within the Bank, although the records do not report their content.[36]

The tensions grew. On March 11, Nugent came to Norman, objecting to having terms "dictated" to him by the Bank. Norman "eventually" persuaded him to be "reasonable" and brought him into "sympathy with [the] need to go slow."[37] With Nugent coming onside, Norman met with Holden two weeks later, "as to prevention of Export of Gold either by agreement or legal prohibition." Holden "will consider [the] whole question," Norman recorded.[38]

Two days later, there was a meeting of "Bankers at [the] Treasury re[garding] Gold Export." "They unanimously asked for an immediate prohibition of export—mainly because they wished a legal reason for refusing gold to any Foreigners who might apply for it," Norman noted in his diary. They did this "in spite of assurance fr[om] Albert Strauss [the Vice Governor of the US Federal

Reserve Board] to [the] Gov[erno]r that [the] US would not facilitate import from here and were about to lift prohibition of export." "Altogether," Norman lamented, it was "a miserable affair."[39]

What did Norman mean by this? On its face, his wording implies that this was "a miserable affair" because the private bankers wanted capital controls and the Bank did not. But this would be a strange turn of events. The prior conversations have shown—and subsequent conversations will show—that the bankers wanted what they almost always want: the freedom to move capital as they saw fit. Moreover, the regime supposedly favored by the bankers was actually the system toward which the government had already moved: the chancellor would grant gold export licenses on a case-by-case basis. The default would be to allow gold shipments for investment, but the government would retain the power to deny them to speculators. This shift toward liberalization could only appear miserable to those who believed, as Norman had put it, that it was "essential to maintain [the] prohib[itio]n ag[ain]st Export of Cap[ita]l."[40]

The confusion was multiplied when Norman touched base with Bradbury two days later. Initially, Norman wrote a summary of the key points under April 7. He later wrote a slightly more detailed summary back under March 31. Several of the points were Bradbury's stalwart (and familiar) recommendations: replace currency notes with banknotes, raise interest rates, and encourage gold inflows from South Africa.[41]

But the key question related to capital controls was left ambiguous. The entry "Bankers gold to be available," written on April 7, was rewritten under March 31 as "Bankers gold here as Export Prohibited." Yet at some point, the "as" was struck through and "export prohibited" was put into parentheses. Certainly, Bradbury had not suddenly changed his mind on this. More likely, this described Norman's old idea that capital controls would ease the Bank's ability to absorb the UK's gold supply.[42]

On April 4, Norman met with Henry Strakosch, the long-serving managing director of South Africa's mining and financial house Union Corporation. Strakosch was not merely wealthy and powerful; he was also among the most prominent commentators on South African finances and the international gold standard system. The empire's gold producers naturally bristled at capital controls and, amid the reduction of other controls, sought to have the gold market more fully liberalized. Thus, Strakosch proposed a partnership between the Bank of England, gold producers, and bankers that would restart this trade even before full liberalization was achieved.

Of course, the concern would have been regulated, but Norman met the request—if not also the man—with suspicion. "He is too clear [i.e., transparent] and frankly wants a monopoly!" Norman exclaimed.[43] This is a far cry from Cunliffe's (premature) promise that the Cunliffe Committee would "do anything [it could] to help the [imperial gold] industry" pump more gold into London.[44] Here again, Norman found reasons to resist the resumption of gold movements.

That summer, the Bank hosted another meeting between the chancellor and the leading private bankers. Norman noted, "Begged Chancellor to end prohibition on export of gold so as to free the machinery of international exchange."[45] But it is unclear *who* begged him thus. Other scholars have assumed that it was Norman.[46] But this would have been a sudden reversal. It could have been Cokayne, although he is not mentioned by Norman in this discussion. Perhaps most likely, the bankers themselves were those who "begged" the chancellor to remove the restrictions on their capital movements.

## Bradbury Liberates Capital

Whatever Norman's skepticism, Bradbury marched on. He drafted a pointed memorandum calling for the government to implement the next steps prescribed by the Cunliffe Committee in its *First Interim Report*. He did not dissimulate. The various capital controls that remained "all form part of a single policy viz. that of compelling liquid capital to remain in this country for financing the war and reconstruction notwithstanding that superior inducements may be offered for its employment abroad."[47]

Bradbury brilliantly eliminated the sense of there being any choice in the matter. "If it were possible to maintain these restrictions in effective operation," he noted, "there would be a good deal to be said for the continuance of this policy, objectionable as it is on all grounds of economic theory."[48] However, he argued quite ingeniously, "we have now reached a point at which [they] can no longer be effectively administered."[49] Now that the government had ceased the wartime postal and cable censorships, it was possible for massive evasion of the controls. The controls would thus prove ineffective and "create serious dissatisfaction in Parliament."[50] Listing the mechanisms of control, Bradbury made his proposal clear: "I am therefore in favor of the immediate repeal of Defence of the Realm Regulations 41D and 30F, the removal of the Customs Prohibition on the Import of Securities and the abolition of all restrictions on dealings in securities which have not been in continuous physical possession in the United Kingdom since the 30th September 1914."[51]

Of course, this would permit capital flight, creating downward pressure on the exchange rate. Defending it would require raising interest rates, both slowing the economy and raising the costs of public borrowing. So much for Lloyd George's hopes of ameliorating the living conditions of the working class. There would have to be "a postponement . . . of any further funding for . . . housing and other reconstruction services."[52]

Such austerity was just what Bradbury sought. "Indeed," he explained, "unless it produces these results it will be ineffective." He did not sugarcoat the consequences: "I fully realize the impossibility from the political point of view of 'the Government putting up money rates against itself,' but I think public opinion is now ripe for taking the initial step towards restoring sound currency in accordance with the recommendation of the Cunliffe Committee."[53]

How did the government respond to this potent prescription? They fully embraced it.

On July 24, Lloyd George's cabinet discussed Bradbury's memorandum at length. The chancellor (Austen Chamberlain) made Bradbury's points as clearly and forcefully as Bradbury had made them. The pair were sure to mention that Cunliffe and Bank Governor Cokayne were in agreement, at least on the point of freeing the private banks to raise interest rates on deposits.[54]

Bonar Law offered some trepidation: "With so many things in a catastrophic condition, he did not want to precipitate any sudden slump in the American exchanges." But Lloyd George responded. "He had seen Mr. Rupert Beckett"— a member of the Cunliffe Committee—"who had urged very strongly that the Government . . . take steps to prevent the financial arrangements from hiding the real facts." He was even "glad that the American Exchange [rate to the British pound] was being allowed to reach its natural level." Chamberlain then chimed in with intelligence from Gaspard Farrer—yet another Cunliffe Committee member—that "most of the financial proposals were for expenditure within the Empire, the greater part of the issue being payable in the Mother Country." So freeing capital would not drive up the US dollar, and it was likely to return in any case.[55]

Lloyd George cut to the chase. "What was gained by taking off [the capital] restrictions at the present moment?" he asked. Bradbury replied by reversing the default: "At least nothing was lost, because the restrictions were rapidly becoming inoperative." Indeed, such was the unstoppable mobility of capital that "he did not attach very great importance to [the capital restrictions'] removal, because . . . they were already becoming increasingly ineffective." Even Bonar Law gave ground here.[56]

So too did Lloyd George. Yet he hoped that those investing abroad would still buy their "machinery, rails, locomotives, &c . . . in this country." "Such restrictions," he admitted, "could not possibly have been enforced before the war, but as the machinery was in operation, it might perhaps be used for this purpose." Thus, it was agreed that these limited restrictions should be continued, but "all the other restrictions should be removed." Just like that, the UK's capital account was almost entirely liberalized.[57]

It was a massive victory for Bradbury. He knew well that the few restrictions that remained were almost totally unenforceable. They would become all the more so as it became increasingly difficult to monitor those transactions after this big bang of capital account opening. The new rules not only affirmed but positively implemented the vision Bradbury had advanced for years. This placed him in the perfect position to enshrine these principles in a final Cunliffe Committee report.

## The Cunliffe Committee Reconvenes

After publishing its *First Interim Report* in the autumn of 1918, the Cunliffe Committee went on hiatus. Its members had finished the lion's share of their work, producing a report that was almost universally hailed. Moreover, Lloyd George had appointed Cunliffe as a British representative on the Reparations Commission. So Cunliffe himself was occupied, at the Paris Peace Conference, for the first portion of 1919.

In the meantime, it became clear that the Cunliffe Committee had left some business unfinished. Obviously, the committee had never seriously considered the theoretical and practical challenges posed by the rather different versions of the gold standard operational in Scotland and Ireland. While the continuation of the war (as a formal matter) had slowed the pace of Westminster's liberalization, Bradbury drove the Treasury steadily along the road. The real dangers derived from the City of London. It quickly became clear that the bankers could prove difficult to control.

There was Norman, of course, who could hardly be trusted, let alone relied upon. He had begun the year committed to extending the capital controls, appears to have supported them over the ensuing months, and in time would explicitly champion them again. In addition, two of the UK's leading bankers—Holden and Goodenough—had also voiced concerns in Cunliffe's absence. Neither was damning, and both broadly sought even *more* orthodoxy rather than less.[58]

While the British press knew better, the American press took the critics at their grandiloquent words. Lumping all of them together, from pure goldbugs to monetary cranks, the American papers suggested that "a large movement has recently been started . . . to change the banking laws of Great Britain."[59] Bradbury had already begun bringing the likes of Holden and Goodenough around to his side behind the scenes; but, he explained to colleagues, "the Government were in a somewhat difficult position. They had a Report to which they naturally attached a great deal of importance but they had some difficulty in acting upon it by reason of the fact that its recommendations were contested by some leading expert banking opinion."[60] Thus, Bradbury concluded, the government needed to silence the dissidents and set the record straight.

Just as Bradbury was pushing his memorandum on capital liberalization through the cabinet, the Cunliffe Committee reconvened. On July 23, the committee laid out its plans: The "Scotch and Irish issues might be cleared out of the way." The committee would then address "the new factors, such as the legal restrictions on the import of gold." Last, it would preempt the critics and issue a final report as soon as possible.[61]

## Bracketing Scotland and Ireland

The church of the Bank of England found few adherents in Scotland and Ireland. Banking had always worked differently there. As the banks' representatives explained to the Cunliffe Committee, these more distant markets had always relied less upon gold and more upon trust and interbank cooperation.[62] The Great War allowed these banks even more freedom from London's control.

The Scots and the Irish proclaimed this wartime experiment a smashing success. One after another they petitioned London to continue the legal tender status of their notes.[63] The Bank of Ireland, together with the private Irish banks, resolved "that a reversion to the prewar position would be from every point of view undesirable."[64]

They were deeply suspicious of new English impositions. The Scots threatened to "defend their legal rights of issue . . . by every means competent to them."[65] The Irish feared a plot to steal their gold. "The Bank of England Note has never been popular in Ireland," one representative explained, "and to force it on the Irish people as the sole Legal Tender would . . . be deeply resented and would tend to bring about a difficult financial position."[66] Another went further: "The Sinn Fein element would undoubtedly . . . say that England was taking all the gold out of Ireland."[67] Given the continuing strife there, this was no small matter.

Hailing from the Bank of Ireland, Andrew Jameson took a softer tact. He assured the Cunliffe Committee that "Irish Bank Notes have only been put into circulation to answer the public demand caused by the high prices of cattle and commodities, and by the abnormal rise in wages paid in Ireland."[68] Like the English bankers, Jameson blamed Westminster's inflationary policies.

Jameson might not have troubled himself. As far as London was concerned, these non-English notes hardly counted. Or at least Bradbury (and his colleagues) did not bother to count them. In his March 1918 tabulations, he reported the statutory maximum of the unbacked issue rather than either the actual issue of unbacked notes or the much larger issue of backed notes, many of which were "backed" by the (largely) unbacked Treasury notes.[69] At that point, as we have seen, the Cunliffe Committee's *First Interim Report* swept the Scottish and Irish notes under the rug.[70] Nothing that happened in the months that followed prompted the Cunliffe Committee to pay any more attention to the quantity of Irish and Scottish banknotes—or to consider the difficulties in removing them.

This became clear when the committee finally spoke with the Scottish and Irish representatives themselves in the summer of 1919. The committee heard from just two representatives from each country, perhaps the minimum required for appearances' sake. And they were hard on each of these witnesses. In particular, they combated the desire to continue the legal tender status of the Scottish and Irish banknotes. Bradbury pressed the witnesses to recognize that "the ultimate [moral] responsibility" "for a legal tender note" "must in practice rest with the Government."[71] The representative of the Royal Bank of Scotland insisted, "We are really assisting the State[,] . . . saving the State a very great deal of money[,] . . . supplying currency for Scotland." But the committee thought him disingenuous. Bradbury highlighted the "conveniences from the point of view of [your] bank," and Cunliffe asked facetiously, "Your fiduciary issue pays you very handsomely, does it not?"[72] Indeed, it did.

More broadly, the peripheral economies could hardly afford the "stigma" that would come from openly challenging the Cunliffe Committee.[73] After all, real money (in the form of investment flows and borrowing costs) was at stake for those countries that did not retain the proverbial "good housekeeping seal of approval" or mind "the company [they] keep."[74] If even the powerful London bankers cowered before the Cunliffe Committee, what should we expect from those in Scotland, Ireland, and beyond—they who had the least to gain and the most to prove?

## The Cunliffe Committee Co-opts Its London "Critics"

When FC Goodenough—the head of Barclays—publicly proposed a "middle course" in which banks produced an "auxiliary currency," the committee knew that it was necessary to hear him out.[75] Ultimately, his proposal did not differ widely from that favored by the Scots and the Irish: private banks should be allowed to issue unbacked notes as legal tender. While the Cunliffe Committee might simply bracket the concerns of the distant Scottish and Irish bankers, it would be far harder to ignore the pleadings of one of London's oldest and most powerful banks.

So the Cunliffe Committee called Goodenough before it in July 1919. The members steered the witness brilliantly. They prompted him to question his proposal by highlighting that shareholders would remain liable for those notes.[76] More important, they maneuvered him into stating—on the record— his commitment to the principles undergirding their report. Goodenough held "the industrial position" as "key to the whole thing." "For that reason we ought to aim at moderately low rates of money," he stated. "But," he continued, "we should have sound currency first and foremost of all."[77] His invocation of the sacred maxim gave the committee an opportunity. Addis got him to agree, first, that high prices were hurting British industry and, second, that prices needed to fall: "Unless . . . prices are brought down to the level of world prices, that vital necessity of the recovery of our international trade will be impossible?" he asked. "That is so," Goodenough testified.[78]

With that, the committee had inoculated itself from this possible critic. Previously, the committee had agreed to interview Holden and Reginald McKenna, but neither of these appearances materialized.[79] Instead, the committee took another hiatus, during which time Bradbury was appointed as the British representative to the Reparations Commission.[80] The committee carried on without its steady, stalwart pilot. It called its last witness—its last potential banking critic—in October: Felix Schuster.

Schuster had complained about the tighter capital and reporting requirements recommended in the *First Interim Report*. Naturally, he insisted that this would favor banks abroad.[81] In a bid to expand their coalition—or at least ensure that rivals were hurt as much as the bankers were—Schuster and some others sought to have these requirements applied to every entity that took deposits or extended credit, right down to department stores.[82] Committee members offered a sympathetic ear but nothing more. They refused to be pulled into metaphysical debates about what a bank is or what counts as "cash."[83]

But without Bradbury there to guide the discussion, the Schuster interview became almost silly at times. In typical orthodox fashion, he insisted upon the centrality of the balance of trade. But he took it to the extreme, past the point of belief. Pigou was baffled by Schuster's meaning. "With regard to the exchanges, you were saying that the trade balance was really the fundamental point?" he asked. "Yes," Schuster replied simply. Pigou's follow-up must be quoted at length: "Is there not also the currency element in it? Supposing that you had got the trade balance perfectly normal, if our currency was depreciated in terms of gold there would still necessarily be an adverse exchange with countries whose currency was not so depreciated, and the mere restitution of the trade balance would not by itself necessarily make the exchange right, would it?"[84]

Schuster gave ground, retreating to a simple orthodox position. "Perhaps not," he responded, "but the ordinary [prewar] remedies . . . would be entirely efficient." The trade balance, he insisted, "is not the whole question but it is the fundamental question. . . . You may have a very sound currency system, but with a continuously adverse trade balance you will break down."[85]

A few moments later, Addis stepped in. He wanted Schuster to agree "that amelioration of the depreciation of the currency would be a very favorable beginning." "Of course; I would not say a word against the appreciation of that," Schuster replied. "I think every possible step should be taken."[86]

To modern eyes, the conversation is mystifying. Like Cokayne before him, Schuster held a bullionist understanding of the relationship between the balance of trade and the quantity and quality of the currency. Pigou knew well enough that an exogenous change in the exchange rate—such as a depreciation against gold—could affect trade patterns. But then the group seemed to get the relationship backward. Schuster insisted that securing a more favorable balance of trade is the "fundamental" factor. But he agreed that an *appreciation* of the exchange rate would advance that objective. Perhaps this banker did not understand the basics of exchange rates—namely, that depreciation promotes exports while appreciation promotes imports. Or perhaps these men were so committed to the principle of a "sound currency" that they believed that any and every conceivable objective depended upon achieving that first.

Ultimately, all that mattered to the Cunliffe Committee was that Schuster embraced their plan: "The measures that are suggested are the best that could be provided."[87] This was enough for them. Another potential heretic had recanted. Schuster had been brought into line. He had espoused their creed.

Thus we see the real modus operandi of the Cunliffe Committee. This was not a consultation by technocrats of a key interest groups or even an epistemic community. This was an inquisition. And like the Church's several inquisitions, the purpose was not to garner perspectives, acquire information, or advance understanding. The purpose was to construct knowledge, disseminate belief, and defend the faith.[88]

## The Cunliffe Committee's Second Set of Tablets

The Cunliffe Committee published its final report in December 1919. It was short and direct. The committee happily concluded, "We have reviewed the criticisms . . . made upon . . . our Report, but we see no reason to modify our opinion. We have found nothing in the experiences of the war to falsify the lessons of previous experience that the adoption of a currency not convertible at will into gold or other exportable coin is likely in practice to lead to overissue and to destroy the measure of exchangeable value and cause a general rise in all prices and an adverse movement in the foreign exchanges."[89]

But as short as it was, the report made a point of expressing the committee's views on the two critical issues of the day: the continuation of the capital controls and the persistence of low interest rates. The committee issued the familiar prescription: fiscal austerity plus the "re-establishing at an early date a free market for gold in London" and "the restoration of the prewar methods of controlling the currency." This meant real capital account liberalization. "The nominal convertibility of the currency note which has been sustained by the prohibition of the export of gold is of little value," the committee argued. It was just as pointed on Bank rate: "An important cause of the depreciation in sterling . . . [is] to be found in the expanded state of credit in this country." Then came an oblique swipe at Norman's new dogma: "The existing expansion is not merely the legacy of the stress of war finance and Government borrowings . . . [but also] of maintaining rates for money in London below those ruling in other important financial centers."[90]

For much of the war—and at its end—Bank rate stood at 5 percent. At the time, sterling traded at about $4.76. It held its value remarkably well into the following summer. As the Treaty of Versailles was signed (June 28), sterling traded at about $4.60—that is, less than 6 percent below parity. Following this, however, there was a boom at home, and the exchange rate slid almost without abatement. By the autumn of 1919, it was clear that this was not a temporary reversal.

So while the Cunliffe Committee was working toward its *Final Report*, Cokayne turned up the pressure on the government. In September, he wrote a formal letter to the chancellor, informing him that the Bank "regard[s] the restoration of the gold standard and the resumption of free gold exports at the earliest possible moment as of vital importance to the Country as a whole and consider[s] that it is well worth a temporary sacrifice to secure that end." What was the required sacrifice? Austerity, of course. Just like the Cunliffe Committee, Cokayne demanded fiscal and monetary contraction. Specifically, he complained that the government's continued borrowing at 3.5 percent had precluded the Bank from making effective the necessary interest rate, which he said would be 5 percent at a minimum. The UK was already suffering under a "virtual abandonment of the gold standard." "Unless remedial measures are quickly taken," Cokayne foreboded, sterling could become "unsalable in many countries."[91]

How did the (largely Conservative) government respond to these calls? It did as instructed. In October, the Treasury raised its interest rate. This allowed Cokayne to take Bank rate all the way to 6 percent, which he did in November.[92]

Cokayne's letter reflected widespread sentiments about the urgency of returning to gold. So when the Cunliffe Committee's *Final Report* was published in December, it was received with as much enthusiasm as had been its *First Interim Report*. Indeed, it inspired a group of Liberal MPs, bankers, and intellectuals to form the Sound Currency Association, "whose objects [were] to get rid of the inflation of the currency, hasten a return to the gold standard, and promote a sound financial policy." In time, this pressure group commanded a loud voice in favor of the orthodoxy.[93]

In mid-December, Conservative chancellor Austen Chamberlain praised the Cunliffe Committee's report in Parliament: The government "agree[s] with the Committee's view that increased production, cessation of Government borrowings, and decreased expenditure both public and private are the first essentials to recovery." Even more important, he affirmed, "the [Cunliffe Committee's] argument as to the exchanges is obviously true." Virtually without exception, Chamberlain committed the government to follow the Cunliffe Committee's recommendations.[94]

Cokayne's rate hikes proved insufficient, as even Keynes argued at the time. By February 1920, sterling had sunk 35 percent below parity to $3.18, its lowest point in history and the lowest it would fall prior to the 1930s.[95] At this point, Governor Cokayne wrote a pointed memorandum to Chancellor Chamberlain. He denounced continued reliance on capital controls and insisted upon further interest rate hikes. Citing the Cunliffe Committee's reports, he declared, "No other practical means for limiting . . . [the] rise in prices has been suggested than the old and well-tried plan of a rise in the Bank rate."[96]

Chamberlain was galvanized. But before raising rates again himself, he pressed the bankers to simply ration credit availability.[97] When they dithered, he made clear "his . . . intention to obtain gradual and continuous deflation—either thro[ugh] action of [the] Banks or by other means of his own."[98] By April, sterling had recovered to more than $3.90, no doubt partly because of the extensive discussion about the imminent rate hikes. When the Bank of France matched the Bank's rate at 6 percent, Chamberlain waited no longer. He raised the rate on Treasury bills to 6.5 percent, leaving Norman to raise

Bank rate to 7 percent. This continuation of Cokayne's policy was one of Norman's first acts as his successor.

This was also the highest that Norman would take interest rates. Far from the 10 percent that Keynes had demanded previously, Norman's hike did nothing to appreciate the exchange rate, which renewed its decline almost immediately. In June, the Federal Reserve raised it rates above the UK Treasury Bill Rate. Norman pressed the Treasury to either follow suit or to allow the Bank to contract the money supply. Within the Bank, Norman always blamed the chancellor for refusing to budge. In public, however, he described the course as "precisely what was advocated in the Report of the (Cunliffe) Committee on Currency and Foreign Exchanges after the War, and adopted by the Government." He praised the chancellor in his Bankers' Dinner speech at Mansion House: "We owe him a debt of gratitude for his consistency—which history will confirm."[99]

Yet, the pound soon began to sink again. By November, sterling was back down to $3.33. But rather than forcing further rate hikes, as Cokayne had done, Norman stayed at 7 percent.[100] At that point, the Conservatives imposed capital controls—seemingly at Norman's behest.

# CHAPTER 9

# Who Would Control Capital?

Where was the UK's working class in all of this? Where was the new, and rising, Labour Party? Where were the old, but increasingly powerful, labor unions? After all, the Cunliffe Committee's mandated deflation would fall hardest upon the shoulders of the working class.

With an eye to these consequences, social scientists might explain the Conservatives' reluctance to implement the Cunliffe Committee recommendations from a materialist standpoint. Perhaps the Conservatives and Liberals in government abandoned their principles and forsook their interests out of an ambition to gain the favor of working people. If it were so, it was mercurial. After the all, the same man who authored these capital controls as a junior minister—Stanley Baldwin—did later remove them as prime minister. Moreover, such an explanation assumes that the working class deprecated the gold standard in 1920. But all of the available evidence shows precisely the opposite.

## Labor Flocks to Gold
### Workers Conceptualize Their Interests

One wonders why the government and its numerous planning committees did not consult the UK's unions—or at least the Trades Union Congress (TUC), the union of unions—on the return to gold. At this point, however, there would have been little point in asking for their formal opinion on the gold standard. Simply put, they did not yet have one. Of course, there were some critics of the gold standard orthodoxy, just as there are heretics in the shadows of every church. But in the summer of 1918, just as the Cunliffe Committee finalized its *First Interim Report*, the *New Statesman* denounced the so-called currency delusions of such fringe thinkers. Invoking the orthodoxy, the editors insisted, "There is no alchemy by which . . . one nation . . . can convert its debts into currency without reducing that currency to next to nothing in exchangeable value." Little did they know that Cunliffe himself had sought to do just that. But here was a leading socialist newspaper denouncing even those reforms proposed by the governor of the Bank of England. Not only did it defend the orthodoxy, but it was at pains to stress that "the Labour Party in this country . . . [is] not responsible for this heresy." Indeed, "It says something for the soundness of the instincts of the Labour Party, and of the British wage-earning class, that they give not the slightest countenance to these currency delusions."[1]

The Fabian socialists behind the *New Statesman* ought to know, not least because they helped to construct the principles at the core of the twentieth-century British labor movement. But whatever the cause, the reality was just as they described it; and the record shows that they were not wrong on this crucial point. The minutes for the TUC's Annual Congress show that they literally had nothing to say about the return to gold at least until 1920. At that point, they arrived at the gold standard by way of questioning the rising cost of living. Until then, questioning the gold standard was akin to questioning gravity.

In the summer of 1920, the "Triple Alliance" (between miners, dockworkers, and transport workers) and the TUC's Parliamentary Committee formed a special Joint Committee on the Cost of Living. It was variously chaired by Edward Lawrence Poulton and James ("Jimmy") Henry Thomas. Its eighteen members included the most powerful men and women from the Parliamentary Committee of the Trades Union Congress, the Co-Operative Union, the Triple Alliance, the Federation of Engineering and Shipbuilding Trades, the National Federation of General Workers, and the National Federation of Building Trades Operatives. It also included Charlie Cramp, the future chair of the Labour Party, and Ramsay Macdonald, the man who would serve as Labour's first prime minister. The committee was, as its secretary noted, "as representative as could possibly be appointed."[2]

Indeed, in the terms of modern social science, the committee represented workers in all four of the broad interest groups delineated by the classic model of "exchange rate politics."[3] The *non-tradables producers* included transport workers, those in the building trades, and "general workers." The *import-com-*

*peting traded goods producers* were the shipbuilders, particularly as industrial rivals in the US and Germany worked to undercut this key UK industry. There were those who depended directly on *international trade*, such as dockworkers and (again) shipbuilders. Crucially, the committee also included Robert Smillie and Frank Hodges, the sometime president and secretary (respectively) of the Miners' Federation of Great Britain. The miners were the quintessential *export-competing traded goods producers*. And, just as our economic models predict, they were the hardest hit by the return to gold. But directly contrary to our political-economy models, they nevertheless endorsed this return. They did this because the miners, like all of these other groups, never imagined that it was possible for the UK to leave the gold standard.

Like the Cunliffe Committee, the men and women on the Cost of Living Committee took their work seriously and consulted broadly. Among others, they interviewed politicians from both Labour and the Liberals, including Reginald McKenna, the former Liberal chancellor of the exchequer. They also examined a prominent banker (Thomas Goodwin) and three major economists: Hugh Dalton (LSE), HD Henderson (Cambridge), and Arthur Pigou (Cambridge). The influence of Pigou was evident in both the content of their ideas and their numerous references to him.

The unions' Cost of Living Committee paralleled the Cunliffe Committee in more ways than one. Over the next year, it published four reports spanning nearly two hundred pages—"the results of the largest investigation ever undertaken by the Labour movement of this country."[4] But like the Cunliffe Committee, most of the Cost of Living Committee's analysis of the gold standard appears in an interim report: the *Interim Report on Money and Prices*, published in August 1920. Incredibly, the two interim reports—the one written by the monetary elites and this one written by the working class—were almost indistinguishable in their assumptions, models, terms, and conclusions.

## The Cost of Living Committee's Orthodoxy, Reported

Like the members of the Cunliffe Committee, the members of the Cost of Living Committee were thoroughgoing monetarists. "The rise in prices," they stated, "is due more to currency expansion than to contraction of production."[5] This defended the working class from employers' accusations that greedy workers had driven up prices by demanding ever-higher wages.[6] Thus, the solution was to "bring to an end inflationist methods of financing Government expenditure."[7] So much for the working class demanding fiscal policy handouts.

The Cost of Living Committee similarly followed the Cunliffe Committee in believing that "the public have become accustomed to the use of Treasury notes."[8] But make no mistake: the workers still embraced the gold standard. The report continues: ". . . though the notes would need to be based on gold held by the national bank."[9]

Other countries might simply abandon their old gold parities, but the UK was different. In fact, it was the exemplar: "Where . . . a country, e.g., the United Kingdom, was within easy reach of re-establishing the prewar parity between currency and gold," the committee insisted, "efforts should be made to return to this parity."[10] What were those "efforts"? Just as the orthodoxy prescribed, the Cost of Living Committee called for "a reduction in the volume of money in circulation," "deflat[ing] it . . . to an extent which will eliminate the depreciation of currency in terms of gold."[11] The committee stated this knowing that in the case of the UK, it meant "a reduction of the general level of prices by about 20%."[12] Here was the UK's working class saying that a 20 percent deflation was going to be "easy." So much for the working class demanding easy monetary policy.

Moreover, the committee fully recognized the painful effects this would have on the economy: "[Such] a drastic restriction of the currency would, we hold, result in widespread unemployment, and, most probably, in a considerable fall in wages."[13] So much for the working class prioritizing unemployment relief over monetary "stability."

Thus the Cost of Living Committee insisted upon restoring the gold standard in the UK even as it acknowledged the enormous dislocation this would bring. How could this possibly be implemented without ravaging the working class? The Cost of Living Committee's proposal was strikingly familiar to that proposed by the Cunliffe Committee. Most simply, it would implement the restoration of the gold standard in stages. Directly following the Cunliffe Committee, this meant "that the amount of the fiduciary issue should be gradually and periodically reduced, by stated amounts at stated intervals of time, until the depreciation of the British paper currency in terms of gold disappears."[14]

At the same time, the Cost of Living Committee "look[ed] to the development of productive capacity all over the world to bring about ultimately a substantial fall in prices."[15] To assuage the painful deflation, the UK would endeavor to grow its economy into the new price level. The Cost of Living Committee declared that through "a steady improvement in productivity (through the participation of all countries in the trade of the world, the improvement of methods and machinery, and a far-reaching reorganization of industry) the standard of life of the people would be maintained and automatically raised as prices fell."[16] So Snowball promised to build a windmill, and Boxer promised to work harder.[17]

Thus, the UK's workers agreed with the monetary elites entirely on the principle objective: returning to gold. They even agreed on the timeline and largely on the means to achieve these objectives. They differed on some points of implementation. Specifically, the workers wanted to force down prices and wages using "controls" (as during the war) and, as necessary, nationalization. They were also more sensitive to the inequities that might follow from the different rates of adjustment. Because so many of the wage agreements included cost-of-living provisions, the TUC became zealous about modernizing inflation calculations. Thus, much of its 144-page *Final Report* was dedicated to building better price indices.[18]

What of the eternal battle between labor and capital, the cleavage that would ultimately lead to the 1926 General Strike? For the most part, the workers' disagreement with capital turned on the responsibility for the inflation: government expenditure on armaments (labor's view) versus organized labor extracting ever-higher wages (capital's retort). This mattered as a normative matter. But it also mattered more practically. Knowing which had been the tail and which had been the dog was seen as key to determining which side ought to move first. Should workers accept lower wages, allowing producers to cut costs? Or should producers cut prices first, allowing workers to accept lower wages? In time, unwinding this spiral became a principal preoccupation of John Maynard Keynes. But this is not where he began, as we shall see.

How did the full TUC respond to these reports by the Cost of Living Committee? One or two members called for greater "public control" and nationalization of the means of production, sometimes citing the example of "Soviet Russia" explicitly.[19] But other than "a few dissentients," the TUC was broadly supportive—including those workers whom political economists predict would have most strongly resisted the policy of deflation.[20] For instance, one representative from the United Plumbers and Domestic Engineers complained that profiteers had "[stolen] the money that I had earned by working." Involved in the service sector, such workers would be hurt considerably by the domestic contraction that would follow. This worker, however, fixated upon the inflated cost of living and on blaming wartime expansionary policy. "The special report now submitted lays the onus and responsibility . . . for the increase in the cost of living upon the shoulders of the right men," he concluded.[21]

## The Workers' Faith

Thus did the commandments of the Cunliffe Committee become the UK's highest law. We know now that it might have been otherwise, that there was more than one way to run a "good" monetary system. But these specific directives became the law—*the* standard. They were exalted as much by the congregation as by the priests who brought them to the people. For all their disagreements with their employers, the UK's working class accepted this most important assumption: the only path to the promised land was this yellow brick road. That the working class blithely accepted this runs directly contrary to conventional accounts of this period.

But should this be so surprising? We have seen that "capital" did not understand the gold standard. The bankers all had their own (irreconcilable) beliefs about the essence of that system. The merchants and manufacturers appeared happy to trade the certainty of short-term deflation for a hope of long-run "currency stability." Even the masters of the Rand gold mines themselves did not understand exchange rates well enough to know that a devaluation would bring a windfall. Why should we expect the miners in the south of Africa and the north of England to meet better the measure of our models? What space was there to marshal the *Principles of Economics* down the shafts, amid the "heat, noise, confusion, darkness, foul air, and . . . unbearably cramped space"?[22] Even if they had the time, space, and peace to illuminate their Smith and their Mill, the workers only would have seen that orthodox monetary theory was every bit as immaterial, impractical, and austere as were the nostrums peddled by their employers.

## Conservative Control

On November 4, 1920, Stanley Baldwin introduced a bill "to control the exportation of gold and silver coin and bullion."[23] At the time, Baldwin was the financial secretary to the Treasury, a junior ministerial post. Soon enough he would go on to higher office, but on this occasion he looked every bit the junior colleague that he was.

It was a difficult bit of business that played out in several heated debates across a month. The bill was not circulated until the morning before its second reading (November 10), and that reading came at the very end of the day. Word of the proposal had nonetheless leaked out, and the bad news traveled fast. One MP, a fellow Conservative, complained that he had heard about it from Calcutta before he was informed about it by his own government in Westminster.[24] In fact, most of the criticism of the bill was espoused by members of Baldwin's own Conservative party, although Donald Maclean also led a Liberal attack with impassioned appeals of his own.

Baldwin downplayed the significance of the bill. "We are proposing nothing new," he insisted. It was "merely . . . the continuation of what now exists." He also (quite disingenuously) suggested that this complied with the actions of "all other principal countries of the world, except the United States of America, whose financial position at this moment is very different from our own." And like a seventeenth-century mercantilist, he attempted to conflate these broad restrictions on the movement of gold and silver with the uncontroversial ban on "defacing . . . and stripping coinage."[25]

It did not work. Baldwin was beset on both sides, as Conservatives and Liberals alike questioned the extension of wartime powers "in perpetuity."[26] They repeatedly stressed the importance of the bill, and they took exception to Baldwin's insinuation that the UK's financial system was comparable to those of its Continental European rivals. "The City of London is still the money pivot of the world," Maclean proclaimed defiantly. "How important it is that the financial world in all countries . . . should know what is the fixed statutory position here with regard to the control of the export of gold," he exclaimed.[27] They also obliged Baldwin with an education in the distinction between "the petty thieves' trick of breaking up the King's coinage" and the forces that drive international gold shipments.[28] The market for melting coins only existed because capital controls had artificially raised the price of bullion above its market value as specie. Under the prewar gold standard system, the two had been kept in equilibrium by the Bank of England's obligation to sell gold at the official rate. All of these arguments were directly in line with the Cunliffe Committee reports.

Baldwin tried, in vain, to justify the rushed timing. The government was "very anxious . . . [because] the control over the export of gold and silver bullion which exists today is regulated by Orders in Council under a provision of 1914, which expires on the conclusion of the last of the Peace Treaties."[29] Historians have bought this line, but Baldwin's colleagues were suitably suspicious.[30] The last treaty of peace, the Treaty of Sevres, had been signed fully three months prior. The government might have become suddenly concerned that Turkey would unexpectedly ratify it, although it never did.[31] Moreover, the left-wing Liberal Harry Barnes argued, the legislative machinery was available to allow the government to extend the required powers as necessary via the Expiring Laws Continuance Bill.[32]

Baldwin assured his colleagues that the government was "as anxious as anyone . . . [to] revert once more to the open [gold] market, which has always been the glory and the strength of finance in this country." Indeed, two years earlier, Baldwin had praised "the most admirable Report of the [Cunliffe] Currency Committee" and told the House of Commons, "the principles which underlie that Report are sound and . . . should guide us."[33] But, now, "having regard to the condition of the exchanges . . . ," he claimed, "there is no expert authority of any kind who will admit that that time is yet come."[34]

Yet Baldwin's own party members decried the shift back toward overt control of markets. They issued the same critique that Bradbury had deployed to such great effect the year prior: the capital controls do little good and much harm. Samuel Samuel, himself an international businessman, insisted that the prohibition "is very injurious to the export trade of this country." "Gold," he lamented, "is . . . very much lacking in this country," but prohibiting gold exports "naturally prohibit[s] the import, because nobody is going to send gold . . . to this country . . . if they know . . . that gold is going to be seized by the Government."[35] "Gold is the most fluid of all commodities," Frederick Alexander Macquisten warned. "It is one of those things, like credit, which can take wings and fly." Newton Moore was didactic: "We want to re-establish London as the chief exchange. . . . I am speaking for people who are actually producing the gold. . . . The Government ought to pay some attention to the people who know something about the subject."[36]

Baldwin tried to play the Tory trump card by invoking the authority of the UK's financial interests, but it backfired terribly. "The bankers of the City of London are unanimous in their desire for this Bill," he insisted in the second debate. Samuel interrupted him, "What bankers?" he asked incredulously. "All the leading banks," Baldwin said vaguely. "Oh no," Samuel snickered.[37] He was sure that "the commercial and financial community wish to get rid of control as soon as they possibly can."[38] Moore proposed an amendment to ensure that imported gold retained the right to be re-exported. And he called Baldwin's bluff. "Since the Second Reading debate," he reported, "I have spoken to several bankers, very important people, and they assure me that the provision which I have now proposed should be inserted in the Bill."[39]

The Liberals, too, were "surprise[d] to learn . . . that the great bankers of this country are prepared to give to all Governments for all time the power . . . to interfere with the export of gold." "That, certainly," Barnes sniped, "is very different from what would be generally done by people who have control of any commodity."[40] Joseph Stanley Holmes argued that the government's request for an indefinite power to block gold exports "is really suggesting a permanent inconvertible paper currency, and that must have a bad effect on our credit."[41] Joseph Kenworthy challenged him outright: "Mr. Baldwin . . . has told us that the whole of the leading bankers are in favor of this Bill, [but] I know at least one important banker, whom I have consulted on the matter, who is not in favor of it." He went further: "I think the officials at the Treasury have slightly misled him in that respect."[42]

Kenworthy was on to something. He just had the wrong locale. The man leading—or misleading—Baldwin and the government was likely none other than Montagu Norman, the governor of the Bank of England. Norman had met with the chancellor between when Baldwin introduced the bill and when the debate commenced.[43] He then met with the chancellor again on November 30, after the second, bruising debate.[44] And he spent an hour with "Baldwin at Treasury as to Gold Export Bill," after the third day of debate, as Baldwin was making the amendments necessary to secure the bill's passage.[45] This should come as no surprise. As Baldwin's biographers suggest, "he was personally devoted to Norman," and Grigg reportedly cast this as Baldwin's "greatest attachment."[46]

What did Norman advise Baldwin and the Treasury to do and to say? With Norman, it is never possible to know for sure. But the simplest explanation is that Norman held the same position at the end of 1920 that he had held in 1918 and 1919 when he wrote that it was "essential to maintain [the] prohib[itio]n ag[ain]st Export of Cap[ita]l."[47] And this would not be the last time that Norman vigorously championed gold export restrictions.

Baldwin's claim in Parliament that the "bankers of the City of London are unanimous in their desire for this Bill" is reminiscent of Norman's account the previous year of unspecified "Bankers" who "unanimously asked for an immediate prohibition of Export."[48] But just who were these unnamed restriction–loving bankers? None of the bankers consulted by Baldwin's fellow MPs wanted to have their capital movements dictated by the government. Not a single one of the bankers who served on or appeared before the Cunliffe Committee had advocated capital controls.

In fact, the Sound Currency Association, which counted several members of the Institute of Bankers among its ranks, publicly denounced Baldwin's bill as soon as debate commenced upon it. In a letter to the *Manchester Guardian*, the association "urge[d] that unflinching opposition should be offered to the . . . Bill." "How can we ever get back to a sound currency unless [the] prewar current of bullion and coin and conversion of one into the other is allowed?" they asked rhetorically. The association was emphatic: "The depreciation of the currency is the principal cause of the unfavorable foreign exchange rates with gold standard countries."[49]

A few days later, the British Bankers' Association published its opinion that "the only hope of relief for the traders of this country was for the Government strictly to limit expenditure." So too did A. W. Kiddy, the editor of *Bankers' Magazine*, celebrate "the advantage we had possessed by our great 'free market for gold.'" Whereas the Bankers' Association had criticized Baldwin's bill only obliquely, Kiddy was explicit: "So long . . . as the regulation prohibiting gold exports . . . was in force, it must have an effect in weakening our financial prestige and retarding a permanent recovery in the exchanges." Kiddy acknowledged that this "was . . . a hard gospel to enunciate, that after four years of strain and suffering we should be called upon to pay the price of such a conflict in economy and harder work." "But," he asked, "on what other basis could we hope to rehabilitate our position?"[50]

And yet Baldwin's Gold and Silver (Export Control) Bill ultimately passed through Parliament and received the royal assent just before the new year. It required significant compromises, and doubtless some whipping of votes, even just to keep the Conservatives on board.[51] Rather than the open-ended authority that Baldwin requested, Parliament would grant the government this power to restrict (some) capital exports for a specified period of time. This, Baldwin's colleagues argued, was vital to helping businesses make their plans. Maclean proposed that the power expire at the end of 1923. In reply, Baldwin again invoked the unnamed "experts" "who are responsible for the protection of our currency and similar matters in the city of London." "Those most competent to judge," he asserted, have concluded that five years (rather than three) "ought to be the shortest period."[52] With that, the deal was made: the capital controls would expire on December 31, 1925. Lord make me chaste—but not yet, as Augustine prayed.

## Norman Proves Dilatory

Before the war, the UK's official reserves totaled just £37 million—3.4 percent of the world's total official reserves. Throughout the war, Cunliffe led the charge to defend, and enlarge, the UK's gold holdings. By the end of it, he had nearly tripled official reserves to £95 million and more than doubled the share of the world's official reserves to 7.6 percent. The Cunliffe Committee estimated that the UK would need £150 million of gold to support the expanded money supply at the prewar gold price. More than likely, the UK over all—including public and private holdings—had surpassed this threshold even before the Cunliffe Committee had published its first report. But Governor Cokayne, Cunliffe's bullionist successor, wanted yet more gold. So he continued this work, raising interest rates and pulling gold into London. By the end of 1920, the UK's official reserves were more than £145 million, fully 10.4 percent of the world's total.[53]

That year, Norman began his term as governor. Previously, he had steered policy from the shadows. Now he would have the chance to set the course on his own. He brought an altogether new approach to the gold standard.

The government, following the Cunliffe Committee's recommendation, centralized the private banks' gold holdings in 1921. This brought the official reserve total to £155 million. That spring, sterling crept back toward $4.00 to

Table 5  English Paper Notes and Gold Reserves, 1913–1927

| | BANK OF ENGLAND | | | | TREASURY | | | OVERALL | | |
|---|---|---|---|---|---|---|---|---|---|---|
| DATE (DEC) | NOTES | FIDUCIARY ISSUE | GOLD RESERVE | COVERAGE RATE | NOTES | GOLD RESERVE | COVERAGE RATE | NOTES | GOLD RESERVE | COVERAGE RATE |
| 1913 | 55.2 | 18.45 | 36.73 | 66.6% | 0.0 | 0.0 | 0 | 55.18 | 36.73 | 66.6% |
| 1914 | 65.5 | 18.45 | 47.05 | 71.8% | 12.8 | 18.5 | 144.23% | 78.33 | 65.55 | 83.7% |
| 1915 | 76.8 | 18.45 | 58.32 | 76.0% | 57.7 | 28.5 | 49.38% | 134.48 | 86.82 | 64.6% |
| 1916 | 73.4 | 18.45 | 54.97 | 74.9% | 122.5 | 28.5 | 23.27% | 195.87 | 83.47 | 42.6% |
| 1917 | 71.9 | 18.45 | 53.49 | 74.4% | 168.6 | 28.5 | 16.91% | 240.52 | 81.99 | 34.1% |
| 1918 | 84.9 | 18.45 | 66.41 | 78.3% | 259.2 | 28.5 | 10.99% | 344.09 | 94.91 | 27.6% |
| 1919 | 103.4 | 18.45 | 84.92 | 82.2% | 333.3 | 28.5 | 8.55% | 436.68 | 113.42 | 26.0% |
| 1920 | 135.1 | 18.45 | 116.65 | 86.3% | 346.1 | 28.5 | 8.23% | 481.24 | 145.15 | 30.2% |
| 1921 | 145.0 | 18.45 | 126.56 | 87.3% | 325.1 | 28.5 | 8.77% | 470.09 | 155.06 | 33.0% |
| 1922 | 144.7 | 18.45 | 126.28 | 87.3% | 296.4 | 27.0 | 9.11% | 441.13 | 153.28 | 34.7% |
| 1923 | 145.4 | 18.45 | 126.92 | 87.3% | 284.2 | 27.0 | 9.50% | 429.62 | 153.92 | 35.8% |
| 1924 | 146.2 | 18.45 | 127.73 | 87.4% | 286.5 | 27.0 | 9.42% | 432.72 | 154.73 | 35.8% |
| 1925 | 165.0 | 18.45 | 146.58 | 88.8% | 290.5 | 0.0 | 0.00% | 455.54 | 146.58 | 32.2% |
| 1926 | 168.3 | 18.45 | 149.83 | 89.0% | 290.6 | 0.0 | 21.61% | 458.86 | 149.83 | 32.7% |
| 1927 | 169.9 | 18.45 | 151.43 | 89.1% | 292.3 | 0.0 | 21.23% | 462.16 | 151.43 | 32.8% |

Millions of Pounds. Source: Forrest Capie and Alan Webber, *A Monetary History of the United Kingdom: 1870–1982* (London: George Allen and Unwin, 1985), 209–14, 326–97.

Note: The 1844 Bank Charter Act (7 & 8 Vict., c. 32) distinguished between the Bank of England's Issue Department and its Banking Department. The former was initially granted the right to emit a £14 million fiduciary issue. By the start of the war, this limit had been raised to £18.5 million. This fiduciary issue was "backed" by securities—government and otherwise—rather than gold. The rest of the Bank's issue was backed one-to-one by gold coin and bullion. Thus, to calculate the gold held by the Bank of England, we subtract its fiduciary issue from its total note issue. When the Treasury began issuing paper notes of its own in 1914, it deposited £18.5 million of gold in a special Currency Note Redemption Account. It added another £10 million of gold the following year. In 1922, this account was reduced to £27 million. The account was transferred entirely to the Bank of England in April 1925, in conjunction with Churchill's resumption of gold convertibility. The figures in this table are for the Bank of England and the UK Treasury exclusively. This does not include the small number of banknotes issued by English banks or the more substantial numbers of banknotes issued in Scotland and Ireland.

the pound. At that point, however, Norman began to systematically cut interest rates. He reduced Bank rate to 6.5 percent at the end of April. He made similar cuts in June, July, and November. Even with Bank rate back down to 5 percent, sterling gradually appreciated. By the end of 1921, the pound stood at $4.20. The next year followed a similar pattern: the sterling-dollar exchange rate rose, even as Norman continued driving down interest rates.

By the start of 1923, conditions for a return to gold had never been stronger. There was £155 million of gold in reserve. The gold value of the pound was within 5 percent of parity. Bank rate was at just 3 percent, granting Norman plenty of headroom. And the Conservatives had just been returned with an outright majority in Parliament. From the standpoint of the Cunliffe Committee, the next steps were obvious: remove the capital controls, announce the return to gold, and then defend the pound by raising interest rates as required.

Norman, however, bucked the directive. Instead, he (quite unconventionally) proposed shipping £100 million of gold to pay down the UK's American debts. He evidently hoped this would force the Federal Reserve to increase its own money supply, thus depreciating the dollar-sterling exchange rate. This was a long shot at best and obviously contradicted the Cunliffe Committee doctrine. Bradbury, of course, rejected the idea, killing it within the Treasury.[54]

That summer, Norman raised Bank rate from 3 percent to 4 percent for reasons that eluded his contemporaries and continue to elude historians.[55] Since the highs in February, sterling had fallen to around $4.55; but this was much higher than it had been when Norman was content to cut rates steadily the year before. Nevertheless, Bank rate was at 4 percent, and there it remained until March 1925, just prior to Churchill's return to gold.

Today, following the Keynesian Revolution, political economists would interpret the central bank's actions in conjunction with their expected effects on employment. But this was decidedly not at the forefront of this particular central banker's mind. Indeed, Norman virtually never broached the unemployment rate in public or in private.[56] But even if he had become conscious of this concern, it is not clear that this would have changed his approach. After all, those who prioritized battling unemployment remained convinced that returning to gold was the best solution to that problem. All of these people—from Conservatives to Labourites, from miners to bankers—believed this because Keynes had not yet revolutionized economic theory.

# CHAPTER 10

# Keynes's Revolution

Seldom have Britons been led worse than when they were pulled along the road back to gold. But this was not due only to the blinkered views of the monetary authorities. Just as often, Britons were let down by failures of imagination on all of the parliamentary benches. Simply put, the UK returned to gold because nobody knew any better. Capital did not know that it could again become the center of the global financial system without a regressive tax regime and a monomaniacal commitment to a single exchange rate valuation. Labor did not know that it could hold capital to account, both to bear its share of the public burdens and to ameliorate the adjustment costs that ever afflict the poorest workers. No one knew that it was possible to reform, let alone leave, the gold standard without suffering hyperinflation. No one in the UK knew this then because John Maynard Keynes had not yet produced and sold these ideas.

The traditional view is that Keynes had little direct influence on macroeconomic policy prior to the Second World War. Passages from several of the most distinguished treatments warrant quoting at length. In his classic account of the national crisis after the return to gold, Williamson argues,

> A common distortion in the study of economic policy . . . is that economists receive a prominence altogether disproportionate to their actual importance. . . . Remarkable is the attention given to Keynes, which is

on a scale explicable only in terms of his subsequent influence. Contemporary politicians might have considered that Keynes had valuable economic ideas, but within the whole context of assessing the practicality of policies . . . he was of no more importance than, say, leading backbench MPs or the editors of *The Times, News Chronicle,* or *Daily Herald.*[1]

Hall's canonical analysis of "Keynesianism across nations" renders Keynes's "economic ideas" as "the principles of countercyclical demand management."[2] The flattening of Keynes himself into the mere prefix of an "-ism" follows from the leveling so common in social scientific analysis. Such essentialization occludes agency in favor of structure. "Prosaic as it might seem," Hall writes, "the orientation of the governing party appears to have been the single most important factor affecting the likelihood that a nation would pursue Keynesian policies. Keynesian policies were much more commonly initiated by parties with particularly strong ties to the working class than by their conservative or bourgeois rivals."[3]

More recently, Seabrooke has modernized this as "agent-centered constructivism." He similarly "question[s] the autonomy of Keynes as a norm entrepreneur from the societal influences around him." "While many constructivist analyses emphasize the power of Keynes' ideas," Seabrooke suggests, ". . . we may give greater recognition to how his 'new liberal' ideas . . . were informed by the experience of the broader population during the 1920s."[4]

In his Pulitzer Prize–winning history, Kennedy took this argument to the extreme:

> This combination of government stimulus to consumption and resumed private capital formation . . . would, in time, constitute the operational heart of 'Keynesian economics.' It was not a conceptually difficult formula to grasp. Indeed, many American policymakers . . . had intuited the essence of these ideas well before Keynes famously put them to paper. To reverse Keynes's notorious dictum . . . that practical men are but the unwitting slaves of some defunct economist, it may be equally true that many economists . . . simply wrap the mantle of academic theory around the practical dictates of instinct and necessity. Surely what the world eventually came to know as 'Keynesianism' grew as much from the jumble of circumstance, politics, and adaptation as it did from the pages of the textbooks.[5]

And thus Keynes is in our textbooks now simply because his recommendations matched the policies embraced by policymakers then, rather than the other way around.

It is true that Keynes was hardly noteworthy in pointing out that the government can moderate macroeconomic cycles using "countercyclical" fiscal policies. After all, did not Joseph advise Pharaoh to do just that?[6] To recognize that Joseph's God was a Keynesian then is to acknowledge that "we are all Keynesians now"—and that we always have been so.[7]

For all of recorded history, policymakers have recognized the intuitive logic of countercyclical demand management.[8] But the gold standard orthodoxy forbade this. All policy, especially fiscal policy, was subordinated to the need to defend the gold value of the currency. This commandment was carved clearly into the tablets that were the Cunliffe Committee's several reports: "If . . . the gold standard [is] to be effectively maintained, it is . . . essential that Government borrowings should cease at the earliest possible moment after the war."[9] Patricians and plebeians of every stripe have always wanted "a free hand to do what is sensible."[10] But nobody in the UK—no political movement, party, or serious actor—believed they could responsibly question the gold standard imperative that precluded this.

That is, until Keynes. By showing that it was possible to move past the gold standard, to allow the gold value of the pound to change over time, Keynes released policymakers from these debilitating "gold fetters." Put another way, the innovation did not come in simply convincing policymakers that they *should* deploy countercyclical demand management. It came in showing them *how* they *could* do so by leaving the gold standard without losing control of inflation. This was only achieved in the 1930s, after Keynes had fully elaborated the theory of this system *and* the unintended experiment of suspending the gold standard showed, empirically, its viability.[11] Thus, the arrival of "Keynesian" fiscal policy turned on Keynes's revolution in monetary policy.

Yet this is not where Keynes began. In fact, as late as 1920, Keynes was even more orthodox than were the governors of the Bank of England. Describing himself then as a "dear money man," Keynes attacked the monetary authorities for their "inflationist" policies and insisted that the Bank of England's interest rate be doubled from 5 percent to perhaps 10 percent.[12] All of this changed in just a few short years, however, as Keynes became the leading—more or less, the only serious—advocate of abandoning the gold standard permanently. How do we explain this first, most profound revolution in Keynes's thought?

Given that so much has been written about Keynes, it is hard to believe that more work has not been done on this critical theoretical development. This is explicable in several ways. First, there is the gravitational force exerted by the so-called Keynesian Revolution itself. Those who do look at Keynes's evolving position on the gold standard are naturally drawn to his later work related to the creation of the Bretton Woods system in the 1940s. In those accounts, Keynes's conversion to monetary heterodoxy is ancient history and thus taken for granted.[13] Last, most of the attention given to Keynes in the early inter-war period understandably fixates upon the themes raised in his marvelous *Economic Consequences of the Peace* and the extensive work on war debts and reparations that followed.

The great biographies of Keynes faithfully present the markers on Keynes's journey into heresy.[14] But the treatments of this issue are small parts of these authors' broader stories, and there appears to be a certain inevitability to this aspect of those stories. It is only by tracing this particular issue across time that we can see how to connect the relevant dots.

It would take a career as fruitful as that of Keynes himself to trace that long and varied journey. This chapter reconstructs the early, critical portion of Keynes's odyssey into world-changing monetary heterodoxy.

## Apostasy

Keynes's first book, *Indian Currency and Finance* (1913), revealed his willingness and capacity to challenge the orthodoxy. Drawing insights from the experience and wisdom of the Indian monetary system, Keynes began to recognize the limitations of England's rarefied hegemonic monetary order. This promising line of inquiry—a possible de-Eurocentrizing of monetary theory—was de-railed by the outbreak of war in 1914. At that point, Keynes became consumed by the practical need to shape the course of events. During the war, Bradbury enlisted him in the struggle to preserve the gold standard as much as possible. As the war ended, Keynes launched his crusade to make the peace compatible with a return to the prewar liberal international order.

In all of this, theory faded into the background. On the one hand, there was the need to proffer policies that were practical and politically salable. But it was not just pragmatism. The old order was in a fight for survival. In the first instance, Keynes looked past the orthodoxy's multiplying contradictions to defend liberalism, broadly construed, against militarism and Bolshevism.[15]

But it was not so simple as that. Keynes's efforts to see the Treaty of Versailles revised, particularly at the Genoa Conference in May 1922, made clear that the liberal order needed more than just shoring up. There was a broad, and growing, range of currency misalignments. While it was fine in theory to suggest that every country simply impose the deflation necessary to restore the prewar gold parities, Keynes recognized that this was hopelessly unrealistic in countries with more than 20 percent depreciation.[16]

There was the problem of war debts and reparations. Rather than simplistic greed, vindictiveness, or bullionism, Keynes came to appreciate that people like Cunliffe were driven by the strictures of the orthodox gold standard to see foreigners' reserves as the salve to their own postwar gold requirements. And there was the challenge of a global redistribution of power, from "the old world" to the "new."[17] This obviously wounded English pride, but it also exposed the misfit between old norms and institutions and the changing material realities. London had the will but lacked the means, and New York had the means but lacked the will. Keynes asked: Would—or could—the liberal economic order function without effective leadership?

In the spring of 1922, Keynes attended (as a news correspondent) the Genoa Conference on Central and Eastern European reconstruction. His immense hopes were disappointed.[18] In the months that followed, the German mark collapsed. It fell from 5,074 to the pound in August to 32,146 in November. As it slid, the German government invited Keynes and several other foreign experts to Berlin to advise on the crisis. After conferring with Bradbury about his perspective and the UK's official position, Keynes set off for Germany.[19]

While in Berlin, Keynes gave a series of private lectures to the Institute of Bankers. The transcript—corrected by Keynes—reveals his unvarnished views, his thinking out loud at the time. For the orthodoxy, the disaster reinforced the importance of sound finance. It was a painful but pedestrian lesson. For Keynes, however, it offered a chance to reconsider the essentials of money.

At this point, Keynes was still motivated by the most orthodox of objectives: exchange rate stabilization. And the means Keynes proposed to effect the stabilization were arguably even more orthodox than were many of the alternatives under consideration. He deprecated attempts to manage the exchange informally using currency intervention. This was the worst of both worlds: "You will preserve the whole of the existing state of uncertainty, and it is quite likely that you would dribble your resources away without having got anything like stabilization because you would not have knocked out speculation."[20] Instead, it was better to make a one-off devaluation (to 15,000 marks to the pound sterling). The Reichsbank would then make an unalterable commitment to the new value, using its gold reserves early and often to keep the market rate at (or near) the official rate. Germany should "abolish all exchange regulations whatsoever and . . . have absolutely free and unfettered dealings" in the exchange market. Most important, the Reichsbank would then implement "a prolonged period of dear money" to create the "incentive to remit money to Germany rather than otherwise." In summary: "We would have absolute fixity, we would have an absolute abolition of exchange regulations, and we would have dear money."[21]

On these points, Keynes could hardly have been more orthodox. Indeed, this approach was more orthodox than that championed by Governor Norman—that of capital controls and cheap money.[22] Moreover, there was an orthodox rationale for such a devaluation. Restoration necessarily put off the day of stabilization. Keynes could argue—and had argued—that the true friends of the gold standard would swallow one-off devaluations of their currencies' gold values to get the gold standard operational again as quickly as possible. Besides, the English orthodoxy seemed to reason, these other countries had sullied reputations in any case.

At the same time, the freedom of thinking outside the box allowed Keynes to develop an altogether new line of analysis: resurrecting the debased mark would prove too disruptive. In a proto-Keynesian move, Keynes invoked the macroeconomic effects of currency appreciation: "a long period of deflation would be a very disastrous thing and might bring German industry almost to a standstill." He intuited, "No modern industrial community could stand the prospect . . . that the legal tender was going to appreciate in the course of the next few years by one thousand percent."[23] It was a brilliant insight, but Keynes stopped short of following it further.

The next week, Keynes considered the compatibility of the lessons across the German and British cases. In England, the metallic standard had been sacrosanct since Locke convinced Parliament that devaluation assaulted the citizenry's property rights in money. Changing that standard would not only redistribute wealth unpredictably and unjustly, but it would also confound all economic arrangements—including, crucially, contracts. To debase the currency, Locke argued, was to fail at the first object of political society and would thus undermine the foundations of the social contract.

Keynes addressed this argument in three ways. First, he invoked historical experience (as Lowndes had done against Locke) to establish that such changes were the norm across time and space. This was particularly true in the wake of major wars. "The burden of the national debt," Keynes explained, "is the measure of what the active earning part of the community have to hand over to the rentier or bond-holding class. . . . The general principles of contract have all through history had to . . . yield to that grand principle of expediency that you cannot increase the claim of the bond-holder . . . beyond a certain extent." Indeed, those who claim that "justice in the matter of contract must be done at all costs are the people who are really the greatest enemies of the sanctity of contract, because policies of that kind are what bring the whole thing into complete disrepute and eventually bring down the entire structure." Taking this haircut, Keynes hinted, might be necessary for the bondholders to ensure they received anything at all.[24] Of course, this was the threat leveled by every bankrupt against his or her creditors. But for Keynes, Central and Eastern Europe provided fresh evidence of the fragility of such unequal social contracts.

Keynes's second argument was more innovative. He disparaged the Lockean/restorationist view as offering a "very technical form of justice." The most significant critique was that few market actors actually conducted market transactions with certain quantities of precious metal in mind. Despite Cokayne's imaginaries to the contrary, gold was often not the medium of exchange used, and acquiring gold itself was seldom market actors' ultimate, or even proximate, object. The very stability of the gold price rendered it sufficiently monotonous that few Britons beyond those in the gold market had any sense of its relative value or absolute price. For most Britons, most of the time, the price of gold was a constant force akin to gravity. But, Keynes pointed out, ensuring that this one price did not vary meant ensuring that all other prices did vary. So while units of currency were stable in terms of gold alone, they were manifestly not stable in terms of the things that people cared about, such as housing, food, and fuel.

Instead, Keynes called for defining justice more holistically. Rather than ensuring that a pound fetches the same quantity of gold, "justice means presumably that you must put . . . people who have entered into contracts into the position which they had reason to anticipate they would be in when they entered into those contracts." Protecting property rights in money, Keynes argued, really meant ensuring that money could acquire the same quantity of goods and services across time. It meant ensuring that overall "purchasing power of the currencies," rather than its gold price necessarily, remained stable.[25]

Last, Keynes argued that there was no longer a single point of reference. At this stage, all valuations—including the value of gold in terms of sterling—had been unstable for nearly a decade. The pound was already depreciated in the market. He explained, "The longer the depreciation lasts the weaker the case [for restoration]. . . . More and more contracts will have been entered into at the depreciated rate, and more and more of the holders even of those contracts which have a history back to prewar times will have changed hands [sic] in the interval."[26] In other words, honoring the letter of the prewar contracts meant violating the expectations encapsulated in the wartime and postwar arrangements.

Yet despite these steps away from the orthodoxy, Keynes still embraced exchange rate stability as the preeminent objective. He defended this maxim in traditional terms. Exchange rate instability creates transaction costs—particularly exchange rate risk—and that reduces bankers' willingness to make foreign loans. This then reduces the quantity of funds available, raising the costs of trade. At the same time, speculators replace bankers in foreign exchange markets, exacerbating the problems of instability.[27]

At the end of the lecture, Keynes raised what would become one of his most important preoccupations: whether the effects of inflation and deflation are symmetric. He concluded, "The modern capitalist world is even less suited . . . for violent fluctuations in the value of money upwards than . . . downwards. Either [action] . . . ought never to be undertaken on purpose."[28] This was a crucial step away from the classical "neutrality of money" and toward the Keynesianism of our textbooks. Keynes now recognized that appreciating a currency was more disruptive than was an equal amount of depreciation.

Keynes continued this exploration in his next lecture. He admitted that unlike those countries that had suffered insurmountable depreciation, "there is no reason why we should not put sterling back to its prewar parity if we wish to." "Owing to our past history and . . . our position as an international financial center," Keynes conceded, there are "special reasons both of self-interest and of pride why we should wish to do so."[29]

Yet Keynes now believed that "the policy of restoring sterling to par was a mistake." It would have been better to have "stabilized, say, somewhere between four dollars and four and a half dollars to the pound sterling."[30] Effectively a devaluation of between 7 and 17 percent, this was a marked departure from his resolution at Genoa that countries with up to 20 percent overvaluation ought to restore their prewar parties.[31] Keynes stated this even while he acknowledged that "it looks as though we shall pursue [restoration] with a considerable measure of success."[32]

To defend this, Keynes trotted out the familiar argument that it would ease the burden of the national debt. But he also emphasized the tremendous transition costs, specifically "the depressing influence of a prospective fall of prices in relation to world prices on trade." Keynes intuited this result, but he had only begun to think about its causes. First, merchants face decreased demand, as "trade will never go ahead until people are certain they have touched bottom." At the same time, they struggle to cut costs. "The business of forcing down certain levels of wages . . . into equilibrium is almost hopeless. . . . The continuance of unemployment is to an important extent due to the fact that we have got the level of wages, particularly the level of wages of the unskilled, out of gear with everything else," Keynes remarked. At this point, however, Keynes still thought principally in terms of international trade. The high wages were problematic because they "compell[ed] [Britain] to ask double for [its] exports when the world level of prices . . . is only about 60% up." "Every hindrance" toward aligning internal and external prices "puts off the day when we shall be in equilibrium, and when we can employ our population." Of course, the decline of exports directly contributed to unemployment given their importance to the British economy. But this was hardly the extent of their effects, as Keynes would recognize soon enough.[33]

As forceful as these arguments were, Keynes advanced them with some trepidation. This concern was "of a more fleeting kind," and, he reckoned, the UK "[had] already borne the greater part of the brunt" of these costs. Moreover, he continued, "it may have been worth it—I do not say it was not."[34]

The same ambivalence—one might say self-contradiction—attended Keynes's discussion of the UK's obligations to restore the prewar parity. He was at pains to demonstrate that "honor" does not require the UK to restore the prewar parity. Several of the arguments were compelling: "Legal tender has constantly been fixed at new values in history," and "There is no other standard in Europe which has lasted for fifty years." But Keynes also suggested, "Even after the wars of Napoleon a change was made. Our standard is the only one which has existed for a hundred years." These claims were specious. As Keynes himself had noted previously in this lecture, the prewar parity was re-established following the Napoleonic Wars.[35] Just as important, the gold value of the pound had been stabilized for not one century but for two, at least. Thus, it simply was not true that "all the precedents are in favor of change." The British precedents—1696, 1819—all pointed to a full restoration. In the next breath, Keynes espoused his support for just that. Even as he maintained that the UK was "under no such obligation," he nevertheless "agree[d] [that] we ought to do it."[36]

At the end of the lecture, Keynes seriously considered the appeal of floating exchange rates. "The advantage of the pegged exchange," he explained, is that "the method of adjustment of a currency to the outside world" "is a slow one." Thus, "a mere seasonal or temporary deficit does not produce an excessive result." But this assumes that the "pegged" exchange rates reflect the long-run relative purchasing power of the currencies in question—that they are not already misaligned and that there will not be significant changes to these long-run relative values. Because "the pegged exchange is so slow in its operation," Keynes explained, ". . . it is dangerous for a country to adopt until it is sure that the basic conditions are fairly sound." But "then, as a correction to the seasonal movement, it is essential."[37]

When the official exchange rates do not accurately reflect "the basic conditions," however, removing the peg allows the market exchange rate to move rapidly toward the level at which there would be purchasing power parity. The conspicuous advantage of these exchange rate movements is that they created equilibrating pressures: "As soon as we import too much or export too little, the exchanges move against us . . . [and] the price of imports and exports is changed almost forthwith." "So," Keynes noted, "the unpegged exchange has one curious advantage which people overlook—it puts the brake on very rapidly." Of course, more than just economic fundamentals—"the basic conditions"—drive the appreciation and depreciation of floating exchange rates, and purchasing power parity is never fully achieved. Keynes admitted this: "The unpegged exchange" is also "sensitive to mere fleeting influences, mere news in the newspapers, or the mere season of the year . . . so that you have home prices bobbing about for reasons which are not permanent causes at all."[38]

Here again, Keynes was only willing to offer tentative conclusions. "The unpegged exchange is so sensitive that it is valuable for certain purposes," he stated, "but it is far too sensitive for other purposes." And he acknowledged the unsettled nature of his thought at this point: "That is an argument which is rather of the opposite tenor to most of what I have been saying in these lectures, but it is of sufficient interest and importance, and has enough relevance on the other side of the case for it to be right that I should mention it in conclusion."[39]

Despite the manifest inconsistencies and tentativeness of the lecture, Keynes sent a copy to Baldwin, now the chancellor of the exchequer. The pair met later that month, but there are scant details of their discussion.[40]

At the same time, Keynes distilled and published some of this analysis in the *Manchester Guardian Commercial*. He still worked mostly in an orthodox mode: exchange rate stabilization should come first; exchange rate instability hurt trade by exacerbating the costs associated with exchange rate risk; and writing effective contracts requires predictable currency values. In this piece published for a British audience, Keynes entirely bracketed his musings on the potential advantages of flexible exchange rates. And he fixed his discussion of the normative dimensions of appreciation and depreciation on the practical political limitations to transferring wealth from the working class to the bondholding class.[41]

He surged forward, however, in elucidating the connections between deflation and unemployment, going beyond just the effect deflation has on export industries. Keynes argued that deflation increases the real burden of private debts. This matters even from a purely domestic standpoint because it raises the costs—and reduces the revenues—of goods and services. Doubling the value of the money "means giving notice to every merchant and every manufacturer that for some time to come his stock and his raw materials will be constantly depreciating on his hands, and that everyone who finances his business with borrowed money . . . will in the end lose 100% on his liabilities." "Modern business being carried on by entrepreneurs largely on borrowed money," Keynes argued, "must necessarily be brought to a standstill by such a process."[42]

The gold standard was heralded as crucial to achieving purchasing power parity—the reality that a quantity of local currency buys the same quantity of goods and services in both the domestic and a foreign market. In theory, sustained imbalances in the balance of payments trigger gold flows, which ought to drive adjustments in money supplies and thus bring price levels back into equilibrium. Since the end of the war, however, the pound had floated vis-à-vis the gold-backed dollar. Untethered to gold, what drove the market exchange rate of the pound? The conventional view, Keynes later recounted, was that speculators bid up (and down) the market exchange rates, allowing their values to become dissociated from domestic macroeconomic conditions.[43] If exchange rates moved independently of shifts in price levels, it was possible to sustain imbalances of trade. For a trade-reliant state like Britain, this could prove deeply disturbing, particularly if the exchange rate appreciated more than the price level fell. The conventional conclusion was that returning to the gold standard, particularly at the prewar level, would force UK prices to fall to more competitive levels.

In the spring of 1923, Keynes began to recognize that this may not have been necessary. In a piece in *The Nation and the Athenaeum*, he examined the relative price levels—compared through the exchange rates at the time—in the United States and the UK since the end of the war. Of course, the exchange rates saw daily swings and an overall seasonality in the shifts. The domestic price levels moved more slowly, more steadily. So on a daily or weekly basis, exchange rates appeared disconnected from overall domestic price levels.[44]

But even when viewed on just a monthly basis, there was usually parity in purchasing power. Across the previous fifty-three months, Keynes found that price levels were within 1 percent of each other in more than two-thirds of the cases. In Keynes's mind, this confirmed that exchange rate movements in the medium and long term were correlated with changes in domestic price levels. So there was little reason to fear that unfixed exchange rates would lead to sustained disequilibrium in the balance of payments. "The modern theory of exchanges," Keynes explained, is that "the rate of exchange depends on the level of prices in America compared with the level of prices here." In other words, the relationship off of the gold standard mirrored the relationship on the gold standard. On the gold standard, domestic prices followed international pressures; but off of the gold standard, domestic shifts simply drove changes in the exchange rate. This insight further reduced the appeal of the gold standard system. If equilibrium and purchasing power parity would be achieved in either case, why not allow one price—the gold price—to fluctuate rather than compelling the entire domestic price level to do so?[45]

Yet there were still the costs created by exchange rate risk. And there was more to say about the connections between deflation and unemployment. In the weeks that followed, Keynes worked through these issues in a sustained fashion as he set to work drafting the *Tract on Monetary Reform*.[46]

## Non-flationism?

As Keynes began work on the *Tract*, Baldwin succeeded Bonar Law as prime minister. Baldwin had more than two years before his capital controls were due to expire, and he had no desire to renew the discussion of monetary policy. But in July, the Liberal MP Hilton Young forced him to declare whether he was a deflationist, an inflationist, or a "non-flationist." Young, who had considerable expertise in finance and connections to Keynes's "Bloomsbury Group," argued vigorously for the latter in terms that paralleled Keynes's own evolving arguments. While inflation "inflict[s] untold hardship on the middle-classes, and all with fixed incomes," Young declared, "deflation brings unemployment." Like Keynes, Young said that policymakers should "endeavor to avoid processes in either direction."[47]

Conceding that he had "but a skin-deep acquaintance with the subject," Baldwin tried (but failed) to evade the question. He could hardly disagree with Young. He announced, "The right policy . . . is to do all in our power to keep prices steady." As if he had been reading Keynes, he argued, "One of the chief causes of unsettlement in industry, whether it be on the part of those who are trying to get orders for business or whether it be on the part of those who work for a weekly wage, has arisen fundamentally from the fact that we have been living in a world of constantly shifting values." Yet on the return to gold, he punted: "Whether we shall be able, within a measurable distance of time, to get back to a gold standard, is a matter which at this moment I do not think can be profitably discussed."[48]

Baldwin's apparent "non-flationism" emboldened Keynes. In a powerful editorial, he denounced what he termed "a secret process of deflation" "of at least 10 percent" as partly responsible for the "weakening of the trade revival and the severe continuing unemployment." He lashed out when the Bank raised interest rates to 4 percent the next day. This "grave mistake" could "cause a million or two of Englishmen to stand idle." Keynes blamed "the Report of the Cunliffe Committee, a document written . . . without any knowledge of all the extraordinary postwar developments, and not containing a single reference to stability of prices and employment." Whereas Baldwin "had rightly committed himself to the contrary," Keynes proclaimed, the Bank of England was still "acting under the influence of a narrow and obsolete doctrine."[49]

In fact, Keynes was wide of the mark. True, Baldwin had described the connection between price instability and unemployment in terms rather similar to those issued by Keynes. But Baldwin did not concede that the UK faced a trade-off between exchange rate stability and domestic price stability. In fact, he—and Young—held the same position that Keynes himself had held for so long: for a trade-dependent, financier state like the UK, exchange rate stability was a necessary precursor to price stability. Keynes might have realized this had he paid closer attention to the rest of the discussion, where Young argued powerfully to this effect. Also, the mandated deflation was hardly a "secret." Indeed, Young had announced to Parliament that "it [was] still necessary to carry further the process of deflation." And Baldwin had not contradicted him.[50]

Yet Keynes had heard what he wanted to hear. Baldwin was talking in Keynes's terms about the effects of price instability on unemployment. Even a year later, Keynes still characterized this comment as a speech announcing a sea change in government policy.

To be fair, Keynes's interpretation was not unreasonable. Baldwin, after all, had been the one to derail the Cunliffe Committee train in 1920 by extending the capital controls. More recently, Keynes had pressed his new ideas upon the new prime minister, and he must have been elated to see them now broached in Parliament. Also, Baldwin still omitted discussing the nonmonetary tools—that is, tariffs—that he and the Conservatives planned to use to stave off deflation while effecting the restoration.[51] So it is understandable that Keynes perceived Baldwin's embrace of "non-flationism" as another step down this progressive road.

Being wrong about Baldwin, however, proved intellectually indispensable for Keynes. It inspired him and gave him the cover required to develop and publish the intuitions he had hit upon in his lectures the previous autumn. Thus, misunderstanding the realm of what was politically feasible gave him the space in which to expand the range of theoretical possibilities.

In the months that followed, most of Keynes's energy went into refining his views for *A Tract on Monetary Reform*. But he did not shy away from pressing his controversial views in the press. He stated his position with ever-sharper clarity. First came the simple diagnosis: "Unemployment today is due to a very considerable extent . . . to a lack of confidence . . . in the existing level of prices." This oversimplification ignored the significant shift in the position of Britain's economy caused by the war, as Keynes subsequently conceded. The concession was significant, since this latter factor would be used by the orthodoxy to justify the deflation: having lost its prewar lead, the UK now needed to drive down its prices in order to compete in foreign markets. Then came the prescription: "This lack of confidence is in some measure remediable by a resolute policy on the part of the Treasury and the Bank of England . . . [of ] not continu[ing] to act . . . on the deflationary recommendations of the Cunliffe Committee."[52]

When commentators balked at the prospect of "abandoning the gold standard" for the sake of maintaining price stability now, Keynes chided them for failing to keep up with the changing times: "It used to be our policy to restore the gold standard. It has become our policy to keep prices stable. We have taken on the new doctrine, without, as yet, discarding the old." "Fortunately," Keynes declared, "we cannot but feel . . . that *The Times*, like *The Economist*, is really with us on the main issue." Moreover, he continued, "*The Times*, like nearly everyone else, shrinks from the practical measures which the old doctrine would require from true believers."[53]

Believing that he was winning the battle of public opinion, Keynes scrutinized the perceived holdouts. "If the Labour Party are interested in remediable causes of unemployment," Keynes proposed, "they would do well to cast their eyes more frequently . . . than they have done hitherto in the direction of monetary policy." So too with the Federation of British Industries, which Keynes called to press the Government "whether . . . the official policy of the Bank of England is the same as that lately acknowledged by the Prime Minister—namely, to promote confidence in the price level." "Failing this," Keynes wrote, "I hope that the Federation of British Industries will call to their assistance the Federation of Trade Unions and push the controversy home."[54]

Of course, Keynes was wrong about Baldwin's policy. But he recognized a reality that we, in a world after Keynes, have struggled to believe: the workers and their employers were united in their zeal for the return to gold. They shared this faith because England's gold standard had been made into a religious, rather than a political, affair; and Keynes was determined to change this. "So long as unemployment is a matter of general political importance," he prophesied, "it is impossible that Bank rate should be regarded, as it used to be, as the secret peculium of the Pope and Cardinals of the City."[55] "We have a right to know what the official policy in fact is," he declared.[56]

Of course they had a right to know, but few beyond Keynes did not already know. The widely hailed Cunliffe Committee's reports were still the official guides to the UK's path forward. Nobody had yet joined Keynes's monetary revolutionary: the (positive) realization that external exchange rate stability often comes at the expense of domestic price stability and the (normative) belief that exchange rate instability was the lesser of the two evils. This was now clear in Keynes's mind. But it was still years away from wide recognition, let alone adoption. To achieve that, the next step was to expound the new, reformed monetary religion.

## The *Tract*: From Orthodoxy to Reform

In December 1923, Keynes published *A Tract on Monetary Reform*. Its title, and much of its tone, belied its radicalism. It offered "the proposal—which may seem, but should not be, shocking—of separating entirely the gold reserve from the note issue."[57] Rather than regulating the supply of money so as to maintain stable exchange rates, Keynes pressed policymakers to prioritize internal price stability. The Bank of England should "'regulate' but not 'peg'" the price of gold. It should set a selling price for gold that was stable in the short run but reserve the right to adjust this rate as occasion required.[58]

This challenged several centuries of orthodoxy, as Keynes well knew. Not since Locke and Newton had this been the rule in England. But here was Keynes proposing to revive the premodern system defended (in vain) by the much-deprecated William Lowndes. Keynes, however, knew better than to hearken back to this ancient practice. He also resisted the temptation to present his proposals as avant-garde. Instead, his brilliant rhetorical strategy was to elucidate its viability and desirability in the present.

### The Importance of Price Stability

Keynes began the work by stating in round terms the importance of minimizing "change[s] in the value of money." The economic organization of contemporary Britain, he argued, "is more dependent than that of any earlier epoch on the assumption that the standard of value would be moderately stable." Recently, however, the standard had fluctuated with "unprecedented violence."[59] "For these grave causes," Keynes concluded, "we must free ourselves from the deep distrust which exists against allowing the regulation of the standard of value to be the subject of deliberate decision. We can no longer afford to leave it in the category of . . . matters which are settled by natural causes."[60]

Keynes's charge that the gold standard failed to maintain internal price stability was not novel. Indeed, Locke (then Smith) had recognized this centuries prior.[61] Even Marshall and Pigou conceded the imperfection of the gold standard in this respect. Simply put, the rate at which precious metals enter the market is independent of the rate of increase of the goods and services available in the economy. So the stability of the gold price meant the instability of everything else. As Keynes put it, "Gold is liable to be either too dear or too cheap. . . . It is too much to expect that a succession of accidents will keep the metal steady."[62] The "moral" of recent experience, he suggested, is "that it is not safe or fair to combine the social organization developed during the nineteenth century . . . with a *laisser-faire* [*sic*] policy towards the value of money. It is not true that our former arrangements have worked well."[63]

Keynes identified two problems with the "fluctuations of the standard." First, they unjustly and unpredictably transferred purchasing power between various groups in society: debtors and creditors, workers and capitalists, and producers and consumers. These effects were indictable simply on the grounds of fairness.[64] More important, inflation and deflation—both when they are expected and when they are unexpected—influence the level at which society's productive resources are employed. "The intensity of production," Keynes posited, "is largely governed in existing conditions by the anticipated real profit of the entrepreneur." But because prices and costs are denominated in nominal terms, changes in "the value of money" between when the entrepreneur's costs are defrayed and revenue from sales, collected, influence the real rate of profit. As a result, "the business world . . . stands to gain by a rise of price and to lose by a fall of price." Hoping to minimize their risk, those in business act on their expectations, and "the fear of falling prices causes [entrepreneurs] to protect themselves by curtailing their operations." While these entrepreneurs merely act to protect their own interests, "it is upon the aggregate of their individual estimations of the risk, and their willingness to run the risk, that the activity of production and of employment mainly depends."[65]

"The best way to cure this mortal disease of individualism," Keynes concluded, "is to provide that there shall never exist any confident expectation either that prices generally are going to fall or that they are going to rise." "The remedy would lie," he suggested, "in so controlling the standard of value that, whenever something occurred which, left to itself, would create an expectation of a change in the general level of prices, the controlling authority should take steps to counteract this expectation by setting in motion some factor of a contrary tendency." Thus, Keynes saw the object of macroeconomic stabilization policy as countering the influence of price changes on employment.[66] The solution, to use the term Young imposed upon Baldwin, was "non-flationism."

What of the exchanges? The orthodoxy held that domestic stability depended upon maintaining external stability.

Keynes agreed that trying to maintain an overvalued or undervalued currency would multiply domestic distortions. But he questioned whether stable exchange rates were necessary in the first instance. Here he was empowered by his previous analysis of real price convergence between the United States and the United Kingdom. Despite the fluctuating exchange rate, Keynes found that the real prices of the two countries tended to converge over the long run. Keynes explained, "The theory of purchasing power parity tells us that movements in the rate of exchange between the currencies of two countries tend . . . to correspond pretty closely to movements in the internal price levels of the two countries each expressed in their own currency."[67] With that, Keynes reversed the causal priority. If the exchange rate were allowed to float freely and domestic stability were targeted, the exchange rates would adjust automatically in due course.

But was not the stable gold price the cornerstone of the UK economy? Again Keynes challenged the conventional wisdom. He minimized the importance of the "stability of exchange" as merely "a convenience which adds to the efficiency and prosperity of those who are engaged in foreign trade." Keynes did acknowledge that some small, trade-dependent states might fare better to prioritize exchange rate stability. But he roundly concluded that "there does seem to be in almost every case a presumption in favor of the stability of prices, if only it can be achieved."[68]

## Keynes's Appeals to Practice

In addition to his theoretical arguments for focusing on internal price stability, Keynes also appealed to the weight of experience. His first appeal bears a striking resemblance to the argument put forth by Lowndes two and a quarter centuries previously. Keynes simply argued that for most of its history, England had utilized exchange rate adjustment as a favorite tool of macroeconomic management. "In 1914," he suggested, "gold had not been the English standard for a century or the sole standard of any other country for half a century." Citing the debasements of Edward III in particular, as Lowndes had done, Keynes explained that these were the product of a fully rational "preference for stability of internal prices over stability of external exchanges."[69]

This trend, Keynes suggested, has been the story of broader monetary history throughout the world: "There is no record of a prolonged war or a great social upheaval which has not been accompanied by a change in the legal tender, but an almost unbroken chronicle . . . of a progressive deterioration in the real value of the successive legal tenders which have represented money." "Moreover," he continued, "this progressive deterioration in the value of money through history is not an accident." According to Keynes, this has been the deliberate, conscious policy of states around the world "back to the earliest dawn of economic record."[70]

But Keynes knew better than to dwell too much upon ancient history, and so he boldly extended this characterization to include contemporary practice. He praised what he referred to as "the postwar method" in Britain and elsewhere, the system under which exchange rates were allowed to adjust freely while domestic prices remained stable.[71] "In truth," Keynes wrote, "the gold standard is already a barbarous relic."[72] He insisted that those orthodox economists and bankers who advocated a return to gold were decidedly out of touch with the times. "Advocates of the ancient standard," he argued, "do not observe how remote it now is from the spirit and the requirements of the age. A regulated nonmetallic standard has slipped in unnoticed. *It exists.*"[73]

Keynes insisted that a nonmetallic standard "exists" in America as well, despite that the United States maintained its gold standard parity. Whereas advocates of the return to gold pointed to the United States as exemplary, Keynes was at pains to demonstrate that the United States was actually violating the orthodox rules of the gold standard game. These conventions specified that central banks govern their discount policy "by reference to the influx and efflux of gold and the proportion of gold to liabilities."[74] But rather than overextending their note issue with respect to their reserves, which was the typical way in which the "rules of the game" were bent, the United States was doing precisely the opposite. Fearing inflation, the United States was unwilling to expand its note issue in due proportion to the gold flowing into its reserves. The result was, as Keynes vividly put it, "the costly policy of burying in the vaults of Washington what the miners of the Rand [had] laboriously brought to the surface."[75]

What does this matter? What were the implications of this new approach to the gold standard? In peak rhetorical form, Keynes exclaimed,

[The gold standard convention] perished, and perished justly, as soon as the Federal Reserve Board began to ignore its ratio and to accept gold without allowing it to exercise its full influence, merely because an expansion of credit and prices seemed at that moment undesirable. From that day, gold was demonetized by almost the last country which still continued to do it lip-service, and a dollar standard was set up on the pedestal of the Golden Calf. For the past two years the United States has *pretended* to maintain a gold standard. *In fact* it has established a dollar standard; and, instead of ensuring that the value of the dollar shall conform to that of gold, it makes provision, at great expense, that the value of gold shall conform to that of the dollar.

The prewar gold standard, Keynes announced, was "as dead as mutton."[76]

This framing considerably softened the apparent radicalism of Keynes's call to leave the gold standard. The proposal would only "appear shocking until the reader realizes that . . . it does not differ in substance from the existing state of affairs."[77] "In practice," Keynes insisted, "we have already gone a long way towards the ideal of directing bank rate and credit policy by reference to the internal price level and other symptoms of under- or over-expansion of internal credit, rather than by reference to the prewar criteria of the amount of cash in circulation (or of gold reserves in the banks) or the level of the dollar exchange."[78] In particular, he extolled "utilizing bank rate as a means of keeping prices and employment steady."[79] By contrast, he continued, "the Cunliffe Report is an unadulterated prewar prescription—inevitably so considering that it was written . . . without knowledge of the revolutionary and unforeseeable experiences of the past five years."[80]

On this point, Keynes was right but for the wrong reasons. The Cunliffe Committee reports *were* thoroughly orthodox in their orientation, and they did describe a set of imaginaries that did not reflect the realities of the postwar world. But this was not because it was impossible to align the imaginary and the reality. The Cunliffe Committee could have imagined managing the monetary system without slavish reliance on gold. Indeed, Cunliffe himself came close to effectively decoupling the money supply from the gold supply. More important, it was still possible to drive reality to that imaginary. Keynes was right that "the gold standard," however imagined, was "dead" in 1923. But as we have seen, the UK had enough gold and more than enough political will to implement the Cunliffe Committee doctrine—to resurrect the orthodox deity.

But Keynes knew better than to get carried away with his own metaphors. He had collaborated with Bradbury for years to effect this salvation; and he knew well his country's capacity to bring it about. So, he bracketed the question of the whether the UK *could* restore the gold standard and instead challenged the assumption that it *should* do so. This meant detailing the costs of imposing a return to gold on an economy that, he insisted, had evolved beyond being tethered to it.

## The Cost of Going Back

The first and most significant costs of restoring the prewar gold value of the pound were the adjustment difficulties that were sure to follow. Keynes estimated that the market value of the pound had depreciated 10 percent below its prewar standard. Insisting that wages and prices were sticky, Keynes argued that such a revaluation would worsen Britain's balance of trade (by making imports more competitive and exports less so) and increase unemployment. Keynes pointed to the Cunliffe Committee's own report to support the latter prediction. "Of all the omissions from the Cunliffe Report," Keynes suggested, "the most noteworthy is the complete absence of any mention of the problem of the stability of the price level." He continued, "And it cheerfully explains how the prewar system . . . operated to bring back equilibrium by deliberately causing a 'consequent slackening of employment.'"[81]

Keynes insisted that the promise of a better future result could not outweigh the costs created by the immediate dislocation. In one of his most celebrated formulations, Keynes attacked the classical economists' fixation on the long-run equilibrium: "But this *long run* is a misleading guide to current affairs. *In the long run* we are all dead. Economists set themselves too easy, too useless a task if in tempestuous seasons they can only tell us that when the storm is long past the ocean is flat again."[82]

There were also geostrategic costs. Returning to gold would significantly strengthen the economic power of the United States. Things are not as they used to be; "the value of gold is no longer the resultant of the chance gifts of Nature and the judgment of numerous authorities and individuals acting independently."[83] The Americans, Keynes reasoned, have so large a share of the world's gold reserves that they can dictate the price of gold and, with it, the internal price level of any nation whose currency is pegged to gold. Keynes concluded, "The reinstatement of the gold standard means, inevitably, that we surrender the regulation of our price level and the handling of the credit cycle to the Federal Reserve Board of the United States."[84]

Keynes must have expected that this last blow would reverberate down Threadneedle Street, the spine of the City of London. But he likely did not imagine the impact it would have, in time, on the City's most powerful pugilist: that great champion of controlling capital, Montagu Norman.

## The World of the Tract

From a political and economic standpoint, the publication of the *Tract* could hardly have come at a less opportune time. The hyperinflation in Central Europe had just peaked, leading to the near total collapse of the German economy. Of course, Keynes saw this as validating his contention that the imposition of reparations was not only wicked but also dangerous. Much to his chagrin, however, elite opinion in Britain took an altogether different lesson from the experience: the *papiermark* had collapsed because it was a paper, rather than a gold, mark. Whatever their foreign obligations, the Germans had failed because they had abandoned the principles of sound finance—because they had abandoned the gold standard.

At home, the *Tract* was born into political upheaval. Hoping for a free hand to raise tariffs, Baldwin had called an early election. He had badly misjudged the temper of the electorate. Just as the *Tract* was coming out, the Conservatives lost nearly one hundred seats, falling from a comfortable majority to a mere plurality. This put Asquith, who had just reunited the Liberal party, in the position of kingmaker. He had little doubt about what he must do: in the name of free trade, the Liberals would prop up a Labour government—Britain's first. In addition to thwarting his ancient rivals, Asquith hoped that this would give the Labour upstarts the opportunity to fail spectacularly.

The "socialist" ascent in Westminster raised pulses on Lombard Street. Whatever appetite there may have been for experimenting with Keynes's monetary reforms vanished.

# PART FOUR

# *Theocracy*

The powers that be are ordained of God. . . . They that
resist shall receive to themselves damnation. . . . For he
is the minister of God to thee for good. (Romans
13:1–4)

# CHAPTER 11

# Understanding "The Norman Conquest of $4.86"

In November 1924, a critic in the *Nation and Atheneaum* decried the impending "Norman Conquest of $4.86." The pithy formulation has stuck, and it has since come to define how we understand the transformation of British monetary policy in the 1920s.[1] Each element plays a crucial role in that canonical story. Beginning at the end, the key objective was to ensure a specific value of the pound in terms of the US dollar. This was both the goal and the measure of success: in the exchange rate market, one pound ought to be worth $4.86. Next, this was a conquest. It began with a struggle between contending claimants for England's throne, but it did not end until many of England's political, social, and economic institutions had been transformed. Finally, that struggle was won, totally and utterly, by Norman—Montagu Norman, governor of the Bank of England.

All this was prescient. The UK did return to the gold standard. Norman did emerge victorious, and he did transform—"Normanize"—the UK's monetary system. But as the received account has become ever further distilled, we have increasingly forgotten the fires that catalyzed this transformation in the first place. There is much more to this rich tapestry than meets the eye. The last part of this book returns to the inferno in which the old golden sovereign was melted away and replaced with the "new" gold standard.

# $4.86

Moggridge's pathbreaking study of the "return to gold" begins thus: "The decision to return to the gold standard at the prewar parity of $4.86 . . . [represents] a watershed in British inter-war economic history."[2] Since then, economic historians have conceptualized British monetary policy in the 1920s as the policy of achieving, and maintaining, a specific dollar value of the pound sterling. For instance, there are many candidates for the point at which the UK left the gold standard in the first place: Was it when the Treasury printed the Bradburys? When the government imposed capital controls across the war? When Parliament extended these controls in peacetime? When Churchill abandoned the gold coinage? But Howson chose March 1919, the moment at which "the government unpegged the exchanges and abandoned the gold standard."[3] Similarly, Sayers read a concern with the dollar value of the pound back into "the Cunliffe recommendations" and the Bank's support for "returning as soon as possible to the gold standard." "In company with the City and the politicians," Sayers wrote, "[the Bank] never thought of this last otherwise than as a return to a dollar parity of 4.86."[4]

But what does the value of the pound to the holders of dollars have to do with the maintenance of the gold standard in England? Why does it matter so much more than, say, the price of tea in China? After all, each was simply a price, and neither was a price that was *necessarily* linked to gold.[5] More to the point, who would have described the binding of the pound to a foreign currency (comprised largely of paper notes) as the restoration of England's ancient gold standard? The answer is startling: before 1923, virtually no one; but by the end of the 1920s, most of the UK's political and economic elites.

Who were the agents of that radical redefinition? That answer is even more startling: John Maynard Keynes and Montagu Norman. The transformation followed from Keynes's revolutionary insight, embraced by Norman, that the US Federal Reserve effectively controlled the world gold market. This meant that a "return" to the "gold" standard was really an adoption of the dollar standard, like it or not.[6]

But this was not how the orthodoxy had understood things, or the course they initially set for the UK. The Cunliffe Committee certainly did not define the gold standard as maintaining some specific dollar value of the pound. Instead, it defined "the essence of" the UK's "complete and effective gold standard" as the reality that "notes . . . always stand at absolute parity with gold coins of equivalent face value, and that both notes and gold coins stand at absolute parity with gold bullion." For the Cunliffe Committee, the parity that mattered was not a specific exchange rate parity but the "parity" with gold itself—the nominal price of gold. The maintenance of stable exchange rates with foreign currencies would be a *consequence* of achieving that primary objective. "When these conditions are fulfilled," the committee stated, "the foreign exchange rates with all countries possessing an effective gold standard are maintained at or within the gold specie points." But the Cunliffe Committee never contemplated that a single exchange rate would become the barometer for assessing the gold value of the pound. In that old world, there was one, and only one, metric: the London gold price.[7]

Churchill continued this fight. Even as he relied upon the new orthodox view, reformed in the wake of Keynes's *Tract*, Churchill was loath to describe the return in terms of the pound's dollar value. In his announcement to Parliament, he did cite the pound's "buoyant" "exchange with the United States" as one of the factors that would ease the return. But he quite explicitly defined the return in terms of the London gold price and the rights of Britons to secure that gold with their pound notes. Churchill maintained the old terms—if not the old forms—of the prewar gold standard: "The Bank of England will be put under obligations to sell gold bullion in amounts of not less than 400 fine [troy] ounces in exchange for legal tender at the fixed price of £3 17s. 10½d. per standard [troy] ounce." Thus, the gold standard was a promise by the government to force the Bank to convert legal tender into sums of gold at the same price that had been specified for centuries. In the first instance, the dollar had nothing to do with it.[8]

Yet Churchill was pouring new wine from the old bottles. His masterful rhetoric to the contrary notwithstanding, Churchill knew well that he was not "restoring" the same old gold standard any more than Parliament "restored" the same old monarchy in 1660. Too much had changed in the interregnum. The "conducting" of the international gold standard symphony had moved from the City of London to Manhattan.[9] Keynes, and the economic historians who followed him, were right to cast the 1925 "return" to the gold standard as an implicit adoption of a dollar standard.[10]

So the gold standard enthroned in 1925 was as different from the prewar sovereign as William I was from Harold—or, more fittingly, as William III was from his father-in-law, James II. In 1914, more than half of the currency in the UK was comprised of gold itself. Particularly in England, getting and using gold had been virtually costless. By 1926, the "new gold standard" had been anointed, and gold itself had virtually vanished from circulation. The minimum "purchase" of gold had been raised more than three thousand times, from half of a sovereign (£0.50) to nearly £1700. It was like the Gutenberg Revolution but in reverse: gold moved from its place as a central physical medium, passing from hand to hand among a sizable portion of the population to an exalted role secured by the authorities and made accessible to the people increasingly through mere symbolic representations alone.

From a nonmaterial standpoint, it matters that the conquest was of "$4.86" rather than of "£3 17s. 10½d." By these means, the identity of "the" gold standard was reconstructed. Even if the new gold standard was a rose by another name, it would be naïve to think that labels do not matter in a country that clings to its Imperial units. It might be that few Britons craved to feel the precious metal itself between their fingers. Yet the symbolism, if not the materiality, of a golden pound was every bit as important as the number of stars on a flag and the color of a passport.

There were substantial material changes as well. The new gold standard brought its high priest, the governor of the Bank of England, to the height of power. He was given the ultimate trump card—"For the sake of our gold standard"—even as the new regime further insulated him from market and political pressure. At the same time, he was given leave to conduct independent diplomacy with his fellow central bankers, particularly those in the United States, as they jointly managed the reformed international monetary order. In the terms of modern social science, it is hard to imagine a more independent central banker than Montagu Norman under the new gold standard.

Perhaps this is the reason that he, as an individual, looms so large.

## Norman-centrism

In discussing the return to gold, it is all too tempting to fixate upon, and point a finger at, Norman. Certainly, those who lived under his rule often did, and that is how they often cast it—as living under Norman's rule. They were not burdened by our textbook political economy models in which central bankers struggle to achieve even a modicum of "independence" from politicians' imperatives. But they also had not yet seen the full depths to which the state's dictates could sink. So it was only in 1939, after nearly two decades of Norman's governing and with some innocence still intact, that one contemporary biographer could write, "It is gradually becoming common knowledge that it is not the Hitlers, Mussolinis, or Stalins . . . who are the real dictators, but the men who lurk in the shadows behind the beflagged and besloganed rostrums— the . . . little-known men who *dictate to the 'dictators.'* Montagu Norman is one of these: perhaps the most powerful of all."[11]

Yet this critic mistakes some important facts.[12] More important, the scale is as wrong as is the domain of the crimes. Norman may have been unsympathetic to those who suffered under his austerity, but he was never murderous.[13]

Still, as monetary authorities go, there has never been—before or since—a host like that of Norman unto himself. It was not for nothing that Norman became the longest-serving, most pivotal, and most powerful central banker in modern history.

Most scholarly accounts similarly accord Norman singular agency. There is little recognition of the tension between his views and those of the Cunliffe Committee. The earliest accounts held that Norman helped to define the Cunliffe Committee's doctrine in the first place.[14] Most gloss over the pivotal Chamberlain-Bradbury Currency Committee, the successor to the Cunliffe Committee.[15] With few exceptions, those that do engage the Chamberlain-Bradbury Committee typically treat its opinions as consonant with those of Norman.[16] Some even get the sequence of events wrong, suggesting that Norman "was supported by" the Cunliffe Committee's reports and that the Chamberlain-Bradbury Committee "accepted the Governor's view on the adequacy of the adjustment of prices" and "proceeded to model its Report closely on [Norman's] latest recommendations."[17]

In fact, the essentials of Norman's dogma were disavowed by the Cunliffe Committee, as we have seen. And, as we shall see, the Chamberlain-Bradbury Committee defied Norman's vigorous resistance and formulated its own conclusions and recommendations. Its report was essentially completed two days before Norman's second testimony. That second invitation was really the committee's attempt to bring Norman into line—to get him to recant his previous position, to commit to not using the loan he had secured from the United States, and to implement the restoration on the terms designed by the Cunliffe Committee.

Thus, it is imprecise, and unfair, to lump together the principal architects of the return to gold—Norman, Niemeyer, and Bradbury—as "the most fanatical and thoughtless advocates of the gold standard to be found anywhere in the country."[18] These three men spent years arguing about the gold standard. Throughout, the ideas of each evolved considerably. They may have been fanatical, but they were not thoughtless. So far from forcing through the early return, Norman was, until the winter of 1925, one of the strongest supporters of extending the capital controls by several years. Perhaps no one was more committed to the Cunliffe Committee dogma than was its principal author: Bradbury. But even Bradbury, in the late summer of 1924, was won over to Keynes's proposed deferral. It was only when the purchasing power of the pound and the dollar appeared to converge quite unexpectedly that Bradbury embraced the gamble of an early return. Then when the return did come, Niemeyer encouraged Churchill to accept all of Norman's recommended limitations on Britons' access to gold. All three of these men accepted the Keynes critique that the prewar gold standard would not, should not, and could not return. It was they who reconstructed a restoration of £3 17*s*. 10½*d*. as adherence to $4.86.

This brings us to the conspicuous diminution of Keynes's role in this drama. As the principal private secretary to the chancellor of the exchequer, Grigg was intimately familiar with Churchill and his decision to effect the return. His memoirs mention Keynes so as to dismiss him:

> [Since] 1918, every Government . . . had proclaimed its intention of working towards the restoration of the Gold Standard as soon as possible, and . . . fiscal and monetary events in these years [were] . . . continuously directed to this end. . . . The opponents of the policy advocated by the Cunliffe Committee were confined to a small number of those who were susceptible to the still small voice of Keynes, and this in spite of the fact that the still small voice was already beginning to be immeasurably amplified by the multiple organ of Lord Beaverbrook.

Thus, the homogenization of the orthodoxy leads to a simple binary: Keynes versus those who supported "the policy"—singular—"advocated by the Cunliffe Committee." That binary was unequal in size: Keynes is virtually alone and has even less support than his coverage in Beaverbrook's newspapers implies. And it was unequal in strength: Keynes's *Tract* only "cast faint doubts on this policy."[19]

Even Keynes's biographers have largely followed Grigg's original denigration. This is particularly true in Skidelsky's account, even in a volume that "tells the story of Keynes's metamorphosis from esthete, philosopher, and administrator into world savior."[20] He writes that "Keynes's argument in the *Tract* against going back to gold had failed to convince," and his "evidence to the Chamberlain Committee was hardly a robust attack on the policy of restoring the gold standard."[21] In fact, the softness of his position actually "helped to crystallize the view that the prewar parity could be regained and maintained without detrimental effect on the real economy."[22] Moggridge's classic account offers a longer, richer discussion. But he agrees that "[Keynes's] was very much a voice in the wilderness, and a very ambiguous one at that." For Moggridge, "the decision to return to the gold standard at prewar par was more or less inevitable, particularly after the rise in the dollar exchange."[23]

It is true that Keynes made "tactical" compromises that, perhaps, proved strategically costly.[24] More important, he blew some of the opportunities he did enjoy to shape the policy discussions. His poor performance in his testimony before the Chamberlain-Bradbury Committee was the most unfortunate of these. It was not just that he was unprepared; he was positively out of touch. He had so thoroughly convinced himself that the Cunliffe Committee dogma was a dead letter that he misunderstood the entire purpose of the Chamberlain-Bradbury Committee: to effect the restoration. More important still, Keynes's theory was still underdeveloped. He had not yet theorized unemployment in equilibrium. Had he done so, he might well have persuaded Churchill to avert course. In other words, Keynes still had plenty of thinking to do; and Churchill's "new" gold standard was still woefully under-reformed. Much of both would be addressed in the years to follow.

Yet we must resist the temptation to simplify this first act too much. After all, Keynes himself had strong incentives to play up his failure in the years that followed. In part, he recognized the need to outflank the counterfactual that might have been issued—namely, that Churchill had compromised and that the consequences followed from that. It does seem extraordinary to suggest that anyone could have thought that Churchill did not go far enough—that, say, reissuing gold coinage would have ameliorated the UK's difficulties. But many extreme goldbugs, such as Bank Governor Cokayne, had suggested that it would be best to force the adjustment as rapidly as possible.[25] By flattening the differences between Churchill's new gold standard and the prewar gold standard, Keynes was able to make the orthodoxy—broadly construed—own the disasters that followed the resumption. Keynes knew well that it was better to play the part of Cassandra than of Hector as Troy burned.[26]

We must be similarly careful in handling the orthodoxy's many explicit renunciations of Keynes. After all, the more seriously the church internalized Martin Luther's critique, the more vigorously it denounced him. So too with Churchill and even Bradbury. In fact, Churchill went to lengths to be sure that he was prepared to rebuff Keynes's attacks. And Bradbury incorporated several of Keynes's own critiques as he reimagined the orthodoxy in 1925. By carefully following the evolution of these leading policymakers' positions, we can look past their professions of faith to the underlying shift in their beliefs. Much can be traced to Keynes's great apostasy.

Following the publication of the *Tract*, there could be no serious discussion of the gold standard without mentioning Keynes. He was on the lips of the major bankers giving speeches, he was invoked repeatedly in the Chamberlain-Bradbury Committee's private discussions, and he was deployed by Churchill in his criticisms of those proposals issued by his subordinates. Keynes was rightly regarded as the most serious heretic and the most serious source of heresy. No one, least of all Churchill's intimates and advisers, doubted that this chancellor took Keynes most seriously. Even if he proved unwilling to implement Keynes's boldest proposals, Churchill's thinking about money and unemployment was shaped more heavily by Keynes than by anyone else.

The more shocking—and completely unrecognized—fact is that the gold standard dogma of the governor of the Bank of England was also profoundly shaped by Keynes. Keynes's assault had landed three critical blows on the prewar orthodoxy. First, the international gold standard system was not automatic but turned on the agency of central bankers, particularly those from the most powerful central banks—such as the US Federal Reserve. As a result, the key metric must be changed from the London gold price to the dollar value of the pound. Last, exchange rate movements were not driven exclusively by material conditions but also depended on market psychology. The combination of these factors pointed to what Keynes called "the ideal state of affairs," "an intimate co-operation between the Federal Reserve Board and the Bank of England" to secure "stability of prices and of exchange . . . at the same time."[27]

Norman followed each of Keynes's criticisms of the old gold standard, and he pursued Keynes's "ideal" with unmatched zeal. We have already seen Norman's support for capital controls following the First World War and his evident reluctance to use Bank rate to appreciate the exchange rate. In the summer of 1924, Norman further defied the Cunliffe Committee in his testimony before the Chamberlain-Bradbury Committee. He proposed extending the capital controls by three years. He emphasized the role of market psychology even more heavily than had Keynes. And he parroted Keynes's argument that the Federal Reserve now defined the world gold supply through its monetary policy (rather than vice versa). At all of these points, Norman had more in common with Keynes than he did with Bradbury, Cunliffe, or Cokayne. This was a new, post-*Tract* view of the gold standard.

When the push for a return became overwhelming, Norman embraced the very methods explicitly denigrated by the Cunliffe Committee: the use of central bank coordination and foreign borrowing. At the beginning of 1924, Norman facilitated a highly irregular, unsecured loan to Germany's new central banker, Hjalmar Schacht. This was an overt effort to sidestep the normal diplomatic channels and forge close inter–central bank links that could withstand political and market pressures alike. At the end of 1924, Norman negotiated an extraordinary $500 million loan from the United States, organized by Benjamin Strong at the New York Federal Reserve. He did this even as his colleagues at the Bank and the Treasury repeatedly told him not to pursue the foreign assistance. So far from leading the charge back to the prewar gold standard, Norman continued his Keynes-ian efforts to push the monetary system past it.

Thus, the "Norman conquest of $4.86" was about far more than just Norman. It is a story of the deep conflicts among the ranks of the advocates of the return to gold. It is a story about Norman's reluctance to carry this particular mantle and his absolute refusal to carry it in the way prescribed by his predecessors and entrenched colleagues. It is a story of Keynes razing less than he hoped but building more than he understood. Ultimately, the return to gold is a story about Montagu Norman in just about the same way that the English Reformation is a story about Henry VIII.

## The Conquest

The Norman conquest is usually seen as a foregone conclusion. Here again, Grigg has set the narrative: Churchill's decision constituted "the final step in the continuous process of restoring the pound to parity, which had been going on ever since the First World War ended."[28] Feavearyear similarly suggests, "Nearly all the recommendations of the Cunliffe Committee were adopted over the next ten years."[29] Manchester explains Churchill's decision in the same simple fashion: "In 1918 the step [of returning to gold] had been recommended by a standing committee of experts [i.e., the Cunliffe Committee] appointed by Lloyd George; a majority of Conservatives, Liberals, and Labourites had then endorsed it. Churchill regarded that endorsement as binding."[30]

The policymakers themselves routinely proclaimed their adherence to the Cunliffe Committee dogma. No surprise, Churchill did not hesitate to emphasize the long continuity of the gold standard, and he did so masterfully in his budget speech. But across the aisle, his predecessor and would-be successor Snowden did the same thing on numerous occasions. Indeed, it was the Labour government that convened the Chamberlain-Bradbury Committee. This government happily maintained the continuity of personnel, appointing the three most outspoken surviving members of the Cunliffe Committee to its successor committee. That committee's twelve-page report referenced the Cunliffe Committee six times. Again and again, the members of the Chamberlain-Bradbury Committee "associate[d] [them]selves with the decided preference expressed by the Cunliffe Committee", which is really saying that Bradbury, Pigou, and Farrer associated themselves with themselves.[31]

But did they really? Did the Chamberlain-Bradbury Committee maintain the same preferences across this period? Did it analyze the same questions in the same terms and offer the same prescriptions? Did this represent the fulfillment of the Cunliffe Committee's promises, the realization of its vision?

The answer to all four questions is the same: no. This is partly due to the reality already examined: there was no such thing as a Cunliffe Committee consensus. No currency committee could fasten its recommendations to the Cunliffe Committee dogma any better than it could fix the pound to silver and to gold simultaneously. The Cunliffe Committee's gold standard was not an element but a volatile compound, an unstable jumble of different notions. And as Keynes had argued, the passage of time had invalidated several of the central assumptions underpinning the Cunliffe Committee's reports.

First, the Cunliffe Committee was wrong in thinking that policymakers would lack the discipline required to push sterling back toward its prewar parity, that the very kinds of capital controls imposed would prompt them to adopt lax fiscal and monetary policies. In fact, the Bank and the Treasury proved adept at concentrating gold in London. They increased the UK's official reserves more than four times between 1913 and 1920, from £36.7 million to £145 million. Thus, the combined Bank and Treasury reserves reached the Cunliffe Committee minimum by 1921. It was then kept around £155 million until the gold standard was restored in 1925. At the same time, the Treasury made significant progress in removing the wartime currency notes from circulation. After reaching a peak of £346 million in 1920, the paper notes were reduced 17 percent to £287 million by the start of 1925. The UK's overall gold-to-note ratio rose from its 1920 low of 26 percent to nearly 36 percent in 1925. All this, despite the arrival of the UK's first Labour-led government.[32]

The *First Interim Report* had warned that delaying the adjustment with capital controls and foreign borrowing "can only render the remedial measures which would ultimately be inevitable more painful and protracted."[33] In fact, Keynes and Norman were right: the capital controls bought time, allowing gradual but steady progress. Contrary to the Cunliffe Committee's predictions of doom and gloom, it would seem that *now there was* something in the UK's experiences since the war "to falsify the lessons of previous experience that the adoption of a currency not convertible at will into gold . . . [would] destroy the measure of exchangeable value and cause a general rise in all prices and an adverse movement in the foreign exchanges."[34]

The Cunliffe Committee was also wrong in its assumptions about just what would be required to bring sterling back to the prewar parity and to keep it there. Even with a six-year running start and these incredible achievements, it still would not be enough to restore the prewar gold standard in the UK. The Cunliffe Committee had depicted the gold standard as a kind of silver bullet. Resumption, it believed, would instantly kill the inflationary spiral and, following this, prices and output would adjust quickly and smoothly. In fact, even making Churchill's attenuated gold standard operable proved far more difficult—and far less necessary—than the Cunliffe Committee expected. Thus, the gold standard was both more costly and less valuable than the orthodoxy had maintained.

By the start of 1925, the pound-dollar market exchange rate was approaching its prewar rate, the US and UK price levels appeared to be converging, the UK's reserves were intact, and the wartime note issue was being reduced steadily. All of this occurred before the miraculous resurrection of the prewar gold standard. For those who insisted that the return itself was requisite, such a contented state must have been unnerving. How did they react? The same way any priest of a false religion reacts when his prophecy is preempted by reality: he pretends the disconfirmation does not exist, suggests the promised miracle has already begun working, and then restates the prophecy in "[contemporary] disguise and borrowed language."[35]

This is the story of 1925. It is a story of constructed continuity and contrived binaries. It is not a story of a King William—either William the Conqueror or William of Orange—simply replacing the head that wears the crown. But nor is it a story of simple conquest—of the orthodoxy slaying Keynes, of progressive ideas being crushed by conservatism, or of finance running roughshod over industry. It is a story of a reformation within the theocracy that ruled Britannia.

This is not far from how Keynes himself saw the course of this history at the time. As each took his turn testifying before the Chamberlain-Bradbury Committee in the summer of 1924, he and Addis exchanged a heady correspondence. On July 25, Keynes vented his exasperation at those

> in authority attacking the problems of the changed postwar world with . . . unmodified prewar views and ideas. . . . Do not be the Louis XVI of the monetary revolution. . . . Enormous changes will come in the next twenty years, and they will be . . . unwisely and even disastrously carried out, if those of us who are . . . agreed in . . . aiming at the stability of society cannot agree in putting forward safe and sound reforms. I am now told . . . that I have become a sort of disreputable figure . . . because I do not agree with the maxims of City pundits. But . . . I seek to improve the machinery of society not overturn it.[36]

Keynes was thinking of France when he ought to have stayed with England. The 1925 "monetary revolution" was less 1789 than it was 1688–1689. But it was a revolution nevertheless, and Keynes played the part of Locke rather than of Rousseau. As with the Glorious Revolution, the old sovereign was not annihilated so much as subordinated. The institutions were not abandoned so much as re-formed. Their new design was not itself determinative. The Bank of England and its governors would hold enormous sway, but as Keynes had put it in the *Tract*, gold would rule "only as a constitutional monarch, shorn of his ancient despotic powers and compelled to accept the advice of a Parliament of banks."[37] The next phase would see Keynes lead the charge to further subordinate the independence of gold. But it remains to recount the monetary revolution that did occur in 1925.

# CHAPTER 12

# Central Bankers as Saviors?

What is the role of the central banker? The answer to that question depends on one's view of the monetary system in place.

For those who clung to the version of the gold standard professed in the Cunliffe Committee's reports, the question itself was provocative. The term "central banker" was anathema to their dogma of a monetary order governed by "rules" rather than "discretion."[1] In theory, the gold standard system needs no such actor. If every country, and every bank in every country, and every banker within every bank within every country, simply follows "the rules of the game," the market will ensure performance. After all, the gold standard is a natural, "automatic" system. It rewards and punishes bankers according to their fidelity. The objective is simple: the purpose of the governor of the Bank of England—a *private* institution—is "to use its resources and engage in activities designed to increase [the Bank's] profits."[2] The means are simpler still: all the bankers need do is protect their reserves. They raise and lower interest rates mechanically—without emotion, agency, or subjectivity—as their gold holdings dictate. So if they could have had a machine to do it, the shareholders of the Bank of England might well have capitalized its instantiation. As it was, they had to nominate one decrepit director after another to serve a two-year term tightening and loosening the purse strings as required to keep the reserves static and the dividends flowing.

Despite being descended from two such directors, Montagu Norman rejected this view categorically. More than any of his predecessors, he recognized the pivotal role that a central banker can play in determining the direction of the economy. He had these views from his earliest days at the Bank. But Keynes's analysis of the US Federal Reserve in the *Tract* seems to have opened Norman's mind to the great possibilities of inter–central bank coordination and intervention. Thus, the answer to the question of the role of the central banker changed radically in this period, in large part due to a most unexpected confluence of outlook between Keynes and Norman. Both would have disclaimed it, but we shall see that Keynes and Norman agreed that central bankers could—and should—serve as "saviors."[3]

## Leading Germany in from the Wilderness

The collapse of the Stanley Baldwin's Conservative government at the end of 1923 happened to coincide with the rise of Hjalmar Schacht to the presidency of Germany's Reichsbank. His ascent was no less surprising than was Baldwin's fall. He was relatively unknown beyond Germany. Within Germany, he was rather better known—infamous—for his questionable financial dealings. Schacht brought equal parts acumen and ambition to all of his endeavors. But he had been molded directly by Gustav von Schmoller—the ultranationalist, the adviser to the Kaiser, and the midwife to Imperial Germany's nationalist mercantilism. Following Schmoller, Schacht scoffed at the classical liberals' attempts to distinguish politics and economics. Au contraire: one must be used to serve the other.[4] Embracing this maxim, in thought and in practice, would similarly take Schacht to the heights of wealth and power as the German Empire rose again.

But in 1915, it cost him his job. Since October 1914, Schacht (under Major von Lumm) had administered banking in occupied Belgium. This gave him direct control over the distribution of millions of francs worth of occupation banknotes. When Deutsche Bank "applied for a very considerable delivery of these notes," Schacht was sure to "procure" some for his sometime employer (the Dresdner Bank) "so that they might not be behind" their competitor. Lumm deemed this "an improper action," and Schacht was forced to resign.[5]

In November 1923, Hitler's Beer Hall Putsch inspired Schacht to return to public service. "I realized," he later recounted, "that Germany was in danger of succumbing to *Communism* and felt it was my duty not to shirk a task which . . . lay within my power to fulfill."[6] Schacht was appointed to the post of commissioner for national currency, where he had the unenviable task of subduing Germany's hyperinflation. He was just the man for the job. His gambit was to issue *retenmarks*, a new currency ostensibly backed by mortgages on land. The program was viewed as a remarkable success, but it was not enough. Schacht set his sights on returning Germany to the gold standard as president of the Reichsbank.

The trouble was that he, by his own account, was almost universally distrusted by the banking and business community in Berlin. Rumors swirled that during the Belgian occupation he had swapped legitimate banknotes for counterfeits and embezzled millions.[7] To clear his name, Schacht used his increasingly powerful political connections to have numerous official inquiries conducted.[8] But their nonfindings simply were not believed. When the Reichsbank board considered his application in December 1923, only three of its forty or so members lent him their support. But it did not matter. President Friedrich Ebert overruled them. He wanted Schacht, and he got Schacht.[9]

Montagu Norman also wanted Schacht. Even before he had met Schacht, Norman seems to have thought that this was a man with whom he could work.[10] Schacht's (essentially) first act as Reichsbank president was to reach out to Norman to request a meeting. Norman invited him to come to London "immediately," which he did.[11] Much to Schacht's surprise, Norman himself received him at Liverpool Street Station late on New Year's Eve, 1923. Schacht was even more surprised when Norman invited him to join him at the Bank the very next morning. "I hope we shall be friends," Norman said warmly.[12]

On January 1, 1924, the two men—virtually alone in the Bank of England—hatched a scheme that is almost unbelievable. With the Dawes Committee on reparations being formed, Norman assumed that Schacht would hope to coordinate their approach. This was true, but Schacht wanted to take bolder, swifter action. Hoping to bypass the "many complications" that come with ratifying such international agreements, Schacht asked Norman for a direct loan immediately. Yet this was not a loan to fund the government or to help Germany manage its billions of pounds of reparations obligations. Schacht wanted the money to found another bank, "based entirely on gold," "*in addition to* the Reichsbank."[13]

But by "on gold," Schacht really meant "on sterling." He would start with a capital of £10 million. Half of that, he assured Norman, he could somehow find in Germany. "The remaining half," Schacht declared, "I should like to borrow from the Bank of England."[14] With the Bank's endorsement, Schacht would then raise at least as much from the private London banks. At the time, the Reichsbank and the German government combined had just over £37 million in gold reserves.[15] Schacht was angling to increase these reserves by

50 percent in one fell swoop. From the standpoint of the Bank of England, a £5 million loan would be nearly 4 percent of its own reserves—hardly an inconsequential sum.[16]

Norman was flabbergasted. Surely Schacht did not intend that the Bank of England should take an ownership position in a new German bank? He did not. Instead, Norman would simply extend a loan for three years. Who would direct this bank? Of course, it would report to the Reichsbank—and thus to Schacht. Who would be its borrowers? Here came the rub: "The loans will chiefly be used . . . to finance Rhinish-Westphalian industries."[17]

At the time, a syndicate of French bankers had joined with Rhinish banks and secured the consent of the German government to set up "their own Central Bank in the Rhineland which will issue their own bank-notes independently of the Reichsbank."[18] They had just written to Norman, asking him to make introductions to English bankers who might participate in the venture. This was precisely the kind of cross-border economic integration at the heart of the European Coal and Steel Community several decades later. Here were commercial liberals trying to make the borders matter less in the mid-1920s.

But to Schacht, the inheritor of Schmoller's ultranationalist mercantilist tradition, it was unacceptable. The financial stabilization of the Rhineland by an Anglo-French-German endeavor would further internationalize the region, encouraging its "regrettable separatist tendencies." German peoples should only look to Germany for their support and direction. "The Reichsbank's attitude is entirely clear and unequivocal," Schacht said. "It is definitely opposed to . . . [any] project which seeks to restrict its own supreme power in matters of currency within the German Reich."[19]

Instead, Schacht's new bank, and the alliance with Norman, would push the francs out of Germania. They would be replaced by pounds. Here came the boldest part of Schacht's scheme. The new bank would not just be capitalized with British capital. It would also issue banknotes *in* pounds sterling.[20]

The proposal was virtually unprecedented. The Bank of England would encourage the central bank of a foreign—sometime belligerent—power to issue its own pounds sterling. Since the Cunliffe Committee, the UK's official policy had been to roll back the rights of private note issue in Scotland and (Northern) Ireland. Yet here was Norman granting this right to the Germans. On paper, that foreign bank would be responsible alone for defending its own issue. But if the Bank of England and English banks had collectively sunk £10 million (or more) into this bank, could Norman really refuse to serve as its lender of last resort?

More important, the Bank of England would have little or no capacity to regulate the behavior of this German bank. Norman ought to have shuddered at the prospect that these pound notes might find their way back to the UK in the form of claims on the Bank's gold holdings. Surely Schacht did not intend to found his bank "on gold," as he had said, by taking the Bank of England's own gold? Schacht promised that its loans and its notes would go to promote "those German industries which are able to resume export trade."[21] That alone would be a tough sell in the UK—the Bank of England rationing credit to the Treasury and producers at home while it funded the industrial redevelopment of the UK's greatest foreign competitors.[22] This is precisely the kind of internationalism decried by those producers who testified before the Cunliffe Committee. And that is merely what Schacht—whom Norman had never met prior—said he would do with the money. Could Norman actually control how Schacht spent the pounds he borrowed or the pounds he printed? It is not as though Germany had ever defaulted on its foreign debts or debased a currency.

Yet after sleeping on it for just one night, Norman threw himself into Schacht's scheme. Over the next several days, Norman took Schacht around London, introducing him to leading policymakers and bankers. Among these, Schacht's reception was often lukewarm; but Norman was undeterred.[23] Within mere days, Norman had arranged the deal. The Bank of England would advance £5 million for three years at just 5 percent interest.[24] At the time, interest rates in Germany, "even for financially sound debtors," were around 10 percent.[25] And "no mention was made of guarantee or security," Schacht happily reported. "Norman was satisfied with an ordinary, simple undertaking on the part of the Reichsbank."[26]

But Norman did not stop there. He steered the private London banks away from the Franco-Rhinish scheme and toward Schacht's new bank. He eventually garnered another £15 million for the Reichsbank. And he showed Schacht the reply he had sent to France: "He was unable to give . . . the name of any English bank that would be willing to join the French syndicate."[27] Norman's letter, Schacht said, "meant the death-blow to Rhineland separatism."[28]

As he journeyed back to Germany, Schacht's secretary remarked, "I have never seen you so cheerful." One does not wonder why. He arrived in England amid persistent rumors of double-dealing and hardly secure in the post of Reichsbank president. He left three days later with half as much in sterling as the German government and Reichsbank (combined) had in reserve. He borrowed this at just 1 percent above Bank rate with no security and perhaps the worse credit in the world.

It is harder to understand Norman's enthusiasm for the scheme. Schacht had sold this as a means to cultivate an Anglo-German alliance at the center of a rehabilitated Europe. "Just think, Mr. Governor," Schacht explained, "what prospects such a measure would afford for economic collaboration between Great Britain's world Empire and Germany."[29]

Those scholars who have investigated this have broadly followed this perspective. Norman's biographer views this as a "practical" effort intended "to end the financial chaos of Germany with or without an agreed political plan."[30] For others, Norman was even more ambitious. He saw this as a means "to strengthen the pound by having other European central banks hold some of their reserves in sterling rather than gold." In these views, "Schacht was only a useful instrument, the means to a greater end" that "Norman went out of his way to cultivate."[31]

Yet from an orthodox perspective, it is hard to see the upside for the Bank of England, let alone how this would bring the world closer to the gold standard. If Schacht's scheme failed, it was a costly venture at a time when the UK could hardly afford it. But what if it succeeded, and the Reichsbank's sterling notes passed interchangeably with the Bank of England's sterling notes? This would not have brought Germany any closer to resuming the gold standard there, any more than "dollarization" today helps a country build its own stable currency. Indeed, this scheme could even become a substitute for a gold standard in Germany, instead of a complement or a precursor to it.

It also reduced Britain's capacity to restore its own gold standard. Prior to this, the Bank of England had attempted to cultivate a "sterling exchange system," encouraging foreign countries to keep sterling balances in London rather than taking gold home. But this was obviously a technique to prop up sterling by *dissuading* capital (especially gold) outflows. From an orthodox standpoint, the outflows to fund Schacht's scheme—and the extra "pounds" he disseminated—would both drive *down* the value of sterling. With the clock ticking, and the race to resume convertibility now underway, it beggars belief that the governor of the Bank of England could have cast its capital across the Channel.

In all of its efforts to cultivate central banks abroad in this period, the Bank of England never proposed that these foreign banks issue sterling banknotes.[32] Indeed, Norman's predecessors and the Cunliffe Committee had taken exception to the emission of "pounds" by even the Scottish and Irish banks. They tolerated their wartime expansion as an "emergency measure," but they wanted to confine their production—especially as legal tender—as much as possible.[33] One can only imagine Cunliffe's reaction to the prospect of Norman sending Bank notes to sometime belligerents so that they could multiply the "pounds" as they pleased. Cunliffe, after all, was the very man who led the charge to impose reparations on Germany. Yet here was his successor returning that gold to Germany. Most broadly, the Schacht scheme directly contradicted the marching orders issued by the Cunliffe Committee: reduce the quantity of sterling notes in circulation, concentrate and grow London's gold reserves, and drive the value of the pound back up to its prewar parity.

Previously, we saw Norman's challenges to Cunliffe personally and to Cunliffe's particular gold standard dogma. We saw his support for capital controls and his resistance to Bradbury's efforts to implement the Cunliffe Committee's prescriptions across 1918, 1919, and 1920. Now we start to see the shape of Norman's positive agenda, the outlines of his own gold standard dogma. Soon enough, he would present this vision explicitly to the successor to the Cunliffe Committee: the Chamberlain-Bradbury Currency Committee.

## Another Cunliffe Committee

In late January 1924, Labour, now a plurality, formed a government in coalition with the Liberals. This was the UK's first Labour government. Keynes's *Tract* had started to make waves, and many wondered aloud whether the new government would be willing to continue the deflation necessary to restore the gold standard. Tom Johnston, a radical Labourite, tested the waters in the first few weeks of Ramsay MacDonald's government. In mid-February, he asked his fellow Scotsman and Labourite if he had considered "the ruinous effects upon trade and employment, caused by the policy of currency deflation and the effort to re-establish a free market for gold in London." He did not assault the gold standard as yet, but he called for the government "to set up a Royal Commission of inquiry into our whole monetary system."[34]

MacDonald ruled it out, out of hand. "The reappointment of a Committee on currency and foreign exchanges at the present time would be premature and inexpedient," he replied. Then came the magic words: "The Government are still guided by the conclusions of . . . the Cunliffe Committee." After all, Baldwin's capital controls were not set to expire for the better part of two years. Arthur Samuel, a Conservative, pressed the issue: "As this is a matter of grave importance, will the Prime Minister state whether he agrees with . . . the question?" But MacDonald did not take the bait: "I confine myself to the answer which I have given."[35]

Beyond the House of Commons, that proved insufficient. In the spring, Schuster "bold[ly] . . . state[d] publicly that a return of the pound sterling to its old parity with the US dollar was . . . not impossible before so very long. That would mean the restoration of the pound sterling to . . . the old sovereign, in fact." At the time, sterling was trading at only $4.38 (10 percent below the prewar value).[36] The suggestion that the prewar standard could be restored "before so very long" caused quite the stir. Schuster expounded this view in a widely-circulated address before the Liverpool Chamber of Commerce.[37]

Schuster offered the chamber a bold restatement of the orthodoxy and an explicit response to the gauntlet thrown down by Keynes. "New theories are in the air," Schuster foreboded, "supported by a very brilliant set of advocates." "The Cambridge School," he termed them, ". . . have set forth their proposals in very eloquent and attractive terms." What is more, the critique was not wrong: "The professors point out . . . not without a certain amount of justice . . . the instability of the value of gold owing to its varying supply and demand." But the trouble lay in their prescribed antidote: "They wish to substitute for [gold] a currency . . . [managed] by an undefined . . . body of men in order to stabilize prices." At best, this was merely "an experiment." More likely, this would prove to be the same fallacy committed by monetary cranks and profligate policymakers across the ages. For the orthodoxy, England's greatest rivals offered the most instructive examples: "The effect . . . of issuing mere paper is . . . terribly demonstrated by what has happened in Russia and Germany."[38]

Schuster was not only one of the world's most powerful bankers, but he was formally connected to industry through his position in the Association of Chambers of Commerce. So he appreciated both perspectives better than most. He categorically rejected Keynes's contention that there was a conflict between the interests of finance and those of industry. "[The producers'] cry has been loud: 'Stabilize your exchanges,'" Schuster stated. "And in some quarters," he continued, "there . . . is still a belief that the City of London . . . had it in its power to do so." But this was wrong. The real power, for good and for evil, resides in Westminster. "The remedy has been pointed out so many times," Schuster declared, ". . . balanced budgets, a currency based on something substantial, something that is of value in the international market, the total cessation of paying for the country's debt by the issue of paper money." All of these things required policymakers, not bankers, to take the difficult but virtuous path.[39]

The good news is that it was well within their means to do so. For one thing, Schuster argued, the "cordial and confidential relations which are known to exist between the Bank of England and the Federal Reserve Board could be depended upon to work in such a way as to prevent movements that might be injurious to either country." But Schuster insisted that the UK could return on its own if necessary. "Is our currency so debased as the pessimists would lead us to believe?" he asked. He then listed the figures of the pound notes in circulation and the various reserves. In total, £153 million of gold backed more than £407 million in notes, a rate of 37.5 percent—"not a bad percentage and,

I think, amply sufficient both for any internal and external demands likely to arise." This sum, Schuster noted gleefully, exceeded the minimum reserve figure specified by the Cunliffe Committee. The time to return, he insisted, was nigh. Would the policymakers have the courage to begin taking overt steps on the road?[40]

At this point, MacDonald came to see that this issue would not be dispatched so easily. With encouragement from the Bank of England, he put the issue onto the agenda. By June, he had formed the Committee on the Currency and Bank of England Note Issues. We know well now that simply implementing the regressive deflation and austerity prescribed by the Cunliffe Committee was bound to harm the working class disproportionately. After all, the return to gold in 1925 did lead to the backlash that was the 1926 General Strike. So with the benefit of hindsight and guided by social scientific theory, we would expect the Labour government to have packed this committee with soft-money heretics—or at least to have included some serious, well-respected critics like Keynes.

In fact, Labour's leaders did just the opposite. They chose exclusively from the list provided by the governor of the Bank of England.[41] And so the newest currency committee was really a rump of the Cunliffe Committee—and the most influential members at that: Bradbury, Pigou, and Farrer. To this, it added Otto Niemeyer, a highly orthodox Treasury official and the wunderkind who had beat out Keynes in the civil service examination two decades earlier.[42] MacDonald asked the former Conservative chancellor Austen Chamberlain to chair the committee.[43] Thus, MacDonald must have had every expectation that this new currency committee, which came to be called the Chamberlain-Bradbury Committee, was really just the same old Cunliffe Committee by another name.[44]

This was not an accident. In June, the Liberal MP Ernest Simon pressed the Labour government for weakness. He queried Chancellor Philip Snowden: "In view of the widely held opinion that the policy of a return to a gold standard by further deflation, as laid down by the Cunliffe Committee, is likely to result in an increase of unemployment, the Government will reconsider their policy on this question?" Simon, it seems, had been reading his Keynes. But Snowden's reply was unequivocal: "We are opposed to inflation[,] . . . we are generally guided by the Report of the Cunliffe Committee, and . . . we hope to see a return to the gold standard as soon as possible."[45] As he had assured a Conservative colleague, "The possibility of an early return to the gold standard is constantly under consideration."[46]

Indeed it was. Three days later the new committee interviewed its first witness: Governor Norman, the archbishop of Threadneedle Street.

# Norman's New Orthodoxy

Norman's testimony in June before the Chamberlain-Bradbury Committee offers new insight into his particular gold standard dogma. Famously enigmatic, Norman was loath to explain himself. He did not write books, as did Keynes, Pigou, and Hawtrey. Nor did he write even extensive memoranda, as did Bradbury. Up to this point, I have reconstructed Norman's views and gleaned his motives from correspondence, speeches, Bank meeting minutes (of sometimes contested accuracy), and his extensive (and infamous) diary entries. Within his extant oeuvre, this testimony constitutes Norman's first sustained discussion of the gold standard. It is all the richer because Bradbury and company had the chance to press the governor, on the record, on his unconventional approach. Having already argued with Norman about capital controls following the armistice, Bradbury must have expected that he and Norman would clash again. But the whole committee must have been floored when it became clear that Norman's actual understanding of the gold standard had more in common with the views advanced by Keynes than with anything in the Cunliffe Committee reports.

Norman made a fine start. "I agree entirely with the [Cunliffe] Committee (whose report I am trying to carry out)," he announced. He similarly believed that "the less internal circulation [of gold] . . . the better." And he wanted there to be "an arrangement with the bankers by which they did not hold gold."[47] Of course, this was a repudiation of the version of the gold standard advanced by his predecessor, Cokayne. But the Cunliffe Committee had endorsed this approach, and it was now the reigning dogma. On this point at least, the Cunliffe Committee reports were still the law of the land.

Thanks to Baldwin's capital controls, however, there had been considerable drift on the all-important sequencing of the restorative actions. The mangling was so profound that the committee's chairman himself remained confused. "It comes as a complete surprise to me," Chamberlain confessed, "that your proposal should be that the first step should be to reestablish the free export of gold and your second step the amalgamation of the notes. . . . I think [the Cunliffe Committee] intended to deal with the note issue first and then as soon as that was done—." Norman interrupted him, explaining that the Cunliffe Committee had specified precisely the reverse sequence.[48] Norman was right about this.

But Norman's plan differed from the Cunliffe Committee plan in a different, more significant way. He claimed to "accept the general statement in the Cunliffe Report . . . [that] we should endeavor to hold 150 millions of gold with open exchanges and free markets for a couple of years" before fixing the fiduciary issue. But that is not at all that he proposed. He insisted that the capital controls, which the Cunliffe Committee had unanimously condemned, be formally extended for "so long a period as three years."[49] "[Even] if, as I should anticipate, the parity were to be reached infinitely more quickly," Norman continued, he did not want the controls to be removed prior to that specified date. This period, with the exchanges legally constrained, was required for the authorities to determine "very reasonably, very fairly, what the fiduciary issue should be." The amalgamation would then occur essentially straightaway— "the day, or the week, or the month after" convertibility was legally restored.[50]

Bradbury must have been shocked. Limitations on capital flows, whether from German submarines or parliamentary acts, insulate the exchange rate from market forces. It was only by working to keep the reserve levels at the required minimum in the face of unbridled market forces that the monetary authorities would learn how many total notes the UK could afford to circulate. Bradbury had formulated these ideas in the earliest days of the Cunliffe Committee meetings, he had fought Cunliffe to have them included in the committee's report, and he would fight Norman, if necessary, to see them embraced here and now.

But Norman's dogma held the dollar value of the pound as the key metric. And he brought to the fore an entirely different view of the workings of exchange rates. For him, the exchange rate is not determined by underlying market conditions but by market psychology. The mere announcement of his plan, he promised, would "immediately" cause the exchange rate to "rise rapidly and strongly."[51] "The great thing . . . to put it to parity," he explained, "is to show we have confidence in [sterling]. At present we are leading the whole world to believe that we have no confidence in it."[52] Speculators, in other words, needed to be reassured that convertibility would be resumed at a clear, inviolable date. The date was distant, of course, but this was necessary to reassure "the man in the street" that he would not have to endure the policies required to raise the exchange rate 12 percent in as many months. Initially, Norman stated that he did "not think [this] would be very reasonable toward the community."[53] But then he clarified that he did "not think [this] would have the *appearance* of being very reasonable."[54] It was thus necessary for Norman to think about what speculators would think about what "the man in the street" would think about what Norman would do. That might seem convoluted, but Norman insisted, "It is much more . . . a question of the psychology of the announcement than of the facts."[55]

This surely figured into Norman's resistance to an early amalgamation of the Bank and Treasury note issues. After all, what could appear worse than the venerable Bank of England suddenly taking on hundreds of millions of pounds of additional liabilities? But Norman also did not see them as his responsibility. When Chamberlain asked him about this specifically, Norman exclaimed, "I should be extremely unwilling . . . that the Bank should assume that great liability which at present the Treasury cannot escape. It is a legacy of the war."[56] The Bradburys were Bradbury's problem, Norman believed.

Of course, this was beside the point. The Treasury's currency notes were legal tender. Crucially, the law also guaranteed that "the holder of a currency note shall be entitled to obtain on demand, during office hours at the Bank of England, payment for the note at its face value in gold coin." In law and in practice these Bradbury notes had the same value as the Bank's notes.[57]

Yet, the regime created in 1914 entailed more than just the formal specifications of the Currency and Bank Notes Act. The informal norms, such as the bankers' use of moral suasion, combined with the formal restrictions under the Defence of the Realm Act and then Baldwin's capital controls (of 1920) to dissuade the holders of all pound notes from trading them for gold to be sent abroad. So the Bank was not (yet) regularly compelled to convert the Treasury notes into gold sovereigns. But the regime also meant that the Bank was not regularly obliged to convert its own notes into gold either. Without new legislation, simply granting gold export licenses more freely would present the Bank with the considerable challenge of converting all types of "pound" notes—Treasury notes and Bank notes—at par.[58] So, Norman was playing for time—and insisting that HM Treasury continue to do the hard work of retiring the Bradburys.

Their namesake was none too pleased. "It is however difficult," Bradbury interjected, as he finally came into the discussion. He was piqued, but he was also disquieted by an apparent contradiction in Norman's analysis: "He told us . . . the immediate effect of such an announcement made with the authority of the Government would be an immediate and substantial rise in the dollar exchange. Then a little later he said, in order to restore parity in twelve months it meant a rise of 1% a month."[59] Norman reasserted his emphasis on the role of the "psychological" effect. "I would not be surprised," Norman declared, "to see it go half way [toward par] within a few days." But Bradbury could hardly swallow this. How could merely *announcing* the resumption of gold exports at some distant date cause sterling to appreciate 6 percent in a matter of days? Moreover, Norman was trifling with the whole of the British economy on the basis of his own subjective views about the "sentimental" factors that move speculators. Bradbury was indignant. "As far as Economics are concerned," he said didactically, "the effect of this policy is to produce something which, from an industrial point of view, would be quasi-catastrophic."[60]

Yet Norman still would not budge. "I do not think it would be quasi-catastrophic," he maintained. Again, he asserted, "the present lowness of the Exchange is in part due to the fact that nobody has any confidence in it."[61]

Rather than material variables trumping the ideational, Norman argued that the psychological factors were themselves driving the real economic consequences. This same fixation on the "sentimental" variables prompted further challenges to the policies enshrined in the Cunliffe Committee reports. Norman agreed that the "desire to have free internal use of gold" was "much weaker . . . than many people suppose."[62] Yet Norman feared the expected "psychological effect" of announcing the suspension of convertibility, of formally eliminating the right to cash notes in for gold sovereigns.[63]

Bradbury scarcely knew how to reply. Norman's fixation on the "psychological" dimension was orthogonal to the mechanistic materialism—the "automatic machinery"—that undergirded the Cunliffe Committee's orthodoxy. In that traditional view, international gold movements "automatically" drove changes in the domestic quantity of money that, in turn, drove changes in domestic prices—and vice versa. The only job of the monetary authority was to ensure that "notes . . . always stand at absolute parity with gold coins of equivalent face value, and that both notes and gold coins stand at absolute parity with gold bullion." There was no need—or room—for central bankers to manipulate this process, to anticipate the "sentiments" of speculators or to manipulate their confidence other than by plainly following these simple rules. Indeed, this was the whole point of the gold standard, as the Cunliffe Committee put it: "The creation of banking credit was so controlled that banking could be safely permitted a freedom from State interference which would not have been possible under a less rigid currency system."[64]

Taken aback by Norman's radical departure, Bradbury redeployed this old model. "Many people, like myself, hold old-fashioned views about currency," he began. Such people argue that "it is absolutely essential to get back to a stable gold exchange and also owing to industrial conditions in Great Britain we cannot contemplate a return to anything except the old gold parity." They believe "that the invasion of America by large quantities of gold" will cause, "sooner or later . . . a general rise in gold prices." Given that assumption, "would it not be better to wait for a bit and get our parity when gold comes down to sterling rather than put sterling up to the present artificial rate for gold?"[65]

Bradbury was alluding to the so-called "rules of the gold standard game," in which surplus countries allowed gold inflows to increase their money supplies and thus depreciate the exchange rate. But Norman questioned this premise. Following Keynes's poignant critique, Norman argued that the gold inflows would not necessarily force the rise of American (and global gold) prices, since "the Federal Reserve people . . . can sterilize the gold . . . for a long time to come."[66] They "have complete control of their prices," and it would thus depend upon political rather than economic factors, Norman insisted.[67]

This was a sharp change in Norman's tune. The previous year, he had lobbied Bradbury to support shipping £100 million of the UK's reserves to reduce its American debts. That obviously contradicted the Cunliffe Committee's dictate to amass reserves. But Norman made an ingenious argument: flooding the United States with gold would pressure the Federal Reserve to emit more dollars, thus appreciating the pound-dollar exchange rate.[68] In the meantime, however, Keynes's *Tract* debunked the orthodox premise that the Federal Reserve needed to, or wanted to, adhere to those old "rules of the game."

Here the dogmatic disagreements between Bradbury and Norman come clearly into view. Bradbury was of the old school, holding "old-fashioned views about currency." As he wrote into the Cunliffe Committee reports, the first move must be to reestablish the free gold market. This was a prerequisite to allowing the pound to "automatically" find its price in terms of other currencies. For those currencies whose monetary authorities followed the same "old-fashioned" approach, their exchange rates ought to remain relatively stable. The Cunliffe Committee's *First Interim Report* was clear: "When these conditions [of gold parity at home] are fulfilled, the foreign exchange rates with all countries possessing an effective gold standard are maintained at or within the gold specie points." And thus the system depended on each country taking the appropriate measures at home—what was sometimes called "self-help."

Norman's dogma was thoroughly internationalist. Shaped by the Keynes critique, Norman recognized that the major central banks routinely broke the rules. Because of its disproportionate share of world gold reserves and its position as a perennial surplus country, the United States effectively controlled the world gold supply. So binding the pound to a specific price of gold really meant binding the UK economy to US monetary policy. In these conditions, Bradbury's "gold standard" became, in effect, a "dollar standard," like it or not. For Keynes, this was reason enough to abandon the orthodoxy entirely. Norman, however, did not give up so easily. For him, the name of the new gold standard game was to steer global gold markets through relationships among leading central bankers. He thus looked past the epiphenomenal global gold market to the substructure of elite networks. In contradistinction to Marx, Norman followed Keynes in "descend[ing] from heaven to earth."[69]

At this point, Pigou intervened. Wearied by the Bank governor's hand-waving, the economist demanded precision. He asked, "How much of the gap between the present level in parity was due to psychology and how far to the comparative price level?" Norman rebuffed him: "I am afraid I cannot divide the two."[70] Pigou then asked, "Do you think it would be possible, by any kind of calculation of purchasing power parity, to give an estimate?" Norman again questioned Pigou's premise: "Personally, I would not know where to turn for such a calculation and I am not sure that I would really believe such calculations if they were made because they are very experimental . . . don't you think?"[71] In fact, he could turn to Pigou himself, who had published several articles on the subject.[72] Pigou knew the limitations of such analyses as well as anyone, and yet this was the necessary starting point. Surprised, and likely offended, Pigou asked if it were not "possible, after consideration, to get some sort of idea?"[73] Again, Norman insisted upon focusing on "the moral side" rather than "the material." "The only way I should try and make a shot at it," he said, "would be to ask a certain number of people in whose opinions I have confidence, add them together and divide, and on the whole I should trust the result."[74] Such a "calculation," Norman maintained, would be more reliable than Pigou's nuanced analysis of meticulously compiled price indices.[75]

The barb must have stung. Norman, who had quit his studies at Cambridge after just a year, appeared to contemn its chair of political economy. So Pigou tried to shift to less contentious ground: politics. "From a political point of view," he asked, "if it was understood you would not meet such a tremendous rise in price it would make things much easier?"[76] "You mean fall in price," Norman snapped back, correcting him. "It would make it much easier, but I do not think you can avoid a big fall in price."[77]

There was no getting around it. These men, despite professing belief in the same faith, had irreconcilable differences over questions of market ontology and economic epistemology. At particularly tense moments, the disagreements boiled over into sharp rebukes, just as they had when Cokayne insulted Cunliffe and Bradbury in his 1918 testimony. So these currency committees were no Camelots. But what ecumenical council is?

## Confession

Norman's perspective and, particularly, his proposals were unusual to say the least. They directly contradicted the Cunliffe Committee doctrine. More broadly, they did not seem designed to speed the UK back onto the gold standard at the prewar parity. Indeed, Norman himself would renounce most of these proposals—although not his dogma—within just a few months. But in the summer of 1924, Norman was determined that the UK should delay its return. As ever, Norman's approach defies easy explanation. But some hints emerge from his unusual—and unusually strong—relationship with Hjalmar Schacht.

Throughout Norman's testimony, the committee thought in terms of macroeconomic conditions that shape long-term patterns of investment. But while the committee was thinking principally about *investors*, Norman was thinking about *speculators*. He stressed, "Not only . . . private individuals [in the UK] . . . send their money abroad to invest it in the United States," but "the Far East spurns sterling now and flies to dollars."[78] Norman also "[knew] of many people in Europe, banking people, countries, who avoid London and send their money to America."[79]

How could Norman be so certain about their thinking? Because he had financially backed them. At one particularly tense moment in his testimony, Norman blurted out, "I myself am lending at this moment several millions of pounds which have been used by the borrowers to obtain dollars, and I say that is very bad for sterling."[80]

The confession is astonishing. Here was the governor of the Bank of England admitting that he had a stake in the direction of the dollar-sterling exchange rate at the same time that he was dictating the approach the British monetary authorities would take. This was not a misunderstanding or a mistranscription. Indeed, this was the *revised* version of Norman's words, after he had carefully edited the transcript. In the original, Norman was recorded as saying that the "several millions of pounds . . . have been used *to secure that country in* dollars."[81]

In the case of Montagu Norman, the country that was "that country" at this point was generally Germany. He was almost certainly referring to the extraordinary £5 million that he had advanced to Schacht a few months prior.[82] Schacht had promised to use the money to found a bank that deepened Anglo-German economic ties, including by issuing sterling notes. His Golddiskontbank was established in March, and he "did print Golddiskontbank notes payable in pounds sterling." But as Schacht later recounted, the notes "were never put into circulation because in the interval the Reichsmark had achieved, and thereafter maintained, its gold parity."[83]

Yet Norman's testimony suggests that there may have been more to this story. If Schacht had spent the pounds to purchase US dollars, it was a bear position against sterling. The generous interpretation is that Schacht had simply concluded that dollars would be more useful to German manufacturers than would be pounds. After having bested Norman in the race back onto gold, the power to emit pounds was far less valuable in the summer of 1924 than it had promised to be just six months prior. In this case, it would merely be a costly transaction for the UK. In his testimony, Norman had complained, "We are contributing to put the whole of Europe on a better plan than ourselves."[84] He warned specifically, "In a few years' time the German Mark will be a far more popular currency than the British pound."[85]

It is also possible that Schacht's maneuver was really an outright speculative attack. Just as Britain's first Labour government came to power, he borrowed £5 million in sterling—not enough to make a difference for Germany but more than enough for a speculator to make a killing. Then, if Norman's testimony were indeed referring to this, Schacht spent those millions of pounds to buy US dollars—adding to the downward pressure on sterling. With an interest rate of just 5 percent and a three-year term (but with no repayment penalty), Schacht was thus perfectly positioned to short the pound. If Norman's proposed announcement of new delays on the return to gold then sent sterling sliding—as orthodox theory would suggest and as Bradbury *did* suggest—Schacht could then use his dollars to buy far more pounds than he had borrowed, keeping the difference as a tidy profit. This was a simple, familiar scheme in which a speculator could use public connections for private gain. It was precisely the kind of malfeasance with which Schacht was charged throughout his career. Certainly, Schacht's many detractors in Berlin had warned that one should expect nothing less from him.

Such was the stuff of international finance in these troubled times. In this period, $150 million of National Defence Bonds were stolen—and never recovered—from the French treasury.[86] More than likely this was an inside job, and the French had nobody to blame but themselves. But they could blame—and they did blame—German-led speculators for the misfortunes of the franc. Throughout the spring of 1924, the French exchanges were in almost constant convulsions, with the franc often shifting more than 10 percent against the dollar in a single day.[87] Much of this followed from the psychological factors Norman had emphasized, as even rumors related to international reparations negotiations could send markets into a frenzy. But the French prime minister, Raymond Poincaré, brought the matter before the National Assembly. He claimed to have documents that proved a "plan for an offensive against the franc."[88] The cabal, he claimed, was headed by German foreign minister Gustav Stresemann—Schacht's old friend and the very man who had convened Schacht's previous exculpatory inquest.[89] Schacht himself ensured that Germany never fell victim to such attacks. When the mark began to slide in April 1924, he preempted the speculators with immediate, unilateral capital controls—just the sort of controls that Norman had defended so vigorously.[90]

Poincaré's claim was convenient, but it was also plausible. With the French marching through the Ruhr, would not the German nationalists "[carry] on the collective struggle for existence with the harshest national egoism, with all the weapons of finance," just as Schacht's mentor Schmoller had instructed them to do?[91] Even after his numerous acquittals by friendly and unfriendly governments alike, even after the "persecution" that attended his denazification, even after (finally) denouncing Hitler, Schacht still refused to apologize for his many efforts to propel Germany past its rivals in the 1920s.[92]

What was Norman's part in all of this? There is no evidence to suggest that Norman personally profited from this or any other such scheme.[93] At first blush, it may seem that Norman was taken in and duped by Schacht. After all, Norman had known the novice central banker for merely a few hours before making the massive loan. In that case, Norman had strong incentives to see the scheme through, lest his own judgment be called into question.[94] To play on Keynes's "old saying," if Schacht had borrowed £5000, he would have been at Norman's mercy; but as Schacht owed the Bank £5 million, Norman was at his—all the more so for a loan that was highly unconventional and entirely unsecured.[95]

But such an interpretation is defied by the fact that the mutual trust—and affection—between Schacht and Norman only increased in the decades that followed. If Norman felt betrayed or used by Schacht, he never showed it. Indeed, the two made common cause in their approach to the Dawes Committee that same summer, even as the stress led to another nervous collapse for Norman.[96] Whatever else it may reveal about Norman, his relationship with Schacht epitomizes the new approach to the international monetary system that these men were pioneering.

As we have seen, Bradbury's "old-fashioned" orthodoxy believed in a world in which monetary authorities reacted to market forces, helping along the largely automatic, natural mechanisms of macroeconomic adjustment. This meant that the specific individuals in authority hardly mattered because they were closely following simple, hard, and fast rules governed by "the market." Last, this orthodoxy conceptualized the international gold standard system as the mere assemblage of national economies operating according to that same set of standard rules. This meant that each country could, and should, implement its commitment to that common standard without regard for the commitments and actions of others.

Schacht and Norman divined a different world. In this world, politics trumped economics; and so the central banker should—must—play politics. In this world, market psychology was irrational, turning less on material facts and logical analysis of cause-effect relationships than on sentiment; and so the central banker should—must—manipulate those market emotions. In this world, every monetary system, on gold or not, was inevitably linked through the global economy; and so every central banker should—must—set that country's policies in conjunction with those existing abroad. This new world, Schacht and Norman believed, should—must—be proactively managed by a small group of elite central bankers from the world's core financial centers.

To be sure, the differences *in practice* were less stark than they were rendered by the apostles of the different creeds. Cunliffe himself was more political, innovative, and internationally oriented than was the idealized monetary authority imagined by the Cunliffe Committee. And Norman was far more diffident, atavistic, and insular than was the idealized central banker he portrayed to the Chamberlain-Bradbury Committee. But Norman's approach redefined his role onto a different scale, even if it was not into a different type. The orthodoxy had some catching up to do.

## Confronting Heresy

If Norman were the first central banker of the modern age, Felix Schuster was the last major banker of the old age. His remarks that spring had galvanized the Labour government to recall the currency committee. With Schuster having appeared twice before the Cunliffe Committee, it was perhaps to be expected that he was among the first witnesses invited by the Chamberlain-Bradbury Committee.

As if to quote chapter and verse, Schuster began his remarks to the Chamberlain-Bradbury Committee by reading from the Cunliffe Committee reports. He "advocate[d] action at once." He warned that delay actually helped the "Americans . . . [get] the advantage over us." More important, the passage of time was likely to make the restoration *more* difficult. "The danger of making a premature announcement would be very great," he admitted, "[but] it may be possible to do it now. In twelve months' time . . . it may not."[97]

Some of the trouble, Schuster explained, came from the threat posed by Keynes. "I confess—we are talking very privately," he told the committee. "I am very much afraid of the inflationary theories . . . for which there is great propaganda made in various quarters—Mr. Keynes' theories in one direction, and people like Mr. Kitson and others writing in the socialist press." While Schuster's faith did not falter, he admitted that "those publications have more influence . . . than we generally give them credit for."[98]

To "counteract them," Schuster proposed "to legalize the whole position as to this currency issue." Sadly, removing the capital controls too quickly posed the "great danger of your losing gold immediately." But it was still possible to take bold steps back toward gold. Instead, he proposed that the Treasury notes be transferred straight away to the Bank of England with an eye to formally fixing the fiduciary limit. This was actually the reverse of the sequence that the Cunliffe Committee had proposed, which would have allowed the reserves to be built up before beating down the inflation. But, Schuster argued, "there is more paper than we need."[99]

It is not surprising that a banker would support deflation. But, quoting the Cunliffe Committee, Schuster insisted that this was absolutely vital to the national interest. Channeling the Keynes critique, Chamberlain addressed this point directly: "[There] are certain . . . perhaps inevitable consequences of an attempt to get back to the gold standard which many representatives of our industry fear very much. . . . They are a little inclined to argue that the return to the gold standard may be in the interests of the City of London . . . but cannot be in the interests of trade."

Schuster was strident: "There cannot be a difference of interests between the City of London and the trade of the country. The two go absolutely together." "I speak now," he added, "as representing the Chambers of Commerce who have discussed this matter first in their Executive Committee and then at a full meeting of their Congress; when all Chambers were represented and there was an unanimous vote in favor of the present proposal." Producers, he emphasized to the committee, "are in a state of uncertainty." But "with a stabilized exchange, that speculative element of uncertainty will be removed; they feel that the cost of raw material will be considerably decreased; that will help to increase our manufactures and thereby our exports."[100]

This fit perfectly with the committee's priors, with their own beliefs. It also fit with all of the guidance the Cunliffe Committee had received. But Chamberlain knew how important it was to be "quite clear about the opinion of the Chambers of Commerce." He wanted to be sure that they recognized "that another step on the same road must be dearer money." He addressed Schuster: "If you had said to them, 'You see, before we reach this end, it will be necessary to have dearer money!' would they have said, 'In that case we do not want to set out at all'?"[101]

Schuster was unequivocal: "No," then added that "they are . . . quite prepared for a maintenance of steady money rates." Besides, he insisted, "traders lose much more by variations in the Exchange than by having to pay a little more for their banking." In his opinion, "far too much is made of that fear of dear money. Whether a trader or manufacturer has to pay 4% or 5% for his advances does not affect his ultimate profits so much, when he has got the certainty of a market and knows exactly on what he has based his calculations of profit, but when the question of Exchange comes in then he is absolutely at sea and does not know."[102]

This was a reasonable, and informed, perspective. After all, even if money rates were dear, producers and traders knew this at the time they borrowed, and they could price this into their calculations. But a swing in the exchange rate of 5 or 10 percent in either direction, in as many months, could overwhelm the predicted profit margin.[103] With the currency hedging market relatively nascent, exchange rate risk was a serious challenge. On this, Keynes and Schuster agreed. "Trade with foreign countries without securing your exchange," Schuster had said in his April address, "has of late years really become one of the wildest and blindest of all gambles, but what is to be done?"[104] Schuster was happy to lead the charge as the UK's producers battled to evade it.

Yet Chamberlain was at pains to get this testament on the record in the clearest of terms. So he asked Schuster yet again to confirm that this view "[was] approved by the General body of Chambers [of Commerce], the most representative body." Schuster was, again, emphatic: "After the Executive meeting, I was asked to propose the resolution agreed to on their behalf to the full meeting, not of the Executive Committee, but of all the Chambers, and there again there was no question raised; there was no opposition; they accepted the resolution unanimously, and it was agreed to send a copy of it to the Prime Minister and Chancellor of the Exchequer."[105]

Schuster knew that this point was crucial. He knew that restoring gold would not be easy, and he knew that politically the committee needed to be sure that business was on board, despite the looming deflation. So he never flagged in his testimony as the committee worked for absolute clarity. This point was so important to him that, after the examination, he followed up with colleagues at the chambers of commerce, put the questions to them, and sent a follow-up (two-page) restatement of their position, with the chambers' president's explicit blessing. Given the importance of knowing the mind of industry at the time, their memorandum to the policymakers deserves quoting at length:

> With regard to the Chairman's question whether the Chambers of Commerce . . . had considered the possibility of a rise in the value of money, i[f] steps towards the restoration of the Gold Standard are taken, I may say that I am a member of the Executive Committee and of the Finance Committee of the Associated Chambers, and therefore in full cognizance of their views . . .
>
> I was asked by the Liverpool Chamber to address them on the question of the Exchanges. . . . Somewhat to my surprise the matter was taken up immediately by a number of Chambers, and the Executive decided of their own initiative and without my moving in the matter that

the question should be brought before the General Meeting of the Association of British Chambers of Commerce held on the 1st May, 1924. At a full meeting of the Executive Committee this was discussed and the Resolution to be submitted decided on, and I was asked to move it. . . . The Resolution was carried unanimously after discussion. From letters I have received and private conversations I feel that the whole Meeting was in full sympathy and well informed as to what the proposal implied.[106]

What more could Schuster have done? His flock was unanimous and unambiguous. If any still wondered whether the gold standard set the industry against the City, soon enough the Federation of British Industries would appear and dispel that myth.

Bradbury was as eager to see Schuster denounce Keynes as Chamberlain was to see Schuster affirm industry's support for the gold standard. He paraphrased both Keynes's critique and his proposal. "We are told," he began, "that . . . a very large part of the gold in the world is now hoarded in the hands of the Americans, according to the present monetary policy of the United States, in a more or less arbitrary fashion." This, the argument ran, "makes it necessary to break away from the gold standard." "Perhaps a country like Great Britain," he continued, "might . . . for the time being fix its currency policy on the basis of maintaining stability of prices . . . and having established . . . a sterling standard . . . wait for the gold using countries to come to this standard." Saying it out loud, Bradbury could not help but admit, "That, of course, is a very ingenious kind of policy." But, he asked, "you think that is a policy which is of very little use and you would be wholly in favor of returning to gold, whatever may be [its] present imperfections?"[107]

Schuster tried evading the question, suggesting that neither he, the other bankers, nor the world had "the intellectual capacity of understanding the working of the [proposed] schemes . . . and how they can be called into practice." But Bradbury persisted: "I do not think Sir Felix does justice either to himself or to his brother bankers. I have no doubt they very thoroughly understand the suggestion." "The point," he explained, "is that the world being what it is, suggestions of this kind do not appear . . . to afford a basis for the—." "No," Schuster interjected. He did not want, or need, the heresy explained to him. Such fantastical flights could always be grounded with a recitation of the orthodox axiom, which he then invoked: "The world at large wants to see currency that is based on something which is of exchangeable value all over the world, and so far we have only gold."[108]

With his wings clipped, Bradbury brought the discussion back to the Cunliffe Committee recommendations. Consideration over the finer points of implementation continued for some time. With the transcription reaching thirty-three pages, Schuster's testimony was one of the longest and most detailed. It was reminiscent of the long, deep discussions in the Cunliffe Committee several years earlier, including Schuster's several appearances before that committee. Across these years, these disciples of gold continued to disagree about crucial specifics, even as they shared a devotion to the desired outcome: restoring the gold standard as swiftly as possible.

Perhaps the most important consequence of the discussion was that it seems to have sparked Keynes's invitation to give evidence. Schuster still lumped Keynes together with Kitson and the other cranks. But he feared the power of these ideas, and he pressed the committee to confront them directly. Bradbury knew that there was more to it than that, and he evidently wanted to have a fuller discussion of these radical, but "ingenious," ideas. Pigou, too, knew better than to ignore the power of Keynes's intellect—and his pen. While he was absent this day, his subsequent work on the committee suggests that he also had been pondering Keynes's critique. So the committee invited Keynes to testify. It marked Keynes's first serious chance since his apostasy to make his case in person. No doubt, Keynes relished the opportunity.

## The Inquest of JM Keynes

In contrast to Norman, Keynes's mind was quite well known by the Chamberlain-Bradbury Committee even before he appeared before them. He had known Pigou since his undergraduate days at Cambridge.[109] He worked at the Treasury (largely under Bradbury) for years during and after the First World War. During that time, he was a stalwart exponent of the old orthodoxy. Indeed, in the first part of 1920, Keynes vigorously pressed Chamberlain (who was then chancellor) to implement the orthodoxy's recommended austerity, raising interest rates as high as 10 percent if necessary.[110]

Much had changed in the ten years since Keynes had rushed down to London to help Bradbury save the gold standard at the war's outbreak. He was now the most serious critic of that system and of the Cunliffe Committee's particular vision of it. His editorials and now his *Tract on Monetary Reform* were attracting ever more attention from the figures at the highest level. So the Chamberlain-Bradbury Committee knew well what Keynes would say. Keynes, however, was wholly unprepared for the committee's response.

Keynes was invited on July 4, 1924, precisely one year after Baldwin's "non-flationist" speech in Parliament. The invitation quoted the committee's terms of reference on "whether the time has now come to amalgamate the Treasury Note Issue with the Bank of England Note Issue."[111] If those terms were ambiguous, the inclusion of the Cunliffe Committee's *First Interim Report* was a strong clue that this new committee intended to implement the very orthodoxy that Keynes had renounced.[112] The next week, however, Keynes visited the committee with entirely the wrong mindset.

Keynes's biggest cognitive block was precisely that which had led him astray the previous summer: he still believed that he had won. After opening remarks, Bradbury pushed against Keynes: "You are really directing your observations to the position which exists so long as the exchange is below parity?" The mention of "parity" caught Keynes unaware. Had not Baldwin abandoned the fixation on "parities" and moved to Keynes's suggested method of targeting price levels instead? Keynes responded, "The existing rule is a relic of the time when it was the policy of the Government to carry out a progressive deflation. . . . That policy, after falling gradually into desuetude, was expressly abandoned by the Government of the day just over a year ago when Mr. Baldwin made his famous non-flationist speech. Unless . . . that policy is reversed, it would be foolish to maintain a rule the object of which is . . . contrary to . . . the policy of the Government."

At the time, Keynes was perhaps the only person who thought that "Baldwin [had] made [a] famous non-flationist speech." As we saw, it was not a speech as much as an evasion. It was not Baldwin but Young who deployed this new standard. And it was hardly "famous."[113] Nevertheless, Keynes launched into his "ideal system," which was really a summary of the *Tract*.[114]

At this point, a perplexed Bradbury asked Keynes to clarify his reference to "the transitional period." "Transitional to what?" Bradbury asked. "Until there has been some final declaration as to . . . our ultimate currency policy," Keynes replied. Evidently, he had missed the Labour prime minister's unambiguous declaration a few months prior that "the Government are still guided by the conclusions of the . . . Cunliffe Committee."[115] Instead, Keynes returned to his starting point: "We are left with a criterion which was explicitly adopted by Mr. Baldwin, on behalf of the Government of the day, a year ago, of maintaining the price level steady." That assumption, which had proved so intellectually useful to Keynes, was now becoming a practical limitation. He had placed far too much stock in Baldwin's refusal to meet Young's challenge, and he was now perilously behind the times politically.[116]

Keynes's homily continued, with only a few brief interruptions, until Chamberlain confronted him with the key question of the day: What will happen when the government resumes the gold standard? As Baldwin's capital controls were really the last vestige of the wartime controls, the question was really this: "What would be the effect of lifting the embargo on the movement of gold . . . restoring the free market in gold for export[?]" Keynes was taken aback. To his mind, the answer was obvious but the question irrelevant. He replied, "A considerable amount of gold would flow, and the exchange would be immediately restored to parity." Chamberlain questioned whether there really were the threat of "a great drain of gold," but Keynes was insistent: "Certainly after a time all the gold would have left the Bank of England and there would still be unsatisfied demands. If you were to offer more gold for sterling and make no other change, the demands for gold at this reduced price for export to America would be bound in the end to swamp you. Therefore that policy would have to be combined with a drastic credit restriction." The further consequences of this would be devastating. "All our exports would cost 12% more in the world market . . . [and] our export trade would be absolutely cut from under our feet," Keynes explained.[117]

It was a troubling prophecy. But it was a possibility that the authorities had considered and ruled out repeatedly. For them, the beneficial effects of exchange rate stability far outweighed the costs of deflation. Their position turned out to be wrong, but it was not unreasonable. Nevertheless, Keynes could hardly believe that the committee was still planning to restore the free movement of gold. And the committee could hardly believe that Keynes could not believe it.

Chamberlain pressed the "practical" question: "The embargo expires on the 31st December 1925. What would you do under those circumstances?" Keynes was taken aback: "This leads into rather big questions." "We are unable to keep them out," Chamberlain exclaimed. Keynes then made explicit the assumption that had guided his thinking for more than a year: "I hold very strongly that the Treasury or the Bank of England . . . [must] in perpetuity keep a hold over both the import and export of gold. I should favor a permanent system of allowing both export and import of gold only by license of the Treasury or the Bank of England. That would mean that the rates at which gold was flowing in or out, and the level of prices and so forth, would be under their control." Denying "the advantages of the supposed free gold market," Keynes insisted, "I see no reason whatever why the existing method of controlling gold imports and exports should not be made a permanent policy."[118]

If the committee members were shocked, they should not have been so. This is just the position that Norman appears to have pressed upon Bradbury across 1919 and 1920: that it was "essential to maintain [the] prohib[itio]n ag[ain]st Export of Cap[ita]l."[119] And it was of a piece with the position that Norman had just vigorously defended a fortnight prior: returning to "the gold standard" required extending Baldwin's capital controls.

Reminded, perhaps, of the governor's analysis, Chamberlain invoked the "psychological" factor that Norman had stressed. Chamberlain worried "that a great many people . . . would treat that as rather a serious declaration . . . [and] as a confession on the part of the British Government of economic weakness." Of course, Keynes did not deny the meaning of such an announcement: "It would be a confession that it was not absolutely certain that we could return to the gold standard by the 1st January 1926." But, Keynes assured the committee, such an announcement was hardly meaningful: "The opinion that we shall return to a gold standard on the 1st January 192[6] is hardly held by anyone."[120]

"Hardly held by anyone"—except for all of the members of this committee, the Labour chancellor and prime minister, the leaders of the Conservative opposition, the City bankers, the speculators, the unions, the workers, the general public, and the foreign exchange market. Empirically, Keynes could not have been more wrong. But theoretically, he could not have been more insightful. The issue is that all of these different actors defined "the gold standard" in radically different, mutually incompatible ways. But the dissensus within the orthodoxy did little to prompt any renunciation of the church or its trappings. Keynes's failing was that he assumed these actors—starting with Baldwin's non-flationist speech—had come to grips with the reality that the gold standard, however imagined, was a false idol.

And so the committee then asked Keynes specifically about that most important icon in this church of England's: the gold sovereign. Chamberlain confirmed that Keynes thought "that we ought not to attempt to restore the old parity of the sovereign." "That is not an essential part of my views," came the reply. "My own belief," Keynes explained, "is that the policy I advocate—price stability—would almost certainly lead to a restoration of the parity of the sovereign, because I . . . believe that American prices will . . . rise in time. . . . I am against hurrying the day." But what about when the two did not go together, Chamberlain and Niemeyer asked. Keynes was clear on the priority. He would grant the monetary authorities the freedom to adjust the official gold price as necessary. "We should then be our own masters," he announced.[121]

Thus, Keynes answered as many iconoclasts had done. He was not insisting upon an end to icons as such. But the casting of that idol, the gold sovereign, must be defined by the true objective, overall price stability, rather than the other way around. In this way, Keynes professed, his reformation would serve the religion's true mission.

It did not take Bradbury long to come to the enormous practical implication of Keynes's radical vision: it gave the monetary authorities unprecedented decision-making autonomy. Just as he had done with Norman, Bradbury challenged this abandonment of the traditional, mechanistic model of central banking. "Mr. Keynes," Keynes's old Treasury superior began, "do you . . . attach any importance at all to the fluctuation in the amount of the reserve in the Banking Department of the Bank of England?" After all, he continued, "the traditional prewar policy of the Bank of England was to determine the credit policy of the Bank with regard to the movements in the reserve in the Banking Department."[122] This idea was the starting point for Bradbury's original proposal to the Cunliffe Committee, and despite Cunliffe's own resistance, Bradbury had made it the governing principle of the Cunliffe Committee's reports. In this traditionalist view, the Bank's reserves alone dictated the money supply of the whole country.[123]

Keynes categorically rejected this principle. "[Even] if gold flowed in or out, while I should attach some importance to the state of the reserve as one of the indications, I should not make it the sole criterion as under prewar conditions," Keynes replied. He went further. In setting monetary policy, the Bank's reserve figures were "useless."[124]

Bradbury might have been appalled by Keynes's summary dismissal of the Cunliffe Committee dogma, but he nevertheless extended an olive branch. Surely Keynes would recognize the value of this symbol in the political realm? "The Bank of England, like other institutions," Bradbury noted, "is susceptible to public opinion." "If a variation of the Bank rate has to be justified to the public," he continued, ". . . the only justification before the War was that the increase had to be effected to protect the reserve of the Banking Department." But again, Keynes stubbornly denied him. This metric was "of very little importance. . . . If the Bank waits to put up its Bank rate, until it can have this justification for the public it will always put it up too late."[125]

How then did Keynes think the Bank ought to set its monetary policy? What did he see as the barometer that the Bank ought to use? Chamberlain himself asked these questions. Instead of one metric, Keynes replied with a bewildering list:

> I should pay great attention to the ease with which the Treasury was able to get its dollars over the exchange. I should watch the level of prices in America. I should watch changes in the form of the assets of the "Big Five" [clearing banks] as between advances, investments and discounts. I should watch the open market rate of discount. I should watch the new issues market, particularly the foreign new issues. . . . I should take into account the relative money rates here and in America, but I should take into account not less the money rates in Germany and France.[126]

He carried on discussing relative price levels, political arrangements (such as the Dawes Plan), and subjective assessments of market confidence. One thing was conspicuously absent: the price of gold. So Bradbury asked him about this specifically. Keynes assured him that he would include this, too, among the many other factors. Bradbury cut to the chase: "You think that the unit of value in this country should be maintained by credit control, plus the taking into account of various economic causes and tendencies, of which no doubt gold value should be one, but possibly not the most important?" Keynes agreed: "That is correct."[127]

For the committee, the implication was clear: Keynes was determined to displace the old laws of Bradbury's mechanistic gold standard with autonomous monetary authorities endowed with discretionary authority. "Would you think that the duty of credit control could properly be left entirely to the Bank of England," "formally a private institution," "in consultation . . . with the Treasury and other people?" Bradbury asked. Keynes answered in the affirmative and added, "I do not regard [the Bank] as a private institution. I regard it as one of our Heaven-sent institutions by which through anomalistic methods we get the advantages both of a private and of a public institution." Just like that, Keynes reconceptualized the historical arc of the covenant of the Bank of England.[128]

When he helped to establish England's permanently fixed exchange rate, Locke's principal argument was that the sovereign had a legal obligation to preserve the metallic value of the currency. The sanctity of contract, the basis of all political authority, required no less.[129] Keynes's suggestion that the monetary authority pursue overall price stability rather than the pound's metallic value thus rejected several centuries of orthodoxy.[130]

Bradbury led the defense of the ancient principle. Was it "entirely consistent with the contract between the bondholder and public creditors of this country generally . . . that emergency currency should be made for the purpose of giving advantages to one party to the contract—the Government—as against the other party?" Keynes was none too worried: "I should regard it as perfectly proper, provided that the Treasury were offering a fair bargain." But the Conservatives' sometime chancellor was plenty worried. "It would be a tremendous power to put in the hands of the Chancellor of the Exchequer or the Government for the time being," Chamberlain exclaimed. It did not help that, at that time, Labour was in power for the first time. "Do you think you can trust the Chancellor of the Exchequer not to fill his Budget deficit or for the purpose of his favorite scheme to use this [opportunity] if he has it?" he asked. "I do not think there are any means of strapping down a really wicked Chancellor of the Exchequer," Keynes responded. Instead, "I should try to throw him out of office." It was a brilliant maneuver: invoking Locke's right of revolution to supplant his monetary rigidity.[131]

There was more than just the questions of contractual rights and obligations. Farrer opened a second front, what Smith (and later Hayek) characterized as a knowledge-problem.[132] Even if we could trust the authorities to use their discretion for the public good, how could any monetary authority possibly deduce the optimum policy from all of the factors that Keynes listed? "Do you think . . . that we have had a breed of people who are capable of taking all those considerations and acting upon them, or do you think we shall have to breed a superman to do it?" Farrer queried. "I do not foresee any particular difficulty with it," Keynes replied, even as he went on to admit that manufacturers, merchants, exporters, "City men" (bankers), and "the great mass of people all through the country" would all struggle to understand the new mechanisms.[133]

The contrast was as stark as that between the Old and the New Testaments. For Bradbury, the principal advantage of the gold standard was that it tied the hands of policymakers by establishing a mechanical relationship between the quantity of gold and the quantity of money. He and the Cunliffe Committee recognized that there must be exceptions to the rules of the game. Indeed, they explicitly acknowledged this in the *First Interim Report*. So too did orthodox theory allow for "suspending" the rules in extenuating circumstances, such as during a financial crisis or the outbreak of war. But such circumstances must be extenuating indeed. For Bradbury, even the outbreak of the Great War and the concomitant financial crisis did not warrant a suspension of the gold standard.[134] Keynes knew this better than anyone. After all, it was the memorandum he drafted, at Bradbury's request, that had changed Lloyd George's mind and saved convertibility then.

But now, ten years later, Keynes was determined to destroy that orthodoxy. He argued that monetary authorities could be judged—and disciplined—by ex post political processes rather than ex ante laws. He had faith in the "Heaven-sent" Bank of England. He believed that the monetary authorities could have the wisdom, and grace, to shepherd their flocks.

For the committee, Keynes's new "system" was utopian. "You are anticipating Paradise in your suggestion," Farrer insisted. As ever, Keynes was indignant: "If the Directors of the Bank of England are as stupid as some people think they are, our currency will break down in any case." It was a snappy retort. But Farrer was not wrong. What "superman" could steer a monetary order unmoored from the "automatic machinery" celebrated by the Cunliffe Committee?[135]

If there were anyone, it was Montagu Norman. Certainly, this is what Norman himself believed. In time, he would establish a new orthodoxy around Keynes's apostasy, one that acknowledged the influence of market psychology and conceded the need for central bankers to collaborate to steer the international system. But first, Norman would have to subdue the counter-reformation being orchestrated by the Chamberlain-Bradbury Committee. Ultimately, it proved easier than he might have expected.

# CHAPTER 13

# Indulgence

None of the witnesses to follow Norman and Keynes at the Chamberlain-Bradbury Committee were remotely challenging by comparison. The several other bankers interviewed gave predictable responses. Walter Leaf had testified before the Cunliffe Committee; and, of course, Harry Goschen had been on the committee itself and contributed meaningfully to drafting its reports. They were, as Leaf put it, "eager for an early restoration of the gold standard."[1] "You do not favor any of these suggestions made in various quarters for establishing some sort of purchasing power parity?" Bradbury asked the Clearing House Committee's representative. The witness was crystal clear: "No. I think every Banker in London is in favor of going back to the gold standard."[2]

The committee also interviewed Robert Horne, the Conservative Scottish MP. As chancellor of the exchequer, he had implemented austerity with remarkable gusto. So the committee could not have been too surprised when he exclaimed, "Nobody realizes better than I do the great advantages that there are in the appreciation in the value of our pound sterling."[3]

Sir George Paish was a Liberal financial writer and sometime Treasury adviser. His views were reminiscent of those of Cunliffe himself. "The depreciation in the pound," he argued "has resulted only in a small degree from an excessive issue of currency notes."[4] Instead, it arose "from the inability of

Great Britain to collect the sums due to her." But, like Cunliffe, Paish agreed "that the really important thing is to get back the free market in gold as soon as possible."[5]

This was tame compared to Edwin Cannan, the renowned economist. When he referred to "an eventual return to the gold standard at the old rate," Farrer asked if he did "not contemplate any immediate return." "No," came the answer. "I should like to see a return tomorrow."[6]

It was no surprise that these men were all eager to return to gold. But what of industry and labor?

The traditional view is that the Chamberlain-Bradbury Committee largely ignored them. Empowered by the chants of finance and enchanted by the chorus of intelligentsia, these elites are said to have overruled the venal interests of the UK's producers. In fact, the opposite was true on both counts. As with the Cunliffe Committee, the members of the Chamberlain-Bradbury Committee were far more reflective and nuanced than we have appreciated. Indeed, even the greatest exponents of the orthodoxy—Pigou and Bradbury—had begun to rethink the gold standard in light of Keynes's devastating critique. They did this even as the representatives of UK industry vigorously cast their lot behind the agenda of the City of London.

## The Committee on the Road to Damascus

Norman was not the only one impressed by Keynes's critique of the orthodox view. Whereas the Chamberlain-Bradbury Committee originally invited Keynes so as to preempt his attacks, his arguments before the committee left a lasting, and positive, impression on its leading members. In the weeks that followed, Pigou went particularly far in reorganizing his approach to the return in light of Keynes's critique. But even the stalwart Bradbury was moved to reconsider the orthodox axiom that the gold standard worked naturally and "automatically." On July 24, he wrote to Farrer, "I am so far impressed by the views of McKenna and Keynes as to think that it may be wise not to pursue a policy of restoring the dollar exchange to parity at the cost of depressing home prices. The odds are that within the comparatively near future America will allow gold to depreciate to the value of sterling—particularly if she realizes that it is the only way by which parity will be restored." With that small seam opened, Bradbury mooted a rather different timetable: "My present feeling is rather in favor of pursuing a credit policy which will aim at keeping the exchange in the neighborhood of [$]4.40 while American prices are steady or falling, and working it back to par when American prices rise." But Bradbury hesitated: "These are not, however, 'settled convictions,' and I am quite ready to modify them after discussion."[7]

The admission marked a decisive twist in England's road to Calvary. Up to this point, the resumption of the free gold market could not come soon enough for Bradbury. This was, after all, the man who had led the charge to save the pound's convertibility in 1914, the man who ensured that the Cunliffe Committee called for "re-establishing at an early date a free market for gold," the man who repeatedly pressed the government for an "immediate repeal" of the capital controls.[8] Yet Keynes had unsettled his convictions and confronted him with the truth of a new vision.

## Backing Business

Social science models predict that there ought to have been a significant divergence in the interests of the financiers in London and the industrialists across the UK. And there was. And its very existence was discussed when the Federation of British Industries (FBI) appeared before the Chamberlain-Bradbury Committee at the end of July. It is crucial to note that Bradbury's first serious flirtation with "the views of McKenna and Keynes" happened a week *before* the FBI's representatives brought their views to the committee. Prior to this, Schuster had been the principal spokesperson for the UK's chambers of commerce and industrial interests. But while neither he nor the committee questioned whether he could speak definitively for the UK's producers, a cynic would surely stress that Schuster was a banker first and (perhaps) foremost. What would happen when the industrialists testified on their own behalf? With Bradbury now seriously contemplating the Keynesian approach, there was never a better time for business to challenge financial orthodoxy. Their beliefs, however, got in the way.

Before appearing, the FBI sent a brief memorandum outlining its concerns. It was as familiar with the particulars of the Cunliffe Committee reports as anyone. It was perturbed by the specter of deflation, rightly arguing that it would cause a "serious temporary dislocation of trade and a probable increase in unemployment due to the effect of the certainty of a period of falling prices upon producers, traders and buyers."[9] Like McKenna, it resisted the idea of an arbitrarily fixed limit to the total supply of currency. And so the FBI proposed "a waiting policy": "In prospect of the undoubtedly serious strain which would be thrown upon Industry in this country by an attempt at drastic deflation, and of the possibility that the position of the sterling exchange will tend to improve in a not too distant future through a rise in American prices without the necessity of such a sacrifice on our part[,] . . . a British initiative in restoring the gold standard at an early date for that purpose would be premature and inadvisable."[10]

But this was hardly a renunciation of the gold standard. The FBI simply did not want to accelerate the return more than was necessary. And even before the inquisition began, the FBI proclaimed its faith in the final salvation:

Since this country is the international clearing house, both for money and goods, a general return to the gold basis by the principal trading countries would, in the opinion of the Federation be greatly to our benefit; it would not only ensure stability to the more important exchanges, but would go a long way towards restoring its prewar mobility to international trade consistently with a reasonable elasticity in our own currency system. Moreover, it is clearly in the interests of this country, as the center of the British Empire within which [by] far the largest portion of new gold from the mines is annually produced, to maintain the position of gold as the monetary standard.[11]

But even with this declaration in print, the Chamberlain-Bradbury Committee wanted its full confession. On July 30, Hugh Chisholm, speaking for the FBI, gave them just that. Putting first things first, Chamberlain asked for, and received, an unambiguous affirmation of the FBI's commitment to "an ultimate return to the old gold standard." He then went on to address the FBI's concerns about the deflation that might be required to effect that return. "Manufacturers," Chisholm replied, "generally have that consideration, not solely but very strongly, in their minds; it seems to outweigh almost anything else."[12] Of course, this undergirded the FBI's "waiting policy." But Chisholm clarified that producers are not "against a reduction in prices in theory, they are more against sudden drops. . . . They would rather have it spread over if it is inevitable."[13]

Chamberlain challenged the perception that there was a meaningful choice in the matter. He asked "whether [the FBI] had in mind the fact that the present embargo on the export of gold is not an embargo until Parliament otherwise determines, but an embargo until . . . the 31st December 1925, and . . . therefore, either we must return to the free gold market on that date or we must have fresh legislation to prolong the embargo?" "We have not discussed it," Chisholm admitted. "[But] if I answer for myself, it would certainly have an effect on my mind."[14]

With that momentum, the inquisitors were ready to ask the FBI's representatives to renounce the heretical teachings of Keynes. "You have no desire to substitute for the gold basis that equation of prices which finds favor with Mr. Keynes?" Chamberlain asked. Chisholm replied, "No." "May I take it," Chamberlain continued, "as being the general and almost universal opinion in the business world, that that is too complicated a system for them to work?" Chisholm agreed: "Certainly."[15]

The next line of questioning followed naturally: What did the FBI mean by "stability," its "great object"? Chisholm evaded the query with the old bromide that "stability of exchanges" and "stability of prices" "comes to the same thing, eventually." But the committee knew well that there was a trade-off between the two, at least in the all-important short run. Chamberlain wanted the FBI to come down definitively on the side of "stability of exchange." Chisholm agreed. "And you do not feel that [the producer] will get that until we get back to the gold basis?" Chamberlain asked. Chisholm was unfaltering: "That is the most advantageous way for us."[16]

The old Bradbury might have left it there. This was just the sort of recantation that he elicited repeatedly on the Cunliffe Committee. Such strong professions of faith would give the government plenty of political space in which to impose the return. But Bradbury's approach had softened considerably, and now he wanted the FBI to endorse his new notion that the return should be deferred, pending American price rises. "You said that you did not approve of the suggestions of Mr. Keynes, that the value of currency should be regulated on some basis of an index figure," Bradbury began. "I take it, however," he continued, "that for the immediate period, until it becomes practicable to reestablish a gold standard, you would suggest that the public credit policy of this country should be based on keeping prices steady, which, in substance surely, is the temporary adoption of Mr. Keynes' principle?" "Mr. Keynes proposes it as a permanent policy," Bradbury explained, "while you propose it as an interim policy pending the time when the fall [rise?] in American prices, as you hope, will enable us to restore the gold standard?"[17]

In fact, that is not what the FBI or Chisholm had suggested. Chisholm had repeatedly said that he wanted an ultimate return to gold. This would prove worth it, even if it involved deflation, because it would give producers the particular type of stability that they prized: exchange rate stability. Moreover, maintaining domestic price stability was almost certainly at odds with achieving exchange rate stability and perhaps even a return to gold itself. After all, even if the United States let its own prices rise, this might not ensure that achieving UK domestic price stability would keep the pound stable relative to either gold or to the dollar.

To say otherwise would be to say that all of the nonmonetary influences on prices (non-gold US prices, non-gold UK prices, and gold prices) were precisely the same across the world. But who would have thought that UK output, US output, and the output of the world's gold mines would move in lockstep or even necessarily converge in the long run? In fact, no one in these discussions suggested this. At least since Locke, the advocates of the metallic standard admitted that the long-term growth of gold and silver supplies diverge from the overall growth of the economy. But because its supply was less volatile over the short term, it was "the best Measure of the alter'd Value of things in a few Years."[18] Smith's oft-bracketed "Digression concerning the Variations in the Value of Silver" was a commentary on the same question. "Corn," Smith wrote, "is at distant periods of time a more accurate measure of value than either silver, or perhaps any other commodity."[19] McKenna had been forceful on this point in his testimony before the committee.[20] Suffice it to say, Bradbury's suggestion that keeping domestic prices stable was a path back to gold was a departure from the orthodoxy. He wanted to implement Keynes's approach but still achieve Locke's outcome. It was an unstable position; from an orthodox viewpoint, it was tantamount to suggesting that we may carry on sinning while we await the arrival of grace.

The subtle distinctions were lost on Chisholm. Having just been pressed to renounce Keynes several times, Chisholm likely did not appreciate being asked now to specify the terms on which indulgence was permissible. But he answered diplomatically—vaguely. "My experience of representatives of manufacturers in the Federation is that they are not keen about Mr. Keynes' theory," he replied, "but, as far as I personally am concerned, I think there is a good deal in it up to a certain point."

Chisholm remained convivial throughout. One might even forget that he represented those capitalists who would suffer the most under the restoration of the prewar price level. If there were grievances, he did not air them. If there were suspicions, he did not reveal them. If there were conflicts, he did not press them.

Indeed, Chisholm denied that any such cleavages existed. Near the end of the questioning, Niemeyer asked him directly, "You do not suggest that there is . . . an ultimate difference in interest between, say, high finance and industry?" "Oh no," Chisholm exclaimed, "any more than the Federation, in spite of its occasional criticism of the policy of the Bank of England as compared with the policy of industry, would contend for a moment that the ultimate interests of the banks were not those of British industry, because, of course, they are." With an eye to posterity—or parliamentary scrutiny, at least—Niemeyer underscored the stakes of the query. "I wanted to be quite clear," he stated. Chisholm had intended his response to be instructive. "Sometimes," he replied, "I know, in utterances of the Federation some misconception has arisen about that, but I can say, perfectly confidently . . . that those who speak for the Federation are just as well aware as anyone that the ultimate banking interest is just the same as the ultimate trading interest."[21]

Clearly this was not the first time British industrial capital and its spokespersons had weighed this crucial question. Chisholm's response was self-reflective but not prepared. It is all the more authentic as a result. In contrast to the schismatic currency committees, British capitalism was, Chisholm maintained, economic ecumenicalism: all the varied denominations of producers were, ultimately, united under the church of England's gold standard.

Smith, and Marx, and modern materialist theory, all tell us that it should not have happened this way. But it did. This was the "ramp" that led back to gold.[22] This was the smoke-filled room in which the fate of the global financial system was decided.[23] This was the producers' opportunity to push back— to invoke the analysis of Keynes and McKenna in the name of sanity, to ask why the reigning dogma was ever inconstant in the name of (theo)logical purity. But they did not. Industrial capital had its chance, and it was found denying Keynes three times. Perhaps Chisholm was incredulous about the creed he mouthed—just as all Christians know that, in his heart, Peter loved Christ. But what mattered more on the road to Calvary—that Peter did know Christ, or that he professed that he did not? And what mattered more to the return to gold—that Chisholm may have harbored doubts, or that he did surrender to his inquisitors?

On this occasion, British labor was, distressingly, not even invited to testify. But it was Labour that had created this committee and appointed its Conservative chair and orthodox members in the first place. More to the point, what might Snowden have said in July that he had not said before and would not say again? Would he simply criticize the government for not moving faster back toward gold, the way that he was about to criticize Churchill a few months hence?

Such is the poisoned chalice of hindsight. Not unreasonably, the industrial and financial interests of the world's sometime hegemon had come to embrace the monetary order that bound them, together, in golden fetters. After a century of ascent, they believed that all good things go together. It is thus folly to disentangle the interests of the different "classes" of this world when the reality is that faith was placed in the hands of a very small group of leading men— all of them, frustratingly, white men in positions of privilege—to define the Restoration.[24] What would be those inventors' bloody instructions?

# Redefining the Restoration

The Chamberlain-Bradbury Committee began drafting its report in August 1924. First, Farrer offered just a few conclusions, and then Pigou circulated a more sustained treatment. It is clear that Pigou had reflected deeply on Keynes's arguments. His draft was brief and did not mention Keynes by name. But this was nevertheless a powerful response to that critique.

The Pigou draft begins by acknowledging the UK's failure to enact the principal recommendations of the Cunliffe Committee:

> The natural starting point . . . is the recommendation of . . . the Cunliffe Committee . . . that the Currency Note issue should be transferred to the Bank of England when it had been ascertained, from experience in a free gold export market, what fiduciary issue is compatible with the maintenance of a central gold reserve of £150,000,000. . . . These conditions have not been fulfilled and we have found it necessary to enter . . . into the questions whether a return to the gold standard is, in present circumstances, no less desirable than at the time of the Cunliffe Committee's Report; whether this is likely to be achieved without further deliberate Government action to that end; and whether experience of the amount of the gold reserve which can be maintained in postwar conditions must necessarily precede the amalgamation of the note issues.[25]

This was a blatant recognition of Keynes's contention that the orthodox gold standard had been suspended, in effect, with the limitations on capital movement during and after the war. There could be no maintenance of the fiction, advanced by Cokayne in 1918, that the gold standard continued to operate despite the capital controls. Since then, as Keynes had put it, the "regulated nonmetallic standard [had] slipped in unnoticed."[26]

Pigou then went on to dispatch with Keynes's proposed alternatives. He summarily dismissed Keynes's compromise position of a one-off devaluation relative to gold. Keynes had intended this to appeal to policymakers, offering the stability of a gold standard without the pain of deflation. But Pigou feared the dangers of such a precedent. One devaluation was a precursor to another, and, the orthodox line went, this would liquidate the credibility built up over two centuries. Such a suggestion "need only be mentioned to be dismissed, it could not be seriously considered as a policy for the United Kingdom."[27]

Keynes's original proposal, "involving the abandonment of the gold standard," was more radical but could not be so easily ruled out. The proposal of "substituting the price level of commodities in general for gold as the regulating principle of the currency," Pigou explained, "has been fully and carefully explained in evidence before us." But Pigou did not want to contend with these arguments explicitly. He did not even summarize them, as they "have been published and are now well known." Instead, he declared, "as a practical present day policy for this country, there is . . . no alternative comparable with a return to the former gold parity of the sovereign." "In this conclusion," he averred, "we are supported by the overwhelming majority of opinion, both financial and industrial, represented in evidence before us."[28]

But to say that Pigou eschewed Keynes's proposed solutions is not to say that he did not take Keynes's critique seriously. Like Keynes, Pigou resisted the desire to rush back onto gold prematurely. At the time, there was "no little apprehension in this country as to the effects of the re-establishment in Germany of a gold standard." But Pigou was skeptical of Germany's capacity to make the gold standard operational and to become the center of a new gold bloc. At the same time, he thought that there was plenty of time for circumstances to evolve—and for the UK to coordinate with the empire and allies—before the capital controls legislation expired at the end of 1925. Given these factors, he "conclude[d] that though a speedy return to the gold standard is highly desirable, there is no immediate and pressing urgency."[29]

It is hard to imagine that this was the same man who, a few years earlier, had written that the deflation "must come about ultimately and any attempt to defeat it would involve subsidence to a pure paper currency. . . . It is a policy which can be postponed by a continuation of loans abroad and the restriction of gold export . . . for some little time after the war period; i.e. the first few months of the reconstruction period." Even before gold movements are resumed, Pigou insisted in 1918, "it will . . . be desirable . . . to begin the process of deflation, bringing up the discount rate and bringing down credits and circulation towards the level they will have to assume when gold exports are released and equilibrium restored."[30]

Why had Pigou's posture and timeline changed so much since the end of the war? It was just as Keynes had said. The intervening years disproved Pigou's dire 1918 prediction that limiting the gold standard would lead immediately to uncontrollable inflation and instability.

Keynes's influence is even clearer in Pigou's analysis of the "routes to the restoration of the gold standard at prewar parity." Two of the routes were familiar to readers of the Cunliffe Committee reports. The onus could be put onto the Bank to "adopt a banking and credit policy calculated to depress prices here." Or the Treasury could force the Bank's hand by removing the gold export embargo, which would deplete the Bank's reserves and force the Bank to contract the money supply. Both approaches, Pigou noted, would "discourage industry and threaten employment." This admission was itself a shift away from the orthodox insistence that the advantages of being on gold more than offset the transitional costs of getting onto that equilibrium.[31] Could it be that Pigou was having a serious crisis of faith?

Pigou went even further, presenting a new, third way. The UK could also "await an expansion of credit in America adequate to bring the dollar exchange to par."[32] This was a leap forward from the old orthodoxy. In the world of the Cunliffe Committee, there were only two paths back to gold: the Bank could proactively defend its reserves by contracting credit, or it could contract credit reactively after it had lost reserves. Indeed, Pigou himself had brought this very point to the fore during the Cunliffe Committee's discussions. "Clearly," he wrote in his 1918 memorandum, ". . . we cannot go on borrowing abroad forever. When we either choose, or are compelled to stop doing this, the embargo on gold exports will have to be removed and either discount rates here raised to the foreign level or all our gold drained abroad."[33] The Cunliffe Committee never considered that the UK's monetary policy depended upon the movements in foreign price levels independent of the movement of gold, which they repeatedly described as "automatic." At that point, Pigou had argued, "equilibrium will be established with a discount rate and a level of prices more or less equivalent to the world gold level." Being on the gold standard means "that our exchanges are within the specie points and our price levels in equilibrium with countries whose currency is at par with its nominal gold value."[34] Now, half a decade later, Pigou's formula had changed. Stability could be achieved by keeping UK prices in line, not with world prices and not with the world gold price, but with US prices. This was a major concession to Keynes's contention that the "gold standard" had been replaced by a "dollar standard."[35] More broadly, Pigou now recognized that the system was not automatic, that much of life was lived between the points of equilibria, in what Keynes famously termed the "tempestuous seasons."[36]

What was the cause of this unnatural disturbance? It was just as Keynes said: the US Federal Reserve. "The normal effect of the accumulation of gold which is taking place in the United States of America," Pigou explained, "would be a general rise in dollar prices, and it is common knowledge that such a rise has only been prevented by the skillful policy of the Federal Reserve Board."[37] If the knowledge were "common," it was only because Keynes had made it so with his incomparable prose in the *Tract*. And while Strong had defended himself to Norman, Norman had accepted this point—and pressed it upon the committee as well.[38] But the orthodoxy would not go down so easily, and Pigou redeployed the orthodoxy's trump card: the long run. "We do not profess to be able to estimate accurately how long [the Federal Reserve] Board will be able to accept and 'sterilize' the surplus gold production of the world," Pigou wrote, "but it is evident that they cannot continue the process indefinitely."[39]

What was the practical implication of this new understanding? For Pigou, it meant that the UK could afford to proceed with caution. Of course, the Bank had to prevent further inflation, but for now, Pigou "conclude[d] that the British Government should not at present take any active steps towards restoring the gold standard." "For another year," Pigou recommended, "the Government should wait upon events. If at the end of 1925 the dollar has not approximated to parity, deliberate Government action to secure that result *may* become necessary."[40] This was a far cry from his demands in 1918 for a swift, bold return to gold.

The last part of Pigou's draft concerned the practical question of "amalgamating" the Bank notes and the Treasury currency notes (the Bradburys). The problem was that the Conservatives' 1920 capital controls, directly contradicting the Cunliffe Committee's dictates, thwarted the operation of the gold market. Pigou was diplomatic in his characterization, but it remained "as true today as five years ago that the permanent fiduciary issue cannot be fixed except with reference to the actual conditions of a free gold market."[41] So in the spirit of the Cunliffe Committee, Pigou proposed that the amalgamation be deferred until several years after the capital controls were removed. Here was yet more stretching of the timeline. This last delay, at least, was less at odds with the Cunliffe Committee recommendations.

How did Pigou's colleagues on the Chamberlain-Bradbury Committee react to this new version of the orthodoxy?

Pigou had gone so far in the Keynes direction that Chamberlain tugged on the reigns. Pigou "hesitates more than I should do," he wrote to the committee. Rather,

> I should . . . like to say definitely that (i) we are strong enough to restore the old gold parity at once and that there would be no exchange danger in announcing the very early removal of the embargo; but (ii) this would involve a sudden fall in prices which industry in its present distressed condition can not stand; and (iii) would be improvident if, as seems likely, American prices must rise, so that the sharp reduction would be in large measure at least only temporary and would have to be followed before very long by a substantial recovery.

"To me," Chamberlain explained, "this is the only reason for not acting now and I should like it put strongly." So Chamberlain too accepted Keynes's warning that the sudden return to gold would be painful—sufficiently painful that it was worth waiting on the hopes of American price rises. But he was determined that the report's rhetoric was strong, even if its recommendation was ultimately guarded.[42]

Bradbury reacted even more strongly against Pigou's "rather flabby" draft. "I think we ought to make it perfectly clear," he insisted,

> that we regard a return to a free gold market at the prewar parity without long delay as of vital importance, but that as this involves either a fall in sterling prices or a rise in gold prices, and as there are indications that a rise in gold prices may be imminent, we think it better to wait for a short time and see whether gold adjusts itself to sterling before taking the steps necessary to adjust sterling to gold, but that we do not propose to wait indefinitely, and if our expectations in regard to American prices are not realized in the near future, we shall be forced to adopt the other alternative.[43]

Bradbury similarly wanted to "lay rather more stress than is laid in the draft report . . . on the importance during this interim period of holding fast to the improvement of sterling which has already been effected."[44]

That very day, Bradbury sent off six pages of proposed revisions to his committee colleagues. First, he inserted those declarations of faith in the orthodoxy requested by Chamberlain. Despite the difficulties following the war, "we entertain no doubt whatever of our ability at any time it may be thought prudent to do so, to restore and maintain the gold standard at the prewar parity." "Further," he added, "we are satisfied that the mere abolition of the prohibition of the export of gold would automatically and rapidly bring about the credit conditions necessary to effect these adjustments, and that the effective gold standard could thus be restored without further danger or inconvenience than that which is inevitable in any period of credit restriction and falling prices."[45]

But this was not just the same old Bradbury. He too had accepted Keynes's contention (seconded by McKenna) that the actions of the US Federal Reserve now effectively dictated the course of the global gold market. He knew well that the implications of this change in perspective were massive. For him, it was not simply that this provided a third way—the wait-and-see approach advanced by Pigou. The reality of a gold standard run by the Federal Reserve created a new danger: What if the UK pushed prices down only to have the US subsequently raise its prices (and thus world prices)? In that case, "we should thus have exposed ourselves to the inconveniences of a double adjustment which a delay in re-establishing the parity would have avoided." So it was not just politically but also economically prudent to await "the possible developments of the American situation."[46]

At the same time, Bradbury was sure to mention, this was "subject to proper safeguards against [the] deterioration of our present position." After all, "in the absence of a free gold market," the normal, "automatic" check against overlending "is absent," and "the domestic supply of banking credit" must be "arbitrarily controlled" to prevent inflation. So Bradbury's version of the committee's recommendation was heavily couched: "For the time being, no drastic action should be taken to restore the sterling exchange to parity, but . . . the credit policy of the Bank of England . . . should be directed to keeping British domestic prices at their existing level in the event of American prices remaining stationary or moving upwards, but on the other hand to securing that any fall in American prices is promptly reflected in the British price Level."[47] Thus, Bradbury's draft advanced a more conservative posture and a more austere tone.

Despite the rhetorical differences, Bradbury and Pigou were on the same side of this reformation. Seeing this, Chamberlain emphasized the consensus in a letter to Young two days later. "Was ever such a happy family?" he wrote. "I wished to say more, Pigou would have liked to say more, Farrar regretted that more was not said—and Bradbury sat down and said (or rather wrote) it!" Chamberlain acquiesced to Bradbury's revisions and instructed Young to effect them in a new draft. Seeing that the committee was still rejecting the bulk of Norman's proposals, Chamberlain also asked Young to send a copy to the governor and to ask him to return for a discussion of it.[48]

Young made several attempts to arrange another meeting with Norman but does not appear to have been successful.[49] At the time, Norman was working seven days a week, principally on "the German loan." The inevitable showdown would have to wait for now.

## Gold on American Terms

Throughout the summer of 1924, Norman had been encouraged by Benjamin Strong at the US Federal Reserve to bring the pound to its prewar dollar value of $4.86. Strong did what he could on his side, effecting easy money in the United States with several rate cuts in the spring and summer. He repeatedly pressed Norman to take bold action, but Norman dragged his feet. It was necessary to "hurry slowly," he explained to Strong.[50]

In October, perceiving that MacDonald was too soft on communism, Asquith withdrew Liberal support from the Labour-led coalition government. The collapse of Labour substantially increased the likelihood that the country would move back toward the right—and, one expects, gold. But Norman remained uncertain, and he blamed his continued dilatoriness on "our sudden and unexpected political upheaval." On October 16, he told Strong that he could not "say how or when our next Government will decide—we must 'wait and see.'" In fact, he still seems to have hoped for a two-year deferment of the restoration, as he had championed before the Chamberlain-Bradbury Committee. In the meantime, he told Strong, "we must get together and devise a plan which will probably need to include some sort of credit operation for steadying or holding the rate of exchange when we get into the 80's."[51]

In late October, Baldwin led the Conservatives to a commanding majority in the general election. This was followed a few weeks later by the Republicans' own victories in the US elections. Taken together, this changed the political landscape. Norman had always styled himself the orthodoxy's champion, even as he found one reason after another to delay the return. But now, Strong expected, Norman could not remain so "hesitant in facing this important matter." "Your political 'upheaval' . . . appears to make plans for a strong policy as to the exchanges and a return to gold payment much easier then would have been the case had not the conservative party had such a sweeping victory and gained such a large majority in Parliament," he wrote in November. He lobbied Norman for bold action. "It is illusory," he wrote, "to expect price readjustments of themselves to effect a recovery of sterling. Sterling cannot return to par and gold payment cannot be resumed without an act of 'force majeure.'"[52]

How could Norman argue with this logic or deflect this pressure? The next day, he approached his colleagues at the Bank to secure leave to arrange a loan from the United States. Norman first broached this with the Bank's Committee of Treasury on November 5. He gained their support for the plan the following week. That same day, the committee nominated Norman to continue for an unprecedented fifth year. At this stage, there was no hint of the opposition within the Bank against Norman and his particular approach to the restoration.[53]

In early December, however, skepticism emerged from the Treasury. On the fourth, Norman informed Niemeyer that he intended to borrow in excess of $300 million in New York. Norman knew well enough that using such exchange rate "credits" abroad, rather than forcing adjustment at home, ran counter to the Cunliffe Committee doctrine. So he preemptively agreed that the Bank should be forbidden by the chancellor to use the loan "until a suffi-ciently large amount of gold had been shipped to America and a sufficiently high rate had been in operation here."[54]

Even with this caveat, however, Niemeyer found it unacceptable. "The more I think of the cushion," he replied, "the less I like it—even on the assumption that it is not used until £100 million has gone in gold, and Bank rate has reached say 6% or 7%." This a "loathsome" step "back . . . to war methods of main-taining exchange," a position they abandoned in 1919. Moreover, all such ef-forts to "keep an unnatural exchange by artificial support" are doomed to fail. "Has anyone ever succeeded in such an enterprise?" Niemeyer asked rhetori-cally. Instead, the United States could help in other ways, not least by provid-ing loans to Europe, saving the UK from having to do so while also redistributing the United States' gold. Moreover, if the cushion were really not meant to be used, what was the point in having it? So far from having a positive effect on the market psychology, Niemeyer asked, "will not the cushion notion simply put into people's heads fears which . . . they probably wouldn't themselves think of?"[55]

But this was Norman's new dogma. Rather than sucking gold into the UK by raising Bank rate, Norman sought to coordinate policy with his like-minded colleagues abroad. Rather than contracting the money supply and imposing deflation, acquiring these credits would allow Norman to sooth the concerns of investors—to steer market psychology, as he saw it. Norman mouthed the creed that the credits could not be a substitute for austerity. But this was just the sort of coordinated action that had become the centerpiece of his new approach to central banking. Just as his loan to Schacht had helped Germany back toward gold, so too might a loan from Strong help the UK along the same path. Strong agreed with Norman and began arranging hundreds of millions of dollars of financial support.[56]

By the end of December, Norman was in New York working directly with Strong, J.P. Morgan, Secretary Mellon, and others to settle terms for the loan. While he was there, Norman's proposed borrowing grew, and he telegraphed London with a "strongly recommended" revised proposal of $500 million.[57] This was equivalent to more than £100 million at the prewar exchange rate and would constitute a two-thirds increase in the size of the UK's "reserves."

Of course, this was not the form of "reserve" that had been prescribed by the Cunliffe Committee. The credits could be used in the United States to prop up the dollar value of the pound. But, obviously, this was different from hav-ing gold in the vaults of the Bank of England that could be paid out to the holders of pound notes (to avert an "internal" drain) and/or to directly ma-nipulate the London gold price. Did the distinction matter?

One's answer to this question turned on one's understanding of the gold standard. The traditional view, which was at the heart of the Cunliffe Committee reports, was that the gold value of the pound was paramount. In a word, the orthodoxy saw gold as the means to discipline the monetary authorities. The Keynes view, adopted by Norman, was that the global gold supply was ultimately driven by the US Federal Reserve and that, in any case, the pound's gold value was just one of many things that mattered. The UK would exercise more control over the international "gold" standard by coordinating its monetary policy with the US Federal Reserve—or, at least, by manipulating the pound-dollar exchange rate. But these kinds of actions insulated central bankers from the harsh discipline of market forces. Today Norman lends to Schacht; tomorrow Strong lends to Norman; and then the day after that, Norman and Schacht help Strong fend off a speculative attack. Share and share alike. All the while, each economy avoids real macroeconomic adjustment. For the old orthodoxy—Locke reincarnated as Schuster—this autonomy enables the monetary authorities to be profligate. The leash must be short and the discipline, austere. The new Keynes-Norman position was that the golden fetters should be softened—if not made "flabby," as Bradbury had put it—to allow for discretion. They insisted that this was not merely desirable but inevitable. Prudence dictated confronting the reality of growing central bank independence—from politics *and from markets*—rather than legislating from, and for, a dreamland.

Back at the Bank of England, Norman's colleagues balked at Norman's significant change in approach. Led by Addis—that Cunliffe Committee alumnus—they rallied around a shared message. There was "much doubt . . . as to the wisdom of obtaining a credit in any form, especially any credit not exclusively arranged with Central Banks." They deployed the old Cunliffe Committee line: "The restoration of the gold standard should follow and not precede the conditions of trade appropriate to the maintenance of a stable exchange." The authorities needed to be "satisfied . . . that the parity of exchange having once been reached could be maintained by the natural play of the market force of supply and demand without resort to any artificial aids." "Until it has been tested by a period of comparatively stable exchange," they insisted, "it would be unsafe to rely on its permanence." This was more than advice. It was a warning: "Some of us would feel reluctant to recommend such a course to [the] British Government."[58] When Norman returned to London, he would have some explaining to do.

# The Chamberlain-Bradbury Committee's Conclusions

The 1924 general election had a significant consequence for the Chamberlain-Bradbury Committee as well: when Chamberlain was made the assistant secretary for foreign affairs, he asked Bradbury to take over as the chairman.[59] At last, Bradbury's formal position would reflect his substantive role in these currency committees. But this was still a post-*Tract* world. Once Keynes upended the orthodoxy's old myths, nothing could fully restore the luster of the prewar gold standard ideal. Bradbury and Pigou had come to accept the reality that, as Keynes had put it, "the value of gold is no longer the resultant of the chance gifts of Nature and the judgment of numerous authorities and individuals acting independently."[60] As their third draft of the Chamberlain-Bradbury Committee report reflected, they now conceded that the UK could not simply resume gold exports unilaterally and expect market forces to naturally align the UK economy with those of its peers.

But across the final months of 1924, two critical developments shifted the terrain. First, the sterling-dollar exchange rate came within striking distance of the prewar rate. This mattered intellectually for the Chamberlain-Bradbury Committee because the contending views—old and new—now led to the same prescription: an early return to gold. From the orthodox view, this was a clear signal that the US and the UK economies were converging in real terms. From the post-*Tract* view, this indicated that market psychology had come to count on an impending restoration. If the former were correct, it was time to ratify with policy the real changes that had occurred in the market. If the latter were correct, proposing an early return was the next necessary step in the courtship of the market's eager anticipations. It did not hurt that this was the result for which Bradbury had pined for a decade.

The second change was the sine qua non of an early return: Norman now supported it. Simply put, the governor of the Bank of England was the single most important figure in setting the agenda for the return to gold. He did not have so much power that he could dictate the outcome, but he was an effective veto player. As Bradbury experienced across 1919 and 1920, Norman could frustrate attempts to restore the gold standard before he felt ready to do so. So in the summer of 1924, the Chamberlain-Bradbury Committee did not have to accede to Norman's demand (at that time) to announce a three-year delay. But the committee also could not propose an early restoration knowing that Norman would resist it. After all, what could imperil the return more than the exposure of such a schism among the monetary authorities? Thus, when Norman embraced the idea of an early return at the end of 1924, the way was cleared for the Chamberlain-Bradbury Committee to accelerate the timetable.

It seemed that the stars had finally aligned. So as Norman negotiated with New York, Bradbury grabbed the reigns of the Chamberlain-Bradbury Committee. Any who had followed Bradbury's decade-long struggle to save the pre-war gold standard could not have been surprised at the conclusion that the committee—now, properly, the Chamberlain-Bradbury Committee—reached in the latest draft of its report:

> We . . . recommend that the early return to the gold basis should without delay be declared to be the irrevocable policy of His Majesty's Government and that it should be definitely stated that the existing restrictions on the export of gold . . . will not be renewed. A general license to export gold should at the same time be given to the Bank of England and the Bank should between now and the date of expiry of the export prohibition avail themselves freely of it whenever the exchange is below the normal export specie point, making good any consequential drafts upon the reserve in the Banking Department in accordance with traditional practice.[61]

The era of "wait and see," of deferral and delay, was finally over. A full and glorious restoration was on the horizon.

But it was one thing to issue the prescription and quite another to explain and justify it. There was more at stake than just winning the support of policymakers and shaping public opinion. The committee recognized that this was a chance to shape the terms on which the UK returned to gold—and the principles by which it would adhere to it. They knew well that Norman's gold standard dogma differed profoundly from their own. Their report was their chance to define the parameters within which Norman would effect the return.

The fourth draft of the committee's report was dated January 26, 1925. It was the first draft written under Bradbury's exclusive leadership. He oversaw significant revisions to this draft—even in the face of resistance from some of the committee's members, even as it meant taking an unconventionally strong stance toward the Bank.[62] Crucially, it was prepared and circulated in advance of Norman's second appearance before the committee.[63] Except for a few changes proposed by Pigou (noted below), it was essentially the committee's final report—dated February 5, 1925, but not published until after Churchill's announcement in April. That printed version weighed in at less than ten pages of large-point text—nothing like the dense analysis of the Cunliffe Committee's *First Interim Report*. Keynes later mocked it as "indolent and jejune."[64] He was right that it remained underdeveloped, and it might be that the report it-self did not matter, that the return became "more or less inevitable . . . after the rise in the dollar exchange."[65] But these last versions of the Chamberlain-Bradbury Committee's report both reflect the significant transformation of the orthodoxy that was already underway and reveal the committee's maneuvers to control the direction of those changes.

The report itself explained the reasons for accelerating the return to gold. Even during the summer of 1924, when the market exchange rate was at least 10 percent below the prewar rate, the committee "entertained no doubt . . . of the ability of Great Britain . . . to restore and maintain the gold standard at the prewar parity." It only required the resolve to implement the necessary austerity:

> A free gold market could readily be established and maintained at the prewar parity, provided that by control of credit we adjusted the internal purchasing power of the pound to its exchange parity and restricted our foreign investments to our real investable surplus. . . . The mere abolition of the prohibition of the export of gold would automatically and rapidly bring about the credit conditions necessary to effect these adjustments, and . . . the effective gold standard could thus be restored without further danger or inconvenience than that which is inevitable in any period of credit restriction and falling prices.

With the end preordained, the committee's report was "confine[d] . . . to answering the questions [of] when and how this restoration is to be brought about."[66]

In the summer of 1924, the report stated, achieving price alignment required "a fall in sterling prices of some 10 or 12% or a similar rise in dollar prices." In that context, it became a question of "whether the undoubted advantages of an immediate return to parity were a sufficient compensation for the inconveniences—temporary though possibly severe while they lasted—of the measure of 'deflation' necessary to bring about the adjustment." The alternative was to wait "at least for a few months longer . . . in the hope that the disparity would disappear through a rise in American prices." The committee concluded that, at that point, the return "could not be regarded as a matter of such extreme urgency as to justify a credit policy calculated to bring down domestic prices if the same practical result could . . . be expected . . . by a policy designed merely to [prevent] them from rising."[67]

It is odd that the committee's report offered these explicit, self-reflective caveats. As Chamberlain suggested, it was rhetorically powerful to suggest that the return could have been effected in even the challenging circumstances of the previous summer. But this also offered a significant shift from the old Cunliffe Committee line that the best medicine was forcing through the changes required to restore the gold standard as soon as possible. This was a frank acknowledgment that there were circumstances in which delaying the return was prudent and that the restoration might require more than just Britons' self-reliance on their own fortitude.

Happily, however, the committee declared that "the favorable course since September of the dollar exchange (which now stands only 1.5% below gold parity) . . . [has] altered the situation."[68] So while the committee had dabbled in the Keynes-Norman school of deferral, this rejuvenated its old conviction that the return could, and should, be effected as soon as possible.

Yet this just begged another question: What had caused this all-important change in the dollar value of the pound? More broadly, what drove the pound-dollar market exchange rate? Was it largely market psychology and speculation, as Keynes and then Norman had argued? Or did it depend on the long-run fundamentals—particularly the relative purchasing power—of the two currencies, as the orthodoxy had always maintained? The answer would define both the real distance to be traversed and the path that the monetary authorities ought to take.

But rather than choosing, the committee deployed both arguments. Sterling's dollar value had appreciated partly due to a real increase in the pound's domestic purchasing power (relative to the domestic purchasing power of the dollar). But market speculation had bid up the value of the pound some amount beyond this. As the committee polished the report, it sometimes blurred these distinctions, describing both the necessary real adjustments and those actions necessary to court speculators' psychology. For instance, the report warned, "If [the adjustment of price levels] is deferred, the exchange will inevitably fall back to the rate justified by the comparative price levels—or below it, since the psychological causes which have operated to force it up will tend to act in the other direction—and a period of fluctuating values is likely to ensue which will be more injurious to trade and industry than the comparatively small sacrifices now required to re-establish the effective gold standard."[69] These were the old axioms recounted using the language and sensibilities of Keynes and Norman.

But what was the relative causal weight of the ideational and the material variables? Or more to the point, how large were the "comparatively small sacrifices" required to make the return sustainable? The fourth draft of the report stated that the pound was overvalued by "not less than 4.5%" at the current exchange rate and would be overvalued "not less than 6%" at parity. This was a clear answer to that all-important question: restoring the pound to parity would require at least a 6 percent appreciation of the purchasing power of the pound. Pigou, however, rewrote this in less certain, and less clear, terms: "We must still be prepared to face a fall in the final price level here of a significant, though not very large amount . . . if the rate of exchange is to be restored to and held at the prewar parity. . . . For the rise in price level required to restore and maintain prewar parity needs to be only some 1.5% larger than that required to hold the exchange at its present rate."[70]

This change elided the baseline. It offered no answer to the crucial question: What was the change in prices required just to keep the exchange rate at its present level? Following Pigou's modification, the committee no longer even estimated this critical figure. Instead, the Chamberlain-Bradbury Committee's final report deployed (three times each) just the 10 to 12 percent figure describing the rate of overvaluation in September and the 1.5 percent difference between the current exchange rate and the official parity. The former was now fourth months out of date, and the latter was the obvious difference between the current market exchange rate and the official prewar parity. Pigou took for granted that the authorities would force through "such price adjustment as may be necessary to maintain the present exchange rate" and to take the steps beyond that to restore the prewar value of the pound. But that was the question being debated, and the report does not even estimate the length of that journey.

It is not as though this issue had escaped Pigou. Indeed, he had been the one to press Norman on this in June.[71] But now Pigou was following Norman's example by simply refusing to answer the question. So the Chamberlain-Bradbury Committee report stressed that this issue was critically important, but it overtly evaded it:

> The appreciation of sterling which has taken place since November, 1924 has been due partly to the belief that an effective gold standard will shortly be restored in this country, and only partly to a lessening of the difference between the purchasing power of sterling and of gold. . . . There has . . . undoubtedly been a considerable element of speculation in connection with that movement, the extent of which cannot be exactly determined. To *this unknown extent* there may be a tendency, when parity has been reached, for realization of the speculative positions to throw a concentrated strain on the exchange.[72]

Thus, to return to gold, Bradbury, Pigou, and company recommended imposing an "unknown" quantity of deflation. From the text of the final report itself, it could be as little as 1.5 percent or as much as 10.5 percent. This was the (rather poor) basis on which policymakers were asked to make a decision. One is reminded of Bradbury's guesses at the money supply and the Cunliffe Committee's haggling over the minimum size of the national reserve—£100 million, or perhaps twice that amount.

We know better now just how problematic this committee's guidance proved to be. With the benefit of hindsight, Moggridge concluded, "An exchange rate perhaps 10% lower than $4.86 would probably have been somewhat more appropriate for sterling."[73] But even without modern statistical analysis, it is clear from the qualitative evidence that the authorities were more uncertain than they were willing to admit. The fourth draft of the report estimated the difference between British and American price levels at 6 percent. One week later, Bradbury inexplicably told Churchill that it was half this size: "not more than 2% or 3%."[74] Previously, Norman had said that the mere announcement of the policy could appreciate the exchange rate 6 percent within a few days. But that was a question of manipulating market psychology and speculative behavior. In this case, Bradbury's construal for Churchill raised the *real* value (purchasing power) of the pound three or four percent.

Thus the Chamberlain-Bradbury Committee broached but refused to answer several crucial questions. How much further appreciation in the exchange rate could be gained from making the announcement now? How much of this appreciation could be sustained by adroitly managing market psychology? How much of this restoration would be achieved by managing the chancellor's own knowledge and understanding of reality?

This leads to another, even more important question: could Chancellor Churchill trust these men? They contradicted each other and themselves as a matter of course. Their models of the determinants of exchange rates were convoluted, and their quantitative metrics and measures varied to serve rhetorical purposes. This was Foucault's "knowledge-power." Or, more precisely, this was Orwell's doublethink: these monetary authorities "use[d] use conscious deception while retaining the firmness of purpose that goes with complete honesty." In the same way that a chocolate ration is "raised" from thirty to twenty grams, so too did Bradbury raise the "real" value of the pound as a part of Winston's process of "learning . . . understanding . . . and acceptance" of the principles of English gold-ism.[75]

And what of the preference hierarchies of those individuals who would lead from within the proverbial Inner Party? Bradbury had been fighting to save the gold standard for a decade. Until quite recently, he had expressed few qualms about driving the pound back to its prewar parity, whatever the cost. Who could say how much deflation he and his colleagues thought was an acceptable imposition on the economy? To be fair, the directive handed to the currency committees was an unenviable one. Who could possibly restore the prewar monetary order? And yet these leading individuals possessed—or at least projected—immense confidence in their ever-shifting assumptions, perceptions, models, and conclusions. They were certain that the "restoration" was necessary, even if they remained uncertain as to why that was so.

With the return all but inevitable, the key questions became these: Who would pilot this journey and by what conveyance? The Chamberlain-Bradbury Committee offered some answer to this last question, at least. Norman would be at the helm, but he would proceed by orthodox means—or, the committee hoped, with at least a strong semblance of the orthodoxy intact.

The committee's report restated the orthodoxy's reservations—dating back to Bradbury's days on the Cunliffe Committee—about reliance on "foreign assistance." It warned, "If [such assistance] took the form of foreign credits to be used . . . to mitigate the effect of the policy upon credit conditions in the United Kingdom, [it] would really serve to counteract the very forces on the operation of which we rely for its success." This admonition was really targeted at Norman, who, the committee feared, hoped to stabilize the exchange rate without forcing through the necessary deflation. That deflation, whatever its size, must not be averted. Yet if the US loan could be utilized symbolically, the committee did see some psychological benefit in Norman's internationalist approach: "The existence of a substantial American credit known to be available for use in sudden emergencies would . . . discourage speculation and . . . creat[e] . . . a general atmosphere of confidence."[76] What speculator would dare to challenge the United Kingdom and the United States working together?

The report specified varied techniques of defense. As a material matter, "the proper safeguard" of the currency "is in the size of the gold reserves and in the resolute use of these reserves."[77] Given the "loyal co-operation of the principal British Institutions which control the supply of credit," the path might be a relatively easy one. "Even though this may involve a temporary increase in Bank rate," the report stated, "a conviction that there will be no hesitation in using [the gold reserves] . . . will go far to obviate the danger we refer to." "Indeed," the report speculated, "such credit restriction as may become necessary to adjust . . . sterling prices to a free gold market may well be less drastic than that which would be required in order to maintain a 'managed' pound in the neighborhood of parity."[78] Thankfully, the Committee was confident "that the existing gold reserves are amply sufficient for this purpose."[79]

So the first line of defense would be shipping gold, avoiding deflation. Or maybe it would be raising interest rates temporarily and keeping the gold. Or, as with the US loan, maybe the return could be saved just by cultivating the perception of a "conviction" to use "resolute[ly]" these tools with "no hesitation." Of course, all of these things pointed in the same direction; but, as with the amount of deflation to be swallowed, the Chamberlain-Bradbury Committee was ambiguous about the type and scale of the intervention required. Likely these differences did not matter to them. Now that the promised moment seemed so near, they themselves had regained the conviction that it was worth doing whatever it took.[80] Besides, such things mostly just took "courage": "British experience of the restoration of the gold standard after the [Napoleonic] [W]ars, 100 years ago, and the recent experience of continental countries which have taken steps, under far more difficult conditions, to rehabilitate their currencies, have shown that a courageous policy in currency matters surmounts apparently formidable obstacles with surprising ease."[81]

The last issue concerned the final elimination of the Bradburys. The Chamberlain-Bradbury Committee "associate[d] [them]selves with the decided preference expressed by the Cunliffe Committee for the principle of a fixed fiduciary issue."[82] Yet, the Chamberlain-Bradbury Committee admitted, "the Cunliffe Committee contemplated a much earlier removal of the prohibition of gold exports than has actually been deemed expedient."[83] But now that Norman was no longer fighting for capital controls, Bradbury had the chance to return to the approach he first devised in the earliest meetings of the Cunliffe Committee. First, the free gold market would be reestablished. HM Treasury would then reduce the quantity of the Bradburys in circulation over several years. When they had made sufficient progress, they would be in a position to determine the appropriate size of the total money supply. This was, simply, the quantity of paper money that could remain in circulation without the exchange rate falling below the prewar rate of $4.86 and without the Bank having to expend reserves to prop it up. At that time, the Bank would be given control over, and responsibility for, the entirety of the money supply.[84]

But Bradbury was forced to compromise elsewhere. In 1914, he had fought harder than anyone to maintain the right of specie redemption: the convertibility of the pound into gold coin. For the orthodoxy, this right was essential to disciplining the monetary authority. By 1925, however, Bradbury had surrendered to the tide of history. The Chamberlain-Bradbury Committee all but eliminated these rights as it redefined the gold standard in the narrowest of terms: "The payment of notes in gold coin upon demand is not in itself essential to the maintenance of the gold standard under modern conditions. An obligation upon the Bank of Issue to buy and sell gold at a fixed price is all that is necessary, and if in fact specie payments had been suspended during the war, we should not have recommended their resumption."[85] The counterfactual caveat—"if . . . specie payments had been suspended"—reconciled Bradbury's old position with the new. It signaled that Bradbury would no longer insist upon imposing that obligation, even as he demurred from being the one to severe those ties now. Instead, he left that world-historic role to Norman.

Thus, Keynes was right: the Chamberlain-Bradbury Committee report was a mess. It was clearly written by a group of individuals in the midst of a reformation. When compared to reports of the Cunliffe Committee, the confusion is multiplied. These were the same individuals answering essentially the same questions across just a few pages, across just a few years. And yet it was impossible to pin down these men on the means, the methods, the modes, the metrics, and the models that were their "orthodoxy." From their views on the interplay of ideational and material variables in markets to the relationship between exchange rates and domestic price levels, most of the major elements were inconstant. Other things—like the UK's minimum reserve threshold—never shifted, even as the monetary conditions evolved significantly. In other words, elements within the "orthodoxy" that ought not to have changed did, and elements within the "orthodoxy" that ought to have changed did not. Such contortion was inevitable as the orthodoxy clung to the shifting tectonic plates of the interwar economic order.

But one must not confuse the reformation of a church with a loss of faith in the religion. Did Martin Luther destroy Christianity, or did he save it? Did Pope John XXIII destroy Catholicism, or did he save it? Did John Bradbury destroy the gold standard, or did he save it?

Of course, the tenets of the new orthodoxy were anything but clear: We ought to restore the gold standard as quickly as possible and impose whatever painful deflation is necessary—that is, by our deeds we earn salvation. But we also ought to wait to receive the grace of American inflation and the increase of the global gold supply—that is, we are saved by faith alone.

But whatever the apparent contradictions, the essential axiom remained: "The assimilation of British currency to the gold currencies of the world is so necessary for the ultimate prosperity of British trade that any temporary disadvantage, if such arise, from the measures necessary to maintain parity will be many times outweighed."[86] Gold shall be our savior. And it is a just and a merciful god.

# Chapter 14

# Deposition and Coronation

Norman returned to England in January, arriving at Paddington Station the evening of January 20, 1925. The next day he was back at the Bank, working to sell his colleagues on the collaborative scheme arranged with the Americans. He spent most of the next week in similar fashion, bouncing between the Bank and the Treasury.[1] Bradbury was sufficiently uncomfortable with Norman's ever-growing proposed US loan that he reconvened the Chamberlain-Bradbury Committee so as to interview Norman formally. With the fourth draft of its report in hand, Bradbury invited Norman to testify on January 28th. Norman's colleagues at the Bank were similarly chary, and so they sent Addis along with Norman to the interview.[2]

But resistance to Norman's conquest proved futile. The Keynes critique had undermined the prewar orthodoxy too deeply. Even the Chamberlain-Bradbury Committee was no longer willing to defend it. Thus, the incumbent sovereign had fled, and Norman's march on that vacant throne proved unstoppable. The likes of Bradbury, Addis, and Niemeyer could only hope to shape his reign following his glorious revolution.

# Why Now?

As with the Chamberlain-Bradbury Committee's report, the first question for Norman was to explain the sudden reversal on the prescribed timing of the return. "The great change," Norman explained to the committee, ". . . is the rise in the Dollar exchange [rate]." This had come about both "naturally" and as a result of American benevolence. The United States was determined to "[get] rid of the surplus gold with which they are now encumbered, but . . . [also] they are interested in the prosperity and stability of the world." The massive $500 million loan was the proof of this.[3] But the credit cut both ways. As Norman knew well, the committee members were concerned that the credit might become a crutch, allowing Norman to avoid implementing the orthodox remedies to speculative attacks. So Norman assured them: "It is . . . specially so stated here that the use of this credit would require progressive exports of gold from here and progressive increases in the [interest] rate. . . . Its chief use is intended to be a warning to the speculator all over the world that . . . it would be useless in view of the magnitude of the credit for any attempt . . . to break . . . the Sterling Dollar exchange." These factors, combined with the prospects for "political stability" in the United Kingdom and the United States, made Norman "greatly in favor of a return during this year." At the same time, Norman warned, the golden opportunity might not last: "If we wait a year or two many things may develop and the opportunity may have gone by."[4]

On the question of timing the announcement, Norman wanted to ensure that the US credits were in place and that the Bank was prepared to raise Bank rate as necessary. Previously, Norman had argued—mystifyingly—that announcing a several-year-long extension of the capital controls would inspire confidence in sterling. But now he voiced the sensible view that "there is so much water to run under the bridge during this intervening period that I do not believe any announcement could be made which would carry full conviction." So instead, the return should be announced in April and then gold export resumed the next day. With that, Norman was content to leave the discussion over to Addis.[5]

But Bradbury intervened. He was surely gratified to see Norman coming around to the position that he had been advancing for years. But Norman's inconstancy made for unpredictability, and Bradbury knew better than anyone Norman's zeal for capital controls. So before Bradbury let Norman give the floor to Addis, Bradbury wanted to be sure that Norman was now fully committed to his version of the orthodoxy. Just what did Norman mean when he said that the announcement would make "to all intents and purposes a free [gold] market"? How "general" would the "general license" be? "Should that license be to all and sundry," Bradbury asked the governor, "or would it be sufficient that it is generally understood that whenever the exchange makes it desirable the Bank should itself export gold and sell it in America?" Norman answered the either-or question by choosing both: "It should be a general license to all and sundry in round amounts. I would not give anybody a license for £100 but I would give anybody a license who wished to take say a hundred thousand ounces." One hundred thousand (fine) ounces, at the prewar price, was equivalent to £424,800 (£140 million at the 2020 gold price). Such a license was hardly "general."[6]

And, as Bradbury immediately replied, it was directly counter to the gold standard. "Might not that get you into a slight technical difficulty in regard to specie payments?" Bradbury asked, putting it diplomatically. "Under the law anybody can go to the Bank and obtain sovereigns in exchange for notes. That has not been altered" (thanks to Bradbury's own great efforts in 1914). After all, the 1920 capital controls (that Norman may have helped Baldwin to design) limited the right to export coin and bullion, but it did not suspend convertibility. It did not limit the right to convert banknotes to coin on demand for internal purposes. If Norman did grant a "general license," then the Bank might be inundated with requests from would-be gold exporters to trade their notes for gold sovereigns, which could then be sent abroad. "Might you not get people attempting to take advantage of that right?" Bradbury asked.[7]

Norman's response could not have surprised Bradbury: "I would have that right, I think, limited to gold packed for export and exported thereupon." But this, Bradbury explained, "would entail an alteration in the law"—either limiting specie convertibility or removing the limit on exporting bullion (obtained from the Bank) but retaining the prohibition on the export of coin. Bradbury was surely pleased when Norman chose the latter. But he was sure to confirm that Norman would not propose extending those limitations yet again: "The prohibition of the export of sovereigns would continue," but "that of course would disappear at the end of the year?" Happily, Norman confirmed this. So bullion could be exported starting in April, and then specie, too, could be exported starting in 1926.[8]

The next questions followed naturally: How would exporters get the gold and at what price? Bradbury assumed that "the Bank would sell bar gold freely to anybody who wanted it . . . at the market price, whatever it may be?" "I think so," Norman replied. And this, Bradbury further assumed, "would presumably be in the neighborhood of the Mint price?" "Very close," Norman answered, but added, "I have not thought out the details of that."[9]

That must have been unnerving for Bradbury. Here they were, weeks away from restoring the gold standard after a decade of controls, and the governor of the Bank of England had not yet thought out the practical details of actually redeeming pound notes in gold. Things—rather, personnel—had changed since 1918, when Norman's immediate predecessor had told the Cunliffe Committee that it was "desirable to encourage the public to seek to exchange their notes for gold."[10] Needless to say, Norman was hardly prepared to meet the standard, extolled by Cokayne, of pound-notes-as-gold-warrants.

Why not? There are several explanations. First, Norman had only come around recently to supporting the early resumption of gold exports. It was natural that he had given it rather less thought than had Bradbury. This also followed from Norman's particular gold standard dogma. Among the advocates of the return to gold, gold itself played the smallest role in his regime. And, it happens, Norman did not expect gold to be claimed and exported in any case.

Norman made this last point to the committee himself. The difference in "the relative price levels" of the United States and the United Kingdom "has so far adjusted itself . . . that even if it presented a difficulty six or seven months ago," "if . . . the exchange were maintained about where it is . . . the price levels would come together of their own motion." So it was as simple as ratifying the underlying trend in the market.[11]

This too was a significant departure from the position Norman had maintained several months prior. At that point, he deprecated entirely such use of comparative purchasing power as a metric, insulting Pigou along the way. Now Norman was a great champion of this tool, so much so that it convinced him to change his policy recommendations as well.[12] He did not offer any reasons for the massive—and massively important—change. The committee did not challenge him on this. But Addis, Norman's Bank colleague and alumnus of the Cunliffe Committee, did.

## The Addis Alternative

"[The] only material change that has taken place," Addis began his remarks to the committee, "has been in America and not here." "Internal prices" in the United States, he contended, have not converged as much as the exchange rate movement implied. This was essential. While "nobody doubt[ed]," "the capacity to return to the gold standard," the persistent distance in the domestic price levels imperiled "your capacity to maintain [the gold standard] after you have reached it." Of course, he was as eager as anyone to see the gold standard restored. But "all of us . . . who have advocated during the last two years a return to the gold standard at the earliest possible moment never had any other idea than that the earliest possible moment was when the conditions were such as to give a reasonable prospect of something like equilibrium being maintained between the relative price levels." Addis admitted that relative purchasing power is "extremely hard to measure." But "the variety of the index numbers which are used to advance the views of one party or the other are so diverse" that he hesitated to "[rely] upon them as a sign that the conditions necessary for the return to the gold standard have been reached."[13]

Addis thus advised caution. He wanted to see the capital controls maintained through the end of 1925. And if the government insisted upon liberalizing movements now, he pressed them to restrict the right to export to a "special and not a general license," one "for the Bank of England only to export gold." Bradbury being Bradbury, he masterfully encapsulated Addis's position: "Your view [is] . . . that the change in the conditions during the last four months is not sufficient fundamentally to justify any departure from the policy we were disposed to recommend on the subject." "Yes," Addis replied. "It is not yet proven." He was right: Norman's new faith in the convergence of price levels was not yet proven.[14]

Addis more than disdained Norman's pursuit of a credit from the United States. Indeed, he had not a positive thing to say about it. There was obviously the prudential concern of "heaping up a debt in the United States." The danger, however, followed from "the temptation to rely upon this credit when . . . more drastic measures were necessary." If they used the credit, "you would have not only an artificial rate of exchange . . . [but you also] might have an artificial bank rate." But even if it were not used, "the mere fact of your having recourse to this credit would interfere with the play of the ordinary market forces which alone can determine the true rate of exchange." This "would not only . . . [prolong] the period when your market would have arrived at a state of equilibrium but [render] it more and more difficult to get back to that state." Addis put it bluntly: "If anybody . . . were to tell me at the outset that he might have to fall back upon a credit I should regard that as a sign of weakness." This was just the argument that Pigou and Bradbury had advanced so forcefully on the Cunliffe Committee; and they did not challenge Addis's logic here.[15]

Addis must have known that Norman would not give up on obtaining the US loan so easily. But the government's announcement—and the Bank's subsequent course of action—could still parade orthodoxy. "The way to produce conviction," Addis insisted, "is to make your statement without ambiguity, without equivocation, in such a way that nobody can misunderstand it, then— and far more important—to support it by the appropriate customary action of the Bank of England which everybody understands." Then "it would become obvious that the object of raising the Bank rate was not to fix the rate of exchange but to frustrate the attempts of speculators to drive it down by any serious amount such as 10 percent." "Otherwise," he added, "I can see no harm in allowing the rate of exchange to continue its own course until you take the final plunge." Evidently, the Cunliffe Committee dogma was alive and well within the body of the Bank of England, if not at its head.[16]

Addis told the committee that he and Norman were "entirely at one" "on the general principle" and "in regard to the general aim." But to clarify the differences in the approach, he "state[d] them as frankly and crudely as possible," "put[ting] them in their baldest form." The contrast was bald, to say the least. Norman wanted to begin liberalizing gold flows in the spring, and Addis wanted to keep the capital controls in place for at least another year, perhaps even longer than that, unless "nothing untoward happens."[17]

The committee was particularly worried by that last proviso. While the government might make even the strongest of declarations in the spring, it was hardly a credible commitment to undertake potentially difficult action the following winter. Talk was cheap, after all, and with the last government falling after less than a year, one knew how quickly the political winds could shift.

Moreover, Addis's relatively "bearish" position would have immediate effects on the market. So Bradbury asked about those psychological factors that Norman had emphasized so heavily. Was the recent rise in the pound-dollar exchange rate "to any extent due to a general impression that there will be an early return to the gold standard?" There was some, Addis agreed, "but I think that effect is greatly exaggerated." This too was a return to the materialism of the Cunliffe Committee dogma.[18]

And Bradbury knew it well. He confirmed Addis's position: "The right policy . . . [is] to arrange money rates [so] as to secure the necessary conditions for a stable exchange. That is to say, equality of price levels by a gold basis in these countries within . . . the next nine months?" Addis agreed. Then came the key question: "There you and the Governor entirely agree?" "Entirely agree." Addis was happy to say so, and the Committee was happy to hear it.[19]

But Norman did not quite agree that they agreed.

## Norman's Last Word

Predictably, Norman's greatest disagreement with his colleagues arose over the question of the credit. "I rather differ from Sir Charles," Norman told the committee, "in thinking that the belief in the minds of the industrialists here and others that the credit exists will cause them to be more lenient in opposing the policy of high rates which will be necessary here in any event." The

formulation was a little clumsy, but the committee heard the refrain that orthodoxy demands: "The policy of high rates . . . will be necessary here in any
event." They pressed Norman to make a robust commitment to treating Bank
rate increases as the first, if not the only, line of defense. Norman acceded to
this, suggesting that the chancellor formally instruct him, "Until you have lost
X millions of your gold the credit is not to be used." Some, such as Farrer, were
still not entirely satisfied. But the loans were already largely negotiated. What
more could Norman do than commit not to use them?[20]

Next, there was confusion over the question of foreign lending. Bradbury
repeated the old line, taken by the Cunliffe Committee, that the solution to
"excessive foreign lending" was "returning to a gold standard." Ostensibly, Norman agreed: "With no regulator . . . [such as] the gold standard the difficulty
of preventing too great an amount of foreign loans . . . would be greater than
we can manage by persuasion." So far, so good. On this, Norman would have
agreed even with Cokayne: easy money had led to the UK lending too much
abroad, and moral suasion alone could not fully dissuade UK lenders and investors from sending the money abroad.[21]

But Norman's next line came out of nowhere. "The continuance of the
managed pound," he said, "would mean that lending to foreign countries could
not be prevented merely by persuasion as has been done during the last few
months."[22] What did he possibly mean by this? The "managed pound" presumably included the restrictions on gold export. But those gold export restrictions did not encourage gold outflows; it prevented them. It also did not
prevent from the Bank from also using moral suasion as well. Never mind that
this was precisely the opposite of Norman's claim a few months earlier that
announcing the extension of the capital controls would increase confidence
and spark the purchase of sterling. This position, on its face, did not make
sense.

Certainly it confused Pigou, who then jumped in. Perhaps Norman was
thinking of a context in which the pound was again sliding? But in that case,
"would not the fall in the exchange itself prevent these foreign loans?" he asked.
This was basic exchange rate theory: if, and as, the pound depreciates, the incentive to move from sterling to other currencies declines. That is one of the
"automatic" elements of the gold standard system. But Norman responded,
"No, there are so many people who want sterling, that are accustomed to borrow here; they want their sterling here. . . . [So] whatever the exchange is,
within reason, they will come here, if they are allowed to do so." This only
confused Pigou further. Did this not just contradict the prior statement? Perhaps more important, had Norman just switched from describing foreign loans
to now describing foreigners who want to borrow to have "their sterling here"?

So Pigou followed up: "He borrows in sterling, what does he do with his loan? Use it in England?" But Norman would not be pinned down. "To a certain extent," he replied, "or to pay off floating debt in his own country which has a depreciated currency or to purchase goods here." The money might be used here. Or it might be sent abroad. Norman could not say. He continued, "I am clear that without a return to gold the present persuasive method of preventing foreign loans could not be indefinitely continued." This statement was indeed clear, but it strained credulity: without removing the legal limit on the export of gold, the Bank of England would not be able to dissuade bankers from lending abroad. So the Bank's ability to discourage foreign lending is increased by granting private banks the legal right to defy the expressed wishes of the Bank of England? And this, from one of the foremost advocates of those very capital controls?[23]

In the midst of this, Bradbury astutely but unhelpfully broached the question of speculation. "The inducement to the foreigner to borrow in London . . . when the exchange is within 1.5 percent of parity," he suggested, "is a great deal stronger than it was when the sterling was at 20 percent discount because in the expectation of sterling going to par he had a premium of 26 percent to pay." This was a reasonable perspective: traders were doing their borrowing now, while the perceived exchange rate risk was low. But it was also possible that speculators thought, as Addis did, that temporary shifts in US policy had led to an unsustainable appreciation of the pound. In that case, they could be happy to borrow in London while the pound was strong, betting that the real burden of their obligations would soon fall as the pound slid from these heights. In June, Norman had given a small homily on the speculators, explaining their thinking and insisting upon their pivotal importance. On this occasion, though, he said nothing about them.[24]

Norman's statements here must have proved immensely frustrating precisely because the issue was such an important one. For Pigou and Bradbury, the point about the "foreign lending" was not about the nationality of the borrowers. The key question was whether the money borrowed in London was, net, sent abroad. If it were, it would create downward pressure on the exchange rate and ultimately the gold reserves. This might be fine in a context in which the classical gold standard was fully operational. The depreciation of the exchange rate would act as a natural (real) buffering mechanism, any gold outflows would trigger the monetary authorities to contract the money supply, and this would cause prices to fall. But, of course, the gold standard was not operational in numerous ways, and, as Addis suggested, the real picture was "obscured" as a result. The price of gold, the pound-dollar exchange rate, and the calculations of purchasing power parity were all dissociated. Certainly, things were not operating in the 1920s as anyone imagined they had done before the war. So Bradbury and Pigou sought to get Norman's perspective on the factors driving one major component of the UK's balance of payments: the capital account. Did the governor of the Bank of England expect that, with free capital movement and the current monetary situation, the UK would over the course of the next year find that capital would tend to flow into, or out of, the UK? Addis had been clear that without tightening policy, the pressure would tend to be outward. As before, Norman had answered this dichotomous question with, essentially, "Both."

To be sure, these are immensely hard questions. Who can say what moves the market today, let alone what will move it twelve months hence? Pigou, Bradbury, and Addis were all willing to admit this and yet still make predictions and offer prescriptions from a comparatively durable set of principles. Norman, however, was incredibly inconstant. Of course, the facts changed, but sometimes even within the span of a few sentences Norman changed his approach, his analysis, his conclusions, and his recommendations. Yet he spoke with uncommon confidence and, sometimes, arresting certainty. Perhaps he was being cagey, deliberately conflating foreigners who borrow to spend in the UK with loans drawn in the UK for foreign investments, so as to bewilder Pigou and Bradbury.[25] Perhaps he did not understand the queries or their significance. Or perhaps he simply misspoke and could not bring himself to admit it.

All of this discussion played out in a particular context. The orthodoxy preached self-reliance and restraint in lending abroad, particularly in difficult times. In short, the orthodoxy celebrated national self-help. Norman had always rejected this as a matter of principle. This question of foreign lending—specifically, Norman's unconventional loan to Schacht—had prompted the sharpest rebukes on both sides. Since then, Norman had continued to work assiduously to arrange loans to Germany both in, and apart from, the Dawes discussions. So the committee did not take seriously his suggestion that he had tried to dissuade foreign lending. When members decried the excessive foreign lending, they were criticizing Norman's particular endeavors. Simply put, they did not want Norman lending to the Germans and borrowing from the Americans. This was not the English orthodox way.

All knew that they were at an impasse. So Bradbury and Pigou gave up getting a clear answer on this. Instead, Pigou simply agreed with Norman that if moral suasion were proving ineffective, "you would have to put up the discount rate higher to have the same effect."[26]

Norman then steered the conversation to the potentially thorny issue of retiring the Treasury's Bradbury notes. Luckily, the committee proved obliging. Norman asked, and was granted, leave to defer the Bank's obligation to manage these notes until the end of 1927. This would provide the perspective needed to determine the appropriate size of the fiduciary (non-gold-backed) currency issue. It would also save the Bank from this additional concern while it was busy defending the exchange rate. This timeline was a vestige of the Cunliffe Committee, and the Chamberlain-Bradbury Committee was pleased to settle with Norman on it.[27]

Feeling, perhaps, that he had worn the committee down, Norman then reopened the discussion of the capital controls. As if the narrowness of his "general license" were not enough, Norman also wanted to impose extensive restrictions on the holding of actual gold outside of the Bank of England. During "the early times," Norman said, while "we are trying to get back and maintain the gold standard," he thought that "there should [not] be anything but a central reserve of gold." "I do not think it should be free to the other banks to hold gold in their reserves or in their tills or to encourage the circulation of gold in the provinces," he added. Niemeyer asked whether he meant "prevented by statute or merely discouraged." As ever, Norman found a way to not answer the question. "I know the Cunliffe Committee said discouraged," but "I think more than discouraged."[28]

Even at this point, the ever-patient Bradbury was still willing to search for common ground. Perhaps the committee could distinguish between private banks' drawing gold directly from the Bank of England and buying gold on the London market. Norman thought "they should do neither." Bradbury tried to assure Norman that the large banks had committed not to hoard gold. But Norman "[did] not think that [went] far enough." So Pigou repeated the original question: "You would have a definite law or a tax on the gold they hold?" Norman just repeated himself again: "The reserve of gold should be at the central bank and for a number of years there should be as little gold as possible in circulation and no gold in their pockets." The interchange was repeated almost verbatim, after which Bradbury tried to break the logjam. "What is the machinery by which you can secure that?" he asked. He then explained precisely why Norman's position proved so problematic: "You can hardly conceive of asking Parliament to pass an Act to say nobody shall have gold in their possession except the Bank," Norman conceded. If "people wish to have sovereigns in their pockets . . . they must have them."[29]

While this might seem to be the best of both worlds, the committee knew that it would prove unworkable. Farrer asked, "Supposing the exchange fell to [the] gold export point and I were to come to you with fifty millions of . . . Treasury notes, have [you] considered whether you would take those fifty millions from the currency reserve or from the Bank of England?" Norman simply replied, "No. I have not considered that." Niemeyer asked if "the right of anybody to take the gold to the Mint to be coined would remain." Again, Norman "had not contemplated it one way or the other."[30]

These were not really questions about private citizens. After all, how many individuals were likely to bring £50 million to the Bank? The committee was asking Norman how he would make these capital controls effective so long as the banknote-to-specie loophole existed. It is telling that, again, Norman could not (or would not) walk the committee through the practical working of gold itself in his prescribed system. Now we see why more clearly. Norman had intended gold to play zero role in "the gold standard" at home. And if Addis were right, Norman also intended to use the credit to minimize its role internationally as well. It is remarkable just how much had changed in this church of England's since it was run by Cunliffe and Cokayne. So too is it remarkable how little had changed in the perennial debate between Bradbury and Norman over capital controls.

In this case, the committee was relieved that Norman had not thought practically about how to remove gold from circulation. Being "old-fashioned," as Bradbury had put it, they thought it would not do to make the pound into an inconvertible paper currency and call that maneuver a "restoration of the gold standard." So it is fitting that the last question brought the discussion back to the defining issue: the removal of the gold export embargo. Unsurprisingly, Farrer was still confused about Norman's position on the essential question: "Would [he] prefer a general license for everyone . . . or confine it to the Bank of England?" Norman answered simply, "I had thought of a general license." Indeed, it would be a "general" license issued at enormous cost to only a select few to export something they were not allowed to possess themselves.[31]

## Alloyage

Sweeping accounts of "capital," "the City," or even "the Bank of England" miss the real richness of the processes by which the monetary order was transformed. We can make a start by decomposing the alloy that emerged, the combination of beliefs and practices that became the new gold standard. But those constituent components are not themselves irreducible, stable elements. It is not as simple as three parts Norman plus one part Addis, inflamed by Keynes in the crucible of the Chamberlain-Bradbury Committee. The views, like several of the figures who advanced them, were not simply mercurial but positively volatile. The appearance of two Bank emissaries arguing vigorously with each other and reconstructing their observations, models, and prescriptions in real time is perhaps the best proof that the Old Lady of Threadneedle

Street was schizophrenic. The disconcerting reality is that there was no singular Bank-of-England position on the return to gold at this most pivotal moment. That Leviathan was as variable as the people who comprised her.

But even if the Bank had issued a single position, it wanted reconciliation with the views of the Chamberlain-Bradbury Committee. Having served with Bradbury, Pigou, and Farrer on the Cunliffe Committee, we might expect Addis to have fallen into line with the Chamberlain-Bradbury Committee's approach to Norman. If political economy were as simple as the binaries of labor and capital or even the continuum of left and right, that might have proved true. But as this was the realm of religious faith, there are as many dimensions as there were adherents. That Bradbury, Pigou, Farrer, and Addis all signed the text of the Cunliffe Committee reports simply meant that they had constructed together sufficient ambiguity, at those moments, to don the same robes. But each remained "orthodox" in his own way.

Addis clung to the materialism of the Cunliffe Committee dogma. For him, the exchange rate was the tail, and the domestic price level was the dog. The only real solution was to bring the note-to-gold ratio back into line with something approaching the prewar rate. Of course, the UK could economize on the use of gold in various ways, with some (Cunliffe) wanting to use less conventional means than others (Bradbury and Pigou). But the monetary authority was still shackled to the same causal chain: gold→ money supply→ domestic prices→ exchange rates (among true gold standard countries). Thus, it was fallacious to target the exchange rate by manipulating market psychology, as Norman advocated. Similarly, there could be no internationalist recourse, no operating the system through inter-central-bank collaboration the way that Norman was attempting to do with his German loans and American borrowing.

Thus, compared to Norman, Addis was far more orthodox in his analysis. And he asked the hard questions about the dissociation between the domestic price levels in the United States and the United Kingdom, the pound-dollar exchange rate, and the gold price. But he came to the unpleasant conclusion that the UK was not remotely close to sustaining the pound at the prewar parity. Of course, it was possible to get to that point, and, in orthodox fashion, Addis was sure that it would be worth doing so. But the adjustment required was massive, and it would take time.

Bradbury might have been willing to accept this as the economic reality. But it proved perilous politically. It proved so *not* because there were concerns about backlash, least of all from Labour or labor. After all, Snowden was about to goad Churchill for dragging his feet. The producers, all told, maintained their faith in the final, golden salvation.

The actual political constraint was created by the Bank of England. For years, the Bank had been pumping the brakes on the return. Bradbury might have thought that this had been due to Norman's supporting capital controls and then keeping Bank rate relatively low despite the dictates of the Cunliffe Committee's reports. But now Norman had reversed his position. Insofar as Addis was sent to speak for the other perspective within the Bank, it became clear that Norman was suddenly the strongest advocate of an early return. Addis's support for delay now, and his refusal to rule out further delays subsequently, surely gave Bradbury pause. He had seen this before: one temporary extension of the capital controls leads to another. Thus, the Addis alternative, however purely conceived, was not an option for Bradbury.

But it was not as simple as the perfect (Addis) standing as enemy to the good (Norman). As Bradbury saw it, Norman's record was highly questionable and his means, thoroughly impure. From the capital controls to Norman's pursuit of a credit, Bradbury had plenty of reason for doubt. It also seemed that Norman's ideal "gold standard" was still leagues away from that envisioned by Bradbury. Despite promising a "general license" to export gold, Norman *still* wanted significant impediments to getting and moving gold. Norman's was a system of essentially irredeemable paper currencies managed by like-minded central bankers using interpersonal trust and interbank lending to thwart speculators and ostensibly to achieve some level of exchange-rate stability. It was a system in which gold movements (and the gold price) were controlled by monetary policy rather than vice versa. It was, largely, the system that Keynes would propose at Bretton Woods. And, arguably, it was the "system [that] worked" in the wake of the 2008 Global Financial Crisis.[32] Yet, in 1925, Bradbury greeted Norman's reforms about as happily as Pope Leo X received Martin Luther's Ninety-five Theses.

But Bradbury was not the pontiff; and so what could he do? Does one expect him to champion the Bank dissenters, who came to a damning prescription for the right reasons, against Norman, who now finally embraced the blessed prescription albeit using impure logic? What would it profit Bradbury to gain the whole Bank but lose its governor?

In the end, Norman's was the gold standard that the Chamberlain-Bradbury Committee could have. And so, like the Immortal Seven of 1688, they invited Norman to save their country. They hoped (prayed) that they could temper the invader's authority and secure his commitment to a new constitution. But they knew that this was not assured, and so they gambled that coronating a new Protestant sovereign was preferable to further indulgence of Catholic debasement.

# CHAPTER 15

# The Sanhedrin

## Churchill's Trials

Given the terrible consequences of England's "return to gold" in 1925, the conventional wisdom is that Churchill, as chancellor of the exchequer, was either a fool or a knave. Many contemporaries and some subsequent scholars have questioned Churchill's financial acumen. Following Leith-Ross and Boyle, Moggridge concludes, "Churchill does not seem to have entered the Treasury with any rigid ideas on financial policy or technical matters." Although Churchill might have "accepted this ignorance," he nonetheless remained a "burden" who "required extensive justifications for every step he had to take."[1]

Both characterizations are unfair to Churchill. His ignorance on these matters, which he habitually averred, was almost certainly overstated—perhaps strategically so. Leith-Ross later reflected, "Many of Churchill's queries . . . were in the nature of chimeras which took a certain amount of trouble . . . but they often represented original ideas that needed consideration."[2] His interactions with policy experts in the winter of 1924–1925 demonstrate both exceptional familiarity with the debate and a strong intuition for the politics of exchange rates.

Indeed, so far from discounting the employment implications of his decision, Churchill actually embraced the gold standard precisely because he thought it would *decrease* unemployment. Churchill seriously engaged Keynes's attacks on the gold standard. That critique, however, focused on the tendency of the gold standard to generate transitional unemployment, whereas Churchill was concerned with the UK's chronic unemployment. As such, Churchill recognized that restoring the gold standard entailed transition costs that might well exacerbate unemployment in the short run. But, desperate to address the root of the UK's postwar woes, Churchill took the gamble that returning to gold would ultimately resolve this problem in the long run.

## Churchill Discovers Gold

At first blush, Churchill's decision to return to the gold standard in 1925 at the prewar parity appears to have been inevitable. His trademark conservative orientation almost certainly predisposed him to favor a "restoration" as such. Even Keynes admitted that the pound's unmatched record of international stability stood as a strong symbol of British financial hegemony. And no one paid greater homage to the symbols of British imperialism than did Winston Churchill. Moreover, the Conservative Party's most powerful constituencies—those of finance and trade—had significant economic interests aligned with the restoration. Last, virtually every major newspaper took the restoration for granted.[3]

Return was indeed Churchill's starting point. In December 1924, shortly after Baldwin had appointed him (unexpectedly) chancellor, Churchill wrote to the prime minister, "The Governor of the Bank will . . . have told you . . . about the imminence of our attempt to re-establish the gold standard, in connection with which he is now going to America. It will be easy to attain the gold standard, and indeed almost impossible to avoid taking the decision, but to keep it will require a most strict policy of debt repayment and a high standard of credit. To reach it and have to abandon it would be disastrous."

As the balance of the letter makes clear, Churchill meant "disastrous" politically (for the Conservatives) as well as economically (for the country). He resisted increasing naval expenditures, which, he insisted, could only come by sacrificing tax cuts "and practically all plans of social reform during the whole lifetime of the present Parliament." He warned Baldwin, "I cannot conceive any course more certain to result in a Socialist victory. If the Socialists win in a tremendous economy wave, they will cut down and blot out all these Naval preparations so that in the end the Admiralty will not get the Navy program for the sake of which your Government will have broken itself."[4] Yet when he got down to the technical business of actually restoring the gold standard, Churchill soon realized that "attaining" the gold standard might be more fraught than he had anticipated.

# Mr. Churchill's Exercise

## The Exercise

Churchill began the business of organizing the return to gold in January 1925. Assuming that the return was a foregone conclusion, he initially set about merely to preempt potential criticism. By the end of January, he had absorbed much of the heterodoxy. He deployed these arguments in a memorandum targeted at the top mandarins in HM Treasury and the Bank.[5] "If we are to . . . remov[e] the embargo on gold export," he explained, "it is essential that we should be prepared to answer any criticisms which may be subsequently made upon our policy. I should like to have set out in writing the counter-case to the following argument."[6]

This "argument" was, in effect, a distillation of Keynes's *Tract on Monetary Reform*. Churchill began by restating Keynes's infamous characterization of the gold standard as a "barbarous relic."[7] He posited, "A Gold Reserve and the Gold Standard are in fact survivals of rudimentary and transitional stages in the evolution of finance and credit." Pointing to the United Kingdom's greater relative stability (vis-à-vis that of the United States) over the last three years, Churchill proposed that domestic credit and price stability did not depend on exchange rate stability. Likewise, British credit abroad depended on financial policy and the health of trade.[8]

Second, Churchill followed Keynes in suggesting that restoring the gold standard might benefit the United States more than it did the United Kingdom. He also queried whether the costs of maintaining the standard would be symmetric between the two states.[9]

Third, Churchill offered an alternative proposal. Rather than using the Bank of England's gold reserves to maintain a given exchange rate, he suggested committing £100 million of those reserves to an immediate payment on the war debt. Not only would this reduce the debt burden, he hypothesized, but it would also trigger a rise in American prices, which would make British trade more competitive abroad.[10] This was largely the same proposal that Norman had advanced at the beginning of 1923. It probed the orthodoxy's commitment to that old assumption that gold flows automatically (via the Humean price-specie-flow mechanism) drive changes in the money supply and thus prices. To deny this would be to admit Keynes's argument that the Federal Reserve had effectively replaced its gold standard with a dollar standard.

Fourth, Churchill pressed the recipients to think beyond the matters of mere finance. He chided them: "The whole question of a return to the Gold Standard must not be dealt with only upon its financial and currency aspects.

The merchant, the manufacturer, the workman and the consumer have interests which, though largely common, do not by any means exactly coincide either with each other or with the financial and currency interests." The consequent rise in Bank rate was more than a mere "inconvenience." It would issue "a very serious check" on trade and employment. Thinking again in Keynes's terms about the political repercussions of the policy, Churchill cautioned that a return to gold was open to the charge that the government had "favored the special interests of finance at the expense of the special interests of production." Eager to find a way to sell the policy, Churchill insisted that this risk must be negated by "very plain and solid advantages."[11]

Fifth, Churchill questioned the urgency of the policy shift. Why now? As he suggested, the export prohibition had been in place for several years and through several different governments. Of course, the policy was not due to expire for nearly a year. How, he asked, was one to justify the urgency?[12]

This gave rise to his final polemic. Given that the United States was so eager to help the UK return to gold, perhaps the UK should delay and demand better terms. Moreover, Churchill invoked the concerns of some that the difficulties of the return could diminish the UK's relative financial position.[13]

The recipients were less than enthused with the chancellor's seemingly pedestrian "exercise." Bradbury questioned Churchill's faith. Writing to Niemeyer, he did not mask his hostility, "The writer of the memorandum appears to have his spiritual home in the Keynes-McKenna sanctuary, but some of the trimmings of his mantle have been furnished by the 'Daily Express.'"[14]

It was a cutting, dismissive remark. But it is hardly surprising. As we have seen, no single individual had done more to effect this return to gold. From his work on the postwar planning committees through to his eventual chairing of the Chamberlain-Bradbury Committee, Bradbury had fought countless battles to see a very specific set of ideas enshrined as "the gold standard." No sooner had he convinced the governor of the Bank of England than he faced losing the chancellor of the exchequer. Was this blustering buffoon—born to privilege with precisely zero financial experience—going to destroy the plans he had laid for nearly a decade, just because Keynes could turn a phrase? Bradbury would not hear of it. And so he prepared to wage yet another campaign in his crusade.

We can understand Bradbury's perturbation. He earned that much. But was he right about Churchill? What was really driving the Chancellor to insist upon explicit refutations of Keynes's arguments?

At this point, Churchill probably did sympathize with Keynes's perspective. But just as much, it seems to have been driven by a careful rhetorical calculus. As he explained, "In setting down these ideas and questionings I do not wish it to be inferred that I have arrived at any conclusions adverse to the re-establishment of the Gold Standard. On the contrary I am ready and anxious to be convinced as far as my limited comprehension of these extremely technical matters will permit. But I expect to receive good and effective answers to the kind of case which I have, largely as an exercise, indicated in this note." Reading between the lines, it would seem that Churchill sought counterarguments—prepared responses that could be deployed to defend the government's decision. Churchill wanted ammunition as much as he wanted explanations.[15]

In this light, Churchill appears to have been far savvier than the members of the Chamberlain-Bradbury Committee. Whereas they had spent the last two months debating among themselves the finer points of the transition they sought to undertake—How general should they make the license to export gold?—Churchill was focused on explaining and justifying the endgame to other policymakers and to the British people. Churchill rightly understood that this could not be done—and the return not successfully sustained—without responding to the robust, convincing arguments issued by Keynes in his *Tract*. Having witnessed the public floggings that comprise *The Economic Consequences of the Peace*, Churchill must have wanted to ensure he was prepared to defend himself.

## Otto Niemeyer, HM Treasury

Much of Keynes's criticism of the proposed return to gold in his *Tract* turned on the premise that the "ancient standard" was a mere "barbarous relic" that had become "remote . . . from the spirit and the requirements of the [present] age."[16] Keynes strategically used this characterization to demonstrate both the viability of his alternative "regulated nonmetallic standard" and to emphasize the costs that would be involved in going all the way back to gold at the pre-war price. Churchill understood this, which is why he began his "exercise" with the rhetorical challenge that the gold standard was passé. This assumption became the main point of contention among the respondents to the chancellor's queries.

Citing the promises made by "Governments of all political shades" to return to gold, Niemeyer insisted that markets at home and abroad had come to count on the restoration of the prewar standard in the UK.[17] Prices, exchange rates, and capital movements, he argued, had all adjusted based on the expectation that the UK would be back on gold by the end of 1925. These expectations combined not only to lower the cost of returning to gold but also to raise the cost of a failure to do so. Niemeyer prophesied:

It would reverberate throughout a world which has not forgotten the uneasy moments of the winter of 1923; and would be the more convinced that we never meant business about the gold standard because our nerve had failed when the stage was set. The immediate consequence would be a considerable withdrawal of balances and investment (both foreign and British) from London; a heavy drop in Exchange; and, to counteract that tendency, a substantial increase in Bank rate. We might very easily reap all the disadvantages which some fear from a return to gold without any of the advantages. With the engine thus reversed, no one could foretell when conditions, political, psychological, economic, would be such that the opportunity would occur again.[18]

Niemeyer's claim that failing to return to gold could indirectly cause a rise in interest rates was a potent rejoinder to Keynes's predictions that high interest rates, deflation, and unemployment would be the necessary casualties on the road back to gold. Citing the forthcoming Chamberlain-Bradbury Committee report, Niemeyer suggested instead that the return "*may* involve a temporary increase in Bank rate." Niemeyer himself added the emphasis on "may."[19]

What of the UK's position as an international financial center? Niemeyer acknowledged that the United States had a considerable share of the world's gold supply. He cited the UK's substantial reserves and stressed that the British Empire was one of the primary producers of gold in the world. Additionally, the increasing movement of other countries back toward gold meant that if sterling were to remain a leading currency in international settlements, it too must be undergirded by a firm commitment to the gold standard. British financial interests, Niemeyer argued, could only be served by a prompt return to gold.[20]

The same was true for the UK's trade sector. "As a great exporting nation," Niemeyer wrote, we "are vitally interested in stable exchanges. With [the] United States, Germany and the main Dominions on gold, we cannot afford to fluctuate in relation to their prices." "Everyone upholds the gold standard, because they believe it to be proved by experience to be best for trade," he argued. Of course, Keynes himself had made these very arguments as few as fifteen months prior. "If it is agreed that we must have the gold standard," Niemeyer asked rhetorically, "is it not better to get over any discomforts at once and then proceed on an even keel rather than have the dislocation . . . still before us?"[21]

Restoring trade, according to Niemeyer, was the key to ensuring the health of the British economy. "No one," Niemeyer argued, "believes that unemployment can be cured by the dole, and palliatives like road digging." He continued: "Every party—not least Labour—has preached that unemployment can only be dealt with by radical measures directed to the economic restoration of trade. . . . On a long view—and it is only such views that can produce fundamental cures—the gold standard is in direct succession to the main steps towards economic reconstruction . . . and is likely to do more for British trade than all the efforts of the Unemployment Committee."[22]

Things were simple for Niemeyer. The British economy needs trade, and trade requires exchange rate stability. Thus, the UK must return to gold.

## John Bradbury

Of course, it was not quite so simple as that. Bradbury did admit that "the scientific advocates of the 'managed pound'"—like Keynes and McKenna—were not mere "inflationists," as were the typical opponents of the gold standard. He acknowledged that it might be possible to devise an alternative system of international settlement comprised of independent, "managed" currencies. He strongly doubted, however, that gold would be removed at any point in the near future from its privileged role as the final means of settlement. In other words, Keynes's vision may be possible, but at this point it was untenable.[23]

Bradbury also questioned whether "managed pounds" could even achieve the internal price stability Keynes prized so dearly. Gold, Bradbury pointed out, fluctuates relatively little in the short term, ensuring predictable price levels for economies that stabilize the value of the currency around the price of gold. "Managed pounds" could only work "if the index on which you work contains a smaller margin of error than the amount by which the real value of gold fluctuates." While it was possible in theory to better stabilize the price level, Bradbury was skeptical that the required index could be produced given the state of the art at that time.[24]

Finally, Bradbury challenged the Keynes claim that adjustment back to gold would be painful and costly. He insisted that the gap between British and American prices was small: "not more than 2% or 3%." Additionally, returning to gold would do so much to restore confidence in the pound that foreign investors would send their capital to London. Bradbury went so far as to suggest that he would "not be at all surprised if very shortly after the restoration of the free gold market a period of cheap money and easy credit becomes necessary to repel an influx of unwanted gold."[25]

## R. G. Hawtrey, HM Treasury

Hawtrey's response followed similar lines. He was, however, more focused on the international dimension of the decision than any of Churchill's other advisers. Pointing to the Genoa Resolutions (1922), Hawtrey argued that the international community had embraced gold and was prepared to cooperate to see it restored as the international medium of exchange. He suggested that London's position as a major financial center would be eclipsed unless the UK joined those countries returning to gold. Whereas Keynes had attempted to reveal a tension between the objectives of price and exchange rate stability, Hawtrey promised that this new gold standard, widely adopted and cooperatively deployed, would "give [the UK] the best of both worlds—stable prices and stable exchanges."[26]

Like the others, Hawtrey was confident that sterling was already nearly at par with the dollar. He echoed Keynes's prediction that the United States would see continued inflation. But while Keynes suggested that this rendered restoration unnecessary, Hawtrey argued that it lowered the cost of restoring gold, making it a more attractive option. Hawtrey also suggested that this inflation would save the UK from having to suffer deflation to raise the pound to the dollar. "No active measures at all need be taken," he posited. By allowing things to continue on their present course, "the exchange will come to par of itself."[27]

## Montagu Norman

Surprisingly, Norman's response was by far the most "orthodox" of any Churchill received. The use of gold in international interchange, he argued, went beyond mere convention. Gold itself constituted the "liquid reserves" required for international interchange. Following Locke (and, more recently, Schuster), Norman insisted, "Gold is the guarantee of [a government's] 'good faith.'" A state, Norman argued, could do without a "gold reserve and the Gold Standard" no more than it could do without "a Police Force or Tax Collectors." He deprecated the "price-level scheme" of "Irving-Fisher [*sic*] and others." "Now," he insisted, "there is no alternative to Gold in the opinion of educated and reasonable men." "The Gold Standard is the best 'Governor' that can be devised for a world that is still human, rather than divine," Norman concluded.[28]

As ever, Norman insisted upon the importance of "psychological" over "fundamental reasons." "The pound sterling," he suggested, ". . . has advanced greatly because the date of free gold is believed to be at hand." Disappointing these market expectations would prove ruinous: "'The financial reputation of Great Britain' is such that the world believes 1925 means 1925 and Gold in 1925 by Act of Parliament means Gold in 1925 in fact. Any other course means a declining pound." While delaying the return "would shatter our Exchange . . . and our international Banking and Finance, there is no reason to suppose it would permanently benefit Trade and Industry."[29]

Norman was franker than the others about the difficult road ahead. "The restoration of Free Gold *will* require a high Bank rate," he admitted. However, he warned Churchill about casting his lot in the wrong direction: "The Chancellor will surely be charged with a sin of omission or of commission. In the former case (Gold) he will be abused by the ignorant, the gamblers and the antiquated Industrialists; in the latter case (not Gold) he will be abused by the instructed and by posterity."[30]

Norman considered and rejected the suggestion that the UK use its gold reserves to pay down its war debt. This directly contradicted the proposal that he himself had advanced across 1923, prior to the publication of Keynes's *Tract.* Norman explained, "the occasion has passed when it might have been possible to embarrass the U.S. by a congestion of Gold." Implicitly following Keynes, Norman argued, "The Federal Reserve Bank [has] learned how to sterilize any amount of Gold we can send." Norman did not dwell on the contradiction between this contention and the assumptions of the currency committees. Instead, he returned to his (and Keynes's) emphasis on the psychological factors. For Norman, depleting the gold reserves would impugn credibility and eviscerate confidence: "Our Note-circulation would probably be discredited at home (as happened e.g. in Germany); specie payment would have to be formally suspended; Exchange would fall . . . and fall; and the world center would shift permanently and completely from London to New York." This was strong stuff. Even at home, Norman prognosticated, the currency would be abandoned.[31]

So, Norman recommended a quick return to gold, lest the UK be beat to it by rivals. The chancellor, he posited, "could hardly assume office with Free Gold in one country and watch half-a-dozen others attain Free Gold . . . without his own" following suit.[32]

Thus, Churchill's advisers suggested that much of the work of returning to gold had already been done by the promises made by the previous governments and the self-fulfilling expectations of the market. Keynes's suggestion that the "spirit of the age" was anything other than golden was incorrect, and testing this hypothesis would be supremely dangerous.

## Churchill Equivocates, Snowden Commits

Churchill read these memoranda with avidity. He found the replies to be "very able," and the Chamberlain-Bradbury Committee's Report furnished "a solid foundation of argument and authority justifying the action proposed." He told Niemeyer, "Your papers and the Report of the Committee marshaled for the first time . . . arguments for the policy you advocate."[33] Never mind that the Cunliffe Committee reports had made many of the same arguments years prior.

Chancellor Churchill, however, was still not entirely satisfied. He was still perturbed by the heterodox contention that the ultimate basis of belief in gold "might . . . be stated as a vulgar superstition." More important, he raised the issue of the timing of the shift. Writing to Niemeyer and Norman, he reported that Frederick Goodenough, the chairman of Barclay's Bank, supported the return to gold but, as Churchill explained, "would deprecate [the] decision being 'rushed.'" Goodenough suggested instead that the pound should be kept at parity for several months before restoring convertibility.[34]

At the same time, Churchill wrote to Chamberlain, enquiring whether he agreed with the conclusions reached by the Chamberlain-Bradbury Committee after his departure.[35] That Churchill knew well enough to ask is a testament to his political intuition. He did not bother to study the Cunliffe Committee's reports because he knew that the Chamberlain-Bradbury Committee's report, whatever its departures, would supersede those dead letters as the new dogma. But he did want to be sure that the current version of the orthodoxy commanded the complete loyalty of its adherents. He knew better than to take this for granted.

Replying along similar lines, Niemeyer and Chamberlain worked to remove all doubts. They worried that attempting to maintain the currency at the prewar value without a full return to the gold standard would bring all of the challenges but none of the advantages of the old regime. The Bank would have to intervene to manage the currency, but markets would remain unsure of the future of the currency. This would confound planning and encourage unnecessary profit taking. Emphasizing the role of expectations, Chamberlain encouraged Churchill: "I feel sure that, if you make your announcement with decisive confidence . . . the operation will now be found . . . an easy one, and that to delay your decision much longer would be to expose you to a serious risk of a renewed fall in sterling. . . . All the world is now expecting us to return to the gold standard. . . . If we do not do it, we shall not stay where we were but inevitably start a retrograde movement."[36]

Niemeyer's response was even starker. Goodenough's proposed delay "would be fatal." As speculators pounced, "the pound would fall to $4 or less," and the UK would exhaust its loan from the United States. He even suggested that "Bank rate would go to 11% or more."[37]

This was hyperbolic. Bank rate had only gone as high as 10 percent in the 1914 financial crisis. Norman had never taken it higher than 7 percent. At the time, Bank rate was only at 4 percent. But Chamberlain and Niemeyer agreed: Churchill must confirm the market's expectations by announcing an early return.

The same day, Labour's shadow chancellor (Snowden) published an editorial calling for an early return to gold. It was a full-throated defense of the gold standard, specifically designed to put pressure on Churchill. But this was not just a political maneuver. This was a core principle of the labor movement, and Snowden genuinely feared the consequences that would follow if Churchill dithered. "This question of the return to gold," Snowden insisted, "is . . . a very practical matter from the point of view of the welfare of the working classes." Most simply, this was necessary to restart the stagnant export industries. "A stable currency is one of the essentials of a healthy state of trade," Snowden explained. More broadly, the working class was reliant on imports as consumers, and the gold standard was necessary to protect them from "the violent changes [in prices] which are inseparable from unstable currencies." More important, there was no alternative option. Espousing the orthodoxy, Snowden acknowledged that it "may for a time present some difficulties." He was quick to add, however, that "they are small compared with the evils from which the world is suffering as a result of . . . fluctuating currencies. . . . Whatever the future may have in store in the form of some new standard base for stable currency, the time has not come to . . . experiment with any one of innumerable alternatives to the gold standard. The world opinion in favor of the return to the gold basis is too overwhelming for any other course to be accepted." "To restore stability," Snowden concluded, "we must bind the currency to gold."[38]

Here was the Conservatives' chancellor of the exchequer expressing serious skepticism about the gold standard, while the sometime Labour chancellor defended the orthodoxy with aplomb. We know now that Snowden's perspective was blinkered and Churchill's intuition brilliant. Not for nothing, we see Churchill—not Snowden—on our pound notes today. So when we cast our gaze back to 1925, we see Snowden through the lens of the 1930s and Churchill through the lens of the 1940s. But when "Winston"—once again—began to question the conventional wisdom, his colleagues saw the failure behind Gallipoli. Nobody could have known that this time Churchill was years ahead of the pack. After all, doubts had crept into even Keynes's own mind.

## Keynes Compromises His Position

Throughout January and February, Keynes remained unaware of Churchill's mulling over the gold standard. At the same time, sterling's appreciation altered the strategic landscape. In late February, Keynes published "The Return towards Gold" in the *Nation and Athenaeum*. He was "more convinced . . . than before" that "monetary reform" was "the most important and significant measure [the UK] can take to increase economic welfare." Yet he also recognized that the "forces of old custom and general ignorance" both strongly advocated for a return to gold. He admitted that the public was not yet ready to reconsider its age-old assumptions. Instead of continuing the head-on attack, Keynes marshaled a rear-guard action: "This is not a battle which can be won or lost in a day. . . . The issue will be determined not by the official decisions of the coming year, but by the combined effects of the actual experience of what happens after that and the relative clearness and completeness of the arguments of the opposing parties." The statement would prove even more prophetic than Keynes might have hoped.[39]

For now, Keynes sought to live to fight another day. Viewing the restoration as a foregone conclusion, he focused instead on the issue of timing. He now sought to delay and prolong the process of return as much as possible in the hope of extending the period of "managed pounds" and smoothing the transition.

While the tactic seemed sensible at the time, Keynes gave up too much ground to his opponents. In the *Tract*, he had forcefully argued that restoration of the prewar parity could not be accomplished without painful, unemployment-generating deflation. In this latest article, however, Keynes explicitly reframed the issue in such a way that suggested that this deflation might not be necessary after all. "Last year," he wrote, "it was a question of whether it was prudent to hasten matters by deliberate deflation; this year it is a question of whether it is prudent to hasten matters by a removal of the embargo against the export of gold." Throughout this editorial, Keynes appears to have been ambivalent about the effect of restoration on employment. At one point, he even doubted "that a somewhat higher bank rate would do any harm . . . to the volume of trade and employment." By conceding these crucial points, Keynes did more than just undercut his previous argument. He also shrunk the stakes of the decision. If widespread deflation and unemployment were a possible result of returning to gold, any decision to return would warrant a second and, perhaps, third examination. If, on the other hand, the potential cost of restoring the pound were merely the export of gold, the risk inherent in returning was considerably less.[40]

Keynes played further into the hands of the restorationists by pinning his proposals on the expectation of future American inflation. Here his prediction was consistent with that issued in the *Tract*: because American prices are likely to rise, simply maintaining the stability of the pound would bring the pound back toward parity in due course. His emphasis, however, changed entirely. Keynes now insisted that he had "maintained for two years past that a return of sterling, sooner or later, towards its prewar parity would be both a desirable and a probable consequence of a sound monetary policy." Technically, Keynes did suggest in the *Tract* that the values of the currencies would move back toward parity, but he certainly did not argue that it should be managed so as to remain at parity. There, he was quite clear that wherever exchange rate stability came at the cost of domestic price stability, deference ought to be paid to the latter. These arguments—the major conclusions of the *Tract*—were largely bracketed in this editorial, replaced by Keynes's overtures that he too had sought to push sterling back "towards its prewar parity."[41]

Keynes also accepted, for the first time, the restorationists' premise that sterling was within striking distance of achieving parity. He scuttled his familiar warnings about the considerable adjustment costs and claimed simply that maintaining stability would prove challenging. He also followed the restorationists in attributing these circumstances to (at least in part) the markets' responses to the expectation of restoration. But while the restorationists insisted that it was necessary to meet these expectations, Keynes suggested that these "abnormal factors" gave reason for pause. The Bank, he pointed out, must be sure it can maintain parity without the help of these speculative capital flows before it commits the nation to that course. Thus, Keynes and Norman agreed that market psychology was crucial; but they disagreed about how to properly steer it.[42]

Keynes did raise new concerns about tying the pound to the inflating American economy. While a boom in the United States would ease the task of raising sterling to the prewar parity, Keynes cautioned against linking "sterling prices to dollar prices at a moment in the credit cycle when the latter were near their peak. . . . For when the American boom broke, we should bear the full force of the slump." "The United States," Keynes wrote, "lives in a vast and unceasing crescendo." Its size and rate of growth, however, soften the blows inflicted by the busts of the boom-bust cycle. The UK is smaller, and its "rate of progress" has slowed. The result is that "the United States may suffer industrial and financial tempests in the years to come, and they will scarcely matter to her; but we, if we share them, may almost drown." While Keynes could not have realized it, this was precisely the concern that sowed Bradbury's doubts the previous summer. It was a crucial point, but it came in the midst of a broader retreat.[43]

Having surrendered on the restoration in general, Keynes was left merely questioning the sequencing of the return. The "orthodox" economists wanted to "hasten" the return by removing the embargo on gold exports. Keynes pressed the government to move more deliberately. Along the lines Goodenough suggested to Churchill—and which Norman had previously espoused—Keynes proposed "to establish the fact [of parity] first and to announce it afterwards, rather than to make the announcement first and to chance the fact."[44]

Elsewhere, Keynes clung to his previous contention that restoration might engender "stern deflation in the effort to keep exchange at parity."[45] He conspicuously cited the "million unemployed" across the UK. This crucial variable, however, remained unexplained. It was still, as Keynes put it, the "paradox of unemployment amidst dearth." Keynes thus invoked the UK's chronic unemployment without attempting to explain it.[46] This is because he *could not* explain it. After all, his understanding of unemployment at this point turned on deflation. And prices had been rising.

This inflation—and the appreciation of sterling vis-à-vis the dollar—challenged Keynes intellectually, as it cut against his expectations. It also raised the risks politically of abandoning an orthodoxy that seemed to explain the course of events so much better. Recognizing this, Keynes largely gave up challenging the wisdom of returning to gold and focused instead on prolonging and smoothing that transition. Hoping to reenter the orbit of policymakers, he reframed his ideas, emphasizing those he held "in common with many others."[47] In doing so, however, Keynes surrendered crucial ground to his opponents. If the return were inevitable, why not "take the plunge"—as Niemeyer put it—sooner rather than later, when the markets were expecting it?[48]

## The Unemployment Question

Despite his retreats, Keynes's latest essay provoked more consternation within HM Treasury than he likely expected. Churchill circulated it to colleagues and, again, demanded a systematic reply. Acknowledging Keynes as "a serious critic of monetary policy," Niemeyer begrudgingly prepared a response.[49] He focused on what he considered to be the most salient features of Keynes's argument. He highlighted Keynes's avowal of the need to raise interest rates in the coming months and agreed with him that it would not affect trade and employment. Niemeyer, however, found Keynes's prediction that American prices would continue to rise to be unfounded. Niemeyer shared Keynes's fear of American domination, but he did not think abandoning gold would furnish sufficient insulation given the cost it would inflict on the UK's trade and financial position. This epitomized Niemeyer's perception of Keynes's position: "Mr. Keynes seems to me to contemplate the main alleged disadvantages of a gold policy (rise of bank rate etc.) while depriving himself, in the interests of an unexplored theory of 'Managed Currency,' of all the advantages."[50]

Niemeyer's summation may have been trenchant, but Churchill found it glib. His frank and unforgiving missive is worth quoting at length:

> The Treasury have never . . . faced the profound significance of what Mr. Keynes calls "the paradox of unemployment amidst dearth." The Governor shows himself perfectly happy in the spectacle of Britain possessing the finest credit in the world simultaneously with a million and a quarter unemployed. . . . This is the only country in the world where this condition exists. The Treasury and Bank of England policy has been the only policy consistently pursued. It is a terrible responsibility for those who have shaped it, unless they can be sure that there is no connection between the unique British phenomenon of chronic unemployment and the long, resolute consistency of a particular financial policy. I do not know whether France with her financial embarrassments can be said to be worse off than England with her unemployment. . . . While that unemployment exists, no one is entitled to plume himself on the financial or credit policy . . . we have pursued.

Churchill declared his confidence in the restorationists, but he still was not ready to agree to the restoration:

> You and the Governor have managed this affair . . . [and] you know more about it than anyone else in the world. . . . [A]lone in the world you have had an opportunity over a definite period of years of seeing your policy carried out. That it is a great policy, greatly pursued, I have no doubt. But the fact that this island with its enormous resources is unable to maintain its population is surely a cause for the deepest heart-searching.[51]

While he did not grasp all of the details or correctly specify the leading characters and the parts they played, Churchill saw the big picture. The Cunliffe Committee reports had been the unquestioned ruling dogma for half a decade, and yet the "chronic unemployment" persisted. Churchill admitted that it was a difficult paradox. "I do not pretend," he confessed, "to see even 'through a glass darkly' how the financial and credit policy of the country could be handled so as to bridge the gap between a dearth of goods and a surplus of labor." He nonetheless made clear his priorities if such a trade-off did exist: "I would rather see Finance less proud and Industry more content."[52]

Churchill's anguish was not lost on Niemeyer. For the first time in the discussion, he understood the importance of explicitly explaining away the correlation between unemployment and the orthodox monetary policy. He replied, "I doubt whether credit policy is even a chief cause, and I at any rate would not advocate, still less be 'happy' with a credit policy which I thought would produce unemployment." The rate of interest, he asserted, could only influence unemployment to a small extent and only in the short-run. He explained, "You can by inflation . . . enable temporarily, spending power to cope with large quantities of products. But unless you increase the dose continually, there comes a time when having destroyed the credit of the country you can inflate no more, money having ceased to be acceptable as value. . . . I assume it to be admitted that with Germany and Russia before us we do not think plenty can be found on this path." Niemeyer thus argued—as such monetarists have always argued—that inflation (and deflation) can stimulate (or depress) employment only when it is unexpected and only before the economy is able to adjust to the new quantity of money. Clinging to the classical perspective, Niemeyer trusted that these transitions were smooth and that equilibrium was restored quickly. This both reduced the efficacy of monetary policy as a tool to influence employment and, at the same time, rendered it less necessary.[53]

Chronic unemployment, he insisted, was the product of underlying economic structure. Some of this structure, and the unemployment it created, was attributable to the "maladjustment of labor supplies" and conditions throughout Europe (particularly tariffs) that reduce trade. The most significant factor, however, was the war. It brought "a great decrease in wealth, and there is consequently less effective demand." Thus, the methods to reduce chronic unemployment in the UK must address these structural causes. Niemeyer proposed three: "The only permanent remedy is to recreate the losses of war—really, not merely by manufacturing paper [money]—and what we have to do . . . is (1) to stabilize our currency in relation to the main trading currencies of the world, (2) to reconstruct the broken parts of Europe and (3) to encourage thrift and the accumulation of capital for industry. These methods and not doles and palliatives are going to remedy unemployment."[54]

In Niemeyer's eyes, then, the only connection between "credit policy" and "chronic unemployment" was found in trade: the level of exchange rate stability influenced the health of trade. Restoring trade, Niemeyer insisted, was "the only way to enable this small island bound to buy and sell largely abroad . . . to support its population."[55]

It was a robust response—one that Churchill could, and would, use to justify the policy. Perhaps now he was ready to face Keynes.

## The Showdown

Several weeks later, the US Federal Reserve raised interest rates from 3 percent to 3.5 percent. Norman followed this with a 1 percent hike in Bank rate to 5 percent on March 5. It might have been merely a response to the US increase, but it nevertheless sparked speculation that an announcement of the much-rumored return was imminent.[56]

The next week, businesses began pressuring Churchill to make a formal commitment to return to gold as soon as possible. The London Chamber of Commerce resolved that it was "glad to note that the policy continuously advocated by the Chamber, namely, a return as soon as possible to prewar regular standards of credit and currency and a free gold market, is that advocated by His Majesty's Government. . . . An announcement at the earliest convenient date would be advantageous."[57] In case Churchill somehow missed the widespread reporting, the chamber passed along its resolution to him directly.

The Federation of British Industries (FBI), so often assumed to have favored leaving the gold standard, took a similar posture. The next day, Roland Nugent, the long-standing director for the FBI, wrote to Churchill directly. There could be no filtering by intermediaries. This was the head of the industrialists' principal mouthpiece writing privately, frankly, and directly to the chancellor of the exchequer. Churchill would have to listen, and indeed he did.[58]

What did Nugent say to Churchill? To be sure, the FBI recognized that there would be significant short-term costs; but as it explained so forcefully to the several currency committees, it thoroughly believed that its long-term interests were united with those of finance and that both would be served by restoring the gold standard. So what did the FBI demand of Churchill? Clarity and coordination. It wanted to know the timeline for restoration and the practical steps that would be taken to effect the return. And it wanted international coordination to ensure that the leading gold standard countries were working together rather than engaging in competitive devaluations. As the thoughtfulness of the FBI's position has been overlooked so regularly, it is worth quoting Nugent's letter to Churchill at length:

> Since [an early return] must obviously involve a period of dislocation, if not of active restriction of credit, which cannot fail for a time at least adversely to affect the operations of Industry, and especially our export trade, the Federation feel that they are justified in pressing His Majesty's Government to make known their intentions at the earliest possible moment, and in the event of an early return to the gold standard being contemplated, to indicate the precise steps by which it is hoped to secure such a return and how, when once achieved, it is to be maintained. . . . It is . . . of such importance to all engaged in Industry, both employers and employed, that the present uncertainty should be dispelled, and that Industry should be able to make its plans for the immediate future with a definite knowledge of the general monetary conditions to be anticipated. . . . As industrialists, the Federation would naturally be inclined to prefer a policy directed to the maintenance of the present stability in prices rather than that Industry should be subjected to the undoubtedly serious strain which must be thrown upon it by restrictive measures. They realize, however, that while a waiting policy might be to the more immediate interests of those engaged in Industry, it may be urged that other considerations make it inexpedient that we should wait indefinitely for the necessary upward movement in American prices. In conclusion, they desire to state clearly that . . . since Great Britain is the principal international clearing house both for money and goods, any step which would lead to a general return to a gold standard by the principal industrial countries in the world would be greatly to the benefit of British Industry, since it would . . . ensure the stability of the more important exchanges, and assist in restoring the prewar mobility of international trade. . . . They would point out, however, that if this country is to act alone, the stability of any newly regained standard must be in constant jeopardy unless some agreement has previously been reached with the central banking authorities in the U.S.A. for regulating the value of gold until such time as it again comes into international general use. . . . Stability cannot . . . be achieved by one country acting alone, but only by a general agreement on the part of the principal trading countries of the world to re-establish a common monetary standard. If, therefore, it is the policy of His Majesty's Government to return to a gold standard at an early date, the Federation would attach the greatest importance to carrying out the recommendations embodied

in the currency resolutions of the Genoa Conference, in particular the measures suggested for avoiding wide fluctuations in the purchasing power of gold, and those for economizing its use.[59]

This is a clear-eyed, incisive analysis. The FBI's position was clearly stated: business interests and industrialists—including those who spoke for exporters—wanted a restoration of the prewar gold standard, they wanted the commitment to be robust, and they were braced for the transition back to it. To what would this bind Churchill? For the most part, it told him what business leaders wanted to hear. They wanted to know the specifics of the restoration—and sooner rather than later. And they wanted to be assured that the UK would push at the international level to bring other countries into line. After years of talk without action, the UK's producers wanted Churchill to do as the Conservatives' 2019 slogan ran: "get [it] done."

It would seem that Churchill had been given his marching orders: embrace the return, inform business leaders, and fight for the UK as it retook its leading position in the international monetary order. Were he simply a mechanism for implementing the will of his constituencies, he might have done just that. But Churchill, more than most, was a thoughtful, savvy, self-assured policymaker. He would not be bullied by business any more than by the experts in the Treasury and at the Bank. He was also far more insightful on this question than most assumed. Having read Keynes and internalized his critique of the orthodoxy, he knew better than the business leaders themselves the difficulties they would face on the road back to gold. And he knew better than most that he needed to take Keynes seriously.

So the same day he received the FBI's letter, he invited Keynes to join him with Niemeyer, Bradbury, and McKenna for dinner.[60] Subsequent scholars have interpreted this meeting as revealing a crisis of confidence or continuing ambivalence on the part of the chancellor. They have assumed that Churchill gathered these men because he was still unsure of the course he ought to take.[61]

It is true that Churchill was never fully comfortable with this course of action, but that would not explain why Churchill did not consult Keynes prior to this. After all, the dinner marked the first time Churchill consulted Keynes himself directly. It was not as though Churchill were unaware of Keynes's interest in the matter. Something further is required to explain why Churchill put off this meeting until this point.

Instead, it seems that Churchill, now planning to return, engineered the meeting so as to help himself anticipate—and mitigate—the criticisms that would follow his decision. Rather than seeking Keynes's perspective, Churchill likely sought to use the meeting to dissuade this likely critic from his expected course. Fully armed with the rigorously vetted responses to Keynes's criticisms, Churchill may have dreamed of swaying the public intellectual. Barring that, he must have figured that if he found Keynes to be incorrigible, he could at least hear the criticisms before Keynes took to the press.[62]

The one evening Churchill and Keynes did spend together discussing the return to gold unfolded along predictable lines. Keynes argued, as before, that a return to the prewar parity was unnecessary and would impose painful adjustment costs. But seemingly invigorated by the opportunity to lobby the chancellor directly, Keynes returned to the hard line he had adopted in the *Tract* (rather than the softer line in "A Return towards Gold" the previous month). He insisted (with support from McKenna) that British prices were closer to 10 percent higher than American prices, not the 2.5 percent implied by the current exchange rate. He reasoned from this that parity could only be restored and maintained by deflating prices by one-tenth. The transition to the new, lower price level would not be easy. Attempts at reducing wages would be met with strikes. Ultimately, stickiness would force adjustment through unemployment.[63]

Bradbury came out swinging. He insisted that the UK was "so near the old parity that it was silly to create a shock to confidence and to endanger our international reputation for so small and so ephemeral an easement." "It was very likely that contractions of the basic industries would have to be faced," he conceded. But this was actually a virtue, as it would force through a reorganization of the British economy away from manufacturing toward postindustrial services. "Having lost the advantage of the flying start which we gained at the time of the Industrial Revolution," Bradbury explained, "we should have to do something of the sort anyhow." "The best future for this country . . . lay in preserving and even developing our international banking, insurance and shipping position . . . in those forms of enterprise where the man was more important than the machine."[64]

The story was compelling. Even McKenna seemed to agree. When Churchill asked the latter, as a former chancellor, what he would do, McKenna replied, "There is no escape; you have to go back; but it will be hell."[65]

# CHAPTER 16

# Judgment

Following his dinner with Keynes, Churchill made moves to restore the gold standard. The first step was to reassure the Federation of British Industries (FBI). On March 19, Churchill drafted a reply to Nugent.[1] This was sent to Niemeyer and then to Hopkins. The former supplied a short analysis of the FBI's statement, switched the voice to Grigg's, and suggested delaying the reply "for a few days, to show how carefully we have digested this letter." He also made a key addition: "The Chancellor . . . observes that in your opinion, since Great Britain is the principal international Clearing House . . . for money and for goods, any steps which would lead to a general return to the gold standard . . . would be greatly to the benefit of British Industry."[2] This was just as Bradbury had done on the currency committees: Niemeyer found, nurtured, and reinforced those of the penitents' statements that fit his dogma.[3] Churchill signed off on this, and Grigg sent this on a few days later.[4] Soon enough, Churchill would address the FBI's concerns directly, in the House of Commons.

The next step was to arrange the plans with the prime minister and the governor of the Bank of England. On March 20, Churchill, Baldwin, and Chamberlain met with Bradbury, Norman, and Niemeyer to make the agreement. They resolved that the decision would be announced in Churchill's upcoming budget speech. Specifically, Churchill would declare that "the power to prohibit exports would not be renewed after December next, and further, that the licenses for the export of gold would be given freely, either from the date of this statement or very shortly afterwards." Thus, the UK would resume gold exports a full eight months earlier than planned. Additionally, the group decided that "the Bank rate should not be put up contemporaneously with the Budget statement." Norman finally received authorization to formalize the US credits. But the amount was scaled back from $500 million to $300 million, and it was agreed that these loans were "for show and not for use." By the end of March, the arrangements were made.[5]

It might have seemed that way. Across the ensuing month, however, Norman tweaked the terms, adjusted the arrangements, and steered the specifics of the "restoration." In the end, a new gold standard emerged. It was far "softer" than the prewar system, with gold playing a reduced role and with access to it heavily constrained. The monetary system was redesigned to be actively managed through international collaboration, with foreign loans and coordination taking the place of mechanistic rules and unilateral self-help. At the same time, Norman reversed the deference paid by the Bank to the Treasury since the start of the war. He made clear that the Bank, despite taking on an even more central role in the new system, would remain private and independent of government oversight. More broadly, Norman's regime overturned centuries of practice and scuttled several of the old regime's most salient features.

With his intuition beholden to Keynes's cogent analysis and still unsatisfied with the Cunliffe Committee dogma, Churchill welcomed all of Norman's innovations. So far from being driven by nostalgia, Churchill "returned" to a reformed, modernized gold standard. But he knew better than to publicly reveal the revolution under way. With the eyes of the world upon him, Churchill packaged the new policies in a compelling—quintessentially Churchillian—address in Parliament. He deliberately smoothed over the complexities inherent in this "restoration," selling the shift as a singular, simple succession to the old, established order.

Beneath the polished rhetoric lay Churchill's deep conviction that the monetary forms and symbols mattered less than did their consequences. Specifically, Churchill was determined to defeat the UK's persistent postwar unemployment. As such, Churchill might have gone even further in the direction of reform. But Keynes's approach proved underdeveloped. Churchill saw a critical flaw in Keynes's argument: if leaving the gold standard would resolve unemployment, and if the gold standard had been "dead as mutton" for half a decade, why was the UK's unemployment rate at its highest level in modern history? More broadly, Keynes's theory was still rooted in monetarism, and he could not yet explain unemployment in equilibrium.

In the event, the return to gold was the wrong choice, as Keynes mercilessly showed in the months that followed. But at the time, it was the best choice given the theory and the evidence available. As bad as it was in 1926, it would have been vastly worse had Churchill "returned" to the gold standard as imagined by Cokayne, as described by the Cunliffe Committee, or as it had existed under Cunliffe before the war. More important, these mistakes taught lessons—to Keynes and Churchill alike—that proved crucial in the decade that followed.

## The Norman Reformation

After the government had committed to the return, Norman moved to impose his design on the restoration. On April 8, he wrote to Niemeyer in the Treasury, "I desire to have your agreement on the following arrangements as needed before either Credit in America can be brought into operation."[6] This was rich: Norman was making stipulations in order to get the credit that Niemeyer never thought he should have requested and was still sure would undermine the return. Of course, several of the seven items on Norman's list were either already agreed (regarding the use of the credit), or they followed necessarily from the agreed plan's design (that the Treasury should provide collateral for the American loans). But two of the items constituted the adoption of Norman's particular gold standard dogma as the new state religion.

The first was truly radical. Norman demanded "satisfactory arrangements by Statute or otherwise to make Notes payable either in gold coin or bar gold *at the option* of the Bank of England and to limit the coining of gold bullion."[7] This would mark the end of the Bank's obligation, dating back to its founding in 1694, to redeem its notes in specie at the request of the note-holder. It would be enacted not in a moment of crisis, as it had been done thrice in the last century, but as a part of the "restoration" of the gold standard. It would not be a temporary deviation from the rules but a permanent addition to the Bank's prerogatives. It was not, as the Treasury had disparaged this possible course in 1914, a "heroic extra-statutory expedient dictated by an appalling and overwhelming danger."[8] Norman would make this the new normal.

At what rate would the Bank redeem its notes? What was the minimum quantity to be redeemed? These questions mattered immensely, as they determined the tightness of the "golden shackles" that the chancellor was placing on the governor. There are no records of the discussions between Norman and the Treasury on this issue at this point. But a few months prior, Norman had told the Chamberlain-Bradbury Committee that he "would not give anybody a license for £100 but [to anybody] . . . who wished to take say a hundred thousand ounces."[9] At that juncture, setting the minimum bullion redemption at £425,000 did not matter as much. After all, banknotes were still redeemable in specie and, Bradbury confirmed at the time, Norman promised to allow the export of specie to resume (as planned) starting in 1926.[10] Now in April, with the return agreed and the announcement imminent, Norman was going to close the specie loophole.

It turns out that Norman was serious when he told the Chamberlain-Bradbury Committee that he intended to concentrate the country's private gold in the Bank as a central reserve. Of course, this had been a long-standing proposition, even proceeding the outbreak of the war.[11] In fact, some of Norman's earliest denunciations of Cunliffe were for his unwillingness to force the private banks to trade their gold for Treasury notes. In 1920, the banks did pay in their gold—a point that Schuster liked to remind all those who questioned the bankers' patriotism.[12] But now Norman demanded of HM Treasury "that existing stocks of Gold, and all Gold received in future, shall be paid in by other Banks to the Bank of England as and when requested." These transfers would now be at the option of the Bank of England, and they would be nonnegotiable.[13]

This was Norman's dogma realized as policy. The Bank of England would have the country's gold, and it would highly limit access to that gold. Instead of global gold flows dictating Bank policy, the Bank would control the flow of gold in and through the UK. By collaborating with a handful of other, like-minded central bankers, Norman believed he could even help to shape the quantity of gold in the global market. If it were not a revolution, it was at least a Reformation.

How did Churchill respond? He went for it. The next week, Niemeyer confirmed the agreement and set to work transforming Norman's "satisfactory arrangements" into legislation.[14] Churchill likely did not realize how much authority he was granting to the Bank of England. These latest adjustments seemed like sensible ways to economize on gold itself. But even if Churchill saw what Bradbury and Niemeyer must have seen, he would not have objected. This chancellor did not, after all, buy the orthodoxy's bogeyman concerns about the need to shackle the "wicked chancellor." Like Keynes, Churchill was content that voters should constrain their leaders rather than that market forces should dictate through the monetary authorities.

As Churchill appeared to be in a generous mood, Norman made one further request of the chancellor: he asked for the Treasury's gold. Per the agreed-upon plan, the Bank would become responsible for retiring the Treasury's currency notes (the Bradburys) two years after Churchill's announcement.

Against those notes, the Treasury held £27 million in gold. Previously, Farrer had suggested transferring the Treasury's gold to the Bank straight away "to fortify its gold holding" (for appearances' sake) and then transferring the currency note obligations subsequently.[15] This is just what Norman proposed in mid-April as the drafting of Churchill's announcement was under way. Niemeyer dutifully passed this on to Churchill, and it too was accepted.[16] Now it just remained to sell this policy to Parliament.

## The Announcement

In the weeks leading up to the announcement, Niemeyer passed drafts and suggested revisions between Churchill and Norman.[17] Then, as planned, the chancellor announced the return in his budget speech on April 28, 1925. It was a pivotal moment, and Churchill knew it. He rose to the occasion with a masterful address.

By the time Churchill came to announce the restoration, he understood the terms of the gold standard debate better than virtually any other member of Parliament. He knew well the varying understandings of the gold standard, the conflicting prescriptions for effecting the return, and all of the arguments for and against the different paths before them.[18] He designed his address to Parliament not to explain or even justify the decision as much as to formally enact the policy and preempt potential attacks. His (relatively short) address on the return marshaled five key themes: inevitability, unanimity, subtlety, attainability, and desirability.

Churchill backed into the announcement in the midst of the budget speech: "Before I come to the prospects of 1925 I have an important announcement. . . . It is something in the nature of a digression, and yet it is an essential part of our financial policy." He then briefly described the wartime capital controls and their extension in the Gold and Silver (Export Control) Act of 1920. He stressed that Parliament had "express[ly]" given the controls "a temporary character," thus ensuring that, upon their expiration, "Great Britain would automatically revert to the prewar free market for gold." This "obliged" the government "to decide whether to renew . . . that Act . . . or to let it lapse." He concluded, "We have decided to allow it to lapse." Thus, it was not that Churchill was changing the policy so much as that the government was choosing not to change it.[19]

Of course, all of this was true, and Churchill described the situation with greater precision and accuracy than did many of his contemporaries. At the same time, doing so served his rhetorical strategy. This was not some bold initiative cooked up by the colorful (critics said "unreliable") and gallant (critics said "foolhardy") Winston. This was a serious chancellor doing serious chancellor-type things in the most conventional (boring) chancellor-y way: heeding the experts as they effected the will of Parliament. Indeed, Churchill would have liked his colleagues to believe that his heroism on this occasion consisted of simply getting out of the way.

Churchill was fully prepared to defend the shift. But he knew it was better to convince his audience that no defense was necessary. The subtle and inevitable policy change was unanimously supported:

> A return to an effective gold standard has long been the settled and declared policy of this country. Every expert conference since the War[,] . . . every expert committee in this country, has urged the principle of a return to the gold standard. No responsible authority has advocated any other policy. No British government—and every party has held office—no political party, no previous . . . Chancellor of the Exchequer has challenged, or so far as I am aware is now challenging, the principle of a reversion to the gold standard in international affairs at the earliest possible moment.[20]

Who could argue with that? Snowden and others could—and would—quibble with the precise timing and the specifics of the journey, but nobody could question the objective or the broad policy. Absent a serious challenge to the mandate, such derision would prove as compelling as sour grapes. Besides, Churchill had anticipated these practical concerns.

"The only questions open," he stated, "have been the difficult and the very delicate questions of how and when." The former had been fully resolved by "a Committee of experts and high authorities"—the Chamberlain-Bradbury Committee—in "a unanimous Report," which Churchill promised to make available after the address. This committee, Churchill reminded his colleagues, had been appointed by the Labour chancellor (Snowden) himself. Its conclusions followed from the evidence given by "a great number of witnesses representing every kind of interest—financial and trading interests, manufacturing interests, the Federation of British Industries and others." Churchill made special mention of the FBI because he knew that industry, particularly exporters, would bear the brunt of the adjustment costs. They had asked for—and Churchill was now providing—a clear statement of the policy as quickly as possible. Soon enough, he would address the producers' concerns about instability, but for now he hammered home the theme of consensus. "There is a general agreement," he said, "even among those who have taken . . . the heterodox view . . . that we ought not to prolong the uncertainty, that whatever the policy of the Government, it should be declared."[21]

This was a powerful paraphrase of the FBI's request from a few weeks earlier that the government "make known their intentions at the earliest possible moment" so that the "present uncertainty [is] dispelled" for "both employers and employed."[22] The FBI had given its litany of supplication, and Churchill had answered directly and publicly. The statement also put potential critics on the back foot. Could Snowden, who still exalted the return to gold, suggest that workers and their employers wanted the uncertainty prolonged? Did Labour stand for instability and unpredictability?

Churchill addressed the question of timing with equal aplomb. So far from this being precipitate, this was a "moment for which the House of Commons has patiently waited . . . the moment at which it was, after long consideration, judged expedient that decisions should be made and actions taken." This was also "the moment most favorable for action": "Our exchange with the United States has for some time been stable, and is at the moment buoyant. We have no immediate heavy commitments across the Atlantic. We have entered a period on both sides of the Atlantic when political and economic stability seems to be more assured than it has been for some years. If this opportunity were missed, it might not soon recur, and the whole finance of the country would be overclouded for a considerable interval by an important factor of uncertainty. Now is the appointed time." These words not only deepened the sense of inevitability, but they broached the question of capability. This was not just something that had to happen. This was something that, at this moment, *could* happen.[23]

Yet the change itself was subtle: "[While] the prohibition on the export of gold will continue in form on the Statute Book until the 31st December," "a general license will be given to the Bank of England for the export of gold bullion from today." Just like that, with a mere shift in ministerial habit, the UK would "resume [its] international position as a gold standard country from [this] moment."[24]

The next part of the address was the most challenging: the list of qualifications. As ever, the devil was in the details, and Churchill knew it. As Bradbury had asked Norman, how general would the license to export be, practically speaking? Would the holders of pound notes retain the right to redeem their notes in specie and take that specie abroad? Would the Bank be obliged to increase the money supply when gold came pouring in from abroad, as Norman and the Chamberlain-Bradbury Committee had predicted?

The answers to every one of these questions surely disappointed any who still clung to the prewar orthodoxy. There would be no gold coinage. There would be no right of redemption. There would be no right of conversion. The Bank of England would determine whether—and how much—gold it bought and how many notes it redeemed. The only good news was that the statutory sale price of bullion (for export) was the same as it had been for centuries: £3 17s. 10½d. (£3.89) per troy ounce of gold at the standard fineness. But the export license was effectively restricted. The minimum purchase was 400 troy ounces of fine gold.[25] In fact, this departed from centuries of practice that had been disrupted by the turmoil of the Great War and, deliberately, only to the smallest extent possible.

But this is not how Churchill presented the changes. "Returning to the international gold standard does not mean that we are going to issue gold coinage," he informed Parliament. "It would be an unwarrantable extravagance," he explained, "which our present financial stringency by no means allows us to indulge in. . . . I must appeal to all classes in the public interest to continue to use notes and to make no change in the habits and practices they have become used to for the last ten years. . . . But now that we are returning publicly to the gold standard in international matters with a free export of gold, I feel that it will be better for us to regularize what has been our practice by legislation."

Note that, again, Churchill frames the policy as maintaining the default: the government is not "going to" undertake the "extravagance" of "issu[ing]" gold coinage. England had been minting the gold sovereign since 1489. The modern gold sovereign (worth £1, or 20 shillings) was introduced after the Napoleonic Wars, in that most earnest restoration of the gold standard. Prior to the First World War, there were around £130 million of gold coins.[26] Since then, many of those coins had been hoarded. Many had been paid in for the war loans and were now at the Treasury, backing the currency notes. But instead of paying these back out to the public, they would be transferred to the Bank of England, as Churchill was about to describe.[27]

Churchill's passing allusion to his Gold Standard Bill hearkened back to the Norman-Bradbury discussion about the nature of Norman's reforms. Norman framed them as "suitable arrangements" to insulate the Bank from market pressure, but Bradbury and Niemeyer recognized that this would require action by Parliament. Churchill slyly described this as "regulariz[ing] what has been our practice by legislation." This was an accurate depiction. But the old orthodoxy might have said, with equal accuracy, that the mere abeyance of ancient rights (since 1914) was not the same as the affirmative surrender of those rights. They might have said that suspending specie convertibility permanently just because the public were not regularly running on the Bank is akin to suspending the right of remonstration simply because the public were not regularly protesting. Such rights chasten authority even when they are not actively exercised. Circulating gold coinage, Churchill posited, "is quite unnecessary for the purpose of the gold standard."[28] This was, indeed, one version of the orthodoxy: the version most vigorously advanced by Norman and tacitly acknowledged by the Chamberlain-Bradbury Committee. But for Norman's predecessors, particularly Cokayne, the Bank's obligations were not just abstract rights but crucial practical mechanisms that guided and disciplined the governors of the Bank of England. Like every other figure considered in this book, Churchill had his own unique assemblage of what was essential and nonessential to being a "believer" in "the gold standard."

Having described what the UK should do, and would do, Churchill next made the case that it was actually possible to do it. He announced the deferral of the amalgamation of the Treasury's currency notes "until we have sufficient experience of working a free international gold market on a gold reserve of, approximately, £150,000,000."[29] That had a much more positive spin than did the language of the Chamberlain-Bradbury Committee in its recommendation of the same course: "The Treasury cannot escape from the responsibility for the existing issue; we doubt whether the Bank would accept it, until the time when effective control can also be given to them."[30] What is more is that the course for the Treasury would be even harder—and that for the Bank even easier—than the Chamberlain-Bradbury Committee recommended. Norman had secured Churchill's commitment to transfer the Treasury's gold to the Bank here and now. While the Bank would have more gold to defend the pound against speculators, the Treasury would face the unenviable task of retiring the currency notes with incoming tax receipts—that is, until it could have the Bank to take on those obligations. In the meantime, the Bank—still a private enterprise paying dividends to shareholders—would have the benefits of the public's capital.

Yet Churchill somehow found a way to sell this arrangement. He chose his words carefully, and they need to be quoted directly:

> We have accumulated a gold reserve of £153,000,000. That is the amount considered necessary by the Cunliffe Committee, and that gold reserve we shall use without hesitation, if necessary with the Bank rate, in order to defend and sustain our new position. To concentrate our reserves of gold in the most effective form, I have arranged to transfer the £27,000,000 of gold which the Treasury hold against the Treasury Note

issue to the Bank of England in exchange for bank notes. The increase of the gold reserve of the Bank of England will, of course, figure in their accounts.[31]

So what would be the total size of the UK's reserve as the restoration proceeded? Would it be £180 million? Or would it just be £153 million? The answer is the latter, lower figure. But Churchill's audience could be forgiven if they had thought that "we" (the authorities) "accumulated a gold reserve of £153,000,000," and then our chancellor (Churchill) "arranged to transfer . . . £27,000,000" of Treasury gold to the Bank "to concentrate our reserves of gold in the most effective form." That was the sequence of Churchill's statements. But it was not the sequence of actions. The transfer happened first, bringing the overall total reserve to £153 million. Churchill was not being deceptive but strategically ambiguous. In a parliamentary system, it was reasonable to expect the shadow chancellor to do his job—to check, and challenge, the figures. If his colleagues wistfully, lazily imagined a larger sum and a more heroic act, could Churchill be blamed?[32]

There is one more point to mention. On this accounting basis, the authorities had achieved this great figure—the Cunliffe Committee minimum—years ago. According to the old dogma, Churchill was no more or less prepared to resume the gold standard than had been his five predecessors. But telling that story would serve Keynes's conclusion: that restoration was now no more realizable and no less arduous than it had been since 1920. To tell that story would sully the gravitas of this moment as the inevitable but decisive culmination of the last half-decade of scrimping and saving, of austerity, of blood, toil, tears, and sweat. All this, Churchill announced, was bolstered by the provision of American accommodation: "Although . . . we are strong enough to achieve this important change from our own resources . . . to make assurance doubly sure, I have made arrangements to obtain . . . credits in the United States of not less than 300 million dollars. . . . We do not expect to have to use them, and we shall freely use other measures in priority. . . . [But] these great credits across the Atlantic Ocean have been obtained and built up as a solemn warning to speculators of every kind and of every hue and in every country."[33]

What could be more compelling to his audience? To his colleagues, it must have conjured that James Montgomery Flagg image from the Great War of Uncle Sam and Britannia, arm in arm, atop the world. To us, it conjures all those great moments from the Second World War and the Cold War thereafter in which Churchill mobilized this "special relationship" to incomparable effect.

Even all this was not enough. In the last part of his address, Churchill put this story into the service of British producers. He knew well their fear of isolation, of peripheralization. "In our policy of returning to the gold standard," he assured them, "we do not move alone." "Indeed, I think we could not have afforded to remain stationary while so many others moved. The two greatest manufacturing countries in the world on either side of us, the United States and Germany, are in different ways either on or related to an international gold exchange."[34]

If invoking the specter of the UK's greatest rivals were not enough, Churchill then listed all of those other countries—friend and foe, imperial and independent—who had moved or would move with London. He continued as if he were speaking directly in response to the FBI's qualms:

> Thus over the wide area of the British Empire and over a very wide and important area of the world there has been established at once one uniform standard of value to which all international transactions are related and can be referred. That standard may, of course, vary in itself from time to time, but the position of all the countries related to it will vary together, like ships in a harbor whose gangways are joined and who rise and fall together with the tide.

And so the return was also desirable:

> The establishment of this great area of common arrangement will facilitate the revival of international trade and of inter-Imperial trade. Such a revival and such a foundation is important to all countries and to no country is it more important than to this island, whose population is larger than its agriculture or its industry can sustain . . . which is the center of a wide Empire, and which, in spite of all its burdens, has still retained, if not the primacy, at any rate the central position, in the financial systems of the world. [35]

Thus did Churchill meet the "interests" of his constituents: as a priest meets those of his congregation. They formed their intercessions, and he performed his rite. He assured them that they were right with the world, and the world was right with them. This was a worthy cause and a cause worthy of them.

## A New "Gold" Standard

The prewar gold value of the pound dates back to Isaac Newton's overvaluation of gold (relative to silver) in his 1717 report. From the 1720s forward, this dictated the market price of gold in London: £3 17s. 10½d. per troy ounce at the standard fineness. The only sustained interruption came with the French Revolutionary and Napoleonic Wars. With the suspension of convertibility in 1797, the price of gold in London rose more than 40 percent above the prewar price.[36] Following the final defeat of Napoleon, Parliament elected to fully restore the prewar gold parity—to ensure that every pound could fetch the same amount of gold as it did before the wars. The Royal Mint was instructed to fashion 20 troy pounds of standard (22 carat, 91.66 percent pure) gold into 934 sovereigns and one half-sovereign. Worth one pound (or 20 shillings) and containing 0.2354 troy ounces of pure gold, the new sovereign defined the gold standard in theory and in practice. But it did not redefine it. The rate was selected quite deliberately to match the prewar (Newtonian) gold price.[37]

To twenty-first century eyes, the flat line of a stable market price for gold drawn across two centuries beggars belief. One is tempted to conclude that this material achievement followed from simplistic materialism: the money made in England was disproportionately made of gold itself. Indeed, more than half of the UK's prewar monetary base was comprised of gold coin.[38] So while most day-to-day transactions were conducted in token and paper currency, gold could be had without cost or inconvenience. Particularly in England, the sovereign was king.

Before the First World War, it was essentially costless for Britons to move between pounds sterling and gold. In law and in practice, anyone who could cobble together ten shillings (equivalent to £58 in 2019 pounds) could get the 0.1176 troy ounces of (pure) gold in a half-sovereign. It was formally illegal to melt coins, but this age-old recourse proved impossible to stamp out. After all, the right to export specie dated back to the 1660s. So the specie could be simply exported and then traded or melted abroad.

All of this changed with Churchill's 1925 Gold Standard Act. Britons could get gold coins only so long as they lasted in the market. The restriction on exporting coin was not explicitly removed in Churchill's new gold standard bill. Instead, actors who would export gold had to obtain it through the Bank of England with a minimum purchase of 400 troy ounces of fine gold. This was several hundred times smaller than the 100,000 (presumably troy) ounces that Norman had pressed upon Bradbury a few months earlier.[39] But it was several thousand times larger than the 0.1176 troy ounces of fine gold in a prewar half-sovereign, the smallest gold coin at the time. The minimum "purchase" of gold had moved from 10 shillings (£0.50) to £1684. Without judging whether this were good or bad, did it substantively matter?

In 1925, the Treasury's official line was that "bullion exports are naturally made in large sums and no inconvenience is anticipated from fixing a 400 ounce unit." The Treasury likewise insisted that, even with the elimination of specie and thus the right to specie redemption, the "obligat[ion] on the Bank to provide gold bullion (in 400-ounce bars) at a fixed price against legal tender . . . secures the maintenance of the gold standard."[40] But the old orthodoxy, from Cokayne to Schuster, had insisted that it would make all the difference in the world. They feared that under the kind of system advocated by Keynes and Norman, the world's leading central banks would be insulated from market pressures and could collectively devalue their currencies.[41] This is why those orthodox figures had fought so hard to save convertibility during and after the war. Churchill's move effectively concentrated the power to "discipline" the monetary authority into the hands of only those actors with access to extremely large sums of liquid capital. Which side of the argument was right?

In the end, the new view prevailed: the use of gold as currency proved unimportant to the mechanisms of the gold standard. Between resumption in 1925 and re-suspension in 1931, Norman did a remarkable job of keeping the pound within a 1 percent band around the prewar pound-dollar exchange rate. He did so while averaging the Cunliffe Committee minimum reserve of £150 million without appreciable gold reserve losses in this period or excessively high interest rates.[42] Despite the vastly diminished gold-to-note ratio from 67 percent to 33 percent, there was no collapse in the pound. There was no uncontrollable inflation. There was no economic Armageddon. In that sense, Norman's new system vindicated Cunliffe's most ambitious vision to save the gold standard by modernizing it. For the revolutionaries-in-waiting—like Keynes and perhaps Churchill—Norman's "new gold standard" shifted the "barbarous relic" ever closer to the ash heap of history.

But while the reforms brought by the new gold standard served to defrock the old orthodoxy, they still did not go far enough to save Britons from the cross of gold.

## The Consequences of Mr. Churchill

When deflation and unemployment continued to rise unabated well into the summer, it became clear that Keynes (and McKenna) had more accurately predicted the difficulty and costs of adjusting back to the prewar parity. Sensing himself vindicated by events, Keynes piled on the chancellor in a series of articles that appeared in the *Evening Standard* that July, which Keynes later published as "The Economic Consequences of Mr. Churchill."

The explanation for the setbacks, Keynes insisted, was simple: "It is a question of relative price here and abroad." Due to the restoration, "the value of sterling money abroad has been raised by 10%, whilst its purchasing power over British labor is unchanged." As a result, "we receive 10% less sterling for our exports; yet our industrialists have to pay out in wages just as much as before, and their employees have to expend just as much as before to maintain their standard of life." Exporters were thus forced to cut prices but unable to reduce wages. This exacerbated class cleavages, pitting desperate industrialists against (understandably) recalcitrant laborers. "It must be war," Keynes warned, "until those who are economically weakest are beaten to the ground."[43]

Keynes laid blame for the crisis squarely on the shoulders of the government in general and Churchill in particular. These "troubles," Keynes insisted, were a uniquely British phenomenon and were indisputably linked to the decision to return to gold at the prewar parity. "This alteration in the external value of sterling money," he argued, "has been the deliberate act of the government and the Chancellor of the Exchequer, and the present troubles of our export industries are the inevitable and predictable consequence of it."[44]

Keynes clarified that his criticisms were not "arguments against the gold standard as such." Instead, he said, "they are arguments against having restored gold in conditions which required a substantial readjustment of all our money values. If Mr. Churchill had restored gold by fixing the parity lower than the prewar figure, or if he had waited until our money values were adjusted to the prewar parity, then these particular arguments would have no force." The problem, in other words, was that the chancellor had undertaken a drastic change in "the value of money" in pursuit of getting back on gold.[45]

"Why did [Mr. Churchill] do such a silly thing?" Keynes asked. He offered three explanations. The first two must have stung: "Partly, perhaps, because he has no instinctive judgment to prevent him from making mistakes; partly because, lacking this instinctive judgment, he was deafened by the clamorous voices of conventional finance." The last explanation—the main explanation—was that "he was gravely misled by his experts."[46]

Keynes identified two "mistakes" made by Churchill's experts. First, "they miscalculated the degree of the maladjustment of money values." This was Keynes's old claim that the yellow brick road back to the prewar parity was a good deal longer than the restorationists suggested. Whereas they suggested that a mild deflation of 2 to 3 percent would be sufficient, Keynes warned of something five times that large. The terrible consequences seemed to confirm his clairvoyance.[47]

His second major criticism was more substantial. Keynes indicted Churchill's advisers for assuming that "bringing about a general reduction of internal money values" would "follow 'automatically' from a 'sound' policy by the

Bank of England." Keynes unpacked their assumptions: "Depression in the export industries . . . coupled if necessary with dear money and credit restriction, diffuse themselves evenly and fairly rapidly throughout the whole community."[48]

Keynes, however, did not think that there was anything "even" or "rapid" about the progress of this depression. Some industries, he explained, were "sheltered" from these effects. Others, like the coal industry, which bought at home and sold abroad, were particularly exposed to the perils of the relative price adjustments. The coal miners, he insisted, were "the victims of the economic juggernaut. They represent in the flesh the 'fundamental adjustments' engineered by the Treasury and the Bank of England to satisfy the impatience of the City fathers to bridge the 'moderate gap' between $4.40 and $4.86." Restoration Road, in other words, was not only longer than promised but also slower going.[49]

Keynes also loathed the means by which the adjustment would be made. Met with "sticky" wages and prices, the constrictive monetary policy could only work by exacerbating unemployment. If a stable cost of living prevented industrialists from reducing wages, they could only cut costs by reducing employment. The government could help to facilitate this "diffusion" by deliberately exposing the sheltered industries to the stress of restricted credit. That too was a "sound," but austere, policy. "Deflation," as Keynes put it, "does not reduce wages 'automatically.' It reduces them by causing unemployment."[50] Restoration Road was thus also rougher and more perilous than promised.

Of course, travel along this path would be easier and faster if prices abroad rose. But what could the UK do to force adjustment abroad? The real problem was that Churchill had committed the UK to swallow this deflation and all of the austerity it entailed. "[That] being the real source of our industrial troubles," Keynes insisted, "it is impossible to recommend any truly satisfactory course except its reversal."[51]

Just as Keynes predicted, deflation and unemployment followed from the decision to (essentially) revalue the currency. When the government ceased protecting miners from falling wages, the Trades Union Congress (TUC) orchestrated a nationwide general strike. Lasting nine days and including upwards of one-fifth of the UK's adult male population, the General Strike of 1926 brought the British economy nearly to a standstill.

Led by Churchill, Baldwin's Conservative government remained steadfast in its commitment to the gold standard orthodoxy. It maintained that the exchange rate must not be adjusted, the government should not attempt to protect those groups (like the coal miners) most affected by intensified international competition, and prices and wages should be left to adjust freely in response to market forces. After a high court judge ruled the strike illegal—thus making the TUC legally liable for the losses the strike had created—the TUC reluctantly backed down. The miners slowly trickled back to work, and by the autumn of 1926 the strike was over.[52]

Of course, the unemployment numbers went from bad to worse over the course of the 1920s. For the UK, the second half of the decade made its first half look positively sublime by comparison.[53] For Keynes, the difference was as simple as the decision to restore the gold standard at the prewar parity. But the orthodoxy explained away these travails as the consequence of the war—and as the penance to be served for the financial and fiscal profligacy that followed in its wake. Thus the conventional wisdom survived: the heyday of the gold standard was the era of low unemployment, and the experiment with exchange rate flexibility in the early 1920s had failed.

## Churchill's Failure

Despite his public overtures that the downturn was unrelated to the restoration, Churchill did come to regret his decision to return to the prewar parity. Even years later, he is reputed to have considered this decision to have been the biggest mistake of his life—which is saying something, given that ten years prior he had masterminded the disastrous invasion of Gallipoli.[54]

Was Churchill so misguided in returning to gold in 1925? It is clear that both of Keynes's major criticisms of the government's policy were on the mark. Sterling was overvalued more than the Treasury and the Bank suggested. Subsequent economic historians have found that overvaluation to be between 5 and 10 percent, rather than the 10 to 15 percent that Keynes suggested. Regardless, the prewar parity proved to be much further beyond reach than Churchill's advisers had promised him.[55]

Keynes was also right that travel along that road would be slower and more arduous than the orthodoxy suggested. The British economy did not adjust "automatically" to the change in the value of money. The revaluation of sterling eviscerated an export sector that had already been weakened by the postwar changes in the global economy. Forced to cut costs to remain competitive, industrialists attempted to lower wages. Resistant workers were forced to choose between "starvation and submission," as Keynes had predicted.[56] After initially braving unemployment and starvation, most workers eventually chose to submit. The UK did go back, but as McKenna predicted, it was hell.

But to say that, in retrospect, Churchill chose the wrong policy is not to suggest that he should have made a different decision given the arguments available to him at the time. It is also not fair to say that Churchill failed to grapple with these dire possibilities. Of course, most of the chancellor's advisers were optimistic about the ease of making the "adjustments" they sought, but there is no evidence to suggest that Churchill was naïve about this impending transition. We know that he took the criticisms of the Treasury's policy seriously—more seriously, it seems, than any of his advisers. He very well may have accepted the possibilities proposed by Keynes as eventualities. Indeed, given Churchill's character, it is likely that he evaluated his decision based on the assumption that the worst was likely to occur.

But if that were the case, why did Churchill choose to go back? The surviving papers reveal that his top priority was addressing the chronic unemployment that had plagued the UK since the end of the war. At the same time, the UK's experiment with the adjustable exchange rate regime did nothing to abate it. While Keynes could praise that approach in theory, Churchill faced the reality of "a million and a quarter unemployed."

While Keynes wrote extensively and passionately about unemployment, his theory told Churchill that stabilizing the pound at its current price would only save the chancellor from creating additional—albeit transitional—unemployment. Keynes offered no solution to the problem of chronic unemployment—unemployment that exists as a stable equilibrium outcome.

It was thus unfair of Keynes to suggest that Churchill lacked "instinctive judgment" and that he unthinkingly bowed to the pressure of the "clamorous voices of conventional finance." Churchill understood the risks he was taking, and he diligently explored the alternatives. Keynes's framework, however, merely promised more of the same, and Churchill wanted to move forward. He calculated that a stable exchange rate would reinvigorate finance and facilitate trade. But, he assumed, these effects would only follow if the government's commitment to exchange rate stability were credible, and this could not be better demonstrated than by restoring the pound to its prewar value. This was the policy, Churchill reasoned, that would best restore the UK's prewar position.

## Keynes's Failure

While Churchill entered office with the intention of returning to gold and keen to find ways to defend that course, it would not have been impossible for Keynes to have changed his mind. Indeed, Churchill's subsequent admission that the policy was misguided demonstrates his open-mindedness. Churchill's exchanges with his advisers show the importance of beliefs in his final decision.

He was fully immersed in the intellectual debate surrounding the decision. Indeed, he took the critics' arguments more seriously than most. In the end, Churchill proceeded only after all of his theoretical concerns had been addressed.

But if Churchill were so open-minded and intellectually curious, why did he fail to converse directly with Keynes prior to his final decision? Why did he limit himself to consulting only Keynes's published work and not also engaging the man himself? Most likely, Churchill saw few advantages of contacting Keynes and several potentially large disadvantages of doing so. We know that Churchill was quite familiar with Keynes's various writings, and he almost certainly noticed that Keynes's radicalism diminished steadily over time. Why, Churchill must have wondered, challenge Keynes directly when isolating him seemed to work so marvelously?

While the advantages of engaging Keynes early on were small, the potential costs of premature engagement were considerable. Churchill was predisposed to support a return to gold, but he began without the technical understanding required to justify it. In person, Keynes would have run circles around him.[57] Perhaps more important, Churchill would have betrayed his limited understanding. Churchill knew that this would have been blood in the water to the author of *The Economic Consequences of the Peace*. Given the harsh treatment Churchill did eventually suffer at Keynes's hand, hindsight confirms that it was wise for Churchill to delay meeting with Keynes until he had a robust, defensible position.

Thus, Churchill's decision turned on his intellectual understanding of how to maximize his overarching policy goal: resolving the UK's chronic unemployment. He pressed his advisers for the ammunition necessary to defend—and explain—the return to gold. These ideas did more than just "cover" Conservative pandering to the party's favorite interest groups.[58] They were the rationale used to explain to the British populace the virtue—and necessity—of the austerity that Churchill expected would follow. Churchill was not prepared to impose these costs without a clear understanding of how doing so would serve the public interest. It was only when he had that understanding that he proceeded to commit the country to that course.

The arguments in favor of restoration were eminently reasonable. Since adopting the fixed metallic standard in 1696, Britons had enjoyed two centuries of unprecedented economic growth, extraordinarily low unemployment, and remarkable social stability. Keynes's vaunted managed exchange rate—like that which followed the First World War—was correlated with anemic growth, high unemployment, and social strife. In light of this evidence, what else could Churchill have concluded? He remained wisely incredulous, but with Norman's reforms, the zeal across the UK to make the restoration work, and the lack of clearly superior alternatives, Churchill resolved to seize the initiative.

The action proved to be a grave mistake. In hindsight, it seems that the orthodoxy had reversed causality. It was not the gold standard that powered the UK's ascent. It was the UK's ascent that enabled Britons to implement their orthodox gold standard(s). Keynes recognized this, but he could not demonstrate it to Churchill in 1925. He did not yet have the unimpeachable evidence to support this conclusion. And, just as perilous, he had not yet worked out the theory required to explain unemployment in equilibrium.

This begs another question: If Keynes had been privy to Churchill's concern with chronic unemployment, would he have been able to persuade Churchill to adopt another course? Had Keynes considered structural unemployment, he would have discovered the principal inadequacy of his policy-making framework at that point. Keynes did not explain chronic unemployment within his framework because he could not. The Keynes of 1925 was still largely a monetarist. He assumed that full employment was the natural result of free markets in equilibrium. Unemployment, he argued, followed from the difficulties of switching between different equilibria. Keynes would have to abandon this framework before he could fully explain unemployment in equilibrium. It would take a more general theory to address this "paradox of unemployment amidst dearth." Over the next decade, Keynes endeavored to develop just that.

# PART FIVE

# *Conclusion*

There are still many people in America who regard depressions as acts of God. I think Keynes proved that the responsibility for these occurrences does not rest with Providence. (Bertrand Russell, *Autobiography*)

# CHAPTER 17

# Faith in History

In the midst of the Second World War, Polanyi reflected on the interwar collapse. "Belief in the gold standard," he wrote, "was the faith of the age.... The war between heaven and hell ignored the money issue, leaving capitalists and socialists miraculously united."[1] We have seen the truth of this characterization throughout this book. The gold standard faith was absolutely central to every discussion of economic policy, and it even permeated many (seemingly) unrelated questions in politics, diplomacy, and security.

While he may have been speaking metaphorically, Polanyi was right to invoke religion. There is no better way to describe the forces, processes, and agents that led England to its cross of gold. All were devoted to achieving the salvation. But none agreed on the means—the beliefs and the deeds—to effect it. So there could be no other way: the course was constructed, and reconstructed, by a cadre of clerics together in their curia, councils, and committees.

## The Past, As It Happened

### Orthodoxy

Whatever their contradictory assumptions and confused logic, the Cunliffe Committee's reports clearly and unambiguously specified the steps that the committee believed were necessary for the UK to return to gold following the First World War. They started with the two axioms of the orthodox gold standard. First, all pound notes must continue to be convertible into gold, as ever before, at the prewar parity. This included the Bank of England notes as well as the Treasury's currency notes (the Bradburys). Second, the import and export of gold must not be hindered by the authorities in any way. Instead, international capital flows could and should be influenced by raising and lowering interest rates.

What of the wartime inflation? Here again, the Cunliffe Committee reports were clear: get rid of it. The first step, of course, was to eliminate the inflationary pressure brought by government borrowing. This meant reversing government budget deficits as soon as the war was over and then, as quickly as possible, consolidating the public debt into longer-term, lower-cost Treasury bills. More broadly, the Cunliffe Committee specified the optimum money supply as whatever quantity could be kept in circulation without both the gold price falling below the prewar parity and the UK's total gold "reserve" dipping below £150 million. Until this could be sustained, interest rates would have to be kept high and the money supply steadily contracted.

As we have seen, the Cunliffe Committee's reports were widely celebrated and, essentially, universally embraced. Throughout the decade that followed, their dictates became the watchwords of UK macroeconomic policy.[2] They were regularly invoked by the monetary authorities in the Bank of England and HM Treasury, in Parliament, and in the popular press. By 1933, at the height of the Great Depression, Arthur Kitson duly noted, "Judged by its effects upon the industrial and social affairs of Great Britain, the Cunliffe Currency Committee's report . . . is the most important document of the late war and postwar periods."[3]

But by the end of 1920, these reports were no longer the UK's touchstones. At that point, the Cunliffe Committee's simple instructions were bracketed, twisted, reversed, and violated. Throughout, organized hypocrisy combined with disorganized misunderstanding and concerted co-option to ensure that lip service, at least, was paid to the Cunliffe Committee. The UK *did* eventually return to a version of the gold standard, but it is a myth that the UK followed the path set forth by the Cunliffe Committee. This persistent myth was central to a web of mythology in which UK monetary policy became ensnared in the years following the First World War.

## Mythology

There was a myth, crafted during the war and propagated vigorously in the interwar period, that there was such a thing as a monolithic, canonical pre-war gold standard, a system to which the UK conceivably could return. As we have seen, this myth bore little resemblance to the actual workings of the monetary systems across the British Isles. Yet the Cunliffe Committee turned a blind eye to these realities. What gaps between seeing and believing might manifest that *faith* cannot bridge?

There is the myth that "class politics" explains the contours of the struggles over macroeconomic policy following the First World War. As Simmons cast it, "Since devaluation cut into the value of investment and creditors' savings, it was avoided by center-right governments and strong independent central banking institutions. On the other hand, trade protection imposed serious costs on the abundant factor of production, labor. The preference of the conservatives was to protect and defend the currency; that of the Left was to devalue and liberalize trade."[4]

In fact, precisely the opposite occurred in the UK following the First World War. The most significant—although inadvertent—departure from the Cunliffe Committee creed came when a small group of Conservatives imposed capital controls at the end of 1920. They did this only after an acrimonious debate in which leading backbench Conservatives and Liberals attacked the Conservative-Liberal coalition government for betraying the UK's financial and business interests. The government, however, had the backing of the (hugely) independent Bank of England, the governor of which insisted upon imposing capital controls over and above the objections of the Treasury.

At the same time, and for good reason, the ever-more-powerful working class preached the Cunliffe Committee orthodoxy. They venerated the Cunliffe Committee's analysis, for it blamed inflation on the government's war-time borrowing (rather than on workers' excessive wage demands, employers' favorite bugaboo). They loudly called for deflationary monetary policy so as to regain control over the ballooning cost of living. They vigorously embraced the return to gold as the best means of revitalizing the UK economy and mitigating unemployment. They celebrated the centrality of London to the global financial system as a distinction that brought them reflected glory.

This was not the first time—and it would not be the last time—that working-class Britons supported ill-conceived schemes to make Britain great again. As Brendan Chilton, the head of Labour Leave, recently put it, "A United Kingdom operating under World Trade Organization rules will be one of the greatest liberating experiences to [be] achieved by this country in modern times." "Free from the shackles of Brussels," he promised, "the next Labour government can embark upon a radical national economic agenda that transforms this country from a nation secluded in Europe to a nation manufactured and secured in global trade in the modern world."[5]

This was not the first time—and it would not be the last time—that a flank of the Conservative Party eschewed Conservative principles and overruled the business and financial interests of its leading members. After all, the Theresa May government largely subordinated City interests in its attempt to deliver Brexit. And this was the compromising—some say "compromised"—view within the Conservative Party. May, at least, paid lip service to the importance of this constituency. Her successor, Boris Johnson, often has not. As he put it in 2018, "Fuck business."[6]

We ought to remember, as Edmund Burke put it, that "Parliament is not a congress of ambassadors from different and hostile interests; which interests each must maintain, as an agent and advocate, against other agents and advocates." It is, rather, "a deliberative assembly of one nation, with one interest, that of the whole."[7] Thus do our trustees represent our shared interest—with unbending firmness in their right, as their gods give each of them to see the right.

The myths of interwar class cleavages over macroeconomic policy have fed into the mythology of the advent of Keynesianism. In this tradition, Keynes's proposals—flattened to merely countercyclical fiscal policy—were obvious and widely championed by the working class, its unions, and its Labour Party. The ascent of Keynesianism came only as a result of Polanyi's "great transformation," only as the working class refashioned the political, social, and economic order from below. The conclusion is that Keynes failed to influence policy for most of his lifetime.

In fact, Keynes began to revolutionize the global monetary order as early as the mid-1920s. Even in the best of times, the "orthodoxy" was not monolithic, stable, or realistic. The constant debates among the monetary authorities—in the Bank, the Treasury, and the successive currency committees—drove home this point. So Keynes's brilliant critique of the gold standard—its arbitrariness, its failure to operate automatically, and its brutal costs—exposed the barren nakedness of gold's *imperium* to those who knew it best. To be sure, those emperors of the (evolving) orthodoxy denounced Keynes's heresy ever more regularly and fulsomely. But we can now see, to paraphrase Queen Gertrude, that Churchill, Bradbury, and Norman did protest too much.[8] In reality, the new, reformed gold standard they adopted in 1925 followed in specific, crucial ways from Keynes's revolutionary rethinking of the old economic orthodoxy.

## Theocracy

The widespread faith in the orthodoxy combined with the extensive mythology surrounding gold and British imperial ascent to exalt the restoration of the prewar gold standard in the 1920s. In the wake of the Great War, "returning to gold" became more than just a monetary policy. It became a metaphor for returning to the antebellum equilibrium—to that Belle Époque when Britannia ruled the waves, when the Clyde Valley was the workshop of the world, and when the Bank of England "conduct[ed] . . . the international orchestra" of global economic order.[9] That this return demanded sacrifice from all classes and sectors—including finance as well as industry—only made it more alluring.

Britons' zeal to restore their mythologized past concentrated power in the hands of a small group of men who battled to set the terms of the return. Beyond the shared objective, they disagreed mightily about the means by which to achieve it. Despite that his name was attached to the highly orthodox Cunliffe Committee reports, Governor Walter Cunliffe was actually the first to recognize the need for reform. He had seen firsthand the challenges of managing the monetary system during the war, and he knew just how far practice had drifted from theory. He would—and did—construe the postwar peace agreements to build England's gold reserves as much as possible. But even this was not enough. He was convinced that the only way to restore the prewar gold parity was by allowing the use of gold substitutes. He believed that it was possible to transubstantiate government debt into currency that was as good as gold. He might have done so, had he not lost control of his own committee.

John Bradbury, the sometime Treasury official, was the real force behind the dogma that powered the Cunliffe Committee doctrine. Together with allies on the committee, he corralled, cajoled, and convinced witnesses representing a huge range of perspectives and interests to accept his tenets and prescriptions. In doing so, he thus constructed the Cunliffe Committee "consensus." This version of the gold standard had much in common with the system that had existed prior to 1914; but it also included critical departures from prewar practices. Crucially, the Cunliffe Committee's "gold standard" essentially eliminated the use of gold as currency. For many, including Cunliffe's own successor as Bank governor (Brien Cokayne), this was anathema to the true orthodoxy.

Following the war, Bradbury convinced the government to embrace and implement the Cunliffe Committee's dictates. He was well on his way to peeling off the wartime capital controls when the Bank's rising deputy governor

(Montagu Norman) began to resist him from within the Bank. Norman appears to have been the force behind the first major departure from the Cunliffe Committee dictates: Stanley Baldwin's 1920 capital controls. All of this was done behind closed doors among this small group, even as fellow Conservative and Liberal MPs alike clamored for liberalization.

This was precisely the kind of priestly rule that Norman extolled. He did not think macroeconomic policy should be subjected to political or market rule. On the contrary, he was convinced that the right central bankers could and should rule the politicians and the market actors alike.

If Norman were a veto player, so too was Churchill. In the summer of 1924, Norman had pressed to have the capital controls extended by several years. Churchill probably could have secured his support for this when he became chancellor that autumn. Certainly, Churchill was not forced to resume gold exports eight months early. In addition, whatever the Cunliffe Committee reports had said—and whatever Baldwin, now prime minister, had promised—Churchill came to recognize that he could define the "restoration" in a broad range of ways.

In the end, Churchill restored a particular—heavily reformed—version of the gold standard. He did this even as he recognized (better than his colleagues) how costly doing so would prove to be. He did this because he was determined to resolve the UK's unemployment problem. So far from failing to grapple with Keynes's analysis, Churchill engaged it more fully than did his advisers. Indeed, he engaged it with such vigor that he came to identify its critical weakness: Keynes could not explain the persistence of unemployment (in equilibrium) across the first half of the 1920s.

Throughout, Churchill's only constraint was issued by the Federation of British Industries. And it only asked to be informed and assured that its sacrifices would serve an international, UK-led endeavor. Churchill being Churchill, he answered this call masterfully.

But as priestly rule often goes, it did not end well. It was not that the people failed to govern their governors. They did their best. And so too did their exalted elites. The problems of the day were just too challenging, and the beliefs just too capacious and too narrow. The wisdom dearly bought by these failures would bear fruit—but only in time.

## The Past, as It Might Have Been

England's return to gold in 1925 proved to be one of the worst political-economic decisions in modern history. Did it have to be this way? Of course not.

One can easily imagine a world in which Churchill made a different decision. Most simply, he might have delayed the return, waiting to see if the exchange rate could have been kept consistently at the official rate before
removing the capital controls. After all, they did not expire for another eight
months. And if necessary, Churchill might have extended the controls beyond
that point. This is precisely what Governor Norman had vigorously advocated
just a few months prior. At the time, Bradbury and company insisted that imposing capital controls would irreparably damage the UK's financial reputation. But this is just what the Conservatives had done in 1920, two years after
the war had ended.[10] Indeed, the junior minister who had authored that legislation, Baldwin, was now the prime minister. Few would have been surprised
if he and Norman had championed their favored approach once again. Given
his own deep misgivings, Churchill would have been happy to punt the decision down the road, especially if the prime minister and the governor of the
Bank of England were visibly the architects of the delay.

More boldly, Churchill might have listened to Keynes. This *would* have been
surprising at the time, but it is not inconceivable in retrospect. Churchill could
have returned to gold at a devalued rate. This would have broken with tradition, but many other countries did just that. Moreover, Churchill's return did
already break from that oldest tradition: the circulation of gold coins. Or, most
boldly, Churchill might have resolved not to return at all, opting instead for a
managed float of the pound. This was, as Keynes argued, the actual state of
things at the time. And following the suspension of gold convertibility in September 1931, this became the state of things once again. One month after that
suspension, the Conservatives were rewarded with the largest electoral mandate in modern British history. Once elected, they betrayed their promise to
re-return to gold and embraced Keynes's managed pound. Thus, leaving gold
in 1931 proved both economically and politically beneficial, particularly to the
Conservatives. How might the course of world history have differed, on everything from reparations to the Great Depression, had Churchill and his Conservative colleagues done the same things in 1925 that they had done in 1920
or that they would do in 1931?

The same can be said for Norman's impact. If he had not ascended in 1920,
things certainly would have been altogether different. Bradbury would have
continued liberalizing the wartime capital controls, even as the exchange rate
slid—just as he had forced through across 1918 and 1919. At the same time,
Cokayne (or a like-minded successor within the Bank such as Lubbock or Addis) likely would have continued the course of interest rate increases. This
would have been a hard test for the orthodoxy. The depreciated exchange rate
would have combined with Bradbury's capital account liberalization to have

eviscerated the UK's gold reserves. And the austerity would have snapped the postwar boom. But the cheap pound also would have promoted exports, and there could be no complaints from investors about their ability to get gold. Who can say whether those "wins" would have proved sufficiently valuable in the minds of the public to garner the political support necessary to continue this ritual sacrifice?

In either case, the results would have been profound. If the gold standard had passed this acid test, it might have found a new birth of commitment and a precedent in favor of austerity. Or, if it had failed, the evidence would have mounted in the opposite direction, and self-flagellation might have been deemed both more painful and less efficacious than had been promised. Crucially, these assessments would have been made before Keynes had theorized the possibility of macroeconomic stability under flexible exchange rates but also before the Central European hyperinflations heightened fears of questioning the orthodoxy.

One of the most interesting counterfactuals concerns Cunliffe: What if he had not died in 1920 but, instead, had the chance to implement his radical reforms? Allowing banks to hold government debt might have released much of their gold reserves into the UK market. At the same time, Cunliffe's willingness to raise Bank rate would have attracted that gold—and much gold from abroad—to the Bank's vaults. If he had also continued to ruthlessly demand that Germany "pay for the war," this too might have appreciated the pound. But one cannot be sure. Such policies of self-help also might have triggered a "great contraction" of the global money supply—as they did with the approach taken by the United States following 1929—with severe consequences for the internationally oriented UK economy.[11] In other words, the scramble for gold and the trade wars of the Great Depression might have come a decade sooner. At the same time, replacing gold with government securities might have triggered capital flight and imperiled the pound.

In all of these cases, it is impossible to know the full cascade of consequences that would follow from these small differences in personnel. After all, much of the course of events depended on actors' reactions at home and abroad. We cannot calculate the probability of landing on one equilibrium or another. For our purposes, the point is that each of these different paths was plausible, that there were multiple viable equilibria. Just as important, we can be certain that each would have brought massively different consequences for the trajectory of the UK and the global economic order. But for a difference in the shape of the pebble, the avalanche would have been different.

Thus, the infamous "Norman conquest of $4.86" was contingent. Cunliffe, Cokayne, and Keynes all might have captured the crown. Even Bradbury might have stamped more than just his signature on the pound. Or, best of all, Keynes might have saved Churchill from his golden Gallipoli. Indeed, each of these figures' competing dogmas was ascendant at different points.

Given that it might have happened another way, why did it happen the particular way that it did? How do we explain the contours of England's twisted, tortuous journey to Calvary? We will not know the answers to these questions until we grapple with the stories of these particular individuals.

This case illuminates a broader point: pivotal agents matter at least as much as the structures of our world. Of course, we must study the effects of norms, interests, parties, law, institutional design, and so forth. But we ought to study with equal vigor the actors who infuse these concepts with meaning and significance, who crystallize these amorphous objects, and who give practical effect to these abstractions.

What does it really mean to "return to gold"? What does it really mean to "take back control"? What does it really mean to "protect and serve"? The answers to these questions are all determined by individuals—sometimes working alone, sometimes working in concert; sometimes in the corridors of power, sometimes in the public square; sometimes as "the state," sometimes against the state.

This book has shown the crucial role played by a small group of remarkably similar men at the very center of the international gold standard system. We cannot understand this world without reference to them, but it is also crucial to remember that recounting their stories is only a starting point. These men are not the only figures we need to consider to understand this case or, indeed, any such important case. The world wants more—and more varied—stories of the diverse cast of characters who, in a wide array of locales, shape the trajectory of global order. Reconstructing all of these stories promises a richer and more accurate account of human experience.

## The Present

There is much that the history of the gold standard has taught us and can teach us still. It is fitting to distill those lessons that might apply to three of the most pressing challenges of our age. Most concretely and practically, the forces that have powered the Brexit movement come more sharply into focus when viewed through the lens of the UK's gold standard. Second, the gold standard itself remains a hotly debated topic. It is not simply the foil against which monetary theory and policy is compared. For many—including leading politicians and policymakers—we ought to return to gold once again. Last, the detailed history told in the pages of this book offers an intimate perspective on the forces that led to Churchill's momentous policy shift. In particular, we have seen that *belief* plays a vastly larger role in political economy than we have generally appreciated.

## Brexit

As with the mandate to "return to gold," the British people have delivered a mandate to "get Brexit done." But what does that mean? There are striking parallels between the debates surrounding the return to gold and the major disagreements about Brexit.

The most obvious is hard versus soft. How "hard" must the gold standard be? How "hard" must the Brexit be? Cunliffe wanted to monetize the debt, keeping the formal link with gold but considerably softening the standard. Cokayne did not think the country would be "on gold" again until gold sovereigns jingled once again in Britons' pockets. Bradbury began near Cokayne's position, but Keynes and Norman persuaded him to acquiesce to something much softer. So too with Brexit. Theresa May wanted to formally withdraw from the EU but to keep intact as many of the old economic ties as possible. Nigel Farage wanted to renegotiate all of these ties. Boris Johnson began near Farage's position, but only time will tell if he and his successors will hold that ground. Whatever his arrangements, there will still be much to play for in the years to come.

What was the right path up Calvary? Keynes (and Norman until 1925) wanted to steer the pound back up to its prewar exchange rate before resuming gold convertibility. On the other extreme, the Cunliffe Committee insisted that the capital controls be removed as a necessary preliminary to finding the pound's real gold value and resuming the vital mechanisms of the price-specie-flow machinery.

So too with Brexit. To avoid a "cliff edge" Brexit, May was determined to establish a transitional agreement with the EU before the UK formally withdrew. Other hardline Brexiteers, however, welcomed a "clean" Brexit, leaving the EU first and then pursuing free trade simultaneously with Europe and beyond.[12]

There is also the question of accountability. Unprecedented deference was given to the monetary authorities in the name of restoring the gold standard. The several currency committees, with their secret meetings, dictated the fate of the global monetary order.

So too with Brexit. Yet May wanted even more authority and less accountability. Initially, she demanded the power to negotiate Brexit without granting Parliament a vote on whatever agreement she reached. This, apparently, was the real meaning of "taking back control"—transforming parliamentary sovereignty into government fiat. For his part, Johnson has simply refused to divulge more than absolutely necessary. Such seems unavoidable when a hugely complicated undertaking is reduced to a simple binary.

Last, how settled was the policy shift? In the case of the gold standard, Churchill resumed gold exports in 1925, but much more was left to be determined than we have usually recognized. Churchill said that restoring several of the previously defining features of the gold standard, such as the circulation of gold sovereigns and unrestricted convertibility, were "out of the question in present circumstances." The wording effectively managed expectations while allowing some hope that a more complete restoration would still come in the future. Churchill also indefinitely deferred the settling of the ultimate size of the money supply "until we have sufficient experience."[13]

So too with Brexit. The UK's formal exit from the EU at the end of January 2020 was attended by much fanfare by Brexiteers. But there remains continued ambiguity about the long-term relationship. In that sense the formal withdrawal was just a first (albeit landmark) step toward a new relationship with Europe, just as Churchill's resumption of gold exports was a first (also landmark) step toward a restoration of the prewar gold standard. It remains to be seen whether Johnson's Brexit will restore the pre-1973 order more fully and durably than Churchill's return restored the pre-1914 order.

Beyond the similarities in form, the very substance of Brexit—the endeavor to restore the old order of things—is itself quintessentially British. Indeed, it is less surprising that Keynes and Niemeyer grappled with the gold standard with reference to Newton and Ricardo than that Churchill did not attempt to tie the gold standard to Magna Carta. Any foreigner who visits or lives in this country is invariably struck by Britons' deep commitment to the "long continuity of [their] institutions"—even if those institutions are sometimes confounding, even if that continuity is sometimes contrived.[14]

If there is any essential principle to the British—as opposed to the English—constitution, it would seem to be the rule of continuity. After all, it is thanks to "the Restoration" that the monarchy exists today. Even the Glorious Revolution, Whigs like Burke maintained, "was made to preserve our *ancient* indisputable laws, . . . liberties, and . . . constitution. . . . The very idea of the fabrication of a new government is enough to fill us with disgust and horror. . . . We wished at the period of the Revolution, and do now wish, to derive all we possess as *an inheritance from our forefathers*. . . . All the reformations we have hitherto made have proceeded upon the principle of reference to antiquity."[15]

This was "the Whig[s'] interpretation of history."[16] On the other side lay the Conservatives, and behind them the old Jacobites who had struggled for decades to restore the Stuarts to the throne(s). The clash of conflicting continuities was the *modus*, if not also the *principium*, of these timeless struggles. So too with the timeless debate between Locke and Lowndes over the metallic standard, which we saw repeated in its essentials between Keynes and Churchill. In lands in which Cromwell and William III still adorn political murals, one shudders at the prospect that Brexit will see "history" weaponized once again. Yet as Brexit proceeds, each faction will quite naturally fight to see its antiquity, its antecedents, its martyrs resurrected.

The resumption of the old monetary disputes obviously presents lower stakes than does the resumption of these kingdoms' internecine violence. But the discussions surrounding Brexit also connect with the exceptional history of the pound sterling.

One of the great surprises in monetary history is that the pound reached such global centrality despite being manifestly inferior at performing one of the three essential functions of money: serving as a unit of account. The myriad (endearing) denominations—pounds, shillings, pence, farthings, florins, guineas, sovereigns, and so forth—and the extensive slang make things hard enough. But the valuations, based on ancient measures and non-base-ten relationships, are intractable to any not inured to them. Who would set out to make their principle currency unit divisible by both twelve and twenty?

Not Thomas Jefferson. Following the American Revolution, Jefferson proposed founding the new nation's currency on a decimalized basis:

> The most easy ratio of multiplication and division is that by ten. . . . Every one remembers . . . be[ing] puzzled with adding the farthings, taking out the fours and carrying them on; adding the pence, taking out the twelves and carrying them on; adding the shillings, taking out the twenties and carrying them on. But when he came to the pounds, where he had only tens to carry forward, it was easy and free from error. . . . Foreigners too who trade or travel among us will find a great facility in understanding our coins and accounts from this ratio of subdivision.[17]

Jefferson's logic rang true, even with his great monetary antithesis Alexander Hamilton. Following Hamilton's institutionalization of the idea in his *Report on the Establishment of a Mint*, one country after another followed this example.[18]

The UK, however, stood apart, bucking the global trend for another two centuries. Jefferson was not wrong about the inconvenience of keeping accounts in the complex pre-decimalized, ever-shifting units. But the pound prevailed because it performed so incomparably well at the other two essential functions of money: storing value and serving as a medium of exchange. Ultimately, it mattered less that the crown, the old sovereign, the guinea, and the other passing (nominal) units changed because the pound (however comprised) was always worth precisely the same quantity of gold. Just as important, the pound commanded goods and services in one of the largest and most dynamic economies in the world. By these means, the UK delayed until 1971 the rationalization that Hamilton had formalized in 1791.

Two years later, the UK joined the European Economic Community. Now that we are undoing that, one wonders how long before a Pound Research Group forms and suggests we undo the decimalization of the pound as well. After all, the prime minister did promise, "We are going to be a fully independent, sovereign country. . . . And that means we are going, once more, to have the freedom to make our own decisions on a whole host of different matters," including "on weights and measures" and "issues like teaspoons."[19] Thus, Brexit will finally grant the chance to restore all of our old weights, measures, and denominations of currency—those ancient "British" units brought here by the Romans.

More seriously, the point is that such labels matter to the people here, whatever Francophile revolutionaries like Jefferson might say. Understanding that is essential to understanding the return to gold in 1925. And grappling with that decision helps us to understand the seemingly irrational but powerful role of beliefs and identities that continues to rule these islands.

## Restoring the Gold Standard, Revisited

From Bitcoin to the future of the eurozone to the renminbi's challenge to the dollar, we are increasingly questioning the future of the international monetary system. All of these discussions are informed by some conventional wisdom about the trajectory of the monetary order over the last several centuries. The gold-backed pound sterling stands as one of the two hegemonic monetary orders against which everything else continues to be compared. For many, the gold standard remains, well, the gold standard of monetary regimes.

For some, gold is prized even beyond that. For them, it is not only the past but also the future of money. The fact that most academics today disdain a return to gold evidently has not curbed the broader goldbug movement or inoculated top policymakers from continuing to consider it. In 2010, the World Bank president proposed in the *Financial Times* that the global monetary "system should . . . consider employing gold as an international reference point of market expectations about inflation, deflation, and future currency values."[20]

President Trump sought to appoint one avowed goldbug after another to the Federal Reserve Board of Governors. One hopes that seriously considering England's return to gold would disabuse us of such dangerous ideas.

Keynes's indictments of the orthodox gold standard are still damning. From whence do we get the gold? To pull it from the earth is not only costly—particularly to the many children in the mines—but also capricious.[21] Must we bind the money supply—and thus the domestic macroeconomic cycle of booms and busts—to, as Marshall put it, "the hazards of mining"?[22] Drawing it from the reserves of our friends and rivals abroad is even more dangerous. At best, it breeds mercantilist trade war. At worst, it leads to the kind of rapacious reparations that sow the seeds of strife. Cunliffe, and the "twenty years' crisis" that followed, were not unique. For centuries, countries have tried to live up to the gold standard ideals. Virtually all nonhegemonic powers have failed perennially. More important, the pursuit itself is perilous. So far from securing domestic stability and cultivating international cooperation—the avowed goals of the gold standard—the worship of gold has wrought dislocation at home and fomented disharmony abroad.[23]

What is said for the gold standard? In an age of distrust and cyber-insecurity, many admire gold for its materiality, its privacy-preserving untraceability, and its decentralized creation. Others place their faith in its high, transhistorical intrinsic value. But the strongest argument is still that which the orthodoxy marshaled in the 1920s: it promises to tie the hands of spendthrift governments and out-of-control central banks alike.

Yet even those arguments fall prey to the gold standard mythology in numerous ways. Simply put, the gold standard *did not* strictly discipline governments. Remember that countries even with primarily metallic currency have regularly debased their currencies. Crucially, this was the norm prior to the Glorious Revolution, as both Locke and Lowndes agreed.[24] Moreover, after Locke prevailed in 1696, Newton, who had argued for devaluation then, still got the better of him with the implicit devaluation of the pound's silver value (relative to gold) in his own reports on the mint.[25] Simply put, if even Locke and Newton clashed to craft the perfect currency, what hope is there for the likes of Ted Cruz and Herman Cain?

Those who celebrate the distributed aspects of a purely gold currency have hit upon some real potential advantages. The trouble is that the market always and everywhere, including in the UK under the gold standard, gravitates away from using gold itself in most transactions. There are numerous reasons for this. It is too risky—imagine traveling to a real estate sale with the payment in gold coins. It is too inconvenient—how are we to conduct global businesses without nonphysical means of payment and settlement?[26] It is too constrained—at today's prices, purchasing a £4 pint of stout would require a "gold" coin that contained just 0.004 ounces of gold. It is too unreliable—if virtually all of the currency we used contains virtually no gold, how could ordinary people be sure that it contains any gold at all? It is too fragile—even if "coin clipping" can be thwarted using high-precision scales in every transaction, how can private actors and hostile powers be prevented from minting impure counterfeits? Again and again, the market has embraced alternatives, and intermediaries, to gold. It has done this even in contexts—like the prewar UK—where there was little question of the reliability of the gold coins themselves. Notably, London's sterling bills, and not the British sovereign, ruled the world's markets. Within England, it is astounding that half of the currency in 1914 took the form of gold coins. At the same time, it is important to remember that half of the England's currency in 1914 did not.[27]

In 1925, Keynes, Norman, and Churchill were confirmed in that bold prediction each had advanced: the public would not much care whether "the gold standard" involved the circulation of gold itself. They recognized that even when actors have ready opportunities to use gold as a medium of exchange, they are just as often found employing the many alternatives to it. The same is true with the use of gold as a store of value. The contention that gold should be our money because its value remains stable in the long run is a red herring. For one thing, the value of gold is not particularly stable with respect to any other commodity or with respect to the overall stock of goods and services. Moreover, nothing is stopping market actors from converting their savings into gold already. They can, and some of them do, use fiat currency to buy gold bars, gold coins, and various types of gold certificates. The fact that most savings is not currently in the form of gold suggests that the free market has not found gold to be the best vehicle for storing wealth. Should the people be "forced to be free" by a state that makes them take the sovereign's sovereign?[28]

The *ultimo ratio* of the gold standard is the "automatic" constraint it is said to impose on the monetary authorities. Again and again, we saw the orthodoxy deploy this argument. Most conspicuously, Schuster led the rejoinder to Keynes, proclaiming, "What the world demands is a currency not managed by any body of men, but resting on something that they understand and something recognized as of intrinsic value all over the world."[29] Then the Chamberlain-Bradbury Committee fell upon Keynes during his testimony, suggesting that it would take "breed[ing] a superman" to manage the monetary system without the gold anchor. "The gold standard," Bradbury explained to Churchill, "was knave-proof."[30] Even Skidelsky suggests that Keynes simply "side-stepped the problem of the Wicked Chancellor."[31]

This view has persisted. Schumpeter conceded this as the "one point about the gold standard that would redeem it from the charge of foolishness": "It imposes restrictions upon governments or bureaucracies that are much more powerful than is parliamentary criticism."[32] Today this remains the principal motivation behind the growing movement to (again) return to gold. Two decades ago, the founder of the Ludwig von Mises Institute (Lew Rockwell) laid out the agenda:

> The difference between our present system and a future gold standard would be a monetary system based on the dollar being backed by a tangible commodity instead of the decisions of macro-managers. . . . Full convertibility must be maintained for every member of the currency-holding public. It is the threat of mass conversion of currency into gold coin that disciplines banks and governments. It would once again be the public's most effective weapon against inflation and unwarranted credit expansion.[33]

Judy Shelton, Trump's most recent goldbug nominee to the Federal Reserve Board of Governors, has issued the same arguments:

> The guarantee provided by gold convertibility not only assures individuals that their purchasing power is not subject to depreciation, it also serves as protection against a runaway, tyrannical government bent on expanding its own power. When citizens accept responsibility for controlling the federal purse strings and literally control the money, government is constrained in the best Jeffersonian tradition. The United States could hardly provide a better example of its political philosophy than to implement a gold standard and promote the benefits of sound money to a world in desperate search of a rational basis for international monetary relations.[34]

Perhaps the principal problem with this argument is that going *on* the gold standard does not itself prevent an authority from going *off* of that standard in a moment of crisis. There are all of those informal mechanisms that can insulate the monetary authorities from market pressures. We must not forget how even the bullionist Cokayne crowed to the Cunliffe Committee that he had maintained the pound's convertibility de jure but eliminated it de facto through moral suasion. But even under the halcyon days of the nineteenth-century gold standard system in the UK, there was nevertheless a ritual—in the vernacular, "securing the chancellor's letter"—by which the Bank could suspend convertibility in times of crisis.[35] That the chancellor only wrote four such letters in a century was due less to the existence of a formal rule "guaranteeing" convertibility than to the dividend of hegemony and the deeply ingrained norms. Whatever the combination of necessary conditions, the suspensions of 1931 (UK) and 1971 (US) both suggest that declining hegemons prove unwilling and/or incapable of abiding these constraints at precisely those moments when markets most fear policymakers' perfidy. After all, if we do not trust the monetary authorities to manage a fiat currency responsibly, why should we expect that they would manage a gold standard any more responsibly? Each is just a promise, the one no harder, no faster than the other.

Constraining the monetary authority by binding the currency to a specific gold price is akin to commanding that rules A and B shall not be broken unless the authority first breaks rule C. It is disingenuous to suggest that metallic standards perform better than do alternatives, provided the authority maintains convertibility. Inflation targeting also works quite well with the same caveat: so long as the authorities do not violate their obligations. The prospect of irresponsible governments abusing their monetary sovereignty is a serious concern, but we set ourselves "too easy, too useless a task" if we just proclaim that governments will respect our property rights so long as they follow our rules.[36]

It is true that a single gold price offers a bright line that is easier for the market to police. But as Keynes argued in the *Tract*, a predesignated price index would provide an equally bright line—one that was less arbitrary and less distortionary.[37]

It would also better address the problem that Keynes, and then Norman, identified in the 1920s: powerful central bankers can use reserves to manipulate the market gold supply itself rather than allowing the market to discipline their monetary policies. Indeed, the history we have considered here shows that the bright line of the London gold price did not constrain the UK monetary authorities as tightly as most goldbugs have assumed. Under both the prewar and the new gold standards, the Bank maintained convertibility, and the London (market) gold price remained at parity. Yet before the war, the Bank maintained a 67 percent gold coverage rate for its notes; and following Churchill's return, the rate hovered at just 33 percent. If the demands of the market were constant, this shows that the prewar Bank and perhaps even the interwar Bank had an excess of reserves. Certainly Cunliffe himself argued as much. But if a 33 percent reserve rate were the minimum across both periods, that is to say that the prewar bank could have doubled its supply of notes without any more difficulty than it faced in the second half of the 1920s.[38] More broadly, how constrained is a bank that can vary its note emission across such a large range? Does this not leave us with a "body of men" determining what credit expansions and contractions are "warrantable"?[39]

Alternatively, if the market's demands had changed between 1914 and 1925, what changed them? Materialists might point to all of those modifications that Norman and Churchill made to the practical working of the new gold standard—those many ways they specifically insulated the Bank from market pressure. Constructivists would emphasize the significant reconstruction of market expectations. This is precisely what Norman promised he would do. Even before this, the Cunliffe Committee's £150 million minimum reserve figure had become, through much recitation, sacrosanct. But, we saw, that figure was derived with essentially no analysis of history, contemporary monetary estimates, or consultation with the speculators themselves. In spirit if not in size, it was Pigou's suggestion, "Say that it should be doubled." It just so happened to align with the quantity of gold that Bradbury thought the UK was capable of centralizing in its reserves in the near future.

If central bankers and currency committees have such power, how can we expect the market to discipline them? In their zeal to protect themselves from the proverbial "wicked chancellor," the advocates of the gold standard increase the peril of "the wicked Bank governor." We saw again and again how the monetary authorities drove even the world's most powerful bankers, gold miners, and industrialists to accept their preordained conclusions—all in the name of the gold standard. If Schuster and Holden could be dominated thus, what chance did the small Scottish and Irish banks have against the leviathan? The irony is that these banking behemoths had themselves grown so large—in the heyday of the gold standard—because the government did not stop them from buying up all of the smaller banks.[40] The greater irony is that the Bank of England was itself still a private institution. As the United States learned with J. P. Morgan, such economies are likely to evolve a "central" bank.[41] The real question is whether the state, let alone the market, is capable of really governing such an actor.

These points matter today because the persistence of the gold standard faith offers false hope and the promise of security, independence, and reliability. The great travesty of the orthodox gold standard was that it was *perceived* as instituting rule-based limitations on authority when it actually centralized decision-making, enshrined discretion, and empowered authority. Quite simply, the dynamics it generated defy our vocabularies of politics and economics. Following contemporaries, only the language of organized religion captures the place of gold in England. Understanding how and why this was true then ought to change the way we approach political economy today.

## The Power of Belief

At the turn of the twentieth century, Georg Simmel powerfully described the process by which individuals increasingly surrendered their agency to broader societal structures. "The individual," he wrote, is "more and more dependent upon the achievements of people, but less and less dependent upon the personalities that lie behind them."[42] Of course, Simmel was hardly the first to emphasize the predominance of structure. His insight was to fixate on money as the central factor in promoting structure over agency. By facilitating impersonal exchange, money serves to depersonalize interpersonal relationships. It grants "the possibility of the individual participating in associations, the objective purpose of which he wants to promote and enjoy, without that connection implying any commitment on his part." "Money," Simmel argued, "has provided us with the sole possibility for uniting people while excluding everything personal and specific." In other words, money provides the means by which individuals can achieve their ends from social relations without having to—without getting to—inject their personalities into those relations. Money thus disintegrates the old social fabric and isolates the individual.[43]

For nearly every individual, this is true. We do (albeit tacitly) consent to place a value on money and thus consent to the manifold consequences that follow.[44] But we are nevertheless price-takers. Money in a commercial world is what rain is in an agricultural society. It is the essence with which—around which—we order our lives. But, like the weather, the money supply is to us capricious: a deluge at one moment, a drought the next.

But what of our monetary authorities—those policymakers who determine money's very essence, specify its operation, and define its value? Creating and destroying money at will, they are wizards who conjure our weather. By decreasing and increasing the money supply, they drain and flood the fields. By regulating and deregulating banks, they build and shape the canals that irrigate our crops. By imposing and removing capital controls, they part the seas for some and release them unto others. By defining what is and what is not money, they transform water into wine and water into blood.

Granted, their sorcery is hardly a science, and they fail more often than they succeed. But their failures only elevate their importance. Our wizards wield forces so great, we perceive, that even they can hardly control this magic. So whenever their spells prove too weak or too overwhelming, the sorcerers insist that they are humble servants of a divinity no human can understand. This both deepens and masks the dominance they achieve through their mastery of money. It simultaneously lowers and exposes humanity. We exist at the behest of the market gods—the god of production, the god of consumption, the god of stability, the god of growth. Whether they be one god with persistent contradictions or many gods with perennial competitions, these are the forces that make and break our world.

Why have we resisted acknowledging this—the power of belief? Most generally, our innate chauvinism has driven us to distinguish ourselves from our history and to deprecate the peoples of "the past." Even the younger Keynes fell prey to this, even as he grappled with the endurance of "the barbarous relic." He set us back (in multiple ways) when, in the preface to the French edition of the *Tract*, he compared the approach of contemporary central bankers to that of "African witch doctor[s]."[45] Keynes was right that these judgments followed from essentially the same mode of analysis: religious, broadly construed. But his Whiggish rhetoric invited the conquest of rationalization and what Hayek called "scientism."[46] By deprecating the influence of beliefs in favor of "economic causes," Keynes also (inadvertently) advanced the conquest of materialism.[47]

Far more blame lies with Marx. He, more than anyone before him, extirpated "religion" from political economy.[48] He believed that our practical emancipation depended upon secularizing not just "the religious spirit" but also our mode of analysis, our critique of political economy.[49] For him, religion was merely a "particular [form] of production" that depended on the "material intercourse of men, the language of real life."[50] Marx's assault reached its most extreme point in the quip that religion has opiated the masses.[51]

If the gold standard orthodoxy opiated the British people, it opiated most of England's elites as well. From the Trades Union Congress to the Federation of British Industries, from Snowden goading Churchill for an early return to Schuster being reconstructed by Pigou and Bradbury, we have seen throughout this book that the coalescence, ascent, and transcendence of the gold standard orthodoxy defies all materialist explanation. The effervescence that was the gold standard was never solid and, so, could not melt. Its holiness was nary profaned. And even when it defied logic and faced manifest disconfirmation, its adherents still were not "compelled to face with sober senses [their] real conditions of life."[52]

Perhaps it is possible to analyze macroeconomics without falling into faith, without the kind of logical self-contradictions and shoddy empirical analysis that were de rigueur for the gold standard orthodoxy. But as analysts of real people, real events, and real decisions, we must be faithful to the fact that those considered here seldom achieved this—despite what they may have thought, despite what they often did say.[53] This book has endeavored to do that, using religious allusions and metaphors as analytic, as well as literary, devices. It contends that England's return to gold is more accurately conveyed à la religious history than political and economic history. This is not to belittle the gold standard orthodoxy as mere religious superstition. The point is to take seriously the role of belief in political economy.

By "belief," I mean more than just the source of constructed preferences and strategies for maximizing those preferences—although beliefs obviously shape both of those as well. We also need to understand the manner in which actors comprehend their reality—specifically, the expectation that there are powerful forces at work making normative judgments about our behavior and defining the consequences of our actions. We have thought that those responsible for England's cross of gold considered macroeconomics as akin to medicine, and so we have studied these actors as if they were "money doctors." With the benefit of hindsight, we have conducted our own postmortem on the British economy, proposed our own remedies, measured the efforts of these money doctors against our prescriptions, and then drawn the natural conclusions as to why they failed to save their patient. That may be what these money doctors believed and said they were doing, but that is not the history that they created.[54] They did not seriously measure the money supply or quantities of gold in the UK before they made their (unflinching) recommendations, which is to say that they did not measure the patient's fever. They did not seriously interrogate the natural experiments of the past or the present, which is to say that they did not craft the treatment plan in the context of a broader epidemiological assessment. And they did not systematically consult price indices and other macroeconomic indicators as they implemented their policies, which is to say that they did not rigorously monitor the patient's vitals as they administered their treatments. Moreover, these policymakers also perennially failed to live up to their own exacting standards, making far fewer material changes than they prescribed for themselves. Parliament did embrace capital controls, Norman did stay the hand of Bank rate increases, and Bradbury did alloy the elements of the gold standard.

This is not to suggest that these actors were disingenuous, dishonest brokers, or antiscience—quite the contrary. They were just men, not heroes or prophets or even philosophers. They were "generously intentioned [men]," but they still had "many of the weaknesses of other human beings." And the burden on their shoulders—to return the world to 1914—proved crushing.[55]

More broadly, the example of the return to gold reveals that even the most thoughtful, best trained, and most analytically rigorous economic advisers are still bedeviled by the inexorable belief that spirits levy final judgment.[56] To some, the UK's money doctors might have been simple plague doctors, a premodern incarnation of their latter-day rationalized, "scientized" iterations. But we have seen how those several currency committees really practiced their art, and it more closely resembles the trials of the inquisitors than the experiments of the alchemists. All those interminable testimonies and discussions were less about examining witnesses and collecting evidence—despite the official designations in the committees' minutes themselves—than they were about purifying the orthodoxy's own beliefs and rooting out heresy.

This will not surprise modern political theorists, particularly those operating in a "critical" mode. Nietzsche, then Keynes and Orwell, and finally Foucault re-inverted Marx's materialist revolution. They recognized that the power to define beliefs and to construct "knowledge" is itself the essence of power and authority. Certainly, "the gold standard" was a form of "governmentality" if ever there were one.[57] Arguably, the gold standard orthodoxy was the quintessential governmentality of political economy.[58] But what sustained—and empowered—the gold standard regime, this self-reinforcing equilibrium of knowledge-power?

Here the relentless reality of religious faith proves indispensable. As Hume put it,

> A purpose, an intention, a design is evident in every thing; and when our comprehension is so far enlarged as to contemplate the first rise of this visible system, we must adopt, with the strongest conviction, the idea of some intelligent cause or author. The uniform maxims, too, which prevail throughout the whole frame of the universe, naturally, if not necessarily, lead us to conceive this intelligence as single and undivided, where the prejudices of education oppose not so reasonable a theory. Even the contrarieties of nature, by discovering themselves every where, become proofs of some consistent plan, and establish one single purpose or intention, however inexplicable and incomprehensible.[59]

As ever, we resist the rule of chaos.[60] We do not want to believe that much of the nature and many of the causes of the wealth of nations lies beyond the realm of human understanding. We do not want to believe that our fortunes depend upon *fortuna*. So when we encounter those less fortunate, we ask whether it was their sin or that of their parents that has thus prostrated their development. We personify market forces; or, at least, we see in them "animal spirits" and so erect idols of the bull and the bear.

More important, we rarefy heroes, prophets, and demigods as those who possess the power to arouse, to steer, and to harness these forces. Their triumphs and tragedies are explained in the same way that our antecedents explained the fates of the Israelites, of Troy, and of the Spanish Armada. "Flavit Jehovah et Dissipati Sunt"—"Jehovah blew, and they were scattered"—read the medals minted in England in 1588. "The market pushed those rates up," Paul Volcker said of his interest rate hikes, which surpassed 20 percent during his tenure as chairman of the Federal Reserve Board.[61] So instead of entreating Jehovah, Zeus, and Christ, we make sacrifices to modernity's god, money, on the altars of central bank restraint, investor confidence, and—Norman's favorite—market psychology. This is not to suggest that "anything flies" in central banking any more than it did in the Sinai Peninsula, the Dardanelles, or the English Channel. But much of our explanations of real, material outcomes turns on preternatural forces: Elizabeth's virtue and thunderous speech at Tilbury conjured the "Protestant wind" just as Volcker's restraint and 1979 announcement "convinced" the market to abate the inflationary spiral. The same impulses that gave us Moses, Solomon, and Joshua gave us Cunliffe, Bradbury, and Norman. And so too did Schuster, Snowden, and Smillie sacrifice their profits on the word of their prophets.

Thus, it is not that the gold standard orthodoxy was a religion fashioned to serve political economy. Nor is it that political economy simply serves our religion. Instead, the two sit on reverse faces of the same coin, operating in the same modes for the same reasons and exerting the same influences. Our belief in progress would have us treat as a puerile atavism what remains a constant in all of our renderings of the social, political, and economic world: we believe that there is some omnipotent, omniscient alien essence that guides and disciplines our actions.[62]

## The Future

What does it mean to grapple with the reality that none of us understands the power of money? What does it mean to know that none of us has known, or will know, how to subdue—or even entreat—this divinity that rules us all?

One rages not against any particular faith. Each was inchoate, incomplete, and inconsistent. One rages against the blind faith in belief—the reality that so many well-meaning, thoughtful people know that they see but "through a glass, darkly," and yet consider resolve to be a substitute for resolution. Money is the most omnipotent and omnipresent divinity of the modern age. It performs more miracles and wreaks more havoc than any of the gods of any (self-described) religion. But we still approach money in our primeval way, erecting churches to one orthodoxy or another. Each believes that his or her particular dogma can describe money's essence and that his or her own religion must prescribe our practice. The cacophonous catastrophe that was England's cross of gold ought to humble us all. But it was less that the solution was awful than that the challenge was overwhelming. Much can be said for those many gold standards advanced in this period. Much more can be said for the systems that came after. But given those two realities—meaningful cross-sectional and cross-temporal variation across ostensibly the same "standard"—it seems that we ought to place less faith in our ability to know and more in our ability to learn.

In that spirit, two exemplary characters stand out: the man who did the most to save the prewar gold orthodoxy, and the man who did the most to destroy it. John Bradbury loved the gold standard. Nobody proved more devoted to it. And yet a few lines in a letter from Bradbury to Farrer after Keynes's testimony in the summer of 1924 are enough to restore one's faith in humanity. Keynes, too, was well practiced at admitting when he had been wrong. Perhaps there was nobody better at doing so. Certainly, there was nobody better known for doing so. Taken together, these old colleagues teach us that sincerely grappling with our mistakes and openly admitting them—what is sometimes called "confession"—is the preliminary to growing beyond them.

So let us be partisans. Let us have faiths. Let us have our zeal, our passion, and our meanings.

But let us also try new things. Let us also change our minds—entertaining more opinions than people in the room. Let us distrust, despise, and disabuse authority.

But most of all, let us also be humble. Let us know that we are uncertain. Let us know that we may not be better today than we were yesterday. But let us still hope that we will not be the same tomorrow.

# Notes

## 1. Genesis and Exodus

1. Across the centuries prior to this, the government had routinely adjusted the metallic content of the currency—as both Locke and his critics agree. William Lowndes, *A Report containing an Essay for the Amendment of the Silver Coins* (London, 1695), 56–57; John Locke, *Further Considerations concerning Raising the Value of Money*, in *Locke on Money*, ed. Patrick Hyde Kelly (Oxford: Clarendon Press, 1991), 458–63. Locke favored a silver standard. In 1717, however, Isaac Newton (who served as Master of the Mint) mistakenly overvalued gold relative to silver. Due to Gresham's Law, this drove the pound from a silver to a gold standard de facto.

2. See Churchill's famous words in an altogether different context. Parliamentary Debates, House of Commons, June 18, 1940, vol. 362, column 60.

3. Parliamentary Debates, House of Commons, April 28, 1925, vol. 183, columns 54–55.

4. Parliamentary Debates, House of Commons, May 14, 1925, vol. 183, column 2027.

5. This was the Treasury's contemporary estimate. NA T 176/13, Restoration of Gold Standard, April 28, 1925.

6. Stanley Baldwin, "Message from the Prime Minister," *Saturday Review of Politics, Literature, Science, and Art*, May 8, 1926.

7. CHAR 22/143/10–12, Churchill to Dawson, May 8, 1926.

8. Melvin C. Shefftz, "The Trade Disputes and Trade Unions Act of 1927: The Aftermath of the General Strike," *Review of Politics* 29, no. 3 (1967): 387–406; Anne Perkins, *A Very British Strike: 3 May–12 May 1926* (London: Macmillan, 2006), 97, 202–7.

9. The UK was not the first country to return to gold, and it would not be the last. But it was the most conspicuous instance of a major economy swallowing significant deflation in order to do so. Many countries, such as France, returned to the gold standard but only after instituting a measurable devaluation (i.e., a reduction in the official gold value of the franc). Those countries that suffered hyperinflation, such as Germany and Austria, restored the gold standard by simply demonetizing their debased currencies. Several countries, such as the United States, did not face much inflation and were thus able to maintain their parities with far less difficulty.

10. Barry Eichengreen, *Golden Fetters: The Gold Standard and the Great Depression, 1919–1939* (New York: Oxford University Press, 1992), xi, 4.

11. John Maynard Keynes, *The Collected Writings of John Maynard Keynes*, ed. Elizabeth Johnson and Donald Moggridge (London: Macmillan, 1971–1989), 25:22.

12. Keynes, *Collected Writings*, 7:349.

13. Barry Eichengreen and Peter Temin, "Fetters of Gold and Paper," *Oxford Review of Economic Policy* 26, no. 3 (Autumn 2010): 370–384.

14. Eichengreen and Irwin show that those countries that embraced the gold standard in the interwar period were more likely to implement mercantilist trade policies. Barry Eichengreen and Douglas Irwin, "The Slide to Protectionism in the Great Depression: Who Succumbed and Why?" *Journal of Economic History* 70, no. 4 (November 2010): 872.

15. Megan McArdle, "Gold-Buggery Takes Center Stage at Republican Debate," *Chicago Tribune*, November 12, 2015, https://www.chicagotribune.com/opinion/commentary/ct-republican-candidates-gold-standard-inflation-20151112-story.html.

16. Stuart Varney, "Donald Trump Welcomes 'Trade War' with China," Fox News, November 10, 2010, http://www.foxnews.com/on-air/your-world-cavuto/transcript/donald-trump-welcomes-trade-war-china. In April 2019, Trump announced that he would appoint Herman Cain to the US Federal Reserve Board. In 2012, Cain had published an editorial in the *Wall Street Journal* that explicitly called for a return to the gold standard. Herman Cain, "We Need a Dollar as Good as Gold," *Wall Street Journal*, May 13, 2012, https://www.wsj.com/articles/SB10001424052702304070304577395891113592150. Cain's nomination faced resistance by four of the Senate's fifty-three Republicans, taking him below the majority needed for confirmation. In the face of this—and, by his own account, the realization that the job does not pay well—Cain withdrew his candidacy. Sam Fleming, "Herman Cain Withdraws as Contender for Federal Reserve Board," *Financial Times*, April 23, 2019, https://www.ft.com/content/dbf5f6e4-651b-11e9-a79d-04f350474d62; Herman Cain, "The Real Reasons I Withdrew from Fed Consideration—Direct from Me, the Only Source You Need," *Western Journal*, April 22, 2019, https://www.westernjournal.com/hermancain/real-reasons-withdrew-fed-consideration-direct-source-need/. With Cain's explanation in mind, who could question whether Cain, Cruz, and Trump should be committed to the "golden straightjacket"?

17. In terms of the classic Goldstein-Keohane typology, the gold standard was closest to a "world view." Defining money itself and the relationship between the world's economies, it was to the international economic order what sovereignty was to the international political order. It incorporated both principled and causal ideas. Judith Goldstein and Robert O. Keohane, "Ideas and Foreign Policy: An Analytical Framework," in *Ideas and Foreign Policy: Beliefs, Institutions, and Political Change*, ed. Judith Goldstein and Robert O. Keohane (Ithaca, NY: Cornell University Press, 1993), 8.

18. This book builds upon—but goes further than—similar studies of the power of the "money doctors" to construct and reconstruct the monetary regimes within states. Kathleen R. McNamara, *Currency of Ideas* (Ithaca, NY: Cornell University Press, 1998); Jeffrey M. Chwieroth, *Capital Ideas: The IMF and the Rise of Financial Liberalization* (Princeton, NJ: Princeton University Press, 2009); Marc Flandreau, ed., *Money Doctors: The Experience of International Financial Advising 1850–2000* (Abingdon, UK: Routledge, 2005); Stephen C. Nelson, *The Currency of Confidence: How Economic Beliefs Shape the IMF's Relationship with Its Borrowers* (Ithaca, NY: Cornell University Press, 2017).

19. The noble was an English gold coin first minted in 1351. The sovereign was the last English gold coin to circulate as currency.

20. Keynes, *Collected Writings*, 9:212.

21. Donald Moggridge, *The Return to Gold, 1925: The Formulation of Economic Policy and Its Critics* (New York: Cambridge University Press, 1969).

22. William Manchester, *The Last Lion: Winston Spencer Churchill: Visions of Glory, 1874–1932* (Boston: Little, Brown, and Company, 1983); Robert Skidelsky, *John Maynard Keynes*, vol. 2, *The Economist as Saviour, 1920–1937*, 1992.

23. To name a few, Liaquat Ahamed, Michael Bordo, Robert Boyce, Susan Howson, Donald Moggridge, Richard Sayers, and Philip Williamson plunged into the archives to piece together individual narratives that propelled the UK through this tumultuous period. Theirs are the stories of pivotal figures who not only transcended their structural constraints but frequently redefined those very structures. Liaquat Ahamed, *Lords of Finance: The Bankers Who Broke the World* (London: Windmill Books, 2010); Michael D. Bordo, "The Gold Standard: The Traditional Approach," in *A Retrospective on the Classical Gold Standard, 1821–1931*, ed. Michael D. Bordo and Anna J. Schwartz (Chicago: University of Chicago Press, 1984), 23–119; Robert Boyce, *The Great Interwar Crisis and the Collapse of Globalization* (New York: Palgrave Macmillan, 2009); Susan Howson, *Domestic Monetary Management in Britain, 1919–1938* (Cambridge: Cambridge University Press, 1975); Moggridge, *Return to Gold*; Donald Moggridge, *British Monetary Policy 1924–1931: The Norman Conquest of $4.86* (New York: Cambridge University Press, 1972); Richard Sayers, *The Bank of England, 1891–1944* (Cambridge: Cambridge University Press, 1976); Philip Williamson, *National Crisis and National Government: British Politics, the Economy, and Empire, 1926–1932* (Cambridge: Cambridge University Press, 2003).

24. The field of international security has produced some notable challenges to this view. Daniel L. Byman and Kenneth M. Pollack, "Let Us Now Praise Great Men: Bringing the Statesman Back In," *International Security* 25, no. 4 (2001): 107–46; Elizabeth N. Saunders, *Leaders at War: How Presidents Shape Military Interventions* (Ithaca, NY: Cornell University Press, 2011). But there are few such parallels emphasizing individual agency in analyses of international political economy. Even those few agent-centered approaches that exist in this field eschew "tell[ing] a story of personalities." Instead, they use "the ideas and tools of modern political economy . . . emphasizing the political and institutional context in which central bankers operate." Christopher Adolph, *Bankers, Bureaucrats, and Central Bank Politics: The Myth of Neutrality* (Cambridge: Cambridge University Press, 2013), 2–3.

25. As Eichengreen and Flandreau put it, *The Great Transformation* remains the "*locus classicus* of political-economy analysis of the gold standard." Barry Eichengreen and Marc Flandreau, introduction to *The Gold Standard in Theory and History*, 2nd ed., ed. Barry Eichengreen and Marc Flandreau (London: Routledge, 1997), 25n. Even Churchill's biographers have fallen into offering the same type of account. Robert Rhodes James, *Churchill: A Study in Failure, 1900–1939* (London: Weidenfeld & Nicolson, 1970), 161–62.

26. Karl Polanyi, *The Great Transformation* (Boston: Beacon Press, 2001), 27.

27. Polanyi, *Great Transformation*, 31.

28. Charles P. Kindleberger, *The World in Depression, 1929–1939* (Berkeley: University of California Press, 1986), 295–304.

29. Krasner offers a parallel account of the evolution of trade policy. He is even more reluctant to name the names of those laggards who initially failed to update as

the global structures evolved. Stephen D. Krasner, "State Power and the Structure of International Trade," *World Politics* 28, no. 3 (1976): 317–47.

30. Beth A. Simmons, *Who Adjusts? Domestic Sources of Foreign Economic Policy during the Interwar Years* (Princeton, NJ: Princeton University Press, 1994), 11–12.

31. To be fair, Simmons's text analyzes the policies of numerous countries and thus sacrifices depth of analysis in any country for global breadth. But insofar as she treats the UK, the leading figures are almost entirely missing. So while the Bank of England appears more than a dozen times, there is virtually no discussion of the governors of the Bank of England. Walter Cunliffe and Brien Cokayne are not mentioned at all. Unconscionably, Montagu Norman appears on just one page. This contrasts with Moggridge, who followed contemporaries in conceptualizing British monetary policy in this period as "the Norman conquest of $4.86." Things are not any different within the government. Of Britain's eight interwar chancellors of the exchequer, five are missing from Simmons's account entirely. Neville Chamberlain, Philip Snowden, and Churchill each appear across a few pages. Given its centrality to not just the UK but to the entire international gold standard system, it is quite surprising that there is no specific analysis of Churchill's pivotal decision to return to gold in 1925. Similarly, of the UK's five prime ministers between the wars, Simmons offers only a few bits of discussion on Chamberlain and MacDonald. Lloyd George, Bonar Law, and Baldwin—who was prime minister for roughly half of the interwar period—are entirely missing from the book. Even Keynes has barely survived this depersonalization of International Political Economy. He is relegated to three footnotes and appears in the main text only twice—once by virtue of a quote from Kindleberger.

32. Eichengreen, *Golden Fetters*, 163. Boyle makes a similar argument. Andrew Boyle, *Montagu Norman: A Biography* (London: Cassell, 1967), 138–39.

33. Eichengreen, *Globalizing Capital: A History of the International Monetary System* (Princeton, NJ: Princeton University Press, 1998), 6.

34. Jeffry Frieden, *Global Capitalism: Its Fall and Rise in the Twentieth Century* (New York: W. W. Norton & Co., 2007), 154.

35. Ruggie famously argued, "The extension of the suffrage and the emergence of working-class political constituencies, parties, and even governments was responsible in part, but demands for social protection were very nearly universal, coming from all sides of the political spectrum and from all ranks of the social hierarchy (with the possible exception of orthodox financial circles)." John Gerard Ruggie, "International Regimes, Transactions, and Change: Embedded Liberalism in the Postwar Economic Order," *International Organization* 36, no. 2 (1982): 388.

36. Peter A. Hall, *The Political Power of Economic Ideas: Keynesianism across Nations* (Princeton, NJ: Princeton University Press, 1989), 376.

37. Eichengreen agrees that the gold standard was "socially constructed." Eichengreen, *Globalizing Capital*, 30. Kunz similarly argued that the gold standard depended upon an underlying "consensus in favor of making major sacrifices" for it. Diane Kunz, *The Battle for Britain's Gold Standard in 1931* (Sydney: Croom Helm, 1987), 184–85. Several scholars—such as McNamara, Eichengreen, and Blyth–extended this analysis to probe the veracity of the Polanyi thesis beyond the confines of the interwar period. McNamara, *Currency of Ideas. Globalizing Capital*, Eichengreen explains, "asks whether Polanyi's thesis stands the test of fifty additional years. Can the inter-

national monetary history of the second half of the twentieth century be understood as the further unfolding of Polanyian dynamics, in which democratization again came into conflict with economic liberalization in the form of free capital mobility and fixed exchange rates?" Eichengreen, *Globalizing Capital*, 5–6, 195–96. Eichengreen, *Golden Fetters*, makes a similar argument but does not invoke Polanyi. Blyth went even further in this direction, entitling his book *Great Transformations*. Mark Blyth, *Great Transformations: Economic Ideas and Institutional Change in the Twentieth Century* (New York: Cambridge University Press, 2002). Polanyi himself may have thought that the "material" variables he stressed followed from a (flawed) set of ideas. I am grateful to Adam Dean for helping me to resolve this apparent contradiction within Polanyi's thought.

38. Williamson, *National Crisis and National Government*, 13.

39. David M. Kennedy, *Freedom from Fear: The American People in Depression and War, 1929–1945* (Oxford: Oxford University Press, 1999), 358.

40. Ikenberry's several powerful treatments are exceptional. G. John Ikenberry, *After Victory* (Princeton, NJ: Princeton University Press, 2001); G. John Ikenberry, "Creating Yesterday's New World Order: Keynesian 'New Thinking' and the Anglo-American Postwar Settlement," in *Ideas and Foreign Policy: Beliefs, Institutions, and Political Change*, ed. Judith Goldstein and Robert O. Keohane (Ithaca, NY: Cornell University Press, 1993), 57–86. Yet his analysis is confined to the late-interwar and postwar period. The analysis here thus complements his work on the later portions of the shift.

41. Readers may be surprised by the use of the formulation "England" rather than "Britain" or "the United Kingdom" here. This is done deliberately, in recognition of the significant variation—and hierarchy—that exists across and within a "country" like the United Kingdom of Great Britain and (Northern) Ireland. More broadly, describing the political and economic units associated with the "British" Isles is no easy task in this period. First and foremost, the familiar demonyms describe different things. "The British Empire" is denoted in the *Oxford English Dictionary* as "the empire consisting of Great Britain and the other British possessions, dominions, and dependencies.". The geopolitical unit "the United Kingdom of Great Britain" was created in 1707 with the Acts of Union between the countries of Scotland and England. The country of Wales had already been subjugated by England and has not been included in the formal name in any way. "Great Britain" is comprised of England, Scotland, and Wales. Notably, it does not include the island of Ireland. So when the Kingdoms of Ireland and Great Britain were unified in 1801, the geopolitical unit was restyled as "the United Kingdom of Great Britain and Ireland." During and after the First World War, Ireland was partitioned with "Southern Ireland" gaining increasing independence and "Northern Ireland" remaining within the United Kingdom. The United Kingdom was then restyled as "the United Kingdom of Great Britain and Northern Ireland." Often the United Kingdom is shortened to simply "Great Britain" or "Britain," and this archipelago is routinely referred to as the "British Isles." But this offends many Irish people, who do not consider themselves to be "British," as well as those in England, Scotland, and Wales who prioritize other identities above their "British" identity. Second, there was significant variation across—if not also within—the units described. And the units themselves were redefined across this period, particularly those related to "Ireland." Moreover, certain formulations carry political

overtones. Despite these challenges—perhaps because of them—these terms have often been used inaccurately. It is obviously wrong to subsume the Scottish and the Irish monetary systems into a "British" monetary system, despite that many of the leading monetary authorities at the time did precisely that. In 1920, for instance, Keynes gave a lecture in Manchester entitled "The Present State of the Foreign Exchanges" in which he categorically used "England" in place of "Britain" or "the United Kingdom." The Scottish and Irish monetary systems were each governed by a different set of statutes before, during, and after the First World War. The banks emitting currency were subject to varying levels of oversight, they operated differently, and the forms of money used in these markets was only about as commensurable as was the currency of any two gold standard currencies at the time. Moreover, given the enormous differences between the operation of money in London and in more distant parts of England, it is too simplistic to think in terms of even a singular "English" monetary system. There are many more examples where conventional demonyms become problematic. Throughout this book, care has been taken to use the most precise formulation possible with these issues in mind. "The UK" will stand in as the generic reference to the collection of European countries ruled, more or less, by the Parliament in Westminster.

42. Costigliola's characterization is typical: "In an economic sense, the United States was the sole victor of World War I. Industrially, commercially, and especially financially, the Great War had strengthened the relative position of the U.S. and weakened that of Britain." Frank C. Costigliola, "Anglo-American Financial Rivalry in the 1920s," *Journal of Economic History* 37, no. 4 (1977): 914. Bayoumi and Bordo illuminate the challenges this created for the UK's 1925 return. Tamim Bayoumi and Michael Bordo, "Getting Pegged: Comparing the 1879 and 1925 Gold Resumptions," *Oxford Economic Papers* 50, no. 1 (1998): 122–149.

43. Polanyi, *Great Transformation*, 31.

44. Keynes, *Collected Writings*, 2:143.

45. Boyle, *Montagu Norman*, 151.

46. England's supposed dearth of gold is broadly assumed to have been an essential structural reality that circumscribed the range of possibilities in the 1920s and 1930s. This book pushes back against the myth of a gold-broke England and reveals the origins of that myth: the UK monetary authorities at the time variously misunderstood and misconstrued these figures to suit their priors and their purposes.

47. Eichengreen, *Golden Fetters*, 3.

48. Novak has shown the political power of such imagined pasts in the US context. William J. Novak, *The People's Welfare: Law and Regulation in Nineteenth-Century America* (Chapel Hill: University of North Carolina Press, 1996).

49. Polanyi, *Great Transformation*, 27.

50. Keynes, *Collected Writings*, 4:155.

51. Economic historians have long recognized that there was no singular gold standard dogma. In his classic discussion, Bordo identified no fewer than "five major schools of thought." Bordo, "The Gold Standard," 23.

52. The leading Liberal politician Hubert Henderson denounced Churchill as "one of the worst Chancellors of the Exchequer of modern times." Hubert Henderson, "Diagnosis and Remedy," *The Nation and the Athenaeum*, May 9, 1925, 167.

## 2. The Road to Calvary

1. George Orwell, *The Road to Wigan Pier* (London: Penguin, 2001), 113–14.

2. Giovanni Capoccia and R. Daniel Kelemen, "The Study of Critical Junctures: Theory, Narrative, and Counterfactuals in Historical Institutionalism," *World Politics* 59, no. 3 (2007): 341–69.

3. The doctrine of free trade is a close second. Recent research pushes the birth of the UK's free trade movement all the way back to the 1780s. James Ashley Morrison, "Before Hegemony: Adam Smith, American Independence, and the Origins of the First Era of Globalization," *International Organization* 66, no. 3 (July 2012): 395–428. But even by that measure, the monetary orthodoxy is another century older than that. The free trade movement was also more highly contested. It was challenged at the time by prominent intellectuals and policymakers. Moreover, one can question whether "free trade imperialism" was really "free trade" at all. Bernard Semmel, *The Rise of Free Trade Imperialism* (Cambridge: Cambridge University Press, 1970). Moreover, when the time came to choose between the gold standard and free trade, as it did in the interwar period, the majority of intellectuals and policymakers proved willing to sacrifice free trade to save the gold standard.

4. Keynes, *Collected Writings*, 7:33. In this instance, Keynes was referring just to the Ricardian doctrine that effective demand is never deficient. But the doctrines are not unrelated, and Keynes said much the same in his many diatribes against the gold standard orthodoxy.

5. P. G. M. Dickson, *The Financial Revolution in England: A Study in the Development of Public Credit, 1688–1756* (London: Macmillan, 1967). Desan powerfully shows that the modern standard only came with Locke in the 1690s (rather than prior, as has been assumed traditionally). Christine Desan, *Making Money: Coin, Currency, and the Coming of Capitalism* (Oxford: Oxford University Press, 2014).

6. Lowndes, *Report containing an Essay*, 56–57.

7. Eric Helleiner, *The Making of National Money: Territorial Currencies in Historical Perspective* (Ithaca, NY: Cornell University Press, 2003).

8. Keynes, *Collected Writings*, 6:274. A large body of literature has bolstered this claim and fleshed out precisely how these arrangements operated. Kindleberger, *World in Depression*, 290; Eichengreen, *Golden Fetters*, 7; Simmons, *Who Adjusts*, 21; Lawrence Broz, "The Domestic Politics of International Monetary Order: The Gold Standard," in *Contested Social Orders and International Politics*, ed. David Skidmore (Nashville: Vanderbilt University Press, 1997), 53–84.

9. In his famous 1943 article, Hayek enumerated some of these advantages. Friedrich Hayek, "A Commodity Reserve Currency," *Economic Journal* 53, no. 210/211 (1943): 176.

10. While it remained *technically* possible to convert pound notes into gold at the Bank of England, difficulty in insuring gold shipments reduced the practical ability to move gold to and from the British Isles. But as Gowa and Hicks show, overall international trade volumes remained high across the war years. Joanne Gowa and Raymond Hicks, "Commerce and Conflict: New Data About the Great War," *British Journal of Political Science* 47 (2017): 653–74.

11. Cunliffe Committee, *First Interim Report*, 5.

12. Philip Snowden, "The Return to Gold," *The Observer*, February 8, 1925.

13. At its most radical, the TUC proposed national management of the financial system. But this was not that far from what the Cunliffe Committee itself had considered. And even this was tempered. The TUC special committee concluded, "The prevention of [currency] amalgamation, however, may not be in the national interest. We have no doubt that industry and commerce have on the whole benefited by the unification which has taken place in the banking world." Trades Union Congress: Joint Committee on the Cost of Living, *Interim Report on Money and Prices* (London: Cooperative Printing Society, 1920), 14. Further discussion below.

14. Contemporaries often referred to the "orthodoxy" that supported the gold standard. Frieden, *Global Capitalism*, 195. Scholars now use the formulation regularly as well. Eichengreen and Irwin, "Slide to Protectionism," 872.

15. M. June Flanders, "A Model of Discretion: The Gold Standard in Fact and in Fiction," *World Economy* 16, no. 2 (1993): 218.

16. Cunliffe Committee, *First Interim Report*, 3.

17. Cunliffe Committee, *First Interim Report*, 11.

18. Cunliffe Committee, *First Interim Report*, 4.

19. GFD Finaeon, "British Pound to US Dollar Exchange Rate (GBPUSD)," Global Financial Data, November 20, 2020; Irene Shrigley, *The Price of Gold: Documents Illustrating the Statutory Control through the Bank of England of the Market Price of Gold, 1694–1931* (London: P. S. King & Son, 1935).

20. Thomas J. Sargent and François R. Velde, *The Big Problem of Small Change* (Princeton, NJ: Princeton University Press, 2003).

21. Discussions of money in the UK are made bewildering for policymakers, market actors, and scholars alike by several things. First, the English tradition mixes multiple systems of measure with similar terms (e.g., pounds sterling, troy pounds, and the customary pounds abbreviated "lbs"), evolving denominations (from pounds, shillings, and pence to decimalized coinage), and even the same names (e.g., "the sovereign") to describe different coins and units of currency. Yet it is necessary to clarify the precise relationship between the nominal unit (one pound sterling) and a given quantity of gold at a given level of purity, as even small changes in the standard had significant implications. Before decimalization, the major units of British currency were pounds, shillings, and pence. Twelve pence made a shilling, and twenty shillings made a pound. From 1817 forward, the (new) sovereign was worth one pound, and the half-sovereign half of that. "Standard" gold was (22 carat) gold used in specie (coins), and "fine" gold was (24 carat) gold as bullion. There are twelve troy ounces in each troy pound. One troy ounce is equal to 1.097 avoirdupois (customary) ounces ("oz") or 31.10 (metric) grams. That gave each sovereign 0.2568 troy ounces, 0.2817 ounces, or 7.99 grams of standard (22 carat) gold. Thus, each sovereign contained 0.2354 troy ounces, 0.2582 ounces, or 7.32 grams of fine (pure) gold. This gives us the gold price used by contemporaries for "standard" gold: £3 17s. 10½d.—that is, three pounds, seventeen shillings, and tenpence halfpenny—per troy ounce. This was often written simply as 77s. 10½d. This also gives us the gold price used by contemporaries for "fine" (pure) gold: £4 4s. 11½d.—that is, four pounds, four shillings, and elevenpence halfpenny per troy ounce. This was written simply as 84s. 11½d. In decimalized terms, the prices are: £3.894 per troy ounce of standard gold, and £4.248 per troy ounce of pure gold. In practice, the Bank of England set its buying price slightly lower than these official ceilings. In September 1919, the market quotes of the London gold

price switched from listing the price of "standard" gold to "fine" gold. This has led to some confusion about the changes in the market price of gold in existing datasets such as the "CMGCGBW" series in Global Financial Data. That dataset appears to have (incorrectly) pooled the figures without accounting for the change in quotation type. It also (incorrectly) reports them in ounces ("oz") rather than troy ounces ("ozt").

22. John Locke, *Some Considerations of the Consequences of the Lowering of Interest and the Raising the Value of Money*, in *Locke on Money*, ed. Patrick Hyde Kelly (Oxford: Clarendon Press, 1991), 263.

23. This was reiterated in the most recent relevant legislation: the Bank Notes (Scotland) Act, 1845 (8 & 9 Vict., c. 38) and the Bankers (Ireland) Act, 1845 (8 & 9 Vict., c. 37). The Cunliffe Committee was reminded of this several times, as discussed below.

24. Adam Smith, *An Inquiry into the Nature and Causes of the Wealth of Nations*, ed. R. H. Campbell, Andrew S. Skinner, and W. B. Todd (Indianapolis: Liberty Classics, 1981), 62.

25. As Blyth might say, orthodoxies do not come with an instruction sheet. Indeed, in the case of the gold standard dictates, even the instructions themselves needed an instruction sheet. Mark Blyth, "Structures Do Not Come with an Instruction Sheet: Interests, Ideas, and Progress in Political Science," *Perspective on Politics* 1, no. 4 (2003): 695–706.

26. Indeed, the supposed inadequacy of the Bank of England's reserves was a mainstay of prewar discussions in financial and political circles. Richard Roberts, *Saving the City: The Great Financial Crisis of 1914* (Oxford: Oxford University Press, 2013), 74. The testimonies of private financial actors considered here show that these debates reached a crescendo as England planned its return to gold.

27. Keynes, *Collected Writings*, 7:161. George A. Akerlof and Robert J. Shiller, *Animal Spirits: How Human Psychology Drives the Economy, and Why It Matters for Global Capitalism* (Princeton, NJ: Princeton University Press, 2010).

28. Frank Knight, *Risk, Uncertainty, and Profit* (Boston: Houghton Mifflin, 1921), 19–20.

29. Jens Beckert and Richard Bronk, *Uncertain Futures: Imaginaries, Narratives, and Calculation in the Economy* (Oxford: Oxford University Press, 2018), 3.

30. Jens Beckert, *Imagined Futures: Fictional Expectations and Capitalist Dynamics* (Cambridge, MA: Harvard University Press, 2016), 9.

31. Morgan shows how uncertainty bedeviled Knight's own efforts to make models. Mary S. Morgan, *World in the Model* (Cambridge: Cambridge University Press, 2012), 150–53.

32. Stephen C. Nelson and Peter J. Katzenstein, "Uncertainty, Risk, and the Financial Crisis of 2008," *International Organization* 68, no. 2 (2014): 362.

33. Morgan, *World in the Model*, 217–18.

34. Beckert, *Imagined Futures*, 10.

35. Nelson and Katzenstein, "Uncertainty, Risk, and the Financial Crisis of 2008," 374.

36. Mark Blyth, *Austerity: The History of a Dangerous Idea* (New York: Oxford University Press, 2013).

37. Robert J. Shiller, *Narrative Economics: How Stories Go Viral and Drive Major Economic Events* (Princeton, NJ: Princeton University Press, 2019), x.

38. Keynes himself deployed this argument and persuaded Lloyd George *not* to suspend specie payments in the 1914 financial crisis. Keynes, *Collected Writings*, 16:11.

39. "The Currency Delusion," *The New Statesman*, August 3, 1918.

40. Richard Bronk, *The Romantic Economist: Imagination in Economics* (Cambridge: Cambridge University Press, 2009); Beckert and Bronk, *Uncertain Futures*.

41. Beckert and Bronk, *Uncertain Futures*, 10.

42. Polanyi, *Great Transformation*, 26.

43. Keynes himself frequently used religious terms, metaphors, and allusions to describe and understand these phenomena, most conspicuously attacking "the orthodoxy" in *The General Theory*. Keynes, *Collected Writings*, 7:xxi. There is not sufficient space here for a proper hermeneutics of Keynes's gold standard discourse; but this book maintains that his reliance on the language of faith, morality, and belief was more than mere rhetorical flourish. In contrast to the social scientists, the historians have followed Keynes's lead. Moggridge concludes, "The 'Norman Conquest of $4.86' was ultimately an act of faith in an incompletely understood adjustment mechanism undertaken for largely moral reasons. It carried with it a belief that any overvaluation of sterling . . . would be removed by reductions in British, or rises in American, prices and costs, that the results would be 'good for trade', if only by inducing stabilizations elsewhere by force of example, and that the resulting stable international environment would provide a basis for expanding trade which would benefit an internationally oriented economy such as Britain's." Moggridge, *British Monetary Policy*, 228. Boyle goes even further: "It would not be pushing the analogy too far to compare the City then, especially with Norman as its Grey Eminence par excellence, to the structure of the Communist party or to that of the Roman Catholic Church. . . . Being a completely closed system, the City spoke out rarely—and then ex cathedra—through its appointed high priest, the Governor of the Bank." Boyle, *Montagu Norman*, 137.

44. Sarah Binder and Mark Spindel, *The Myth of Independence: How Congress Governs the Federal Reserve* (Princeton, NJ: Princeton University Press, 2017).

45. Paul Tucker, *Unelected Power: The Quest for Legitimacy in Central Banking and the Regulatory State* (Princeton, NJ: Princeton University Press, 2018).

46. Cf. Keynes, *Collected Writings*, 7:32.

47. Further discussion below.

48. The Trades Union Congress subsequently made this point, but only parenthetically: "The action of the Government in borrowing money at high and increasing rates of interest (though it adopted the conscription of men) must be held responsible in some measure for the rise in prices." TUC, Cost of Living Committee, *Interim Report*, 14.

49. Charles Tilly, *Coercion, Capital, and European States, AD 990–1990* (Cambridge: Basil Blackwell, 1992), chap. 3, 157.

50. Keynes, *Collected Writings*, 2:143.

51. Keynes, *Collected Writings*, 2:27.

52. Milton Friedman, "The Case for Flexible Exchange Rates," in *Essays in Positive Economics* (Chicago: University of Chicago Press, 1953), 167–70.

53. Forrest Capie and Alan Webber, *A Monetary History of the United Kingdom: 1870–1982* (London: George Allen and Unwin, 1985): 211–12.

54. Keynes, *Collected Writings*, 7:349.

55. He was particularly close to Benjamin Strong in the United States and Hjalmar Schacht in Germany. Indeed, he stood as godfather to Schacht's grandson, who was himself named after the two men: Norman Hjalmar. Hjalmar Horace Greeley Schacht, *My First Seventy-Six Years*, trans. Diana Pyke (London: Allen Wingate, 1955), 200. He had good relations with George L. Harrison as well. Famously, he had a difficult relationship with France's Émile Moreau.

56. Antony Lentin, "Lord Cunliffe, Lloyd George, Reparations and Reputations at the Paris Peace Conference, 1919," *Diplomacy and Statecraft* 10, no. 1 (1999): 55–56, 71.

57. He has attracted little scholarly attention. There is no entry for Cokayne in the *Dictionary of National Biography*. Even his name has been variously misspelled by previous scholars—a testament to his low profile. The mistakes begin with Boyle, who referred to him as "Brian Cockayne" throughout. Boyle, *Montagu Norman*. Moggridge gives varied spellings across his work. In his 1969 book, Cokayne is simply "Cockayne." Moggridge, *Return to Gold*, 14. His second book uses the correct forename (Brien) but continues with the incorrect surname. Moggridge, *British Monetary Policy*. His 1992 biography of Keynes gives the surname correctly but switches the forename to "Brian." Donald Moggridge, *Maynard Keynes: An Economist's Biography* (New York: Routledge, 1992). More recently, Ahamed gets both names wrong ("Brian Cockayne"). Ahamed, *Lords of Finance*, 82. Cokayne was made Baron Cullen of Ashbourne in 1920.

58. Taken together, this presents the chiasmatic irony that Cunliffe sought to save the "Bradburys" that Bradbury despised, and Bradbury (largely) authored the Cunliffe Committee reports that Cunliffe deprecated.

59. While such cooperation had proven vital (in fact) to the prewar gold standard, the Cunliffe Committee reports do not mention international collaboration a single time. Eichengreen, *Golden Fetters*, 7.

60. Jens Beckert and Richard Bronk, "Uncertain Futures: Imaginaries, Narratives, and Calculation in the Economy," Watson Institute for International and Public Affairs, Brown University (October 24, 2019), https://youtu.be/FseT_EU-EbI.

61. Recently, Beckert and Bronk were asked this question at Brown University following a presentation of their edited volume. Beckert conceded, "Nobody in this book . . . [has] a theory on this. . . . [I question] whether it is possible to have a general theory on this issue simply [because of] the complexity of issues that are involved." Beckert and Bronk, "Uncertain Futures."

62. Beckert and Bronk, "Uncertain Futures."

63. Again, one thinks of the many plausible versions of "Brexit."

64. I am grateful to Duncan Snidal for provocative discussion on this question.

65. Karl Marx, *The German Ideology*, in *Karl Marx: Selected Writings*, 2nd ed., ed. David McLellan (Oxford: Oxford University Press, 2000), 175–208. See also Frieden, *Global Capitalism*, 33, 154.

66. Michel Foucault, *The History of Sexuality: Volume I: An Introduction* (New York: Vintage, 1990), 98. Beckert and Bronk have embraced this latter view. In response to an audience question, Bronk replied, "In order to think about how economic actors in practice think about their interests, you have to consider the technologies of future-making in which they envisage their own interests." Beckert explained further: "The way interests are formulated and pursued is not just simply a 'base'—to use the Marxian formulation—phenomenon but somehow the superstructure plays a role in this. . . . In these situations of uncertainty, actors often do not know

themselves what is in their best interest. Their ideas . . . are neither false nor correct. . . . Once you bring in the power aspect . . . then you are much more in a discourse where you can bring [in] notions of ideology, or governmentality—the Foucauldian term." Beckert and Bronk, "Uncertain Futures."

67. For instance, the subsequent chapters will show how Edward Holden, the man who built the London City and Midland Bank into the largest bank in the world, is variously ignored, bracketed, and ultimately overruled by the Cunliffe Committee. The case of Felix Schuster, another one of the UK's most powerful bankers, is even more extreme.

68. For example, Pigou proved influential in these discussions principally because he was on the Cunliffe Committee. External scholars who submitted memoranda were largely ignored. And even Pigou, the Professor of Political Economy at Cambridge, was routinely led by Bradbury, as the discussion below shows. This is in sharp contrast to the "epistemic communities" literature in which "policy paradigms" are created by "ideas entrepreneurs" and then pushed onto policymakers in accordance with evolving societal norms. Peter M. Haas, "Introduction: Epistemic Communities and International Policy Coordination," *International Organization* 46, no. 1 (1992): 1–35; Hall, *Political Power of Economic Ideas*; Martha Finnemore and Kathryn Sikkink, "International Norm Dynamics and Political Change," *International Organization* 52, no. 4 (1998): 887–917; Leonard Seabrooke, "The Everyday Social Sources of Economic Crises: From 'Great Frustrations' to 'Great Revelations' in Interwar Britain," *International Studies Quarterly* 1, no. 51 (2007): 795–810.

69. This was their lived experience, even if we might think that they were actually being "disciplined" rather than "punished." Michel Foucault, *Discipline and Punish: The Birth of the Prison*, 2nd ed. (New York: Vintage, 1995).

70. Marx, "Towards a Critique of Hegel's *Philosophy of Right*: Introduction," in *Karl Marx*, 72. In this view, the "scientization" of political economy—to invoke Hayek—actually worked against the hegemony of the orthodoxy. After all, even the performance of science, let alone an actual "scientific" approach, admits empirical testing and logical counterargument, whereas faith subordinates both. Friedrich Hayek, *The Counter-Revolution of Science: Studies on the Abuse of Reason* (Glencoe, IL: Free Press, 1952), 15–16. Bordo suggested, "The evolution of the interpretation of the gold standard has many of the characteristics of a Kuhnian scientific revolution." Bordo, "The Gold Standard," 29. The narrative developed here, by contrast, suggests that these interpretive debates are better analogized to religious rather than scientific revolutions.

71. Bank of England, ADM 34/5, diary of Montagu Collet Norman, December 12, 1917.

72. Omarosa Manigault Newman, *Unhinged: An Insider's Account of the Trump White House* (New York: Simon & Schuster, 2018); Anthony Scaramucci, *Trump, the Blue-Collar President* (New York: Center Street, 2018); Michael Wolff, *Fire and Fury* (London: Hachette UK, 2018).

### 3. The Cunliffe "Consensus"

1. Cunliffe Committee, *First Interim Report*.

2. Keith Grieves, "James Lyle Mackay, First Earl of Inchcape," *Oxford Dictionary of National Biography*, online (Oxford: Oxford University Press, 2008).

3. NA T 185/1, Press Notice.

4. Cunliffe Committee, *First Interim Report*, 5.

5. Cunliffe Committee, *First Interim Report*, 3.

6. Arthur Kitson, *The Bankers' Conspiracy! Which Started the World Crisis*, (London: Elliot Stock, 1933.

7. Moggridge, *British Monetary Policy*; Moggridge, *Return to Gold*; Eichengreen, *Golden Fetters*, 51; Simmons, *Who Adjusts*, 36–37; Ahamed, *Lords of Finance*, 220.

8. These materials are stored principally in the (UK) national archives collections T 185/1 and T 185/2. T 185/3 provides another hundred pages of material specifically on the question of silver coinage.

9. Moggridge's first book (published in 1969) deals directly with the 1925 return to gold. Unfortunately, these materials could not be located at the time that book was written. Moggridge, *Return to Gold*, 12n. They became available in time for Moggridge's second book (published in 1972). But because that book continues the narrative, tracing monetary policy from 1924 to 1931, the Cunliffe Committee's internal workings in 1918–1919 are less directly relevant. Moggridge, *British Monetary Policy*, 17–21. Howson provides some details and background as well. Howson, *Domestic Monetary Management*, 13. Boyce offers the fullest discussion of these materials to date. Robert Boyce, "Creating the Myth of Consensus: Public Opinion and Britain's Return to the Gold Standard in 1925," in *Money and Power: Essays in Honour of L. S. Pressnell*, ed. P. L. Cottrell and Donald Moggridge (London: Palgrave Macmillan UK, 1988), 173–97.

10. In his magisterial *History of Economic Analysis*, Schumpeter used the Cunliffe Committee's apparent simpleness as a foil to emphasize the complexity and subtlety of their forebears a century before. Joseph A. Schumpeter, *History of Economic Analysis* (London: Routledge, 1954), 692. Initially, Moggridge followed the committee's line: "Thus the Cunliffe Committee was merely echoing the opinion of its witnesses." Moggridge, *Return to Gold*, 12. Upon accessing the Cunliffe Committee's papers, however, he updated his conclusion: "Thus the Committee might be said to be somewhat divided and uncertain as to the best short-term policy but united on long-term goals." Moggridge, *British Monetary Policy*, 21. Eichengreen describes the source of the committee's fixation on the use of interest rate adjustment but does not describe the debates within the committee over alternatives. Eichengreen, *Golden Fetters*, 37–38, 51. Boyce rightly challenges this myth, although the lines of disagreement have not yet been fully or clearly specified. Also, difficult questions remain about the producers' voice and influence. Further discussion below. Boyce, "Creating the Myth of Consensus."

11. For some reason, the several reports written by the Joint Committee on the Cost of Living—and published by the Trades Union Congress—have not been discussed by previous scholars working on the return to gold.

12. Milton Friedman, *Capitalism and Freedom* (Chicago: University of Chicago Press, 2002), 133–36.

13. NA T 185/2, Discussion following Schuster Testimony, October 16, 1919, 732.

14. Alexander Hamilton, *The Works of Alexander Hamilton*, ed. Henry Cabot Lodge (New York: G. P. Putnam's Sons, 1904), 2:283, 3:388–443.

15. See James 3:12.

16. Churchill is reputed to have said, "If you put two economists in a room, you get two opinions, unless one of the economists is Keynes, in which case you get three opinions."

## 4. Atop Sinai

1. Walter Bagehot, *Lombard Street: A Description of the Money Market* (New York: Scribner, Armstrong, 1873), 4; Keynes, *Collected Writings*, 11: 284–86; Roberts, *Saving the City*, 29–32.

2. Roberts, *Saving the City*, 24.

3. Roberts, 95–96.

4. Keynes, *Collected Writings*, 11:246.

5. Roberts, *Saving the City*, 200–201.

6. Keynes, *Collected Writings*, 11: 245–46.

7. Keynes, *Collected Writings*, 11: 241–42.

8. Roberts, *Saving the City*, 44.

9. Sargent and Velde described this perennial problem as "the big problem of small change." They end their study in 1850, by which point two components of the solution were widespread: modern monetary theory and sophisticated means of producing token coins that were difficult to counterfeit. Sargent and Velde, *Big Problem of Small Change*, 6. The case of 1914 suggests that there is a third requirement: the willingness of the monetary authorities to produce token currency valued on a par with gold specie.

10. NA T 185/2, Bradbury, "Future Dimensions of the Fiduciary Issue," March 9, 1918.

11. This was deliberate. Having associated small denomination notes with the easy money era during the Napoleonic Wars, the Bank of England instinctively resisted producing the cheaper currency notes.

12. Roberts, *Saving the City*, 59–61.

13. M7/158, Osborne, *The Bank of England, 1914–1921*:105–18; Sayers, *Bank of England*, 1:67–76.

14. Currency and Bank Notes Act, 1914 (4 & 5 Geo. 5, c. 14).

15. Roberts, *Saving the City*, 125–28.

16. Parliamentary Debates, House of Commons, August 5, 1914, vol. 65, column 1992.

17. Sayers, *Bank of England*, 1:67–76.

18. NA T 185/2, Bradbury, "Future Dimensions of the Fiduciary Issue," March 9, 1918.

19. Cf. Governor Cokayne's minority opinion in his testimony to the Cunliffe Committee, discussed at length below.

20. In its original incarnation, Eichengreen and Hausmann defined "original sin" as "a situation in which the domestic currency cannot be used to borrow abroad or to borrow long term even domestically." The UK Treasury faced this constraint during and after the war. Barry Eichengreen and Ricardo Hausmann, "Exchange Rates and Financial Fragility," National Bureau of Economic Research, Working Paper 7418, 1999: 3, http://www.nber.org/papers/w7418. But it was also "original sin" in the sense of inherited sin that followed after Britons ate of the forbidden fruit of (essentially) unbacked paper currency.

21. For some actors, such as Bank Governor Cunliffe, the declining gold reserve ratio constituted a crisis, a situation "which agents intersubjectively interpret as necessitating change." Wesley W. Widmaier, Mark Blyth, and Leonard Seabrooke, "Exogenous Shocks or Endogenous Constructions? The Meanings of Wars and Cri-

ses," *International Studies Quarterly* 51, no. 4 (November 2007): 748. Cunliffe thus proposed a radical new approach to the gold standard. For others, the situation demanded merely stronger doses of the same old medicine.

22. NA T 185/1, Minutes, February 18, 1918.

23. NA T 185/1, Minutes, February 18, 1918.

24. NA T 185/1, Minutes, February 25, 1918.

25. NA T 185/1, Minutes, February 25, 1918.

26. NA T 185/1, Minutes, February 26, 1918.

27. Bank of England, ADM 34/6, diary of Montagu Collet Norman, February 27, 1918. Of course, Norman was hardly an unbiased observer. He was particularly vitriolic toward Cunliffe.

28. NA T 185/1, Minutes, March 4, 1918.

29. NA T 185/1, Minutes, March 4, 1918.

30. In another memorandum, Pigou ruled out various schemes to limit the nonmonetary use of gold and to direct all inflows to the Bank of England. He also deployed the centuries' old argument that attempts to limit smuggling were futile. NA T 185/1, Pigou, Note on Prohibiting Gold Import, March 6, 1918.

31. NA T 185/1, Minutes, March 4, 1918.

32. NA T 185/1, Minutes, March 5, 1918.

33. NA T 185/2, Bradbury, "Future Dimensions of the Fiduciary Issue," March 9, 1918. All of these figures are from Bradbury himself. Some are official figures, but others—such as private banks' gold holdings, or the quantity of gold held privately by Britons—were his rough calculations made at the time. While subsequent analysis reveals the limitations of these estimates, Bradbury's figures are important, as they became the basis for the next decade of policy.

34. NA T 185/2, Bradbury, "Future Dimensions of the Fiduciary Issue," March 9, 1918.

35. NA T 185/2, Bradbury, "Future Dimensions of the Fiduciary Issue," March 9, 1918.

36. Forrest Capie and Alan Webber, *A Monetary History of the United Kingdom: 1870–1982* (London: George Allen and Unwin, 1985), table III (6).

Capie and Webber, *Monetary History*, 460–63.

37. Capie and Webber, *Monetary History*, 269.

38. Despite Cunliffe's subsequent resistance, this formulation made it into the Cunliffe Committee's report. It was echoed again in 1925 by the Chamberlain-Bradbury Committee. NA T 185/2, Bradbury, "Future Dimensions of the Fiduciary Issue," March 9, 1918.

39. Bradbury subsequently drafted a separate (undated) memorandum that proposed the practical process by which the Bank of England could obtain the gold reserves and achieve a monopoly of note issue. NA T 185/2, Bradbury, "Suggested Arrangements for Transitional Period," 1918.

40. NA T 185/2, Bradbury, "Future Dimensions of the Fiduciary Issue," March 9, 1918.

41. NA T 185/1, Pigou, Note on Cunliffe's Plan.

42. NA T 185/1, Pigou, Memorandum on Fiduciary Note Issue.

43. NA T 185/1, Pigou, Memorandum on Fiduciary Note Issue.

44. NA T 185/1, Pigou, Memorandum on Fiduciary Note Issue.

45. NA T 185/1, Pigou, Memorandum on Fiduciary Note Issue.

46. NA T 185/1, Pigou, Memorandum on Fiduciary Note Issue.

47. NA T 185/1, Pigou, Memorandum on Fiduciary Note Issue.

48. NA T 185/1, Pigou, "Effect of Amalgamating the Issue and Banking Departments of the Bank of England."

49. NA T 185/1, Pigou, "Effect of Amalgamating the Issue and Banking Departments of the Bank of England."

50. NA T 185/1, Minutes, March 11, 1918.

51. NA T 185/1, Minutes, March 12, 1918.

52. NA T 185/1, Gibbs, Memorandum on Banks' Issue of Currency Notes against Government Debt.

53. NA T 185/1, Gibbs, Memorandum on Banks' Issue of Currency Notes against Government Debt.

54. NA T 185/1, Minutes, March 18, 1918.

55. NA T 185/1, Minutes, March 18, 1918.

56. The memorandum itself includes no date. Subsequently, however, Bradbury referred to his "memorandum of the 9th March, 1918, on the future basis of the fiduciary Note issue." NA T 185/2, Bradbury, "Suggested Arrangements for Transitional Period," 1918.

57. NA T 185/1, Minutes, March 18, 1918.

58. NA T 185/1, Minutes, March 19, 1918.

59. NA T 185/1, Minutes, March 19, 1918.

60. NA T 185/1, Minutes, March 19, 1918.

61. NA T 185/1, Minutes, March 19, 1918.

62. NA T 185/1, Minutes, March 19, 1918.

63. Bank of England, G8/53, 1918, 3–20.

64. Bank of England, ADM 34/6, March 20, 1918.

65. The minutes simply note that the standing committees would not be appointed until after the new Committee of Treasury had been appointed—according to Cokayne's new scheme—and after Cunliffe had been replaced. Bank of England, G4/140, March 21, 1918.

66. Bank of England, ADM 34/6, March 21, 1918.

67. The several scholars to consider these events have not appreciated the significance of this threat. Kynaston, for instance, quotes virtually the entirety of Norman's diary entry on these events, but he excludes the third, and most important, point. David Kynaston, *The City of London*, vol. 3, *Illusions of Gold, 1914–1945* (London: Pimlico, 2000), 36; David Kynaston, *Till Time's Last Sand: A History of the Bank of England, 1694–2013* (London: Bloomsbury, 2017), 287. Sayers gives the whole list, but, following this, he writes, "[Cunliffe's] colleagues were forgiving enough to follow custom by giving him a place in the Committee of Treasury for his remaining two years. . . . His relations with Lloyd George and Bonar Law were sufficiently reestablished for him to have been appointed Chairman of the Committee on Currency and Foreign Exchanges after the war." Sayers, *Bank of England*, 1:108–9. This implies that Cunliffe's appointment to the Cunliffe (Currency) Committee followed his ignominious departure as bank governor. But this gets the timeline backwards. In fact, Cunliffe had been appointed to head up the committee when it was created in December. The confrontation in late March was the crescendo in Cunliffe's ploy to use his position on

that external Currency Committee to regain control over the Bank of England from without.

68. NA T 185/1, Minutes, March 22, 1918.

## 5. The Golden Calf

1. Boyce, *Great Interwar Crisis*, 87.

2. According to Ferguson, the capital of N. M. Rothschild & Sons fell from £7.8 million in 1913 to £3.6 million in 1918. Midland's capital rose from £4.3 to £7.1 million across the same period. Ferguson attributes the Rothschilds' decline to their "strategic error . . . not to establish a Rothschild house on the [American] side of the Atlantic." Niall Ferguson, *The House of Rothschild: The World's Banker, 1849–1999* (London: Penguin, 2000), 454–56. This fits the familiar tale of torch-passing from London to New York, but it does not explain Holden's ascent, which depended on consolidation within the UK. Anthony Ralph Holmes and Edwin Green, *Midland: 150 Years of Banking Business* (London: BT Batsford, 1986), chapter 5.

3. Edwin Green, "Edward Hopkinson Holden," *Oxford Dictionary of National Biography*, online (Oxford: Oxford University Press, 2004).

4. NA T 185/1, Holden, "Testimony," April 8, 1918, 4.

5. NA T 185/1, Holden, "Testimony," April 8, 1918, 17.

6. NA T 185/1, Holden, "Testimony," April 8, 1918, 19.

7. NA T 185/1, Holden, "Testimony," April 8, 1918, 10.

8. NA T 185/1, Holden, "Testimony," April 8, 1918, 12.

9. NA T 185/1, Holden, "Testimony," April 8, 1918, 3.

10. NA T 185/1, Holden, "Testimony," April 8, 1918, 1–2.

11. NA T 185/1, Holden, "Testimony," April 8, 1918, 12–13.

12. Following a merger in 1918, the National Provincial and Union Bank was one of the "big five" clearing banks. Richard Davenport-Hines, "Felix Otto Schuster," *Oxford Dictionary of National Biography*, online (Oxford: Oxford University Press, 2010).

13. NA T 185/1, Schuster, "Testimony," April 9, 1918, 4. Despite the fixation on the balance of trade, Schuster was a committed free trader. Davenport-Hines, "Felix Otto Schuster."

14. NA T 185/1, Schuster, "Testimony," April 9, 1918, 7.

15. NA T 185/1, Schuster, "Testimony," April 9, 1918, 3.

16. NA T 185/1, Schuster, "Testimony," April 9, 1918, 20.

17. NA T 185/1, Schuster, "Testimony," April 9, 1918, 15.

18. NA T 185/1, Schuster, "Testimony," April 9, 1918, 2.

19. NA T 185/1, Schuster, "Testimony," April 9, 1918, 3.

20. NA T 185/1, Benson, "Testimony," May 6, 1918, 5.

21. NA T 185/1, Benson, "Testimony," May 6, 1918, 16.

22. NA T 185/1, Benson, "Testimony," May 6, 1918, 6.

23. NA T 185/1, Benson, "Testimony," May 6, 1918, 5, 16.

24. NA T 185/1, Benson, "Testimony," May 6, 1918, 1.

25. NA T 185/1, Benson, "Testimony," May 6, 1918, 9.

26. NA T 185/1, Benson, "Testimony," May 6, 1918, 14–16.

27. NA T 185/1, Benson, "Testimony," May 6, 1918, 16.

28. NA T 185/1, Benson, "Testimony," May 6, 1918, 17.

29. NA T 185/1, Benson, "Testimony," May 6, 1918, 5.

30. NA T 185/1, Benson, "Testimony," May 6, 1918, 17.

31. NA T 185/1, Benson, "Testimony," May 6, 1918, 21–22.

32. NA T 185/1, Nugent, "Testimony," May 7, 1918, 1.

33. NA T 185/1, Nugent, "Testimony," May 7, 1918, 10.

34. NA T 185/1, Nugent, "Testimony," May 7, 1918, 23.

35. NA T 185/1, Nugent, "Testimony," May 7, 1918, 26.

36. NA T 185/1, Nugent, "Testimony," May 7, 1918, 5.

37. Invoking J. S. Mill, Nugent argued that "the circulation of notes in the preliminary stage will not cause inflation." NA T 185/1, Nugent, "Testimony," May 7, 1918, 8. Insofar as there was inflation, Nugent declared, "I do not trouble myself about contracting the notes . . . because I am not a believer in the theory that it is an unhealthy inflation." NA T 185/1, Nugent, "Testimony," May 7, 1918, 28.

38. NA T 185/1, Nugent, "Testimony," May 7, 1918, 2.

39. NA T 185/1, Nugent, "Testimony," May 7, 1918, 24.

40. NA T 185/1, Nugent, "Testimony," May 7, 1918, 21.

41. NA T 185/1, Nugent, "Testimony," May 7, 1918, 12.

42. NA T 185/1, Nugent, "Testimony," May 7, 1918, 9.

43. NA T 185/1, Nugent, "Testimony," May 7, 1918, 20.

44. NA T 185/1, Nugent, "Testimony," May 7, 1918, 4.

45. NA T 185/1, Nugent, "Testimony," May 7, 1918, 29.

46. NA T 185/1, Nugent, "Testimony," May 7, 1918, 28.

47. NA T 185/1, Nugent, "Testimony," May 7, 1918, 29.

48. NA T 185/1, Nugent, "Testimony," May 7, 1918, 29.

49. NA T 185/1, Nugent, "Testimony," May 7, 1918, 18.

50. NA T 185/1, Nugent, "Testimony," May 7, 1918, 12.

51. NA T 185/1, Nugent, "Testimony," May 7, 1918, 21.

52. NA T 185/1, Nugent, "Testimony," May 7, 1918, 14.

53. NA T 185/1, Nugent, "Testimony," May 7, 1918, 12.

54. NA T 185/1, Nugent, "Testimony," May 7, 1918, 18.

55. NA T 185/1, Nugent, "Testimony," May 7, 1918, 14.

56. William C. Lubenow, "Walter Leaf," *Oxford Dictionary of National Biography*, online (Oxford: Oxford University Press, 2010).

57. Lubenow, "Walter Leaf."

58. NA T 185/1, Leaf, "Testimony," May 27, 1918, 3.

59. NA T 185/1, Leaf, "Testimony," May 27, 1918, 4.

60. NA T 185/1, Leaf, "Testimony," May 27, 1918, 3.

61. NA T 185/1, Leaf, "Testimony," May 27, 1918, 3.

62. NA T 185/1, Leaf, "Testimony," May 27, 1918, 3.

63. NA T 185/1, Leaf, "Testimony," May 27, 1918, 6.

64. NA T 185/1, Leaf, "Testimony," May 27, 1918, 11.

65. NA T 185/1, Leaf, "Testimony," May 27, 1918, 8.

66. NA T 185/1, Leaf, "Testimony," May 27, 1918, 5.

67. NA T 185/1, Leaf, "Testimony," May 27, 1918, 10.

68. NA T 185/1, Leaf, "Testimony," May 27, 1918, 10.

69. NA T 185/1, Leaf, "Testimony," May 27, 1918, 11.

70. NA T 185/1, Leaf, "Testimony," May 27, 1918, 11.

71. NA T 185/1, Leaf, "Testimony," May 27, 1918, 11.

72. NA T 185/1, Leaf, "Testimony," May 27, 1918, 15–16.

73. NA T 185/1, Leaf, "Testimony," May 27, 1918, 16.

74. NA T 185/1, Leaf, "Testimony," May 27, 1918, 16.

75. NA T 185/1, Leaf, "Testimony," May 27, 1918, 17.

76. NA T 185/1, Leaf, "Testimony," May 27, 1918, 17.

77. NA T 185/1, Leaf, "Testimony," May 28, 1918, 2.

78. NA T 185/1, Leaf, "Testimony," May 28, 1918, 2.

79. NA T 185/1, Leaf, "Testimony," May 28, 1918, 3.

80. NA T 185/1, Leaf, "Testimony," May 28, 1918, 11.

81. The subcommittee's version originally read, "The first condition of the restoration of a sound currency and of the exchanges is the reduction of existing credit inflation." This was changed to avoid confusion. Pigou and Bradbury insisted that they be clear that the "credit inflation" was itself a symptom of the deeper problems. NA T 185/1, Minutes, May 28, 1918; NA T 185/1, Summary of Provisional Conclusions.

82. NA T 185/1, Summary of Provisional Conclusions.

83. NA T 185/1, Minutes, May 28, 1918.

84. NA T 185/1, Minutes, May 28, 1918.

85. NA T 185/1, Minutes, May 28, 1918.

86. NA T 185/1, Summary of Provisional Conclusions. NA T 185/1, Discussion, June 4, 1918.

87. NA T 185/1, Summary of Provisional Conclusions. NA T 185/1, Discussion, June 4, 1918.

88. NA T 185/1, Discussion, June 4, 1918.

89. Roger T. Stearn, "Simpson, Sir John Hope," *Oxford Dictionary of National Biography*, online (Oxford: Oxford University Press, 2012); "Finding Aid for 'Bank of Liverpool, 1831–1919,'" Archives Hub, November 20, 2020, https://archiveshub.jisc.ac.uk/data/gb2044-bb25/2.

90. NA T 185/1, Simpson, Memorandum of Evidence, May 27, 1918, 1.

91. NA T 185/1, Simpson, Memorandum of Evidence, May 27, 1918, 2.

92. NA T 185/1, Simpson, Memorandum of Evidence, May 27, 1918, 2.

93. NA T 185/1, Simpson, Memorandum of Evidence, May 27, 1918, 5.

94. NA T 185/1, Simpson, "Testimony," June 3, 1918, 22.

95. NA T 185/1, Simpson, "Testimony," June 3, 1918, 2.

96. NA T 185/1, Simpson, "Testimony," June 3, 1918, 2.

97. NA T 185/1, Simpson, "Testimony," June 3, 1918, 2.

98. NA T 185/1, Simpson, "Testimony," June 3, 1918, 12.

99. NA T 185/1, Simpson, "Testimony," June 3, 1918, 11.

100. NA T 185/1, Simpson, Memorandum of Evidence, May 27, 1918, 5–6.

101. NA T 185/1, Simpson, Memorandum of Evidence, May 27, 1918, 6.

102. NA T 185/1, Simpson, Memorandum of Evidence, May 27, 1918, 4.

103. NA T 185/1, Simpson, "Testimony," June 3, 1918, 22.

104. NA T 185/1, Simpson, "Testimony," June 3, 1918, 5.

105. NA T 185/1, Simpson, Memorandum of Evidence, May 27, 1918, 6.

106. NA T 185/1, Simpson, "Testimony," June 3, 1918, 22.

107. NA T 185/1, Simpson, "Testimony," June 3, 1918, 11.

108. NA T 185/1, Simpson, "Testimony," June 3, 1918, 13.

109. NA T 185/1, Simpson, "Testimony," June 3, 1918, 14.

110. NA T 185/1, Simpson, "Testimony," June 3, 1918, 25.

111. W. R. Scott and John Maloney, "Nicholson, Joseph Shield," *Oxford Dictionary of National Biography*, online (Oxford: Oxford University Press, 2004).

112. NA T 185/1, Nicholson, Memorandum on Currency, 1.

113. NA T 185/1, Nicholson, Memorandum on Currency, 2.

114. NA T 185/1, Nicholson, Memorandum on Currency, 4.

115. NA T 185/1, Nicholson, Memorandum on Currency, 2.

116. NA T 185/1, Nicholson, Memorandum on Currency, 3.

117. NA T 185/2, Nicholson, Answers to Cunliffe Committee Questions, June 15, 1918, 3–5.

118. NA T 185/1, Nicholson, Memorandum on Currency, 1–2, 5; emphasis added.

119. NA T 185/1, Nicholson, Memorandum on Currency, 3.

120. NA T 185/2, Nicholson, Answers to Cunliffe Committee Questions, June 15, 1918, 2.

121. NA T 185/2, Nicholson, Answers to Cunliffe Committee Questions, June 15, 1918, 8.

122. NA T 185/2, Nicholson, Answers to Cunliffe Committee Questions, June 15, 1918, 4.

123. NA T 185/1, Nicholson, Memorandum on Currency, 6.

124. NA T 185/2, Nicholson, Answers to Cunliffe Committee Questions, June 15, 1918, 5.

125. NA T 185/2, Nicholson, Answers to Cunliffe Committee Questions, June 15, 1918, 4.

126. NA T 185/2, Manchester Chamber Commerce, "Report on . . . Reforms . . . Desirable . . . [for] the Bank of England," July 10, 1918, 534; NA T 185/1, Samuel, "Scheme for Reform of the Bank of England," April 26, 1918, 202.

127. Indeed, when the UK *did* leave the gold standard in 1931, the gold mines' profits soared. One historian of the South African gold producers calculated that (previously) the Gold Fields Group "had been hard pressed to show a profit of £438,879 on a capital of £6,500,000. Its profit for the year ending 30 June 1933 was £933,841. The following year it soared to £1,388,060." In other words, the suspension of the gold standard tripled the Gold Fields Group's profit rate from less than 7 percent to more than 21 percent. Alan Patrick Cartwright, *Gold Paved the Way: The Story of the Gold Fields Group of Companies* (London: Macmillan, 1967), 201. Such was the role of fortune in the making of these fortunes. Throughout, Cartwright regales his readers with the "adventures" of the "Empire-builders" who persisted in their "courageous prospecting," even when "lost in the desert . . . and about to die of thirst," so that they could "persuade" the African authorities to sign "concession[s]" to their mineral rights. But then, he concedes, the book was "written with the co-operation of Consolidated Gold Fields Limited. . . . [It] is *their* book." Cartwright, *Gold Paved the Way*, ix; emphasis in the original.

128. Katherine Prior, "Harris, George Robert Canning, Fourth Baron Harris," *Oxford Dictionary of National Biography*, online (Oxford: Oxford University Press, 2006).

129. Cartwright, *Gold Paved the Way*, 98.

130. For instance, Cartwright describes some of the invoices—for military expenses and "fines"—issued from the British South Africa Company to Rhodes's Gold Fields Group. Cartwright, *Gold Paved the Way*, 91. The company, after all, was not just responsible for governing. It was accountable to its shareholders as well.

131. NA T 185/2, Harris, "Testimony," June 11, 1918, 3.

132. NA T 185/2, Harris, "Testimony," June 11, 1918, 3.

133. NA T 185/2, Harris, "Testimony," June 11, 1918, 3.

134. David A. Steinberg, *Demanding Devaluation: Exchange Rate Politics in the Developing World* (Ithaca, NY: Cornell University Press, 2015).

135. NA T 185/1, MacIndoe, Memorandum of Evidence..

136. NA T 185/1, MacIndoe, Memorandum of Evidence.

137. NA T 185/1, MacIndoe, "Testimony," June 10, 1918, 7.

138. NA T 185/1, MacIndoe, Memorandum of Evidence.

139. NA T 185/1, MacIndoe, Memorandum of Evidence.

140. NA T 185/1, MacIndoe, "Testimony," June 10, 1918, 7.

141. NA T 185/1, MacIndoe, "Testimony," June 10, 1918, 6–7.

142. NA T 185/1, MacIndoe, "Testimony," June 10, 1918, 8.

143. NA T 185/1, MacIndoe, "Testimony," June 10, 1918, 6.

144. NA T 185/1, MacIndoe, "Testimony," June 10, 1918, 6.

145. NA T 185/1, MacIndoe, "Testimony," June 10, 1918, 2.

146. NA T 185/1, MacIndoe, "Testimony," June 10, 1918, 3.

147. NA T 185/1, MacIndoe, "Testimony," June 10, 1918, 2.

148. NA T 185/1, MacIndoe, "Testimony," June 10, 1918, 5.

149. NA T 185/2, Bell, "Testimony," July 11, 1918, 6.

150. NA T 185/2, Bell, "Testimony," July 11, 1918, 2–3.

151. NA T 185/2, Bell, "Testimony," July 11, 1918, 2–3; David Hume, "Of Money," in *Essays: Moral, Political, Literary*, ed. Eugene F. Miller (London: Liberty Fund, 1987), 281–94. See also Keynes, *Collected Writings*, 7:343.

152. NA T 185/2, Bell, "Testimony," July 11, 1918, 6.

153. NA T 185/2, Bell, "Testimony," July 11, 1918, 4–5.

154. NA T 185/2, Bell, "Testimony," July 11, 1918, 7.

155. NA T 185/2, Bell, "Testimony," July 11, 1918, 8.

156. NA T 185/2, Bell, "Testimony," July 11, 1918, 11.

157. NA T 185/2, Bell, "Testimony," July 11, 1918, 9; emphasis added.

158. NA T 185/2, Bell, "Testimony," July 11, 1918, 8–10.

159. NA T 185/2, Manchester Chamber Commerce, "Report on . . . Reforms . . . Desirable . . . [for] the Bank of England," July 10, 1918, 1.

160. NA T 185/2, Manchester Chamber Commerce, "Report on . . . Reforms . . . Desirable . . . [for] the Bank of England," July 10, 1918, 1.

161. NA T 185/2, Manchester Chamber Commerce, "Report on . . . Reforms . . . Desirable . . . [for] the Bank of England," July 10, 1918, 1.

162. NA T 185/1, Summary of Provisional Conclusions.

163. NA T 185/1, Samuel, "Scheme for Reform of the Bank of England," April 26, 1918, 1.

164. NA T 185/1, Samuel, "Testimony," June 10, 1918, 2.

165. NA T 185/1, Samuel, "Testimony," June 10, 1918, 5.

166. NA T 185/1, Samuel, "Testimony," June 10, 1918, 15.

167. NA T 185/1, Samuel, "Testimony," June 10, 1918, 17.

168. NA T 185/1, Samuel, "Testimony," June 10, 1918, 3.

169. Boyce, "Creating the Myth of Consensus," 196.

170. NA T 185/2, London Chamber of Commerce, Memorandum, July 1918, 478.

171. NA T 185/2, Begg, "Testimony," July 11, 1918, 12.

172. NA T 185/2, Begg, "Testimony," July 11, 1918, 13.

173. NA T 185/2, Begg, "Testimony," July 11, 1918, 6.

174. NA T 185/2, Begg, "Testimony," July 11, 1918, 6.

175. NA T 185/2, Begg, Testimony at London Chamber of Commerce (draft), June 1918.

176. NA T 185/2, Begg, Testimony at London Chamber of Commerce (draft), June 1918, 453–56.

177. NA T 185/2, Begg, "Testimony," June 11, 1918, 3.

178. NA T 185/2, Begg, "Testimony," July 11, 1918, 3.

179. NA T 185/2, Begg, Testimony to London Chamber of Commerce (printed), June 1918, 12.

180. NA T 185/2, Begg, "Testimony," July 11, 1918, 10.

181. NA T 185/2, Begg, "Testimony," July 11, 1918, 18.

182. NA T 185/2, Begg, "Testimony," July 11, 1918, 18.

183. NA T 185/2, Begg, Testimony to London Chamber of Commerce (printed), June 1918, 8.

184. NA T 185/2, Begg, "Testimony," June 11, 1918, 10.

185. NA T 185/2, Begg, "Testimony," July 11, 1918, 11.

186. NA T 185/2, Begg, "Testimony," July 11, 1918, 2.

187. NA T 185/2, Begg, "Testimony," July 11, 1918, 18.

188. NA T 185/2, Begg, Testimony to London Chamber of Commerce (printed), June 1918, 3.

189. NA T 185/2, Begg, "Testimony," July 11, 1918, 20.

190. Boyce, "Creating the Myth of Consensus," 177. Boyce has done the most work to reconstruct the FBI's position. Robert Boyce, *British Capitalism at the Crossroads, 1919–1932: A Study in Politics, Economics, and International Relations* (Cambridge: Cambridge University Press, 1987), 37–38; Boyce, *Great Interwar Crisis*, 88. The interpretation offered here differs markedly. It also draws on material that Boyce minimizes, such as the FBI's crucial letter to Churchill in March 1925, quoted at length below.

191. NA T 185/2, FBI, "Foreign Exchange after the War," July 10, 1918, 1.

192. NA T 185/2, FBI, "Foreign Exchange after the War," July 10, 1918, 1–2.

193. NA T 185/2, FBI, "Foreign Exchange after the War," July 10, 1918, 2.

194. NA T 185/2, FBI, "Foreign Exchange after the War," July 10, 1918, 4, 7.

195. Committee on Financial Facilities, *Report*, Cd. 9227 (London: His Majesty's Stationery Office, 1918), 2–3. This committee and its report have been missed almost entirely by scholars. Moggridge mentions the report one time in his second book. Moggridge, *British Monetary Policy*, 22. Pollard and Peden do as well. Sidney Pollard, "Introduction," in *The Gold Standard and Employment Policies between the Wars*, ed. Sidney Pollard (London: Methuen, 1970), 2; G. C. Peden, *The Treasury and British Public Policy, 1906–1959* (Oxford: Oxford University Press, 2000), 121. Boyce provides insight into the subsequent struggles of British industry, but he minimizes the degree to

which the industrialists were consulted by these wartime committees (i.e., the Cunliffe Committee and the Committee on Financial Facilities). Boyce, *Great Interwar Crisis*, 87; Boyce, *British Capitalism at the Crossroads*, 37–38; Boyce, "Creating the Myth of Consensus," 175–76. The materials from the Committee on Financial Facilities are available at the UK National Archives in RECO 1/860.

196. Committee on Financial Facilities, *Report*, 6.

197. This report was published in late November 1918, three months after the Cunliffe Committee's *First Interim Report*.

198. Committee on Financial Facilities, *Report*, 6.

199. Cf. Boyce, *Great Interwar Crisis*, 87.

## 6. Commandments

1. Henry Clay, *Norman* (New York: Macmillan, 1957), 112; Boyle, *Montagu Norman*, 128.

2. Bank of England, G4/141, June 27, 1918.

3. Clay, *Norman*, 112.

4. Bank of England, G4/141, June 27, 1918.

5. Bank of England, G4/141, June 27, 1918.

6. Clay, *Norman*, 112. Clay does not cite the source of these proposed amendments. The only copy found in the Bank's archive does not include marginalia. The comments may have come from an interview. Moggridge similarly cites Clay. Moggridge, *British Monetary Policy*, 201.

7. There is no record of the content of the Bank's several discussions of these drafts. Cunliffe missed these several meetings. Bank of England, G8/54, June 19, 1918; Bank of England, G4/141, June 13 and 20, 1918.

8. NA T 185/2, Cokayne, "Testimony," July 8, 1918, 4.

9. NA T 185/2, Cokayne, "Testimony," July 8, 1918, 3–4.

10. Locke, *Some Considerations*, 266.

11. NA T 185/2, Cokayne, "Testimony," July 8, 1918, 2–3, 23.

12. Smith, *Wealth of Nations*, 295–96, 321.

13. NA T 185/2, Cokayne, "Testimony," July 8, 1918, 5.

14. NA T 185/2, Cokayne, "Testimony," July 8, 1918, 5.

15. NA T 185/2, Cokayne, "Testimony," July 8, 1918, 4.

16. NA T 185/2, Cokayne, "Testimony," July 8, 1918, 4.

17. NA T 185/2, Cokayne, "Testimony," July 8, 1918, 7.

18. NA T 185/2, Cokayne, "Testimony," July 8, 1918, 13; emphasis added.

19. NA T 185/2, Cokayne, "Testimony," July 8, 1918, 12.

20. NA T 185/2, Cokayne, "Testimony," July 8, 1918, 14.

21. NA T 185/2, Cokayne, "Testimony," July 8, 1918, 18.

22. NA T 185/2, Cokayne, "Testimony," July 8, 1918, 19.

23. NA T 185/2, Cokayne, "Testimony," July 8, 1918, 18.

24. NA T 185/2, Cokayne, "Testimony," July 8, 1918, 18.

25. NA T 185/2, Cokayne, "Testimony," July 8, 1918, 24–25.

26. NA T 185/2, Cokayne, "Testimony," July 8, 1918, 7.

27. Sayers, *Bank of England*, 1:100–101. Ahamed and Kynaston both repeat the slight. Ahamed, *Lords of Finance*, 81; Kynaston, *Till Time's Last Sand*, 259.

28. NA T 185/2, Cokayne, "Testimony," July 8, 1918, 1.

29. NA T 185/2, Cokayne, "Testimony," July 8, 1918, 1.

30. NA T 185/2, Cokayne, "Testimony," July 8, 1918, 25.

31. NA T 185/2, Minutes, July 9, 1918, 1, 3.

32. NA T 185/1, Amended Summary of Provisional Conclusions.

33. Cunliffe Committee, *First Interim Report*, 11.

34. There has been almost no previous scholarship systematically analyzing the *First Interim Report* itself.

35. David Hume, "Of the Balance of Trade," in *Essays: Moral, Political, Literary*, ed. Eugene F. Miller (London: Liberty Fund, 1987), 308–26.

36. Cunliffe Committee, *First Interim Report*, 3.

37. Cunliffe Committee, *First Interim Report*, 9.

38. Cunliffe Committee, *First Interim Report*, 3.

39. Cunliffe Committee, *First Interim Report*, 6.

40. Cunliffe Committee, *First Interim Report*, 4.

41. Donald Moggridge, "The 1931 Financial Crisis: A New View," *The Banker* 120, no. 534 (1970): 832–39.

42. Cunliffe Committee, *First Interim Report*, 4.

43. Cunliffe Committee, *First Interim Report*, 5.

44. Cunliffe Committee, *First Interim Report*, 5.

45. Cunliffe Committee, *First Interim Report*, 8.

46. Cunliffe Committee, *First Interim Report*, 6.

47. Cunliffe Committee, *First Interim Report*, 3.

48. Cunliffe Committee, *First Interim Report*, 6.

49. Cunliffe Committee, *First Interim Report*, 6.

50. Cunliffe Committee, *First Interim Report*, 7.

51. Cunliffe Committee, *First Interim Report*, 7.

52. Cunliffe Committee, *First Interim Report*, 7.

53. NA T 185/1, Minutes, March 11, 1918.

54. Cunliffe Committee, *First Interim Report*, 3, 5.

55. Cunliffe Committee, *First Interim Report*, 7.

56. Cunliffe Committee, *First Interim Report*, 9–10.

57. Before the war, the Scottish and Irish banks circulated £11.6 million of notes fully backed by reserves. By the end of 1918, they were circulating £56 million against £51 million in reserve. How did they increase their reserves so markedly? The answer probably lies in the different regulatory and reporting standards applied to these banks. In England, almost all of the currency was issued by the Bank of England and the Treasury, which counted only gold coin and bullion as reserve. Most of the currency increase took the form of (essentially unbacked) Bradburys. Because the Bradburys were treated as legally equivalent to gold-backed Bank of England notes and gold coin, the private banks were able to count Bradburys as reserve. Most likely, the bulk of the quintupled Scottish and Irish reserves took that form. If so, the increase in their reserves, while perfectly legal, would not have affected the total gold reserve rate. On the other extreme, if the entirety were comprised of gold coin and bullion not counted elsewhere, this would have shifted the overall national reserve rate to 73 percent, more than doubling the rate implied by the Cunliffe Committee. Bradbury

essentially ignored this puzzle. This is discussed further in an online appendix available at http://jamesashleymorrison.com/bradbury_money_supply_estimates.

58. NA T 185/2, Bankers Clearing House to Bradbury, July 17, 1918; NA T 185/2, Jameson, Memorandum on Irish Banks, 1918. If the figures were circulated or discussed among the Cunliffe Committee members, there is no record of it. NA T 185/2, Upcott to Bradbury, July 19, 1918.

59. At that point, Keynes estimated that the South African gold mines sent about £36 million of gold to London annually. Keynes, *Collected Writings*, 17: 178.

60. Capie and Webber, *Monetary History*, 211–12, discusses the 1920 gold seizure. For the calculations of total reserves, see table 5. The shares of global gold reserves are provided by the US Federal Reserve. US Federal Reserve, *Banking and Monetary Statistics: 1914–1941* (Washington: Board of Governors of the Federal Reserve System, 1976), 544–55. The Federal Reserve's figures for the UK's reserve holdings are a bit higher than those derived from Capie and Webber, but the Federal Reserve reports its figures in the USD gold price and does not explain how it handles the changes in exchange rates and the UK's change in gold price quoting after the war.

61. Foucault, *History of Sexuality*, 98.

62. NA T 185/2, Bankers Clearing House to Bradbury, July 17, 1918; Cunliffe Committee, *First Interim Report*, 4; NA T 185/2, Bradbury, "Future Dimensions of the Fiduciary Issue," March 9, 1918.

63. NA T 185/2, Young to Minister of Reconstruction, August 22, 1918.

64. "Currency and Exchange—Report of Lord Cunliffe's Committee," *Manchester Guardian*, October 30, 1918.

65. NA T 185/2, Meredith Company, Financial Comments, November 1, 1918.

66. NA T 185/2, Meredith Company, Financial Comments, November 1, 1918.

67. NA T 185/2, Meredith Company, Financial Comments, November 8, 1918.

68. NA T 185/2, Meredith Company, Financial Comments, November 8, 1918.

69. NA T 185/2, Meredith Company, Financial Comments, November 1, 1918.

70. When this special committee was renewed the following April, Norman was not among those appointed to it. Bank of England, G4/142, April 3, 1919.

71. Bank of England, G4/141, November 26, 1918.

## 7. Myths

1. Boyce, by contrast, emphasizes the importance of "international conditions" rather than the dynamics between the Cunliffe Committee's directives and the capital controls extended by the Conservatives. Boyce, "Creating the Myth of Consensus," 189.

2. Parliamentary Debates, House of Commons, April 28, 1925, vol. 183, columns 54–55.

3. Gold and Silver (Export Control, &c.) Act, 1920 (10 & 11 Geo. 5, c. 70).

4. Clay simply follows Norman's line that they were demanded unanimously by the private banks. Clay, *Norman*, 116. Atkin's more extensive treatment nevertheless brackets the discussions that generated these significant policy changes. John Atkin, *The Foreign Exchange Market of London: Development since 1900* (New York: Routledge, 2004), 27–31. Others discuss the emergence of the controls only in passing. Boyle,

*Montagu Norman*, 125–27; Moggridge, *Return to Gold*, 14; Moggridge, *British Monetary Policy*, 23; Ahamed, *Lords of Finance*, 210.

5. Sayers, *Bank of England*, 1:116–17; 3:55–56.

6. Keynes, *Collected Writings*, vol. 17: 185.

7. Ronald Rogowski, *Commerce and Coalitions: How Trade Affects Domestic Political Alignments* (Princeton, NJ: Princeton University Press, 1989); Jeffry Frieden, "Exchange Rate Politics: Contemporary Lessons from American History," *Review of International Political Economy* 1, no. 1 (1994): 81–103.

8. Bradbury highlighted this point to the Cabinet in 1919. NA CAB 27/71, Appendix: 1.

9. Thomas Oatley, "How Constraining Is Capital Mobility? The Partisan Hypothesis in an Open Economy," *American Journal of Political Science* 43, no. 4 (1999): 1008.

10. Perhaps the social scientists can be forgiven for this oversight as even Baldwin's biographers have missed this point. In general, they have minimized his role in the return to gold. In their 1,100-page biography, Middlemas and Barnes mention the gold standard fewer than two dozen times, despite that the 1925 return was one of the most consequential policies of his second government. They write, "Essentially, the decision to return was taken when the Report of the Cunliffe Committee was published in 1918," and "The chief responsibility rested with . . . Norman . . . and Churchill." Keith Middlemas and John Barnes, *Baldwin: A Biography* (London: Weidenfeld & Nicolson, 1969): 302. Williamson also does not discuss Baldwin's introduction of the 1920 capital controls. Similarly, he notes, "Baldwin himself did not assess his career in terms of imperial or economic policies." Philip Williamson, *Stanley Baldwin: Conservative Leadership and National Values* (Cambridge: Cambridge University Press, 1999): 358.

11. Alberto Alesina, Vittorio Grilli, and Gian Maria Milesi-Ferrett, "The Political Economy of Capital Controls," National Bureau of Economic Research, Working Paper 4353, 1993, https://www.nber.org/papers/w4353.

### 8. Liberalization

1. Termination of the Present War (Definition) Act (8 & 9 Geo. 5, c. 59), 1918.

2. Governor "Brian Cockayne [*sic*]" appears on one page. Deputy Governor Lubbock is not mentioned at all. Charles Addis gets several mentions in passing, despite that his explicit disagreements with Norman were put on display—and on the record—in their joint testimony before the Chamberlain-Bradbury Committee in 1925. The sole mention of that committee mischaracterizes its principle conclusion as "recommend[ing] a delay of some years." Ahamed also asserts that Bradbury and Niemeyer were "both . . . well established in the Norman camp" in 1925. Ahamed, *Lords of Finance*, 82, 220, 233–34.

3. Under the Act for the Encouragement of Trade (15 Car. 2, c. 7, 1663), foreign coin and gold and silver bullion could be exported without tax or limitation. Exports simply needed to be logged in a customs house.

4. Locke's arguments to permanently fix the exchange rate took for granted that it was practically impossible to effectively limit bullion flows. Locke, *Further Considerations*, 432–33, 474; John Locke, "Answer to My Lord Keepers Queries," in *Locke on Money*, 387–88.

5. NA T 185/2, Cokayne, "Testimony," July 8, 1918, 12. Sayers follows this line. Sayers, *Bank of England*, 3:55. Technically, it was not "prohibited," but it was increasingly restricted and strongly discouraged.

6. The act gave to "His Majesty in Council" (in effect, the wartime cabinet) sweeping authority to make whatever regulations necessary to prosecute the war. The government expounded these in iterated versions of the DORA "manual." Charles Cook, ed., *Defence of the Realm Manual, Revised to March 31st, 1919*, 7th ed. (London: His Majesty's Stationery Office, 1919).

7. Atkin, *Foreign Exchange Market of London*, 30–31. Osborne mistakenly lists December 21, 1917, as the date of enactment. Bank of England, M7/159: 204.

8. Sayers, *Bank of England*, 1:98n.

9. NA CAB 27/71, Appendix: 1.

10. NA CAB 24/5/37, 2.

11. NA CAB 24/75/87, 5.

12. NA CAB 24/75/20, 1.

13. NA CAB 24/75/20, 3.

14. NA CAB 24/75/20, 4.

15. NA CAB 24/75/20, 6.

16. NA CAB 24/75/87, 4.

17. NA CAB 24/75/87, 1–2.

18. NA CAB 24/75/87, 7.

19. NA CAB 24/75/87, 7.

20. NA CAB 24/75/87, 5.

21. NA CAB 24/75/87, 5, 11.

22. NA CAB 24/75/87, 15–16.

23. Auckland Geddes's 1919 report is not to be confused with that authored by his brother (Eric) several years later. Infamous for its cuts to public expenditure, the latter became known as the "Geddes Axe." The earlier Geddes report has received rather little scholarly attention. As usual, Howson's treatment is exceptional. Howson, *Domestic Monetary Management*, chapter 2.

24. NA CAB 24/5/37, "Unemployment and the State of Trade," March 14, 1919, 2.

25. NA CAB 24/5/37, "Unemployment and the State of Trade," March 14, 1919, 2.

26. NA CAB 24/5/37, "Unemployment and the State of Trade," March 14, 1919, 3.

27. NA CAB 24/5/38, 2.

28. Howson, *Domestic Monetary Management*, 11.

29. The Cunliffe Committee did suggest that it might take upwards of a decade to discern that figure. But it did *not* intend that resumption of capital movement should be deferred for a decade.

30. Cook, *Defence of the Realm Manual*, 30F.

31. NA CAB 24/5/38, 1.

32. Tellingly, several of the items were explicitly connected in this list to Bradbury; later, Norman elaborated them in terms of the interchanges he had with Bradbury.

33. Bank of England, ADM 34/8, 1.

34. Bank of England, ADM 34/8, March 1, 1919.

35. Bank of England, ADM 34/8, March 6, 1919.

36. Bank of England, ADM 34/8, March 10, 1919, and March 17, 1919.

37. Bank of England, ADM 34/8, March 11, 1919.

38. Bank of England, ADM 34/8, March 25, 1919.

39. Bank of England, ADM 34/8, March 27, 1919.

40. Bank of England, ADM 34/8, 1.

41. Bank of England, ADM 34/8, March 29, 1919, and April 7, 1919.

42. Norman revisited these entries several times. The entries were originally written in black ink. In the margins (with red ink), Norman indicated that the meeting with Bradbury had taken place on the twenty-ninth and that these provisions were "agreed [the] 1st." With a pencil, he drew an arrow connecting the two sets of entries. At the top of those on the thirty-first, he wrote, "? [sic] Two Shifts Begin." It is unclear just which two of the many shifts attracted Norman's attention. Bank of England, ADM 34/8, March 29, 1919, and April 7, 1919.

43. Bank of England, ADM 34/8, April 4, 1919.

44. NA T 185/2, Harris, "Testimony," June 11, 1918, 3.

45. Bank of England, ADM 34/8, July 11, 1919.

46. Boyle, *Montagu Norman*, 126. In presenting this, Boyle contrasts Norman's "unfashionable pessimism" with Lloyd George's "mood . . . of unreasonable, un-shakable optimism." But would a pessimist have opened the UK's financial system to global market forces? The previous week, Norman recorded, "I begged [the] C[hancello]r . . . to have a compulsory Loan in [the] Autumn." Bank of England, ADM 34/8, July 7, 1919. The act of "begging" was the same, but the nature of the action being requested could not have been more different: forcing capital to loan its money to the government versus granting capital the freedom to send its money abroad.

47. NA CAB 27/71, Appendix: 1.

48. NA CAB 27/71, Appendix: 1.

49. NA CAB 27/71, Appendix: 1.

50. NA CAB 27/71, Appendix: 2.

51. NA CAB 27/71, Appendix: 2.

52. NA CAB 27/71, Appendix: 4–5.

53. NA CAB 27/71, Appendix: 3.

54. NA CAB 27/71, 2, 6.

55. NA CAB 27/71, 3–4.

56. NA CAB 27/71, 6–7.

57. NA CAB 27/71, 7–8.

58. After the Cunliffe Committee rejected Holden's proposals, he developed a new approach. In January 1919, he proposed authorizing the Bank of England "to issue notes on the security of gold *and* bills of exchange." Emphasis added. The previous April, he had deprecated issuing notes against bills of exchange. NA T 185/1, Holden, "Testimony," April 8, 1918, 22. This proposed innovation is reminiscent of Cunliffe's proposal to issue notes against government securities. But Holden specifically es-chewed the issuing of notes against securities. NA T 185/1, Holden, Speech, January 29, 1919, 33–34, 37–38. Compared to the most orthodox members of the Cunliffe Committee, Holden wanted an even larger gold reserve and an even stronger gold backing for all British notes. But rather than pooling all of Britain's reserves in the Bank of England, he insisted that joint stock banks, such as his own, should keep their own gold holdings as a secondary reserve. At the same time, the British government should also acquire an extra £100 million or so to provide a one-to-one gold backing for British notes. NA T 185/1, Holden, Speech, January 29, 1919, 59–61.

59. "Allied Government Banks and Allied Money," *Washington Herald*, January 27, 1919; "Currency Report Condemned by Critics," *Wall Street Journal*, March 15, 1919.

60. NA CAB 27/71, 4; NA T 185/2, Discussion following Wright Testimony, July 23, 1919, 664.

61. NA T 185/2, Discussion following Wright Testimony, July 23, 1919, 665.

62. NA T 185/2, Jameson, "Testimony," July 22, 1919, 637; NA T 185/2, Wright, "Testimony," July 23, 1919, 669.

63. NA T 185/2, Robb, "Testimony," July 23, 1919, 679; NA T 185/2, Johns, Memorandum of Testimony, November 1, 1918, 628; NA T 185/2, Jameson, "Testimony," July 22, 1919, 640.

64. NA T 185/2, "Meeting of Representatives of the Irish Bank," September 16, 1919, 725.

65. NA T 185/2, Wright, "Testimony," July 23, 1919, 672.

66. NA T 185/2, Johns, Memorandum of Testimony, November 1, 1918, 617.

67. NA T 185/2, Jameson, "Testimony," July 22, 1919, 629.

68. NA T 185/2, Jameson, Memorandum on Irish Banks, 1918, 607.

69. NA T 185/2, Bradbury, "Future Dimensions of the Fiduciary Issue," March 9, 1918.

70. Cunliffe Committee, *First Interim Report*, 5.

71. NA T 185/2, Wright, "Testimony," July 23, 1919, 672. See also NA T 185/2, Johns, Memorandum of Testimony, November 1, 1918, 660; NA T 185/2, Robb, "Testimony," July 23, 1919, 682.

72. NA T 185/2, Wright, "Testimony," July 23, 1919, 678.

73. Ayşe Zarakol, *After Defeat: How the East Learned to Live with the West* (Cambridge: Cambridge University Press, 2011), 3–5.

74. Michael D. Bordo and Hugh Rockoff, "The Gold Standard as a 'Good Housekeeping Seal of Approval,'" *Journal of Economic History* 56, no. 2 (1996): 389–428; Julia Gray, *The Company States Keep: International Economic Organizations and Investor Perceptions* (Cambridge: Cambridge University Press, 2013).

75. NA T 185/2, Goodenough, "Testimony," July 29, 1919, 685, 689.

76. NA T 185/2, Goodenough, "Testimony," July 29, 1919, 690.

77. NA T 185/2, Goodenough, "Testimony," July 29, 1919, 693.

78. NA T 185/2, Goodenough, "Testimony," July 29, 1919, 694.

79. NA T 185/2, Discussion following Wright Testimony, July 23, 1919, 664.

80. NA T 185/1, Minutes, October 15, 1919.

81. NA T 185/2, Schuster, "Testimony," October 16, 1919, 746.

82. See in particular the discussion with Bell from Lloyd's of London. NA T 185/2, Bell, "Testimony," July 31, 1919, 715.

83. NA T 185/2, Discussion following Schuster Testimony, October 16, 1919, 732.

84. NA T 185/2, Schuster, "Testimony," October 16, 1919, 14.

85. NA T 185/2, Schuster, "Testimony," October 16, 1919, 14.

86. NA T 185/2, Schuster, "Testimony," October 16, 1919, 15.

87. NA T 185/2, Schuster, "Testimony," October 16, 1919, 737.

88. Carlo Ginzburg, *The Cheese and the Worms: The Cosmos of a Sixteenth-Century Miller* (Baltimore: Johns Hopkins University Press, 1992).

89. Cunliffe Committee, *First Interim Report*, 3.

90. Cunliffe Committee, *First Interim Report*, 3.

91. Bank of England, G4/142, September 25, 1919.

92. Bank of England, G8/54, November 5, 1919.

93. "British Currency Question," *Manchester Guardian*, December 16, 1919.

94. The only caveat came with trade policy, which the Conservatives planned to craft in conjunction with diplomacy. Parliamentary Debates, House of Commons, December 1919, vol. 123, columns 43–46.

95. GFD Finaeon, "British Pound to US Dollar Exchange Rate (GBPUSD)."

96. NA T 172/1384, "Memorandum as to Money Rates," February 10, 1920.

97. This material is contained in the collection NA T 172/1384.

98. Bank of England, ADM 34/9, March 30, 1920.

99. Clay, *Norman*, 127–30.

100. GFD Finaeon, "British Pound to US Dollar Exchange Rate (GBPUSD)."

## 9. Who Would Control Capital?

1. "The Currency Delusion," *The New Statesman*, August 3, 1918.

2. TUC, *Annual Report* (1920), 293–94.

3. Frieden, "Exchange Rate Politics," 85.

4. TUC, *Annual Report* (1921), 154.

5. TUC: Cost of Living Committee, *Interim Report*, 20. The committee quoted Keynes—still then a monetarist—showcasing the veracity of the quantity theory of money (8).

6. See the committee's systematic response (published separately) to such claims made by the Federation of British Industries. TUC: Cost of Living Committee, *Wages and Prices*.

7. TUC: Cost of Living Committee, *Interim Report*, 7.

8. TUC: Cost of Living Committee, *Interim Report*, 16.

9. TUC: Cost of Living Committee, *Interim Report*, 16.

10. TUC: Cost of Living Committee, *Interim Report*, 18–19.

11. TUC: Cost of Living Committee, *Interim Report*, 12, 20.

12. TUC: Cost of Living Committee, *Interim Report*, 21.

13. TUC: Cost of Living Committee, *Interim Report*, 21.

14. TUC: Cost of Living Committee, *Interim Report*, 13.

15. TUC: Cost of Living Committee, *Interim Report*, 21.

16. TUC: Cost of Living Committee, *Interim Report*, 21.

17. George Orwell, *Animal Farm: A Fairy Story* (New York: Signet Classic, 1996.), chapters 5–6.

18. TUC: Cost of Living Committee, *Final Report*.

19. TUC, *Annual Report* (1920), 301.

20. TUC, *Annual Report* (1920), 301.

21. TUC, *Annual Report* (1920), 298.

22. Alfred Marshall, *Principles of Economics: An Introductory Volume*, 8th ed. (London: Macmillan, 1920), 574–75; Orwell, *Road to Wigan Pier*, 18.

23. Parliamentary Debates, House of Commons, November 4, 1920, vol. 134, column 577.

24. Parliamentary Debates, House of Commons, November 10, 1920, vol. 134, columns 1320–26.

25. Parliamentary Debates, House of Commons, November 10, 1920, vol. 134, columns 1321–22.

26. Parliamentary Debates, House of Commons, November 29, 1920, vol. 135, column 1043.

27. Parliamentary Debates, House of Commons, December 13, 1920, vol. 136, columns 118–19.

28. Parliamentary Debates, House of Commons, November 29, 1920, vol. 135, column 1057.

29. Parliamentary Debates, House of Commons, November 10, 1920, vol. 134, column 1321.

30. Sayers, *Bank of England*, vol. 3, appendix 6, 55.

31. It was superseded by the Treaty of Lausanne in 1923.

32. Parliamentary Debates, House of Commons, November 29, 1920, vol. 135, column 1062. Barnes was considered a radical by many Liberal colleagues. By the 1930s, he was elected (locally) on Labour's ticket. "Major Harry Barnes," *The Times*, October 14, 1935.

33. Parliamentary Debates, House of Commons, November 14, 1918, vol. 110, column 2972.

34. Parliamentary Debates, House of Commons, November 10, 1920, vol. 134, column 1321. Here again, historians have bought this line. Sayers, *Bank of England*, 3:55. Baldwin's own words controvert his biographers' claim that extending the capital controls beyond 1925 was unthinkable. They write, "In Baldwin's opinion, the admission of failure, implicit in extending the suspension, would damage confidence in sterling and lead to a long reversion towards violent currency fluctuation in Europe . . . Such a dereliction of what he recognized as a British duty, was impossible." Middlemas and Barnes, *Baldwin*, 303.

35. Parliamentary Debates, House of Commons, November 29, 1920, vol. 135, columns 1043–44.

36. Parliamentary Debates, House of Commons, December 6, 1920, vol. 135, columns 1849–51.

37. Parliamentary Debates, House of Commons, November 29, 1920, vol. 135, column 1051.

38. Parliamentary Debates, House of Commons, November 29, 1920, vol. 135, column 1042.

39. Parliamentary Debates, House of Commons, December 6, 1920, vol. 135, columns 1849–50.

40. Parliamentary Debates, House of Commons, November 29, 1920, vol. 135, column 1062.

41. Parliamentary Debates, House of Commons, November 29, 1920, vol. 135, column 1055.

42. Parliamentary Debates, House of Commons, November 29, 1920, vol. 135, column 1057. It is worth noting that Kenworthy was sufficiently far to the left that he resigned from the Liberal party and joined Labour a few years later.

43. Bank of England, ADM 34/9, November 5, 1920.

44. Bank of England, ADM 34/9, November 30, 1920.

45. Bank of England, ADM 34/9, December 8, 1920.

46. Middlemas and Barnes, *Baldwin*, 305.

47. Bank of England, ADM 34/8, 1.

48. Bank of England, ADM 34/8, March 27, 1919.

49. "Gold Export Control: Government Bill Condemned," *Manchester Guardian*, November 15, 1920.

50. "Britain's External Debt: What the Facts Demand," *Manchester Guardian*, November 27, 1920. There are striking similarities to the language Cokayne used in his letter to Chamberlain the previous autumn. See above.

51. In particular, the government promised that gold producers would be allowed to re-export refined gold.

52. Parliamentary Debates, House of Commons, December 13, 1920, vol. 136, columns 117–20.

53. Capie and Webber, *Monetary History of the United Kingdom*, 209–14; US Federal Reserve, *Banking and Monetary Statistics*, 544–555.

54. Sayers, *Bank of England*, 1:126–29.

55. Sayers, *Bank of England*, 1:129–31.

56. Boyle, *Montagu Norman*, 142.

## 10. Keynes's Revolution

1. Williamson, *National Crisis and National Government*, 13.

2. Hall, *Political Power of Economic Ideas*, 6–7.

3. Hall, 376.

4. Seabrooke, "Everyday Social Sources of Economic Crises," 797.

5. Kennedy, *Freedom from Fear*, 358.

6. Genesis 41.

7. Cf. the infamous comment made by Friedman and repeated (in truncated form) by Nixon. "We Are All Keynesians Now," *Time*, December 31, 1965; Milton Friedman, "Letter to the Editor," *Time*, February 4, 1966. Hayek (among others) disagreed, questioning whether even Keynes himself were a "Keynesian." Friedrich Hayek, "Interview with Leo Rosten, November 15, 1978," in *Nobel Prize-Winning Economist: Friedrich A. von Hayek* (Los Angeles: Oral History Program, University of California, Los Angeles, 1983), 121.

8. In the main, Joseph proposed buffering stocks. But the suggestion that Pharaoh "take one-fifth" implies fiscal policy. Joseph's insight was that the public lean against the winds: saving in good times and spending in hard times.

9. Cunliffe Committee, *First Interim Report*, 6.

10. Keynes, *Collected Writings*, 9:245.

11. James Ashley Morrison, "Shocking Intellectual Austerity: The Role of Ideas in the Demise of the Gold Standard in Britain," *International Organization* 70, no. 1 (2016): 175–207.

12. Keynes, *Collected Writings*, 17:184.

13. Benn Steil, *The Battle of Bretton Woods: John Maynard Keynes, Harry Dexter White, and the Making of a New World Order* (Princeton, NJ: Princeton University Press, 2013).

14. Moggridge, *Maynard Keynes*, chapter 17; Robert Skidelsky, *John Maynard Keynes*, vol. 2, *Economist as Saviour, 1920–1937* (London: Macmillan, 1992).

15. Keynes, *Collected Writings*, 17:372–73.

16. Keynes, *Collected Writings*, 17:384.

17. Keynes, *Collected Writings*, 2:13.

18. Keynes, *Collected Writings*, 17:398–410; 18:70–84.

19. Keynes, *Collected Writings*, 18:61–63.

20. Keynes, *Collected Writings*, 19:40.

21. Keynes, *Collected Writings*, 19:34–38.

22. No surprise, then, that Bradbury himself had accepted devaluation of the mark as inevitable. Keynes, *Collected Writings*, 18:62.

23. Keynes, *Collected Writings*, 19:38.

24. Keynes, *Collected Writings*, 19:47.

25. Keynes, *Collected Writings*, 19:45.

26. Keynes, *Collected Writings*, 19: 46.

27. Keynes, *Collected Writings*, 19:53.

28. Keynes, *Collected Writings*, 19:60.

29. Keynes, *Collected Writings*, 19:60–61.

30. Keynes, *Collected Writings*, 19:61.

31. Keynes, *Collected Writings*, 17:384.

32. Keynes, *Collected Writings*, 19:61.

33. Keynes, *Collected Writings*, 19:63–67.

34. Keynes, *Collected Writings*, 19:64–65.

35. Keynes, *Collected Writings*, 19:61.

36. Keynes, *Collected Writings*, 19:74.

37. Keynes, *Collected Writings*, 19:75–76.

38. Keynes, *Collected Writings*, 19:75–76. This justification formed the kernel of Friedman's famous defense of flexible exchange rates." Friedman, "Case for Flexible Exchange Rates."

39. Keynes, *Collected Writings*, 19:76.

40. Keynes, *Collected Writings*, 18:99; Keynes, *Collected Writings*, 19:76.

41. Keynes, *Collected Writings*, 18:70–84.

42. Keynes, *Collected Writings*, 18:76.

43. Keynes, *Collected Writings*, 19:87–91.

44. Keynes, *Collected Writings*, 19.

45. Keynes, *Collected Writings*, 19:87–91.

46. Keynes informed his mother that work had begun on the *Tract* in late June. Keynes, *Collected Writings*, 18:179.

47. Parliamentary Debates, House of Commons, July 4, 1924, vol. 166, columns 482–83.

48. Parliamentary Debates, House of Commons, July 4, 1924, vol. 166, column 576.

49. Keynes, *Collected Writings*, 19:100–103.

50. Parliamentary Debates, House of Commons, July 4, 1924, vol. 166, columns 483–86.

51. Baldwin called for protection that October.

52. Keynes, *Collected Writings*, 19:116–17.

53. Keynes, *Collected Writings*, 19:106.

54. Keynes, *Collected Writings*, 19:109–112.

55. Keynes, *Collected Writings*, 19:105.

56. Keynes, *Collected Writings*, 19:112.

57. Keynes, *Collected Writings*, 4:154.

58. Keynes, *Collected Writings*, 4:149–50.

59. Keynes, *Collected Writings*, 4:1–3.

60. Keynes, *Collected Writings*, 4:36.

61. Locke, *Some Considerations*, 263; Smith, *Wealth of Nations*, 195–264.

62. Keynes, *Collected Writings*, 4:133.

63. Keynes, *Collected Writings*, 4:16.

64. Keynes, *Collected Writings*, 4:1–3.

65. Keynes, *Collected Writings*, 4:32–34.

66. Keynes, *Collected Writings*, 4:35–36.

67. Keynes, *Collected Writings*, 4:87–88.

68. Keynes, *Collected Writings*, 4:126.

69. Keynes, *Collected Writings*, 4:8, 131; Lowndes, *Report containing an Essay*, 13.

70. Keynes, *Collected Writings*, 4:8.

71. Keynes, *Collected Writings*, 4:130.

72. Keynes, *Collected Writings*, 4:138.

73. Keynes, *Collected Writings*, 4:138.

74. Keynes, *Collected Writings*, 4:155.

75. Keynes, *Collected Writings*, 4:134.

76. Keynes, *Collected Writings*, 4:155; emphasis in the original.

77. Keynes, *Collected Writings*, 4:151.

78. Keynes, *Collected Writings*, 4:146.

79. Keynes, *Collected Writings*, 4:152.

80. Keynes, *Collected Writings*, 4:153.

81. Keynes, *Collected Writings*, 4:153.

82. Keynes, *Collected Writings*, 4:153; emphasis in the original.

83. Keynes, *Collected Writings*, 4:134.

84. Keynes, *Collected Writings*, 4:139.

## 11. Understanding "The Norman Conquest of $4.86"

1. Moggridge, *British Monetary Policy*, 228. Consider the apt subtitle of this, Moggridge's second book: *The Norman Conquest of $4.86*.

2. Moggridge, *Return to Gold*, 9.

3. Howson, *Domestic Monetary Management*, 11.

4. Sayers, *Bank of England*, 1:118.

5. Indeed, the pound-dollar exchange rate had been stable only since the 1870s, when the United States resumed gold convertibility. Compare that to the stability of the London gold price, which went back 150 years before that.

6. Keynes, *Collected Writings*, 4:155.

7. Cunliffe Committee, *First Interim Report*, 4.

8. Parliamentary Debates, House of Commons, April 28, 1925, vol. 183, column 54. Cf. Moggridge, who writes that "Churchill . . . [told] the House of Commons of the decision, effective immediately, to return to the gold standard at the prewar parity of $4.86." Moggridge, *British Monetary Policy*, 1.

9. Albert Feavearyear, *The Pound Sterling: A History of English Money*, 2nd ed. (Oxford, UK: Clarendon Press, 1963), 351–52.

10. Thus, the contention is not that Moggridge, Howson, and Sayers were wrong to fixate on $4.86. Our task is to trace the ascent of $4.86 as the explicit target. Writing in the twilight of the Bretton Woods system, these scholars knew well that a stable relationship to the dollar did not guarantee a stable relationship to gold.

11. John Gordon Hargrave, *Professor Skinner, Alias Montagu Norman* (London: Wells Gardner, Darton & Co., 1939), 2–3.

12. Such as when Norman became the deputy governor of the Bank of England (writing "1915" instead of "1918"). Hargrave, *Professor Skinner, Alias Montagu Norman*, 235.

13. Boyle, *Montagu Norman*, 142.

14. Clay, *Norman*, 112; Boyle, *Montagu Norman*, 128.

15. Feavearyear, *Pound Sterling*, 358; Kunz, *Battle for Britain's Gold Standard*, 15; Peden, *Treasury and British Public Policy*, 198; Alec Cairncross and Barry Eichengreen, *Sterling in Decline: The Devaluations of 1931, 1949 and 1967* (Oxford, UK: Basil Blackwell, 1983), 39.

16. Boyce, "Creating the Myth of Consensus," 183; Skidelsky, *Economist as Saviour*, 197. Moggridge, *Return to Gold*, is exceptional.

17. Stephen V. O. Clarke, *Central Bank Cooperation: 1924–31* (New York: Federal Reserve Bank of New York, 1967), 72–73; Sayers, *Bank of England*, 1:144.

18. Pollard, *Gold Standard and Employment Policies*, 7.

19. P. J. Grigg, *Prejudice and Judgment* (London: Jonathan Cape, 1948), 181–82.

20. Skidelsky, *Economist as Saviour*, xv.

21. Skidelsky, *Economist as Saviour*, 189, 193.

22. Skidelsky, *Economist as Saviour*, 193.

23. Moggridge, *Return to Gold*, 67–68.

24. Skidelsky, *Economist as Saviour*, 189–193.

25. In fact, contemporary goldbugs suggest that the problems of this "new" gold standard—like the Great Depression—followed from the attenuation of the use of gold itself. Joseph T. Salerno, "Free Banking the Gold Standard," in *Gold and the International Monetary System: The Contribution of Michael A. Heilperin*, ed. Llewellyn H. Rockwell Jr. (Auburn, AL: Ludwig von Mises Institute, 1992).

26. Keynes, *Collected Writings*, 6:346.

27. Keynes, *Collected Writings*, 4:158.

28. Grigg, *Prejudice and Judgment*, 180–81.

29. Feavearyear, *Pound Sterling*, 350.

30. Manchester, *Last Lion*, 1:791–92.

31. Chamberlain-Bradbury Committee, *Report*, 9.

32. Capie and Webber, *Monetary History*, 209–14. This aligns with contemporary figures. US Federal Reserve, *Banking and Monetary Statistics*, 544–555.

33. Cunliffe Committee, *First Interim Report*, 7.

34. Cunliffe Committee, *First Interim Report*, 3.

35. Cf. Marx, *The Eighteenth Brumaire of Louis Bonaparte*, in *Karl Marx*, 329–55. When Churchill raised this point, Norman, now eager for the return, retorted, "These three years of 'managed' finance have been possible only because they have been made up of . . . deliberate steps . . . towards a golden 1925." NA T 172/1499B, Norman, "Commentary," February 2, 1925.

36. Keynes, *Collected Writings*, 19:272.

37. Keynes, *Collected Writings*, 4:138.

## 12. Central Bankers as Saviors?

1. Describing the new, zealous "movement for central banking" in this period, the Chicago economist Henry Simons crystalized the debate in these terms. Henry C. Simons, "Rules versus Authorities in Monetary Policy," *Journal of Political Economy* 44, no. 1 (1936): 3, 12.

2. Friedman, *Capitalism and Freedom*, 133.

3. Skidelsky, *Economist as Saviour*.

4. Schacht's dissertation, entitled *The Theoretical Quality of English Commerce*, emphasized the practical aspects of the early modern English mercantilists. After finishing at the University of Kiel, Schacht went on to what he called "the Schmoller Training College." Schmoller became Schacht's "most valued teacher," and Schacht published numerous articles in Schmoller's *Jahrbuch*. Schacht, *My First Seventy-Six Years*, 81–96.

5. Predictably, Schacht returned to "[his] work in the Dresdner Bank," where it was "intimated that [he] would be appointed a regular member of the board at the earliest opportunity. . . . That [he] had done some successful work as deputy manager in occupied Belgium had doubtless more than a little to do with it." Schacht, *My First Seventy-Six Years*, 137–39. Even decades later, Schacht struggled to see why his dealings in Belgium had been viewed as improper.

6. Schacht, *My First Seventy-Six Years*, 182; emphasis added.

7. Ahamed, *Lords of Finance*, 512.

8. Schacht, *My First Seventy-Six Years*, 137–38.

9. Schacht, *My First Seventy-Six Years*, 190.

10. Boyle, *Montagu Norman*, 170.

11. Schacht, *My First Seventy-Six Years*, 191.

12. Schacht, *My First Seventy-Six Years*, 194–95.

13. Schacht, *My First Seventy-Six Years*, 196–97; emphasis in original.

14. Schacht, *My First Seventy-Six Years*, 196.

15. US Federal Reserve, *Banking and Monetary Statistics*, 545.

16. See table 5.

17. Schacht, *My First Seventy-Six Years*, 197.

18. Schacht, *My First Seventy-Six Years*, 198.

19. Schacht, *My First Seventy-Six Years*, 198–99.

20. Schacht, *My First Seventy-Six Years*, 197.

21. Schacht, *My First Seventy-Six Years*, 196.

22. NA T 185/1, Samuel, "Testimony," June 10, 1918, 15.

23. This suggestion comes from Boyle, *Montagu Norman*, 170, based on interviews.

24. At the time, Bank rate was at 4 percent. The loan was approved retroactively by the Committee of Treasury. Bank of England, G8/55, January 9, 1924. Presumably, the loan was mentioned to the Court of Directors as part of the weekly advances and discount, but there is no record of further discussion of it. Bank of England, G4/146, January 10, 1924.

25. Schacht, *My First Seventy-Six Years*, 201.

26. Schacht, *My First Seventy-Six Years*, 201.

27. Schacht, *My First Seventy-Six Years*, 202.

28. Schacht, *My First Seventy-Six Years*, 202.

29. Schacht, *My First Seventy-Six Years*, 197.

30. Boyle, *Montagu Norman*, 169–71.

31. Boyle, *Montagu Norman*, 169–71; see also Sayers, *Bank of England*, 2:184.

32. Sayers, *Bank of England*, 1:208.

33. Cunliffe Committee, *First Interim Report*, 4.

34. Parliamentary Debates, House of Commons, February 18, 1924, vol. 169, column 1309.

35. Parliamentary Debates, House of Commons, February 18, 1924, vol. 169, columns 1309–10.

36. GFD Finaeon, "British Pound to US Dollar Exchange Rate (GBPUSD)."

37. The speech was subsequently published in the *Bankers' Magazine*, by which means it reached the monetary authorities in London. NA T 160/197/3, Schuster, "Currencies: Foreign and Our Own," April 30, 1924.

38. NA T 160/197/3, Schuster, "Currencies: Foreign and Our Own", April 30, 1924.

39. NA T 160/197/3, Schuster, "Currencies: Foreign and Our Own", April 30, 1924.

40. NA T 160/197/3, Schuster, "Currencies: Foreign and Our Own", April 30, 1924.

41. Moggridge, *Return to Gold*, 25; NA T 160/197/2, Treasury Minute, June 10, 1924; NA T 160/197/2, Norman to Niemeyer, April 16, 1924.

42. Skidelsky, *Hopes Betrayed*, 175.

43. When Baldwin lead the Conservatives to victory in the general election that autumn, Chamberlain was made secretary of state for foreign affairs. At that point, Bradbury himself took over the chair and led in the production of the committee's final report.

44. The committee sent a copy of the Cunliffe Committee's *First Interim Report* to its witnesses. Keynes, *Collected Writings*, 19:238–39.

45. Parliamentary Debates, House of Commons, June 26, 1924, vol. 175, columns 586–87.

46. Parliamentary Debates, House of Commons, June 23, 1924, vol. 175, column 78.

47. NA T 160/197/6, Norman, "Testimony," June 27, 1924, 4.

48. NA T 160/197/6, Norman, "Testimony," June 27, 1924, 6.

49. NA T 160/197/6, Norman, "Testimony," June 27, 1924, 7.

50. NA T 160/197/6, Norman, "Testimony," June 27, 1924, 8.

51. NA T 160/197/6, Norman, "Testimony," June 27, 1924, 9.

52. NA T 160/197/6, Norman, "Testimony," June 27, 1924, 9.

53. NA T 160/197/6, Norman, "Testimony," June 27, 1924, 14.

54. NA T 160/197/6, Norman, "Testimony," June 27, 1924, 14; emphasis added.

55. NA T 160/197/6, Norman, "Testimony," June 27, 1924, 14.

56. NA T 160/197/6, Norman, "Testimony," June 27, 1924, 15.

57. Roberts, *Saving the City*, 125–28; Keynes, *Collected Writings*, 11:256; Currency and Bank Notes Act, 1914 (4 & 5 Geo. 5, c. 14).

58. Norman might have contemplated the radical possibility that Treasury notes be redeemed at a discount vis-à-vis the Bank's notes. But to depreciate the Treasury's pound notes might have imperiled the credibility of the Bank's pound notes. The holders of the Bank's notes would have to ask, "Shall we be next?"

59. NA T 160/197/6, Norman, "Testimony," June 27, 1924, 15.

60. NA T 160/197/6, Norman, "Testimony," June 27, 1924, 16.

61. NA T 160/197/6, Norman, "Testimony," June 27, 1924, 16.

62. NA T 160/197/6, Norman, "Testimony," June 27, 1924, 25.

63. NA T 160/197/6, Norman, "Testimony," June 27, 1924, 25.

64. Cunliffe Committee, *First Interim Report*, 4.

65. NA T 160/197/6, Norman, "Testimony," June 27, 1924, 16–17.

66. NA T 160/197/6, Norman, "Testimony," June 27, 1924, 17; Keynes, *Collected Writings*, 4:134.

67. NA T 160/197/6, Norman, "Testimony," June 27, 1924, 17.

68. Sayers, *Bank of England*, 1:126–29.

69. Marx, *The German Ideology*, 180.

70. NA T 160/197/6, Norman, "Testimony," June 27, 1924, 19.

71. NA T 160/197/6, Norman, "Testimony," June 27, 1924, 19.

72. Arthur Cecil Pigou, "Some Problems of Foreign Exchange," *Economic Journal* 30, no. 120 (1920): 460–72; Arthur Cecil Pigou, "The Foreign Exchanges," *Quarterly Journal of Economics* 37, no. 1 (1922): 52–74.

73. NA T 160/197/6, Norman, "Testimony," June 27, 1924, 19.

74. NA T 160/197/6, Norman, "Testimony," June 27, 1924, 20.

75. In making explanations for Norman, Sayers inadvertently repeats Norman's disparagement of Pigou. Sayers, *Bank of England*, 151–52. This overstates Norman's commitment to this position as a matter of principle. In his subsequent appearance before the committee, he vigorously defended such calculations even against the skepticism of his Bank colleagues (such as Addis). More broadly, Norman did not want for offers of "expert technical analysis" from Pigou (and presumably others). Like any governor, Norman had access to all of the expertise he thought he needed.

76. NA T 160/197/6, Norman, "Testimony," June 27, 1924, 20.

77. NA T 160/197/6, Norman, "Testimony," June 27, 1924, 20.

78. NA T 160/197/6, Norman, "Testimony," June 27, 1924, 28.

79. NA T 160/197/6, Norman, "Testimony," June 27, 1924, 28.

80. NA T 160/197/6, Norman, "Testimony," June 27, 1924, 28.

81. NA T 160/197/6, Norman, "Testimony," June 27, 1924, 28.

82. It is difficult to determine who else could have been the recipient of millions of pounds of Bank loans. Other countries, such as Hungary, had requested loans from the Bank at the same time but had been denied. Bank of England, G8/55, January 9, 1924.

83. Schacht, *My First Seventy-Six Years*, 205–6.

84. NA T 160/197/6, Norman, "Testimony," June 27, 1924, 2.

85. NA T 160/197/6, Norman, "Testimony," June 27, 1924, 2.

86. Ahamed, *Lords of Finance*, 203.

87. Ahamed, *Lords of Finance*, 204–5.

88. Ahamed, *Lords of Finance*, 204.

89. Schacht, *My First Seventy-Six Years*, 189.

90. Schacht, *My First Seventy-Six Years*, 214–15.

91. Gustav Schmoller, *The Mercantile System and Its Historical Significance Illustrated Chiefly from Prussian History* (New York: Macmillan, 1896), 75–76.

92. The formulation is Schacht's, of course, and not mine. Schacht, *My First Seventy-Six Years*, 510.

93. As for Schacht, seizures by the Gestapo and then the Red Army left him with nothing by the end of the Second World War. Schacht, *My First Seventy-Six Years*, chapter 60.

94. This would explain Norman's otherwise bizarre position that it was better for sterling if the Labour government were to announce a several-year-long delay of the restoration. It would also explain Norman's sense of urgency—the supposed threat that if the government's announcement did not come quickly, the exchange would fall. NA T 160/197/6, Norman, "Testimony," June 27, 1924, 27.

95. Keynes, *Collected Writings*, 24:128–131.

96. Boyle, *Montagu Norman*, 176–77.

97. NA T 160/197/6, Schuster, "Testimony," July 3, 1924, 1–2.

98. NA T 160/197/6, Schuster, "Testimony," July 3, 1924, 2–3.

99. NA T 160/197/6, Schuster, "Testimony," July 3, 1924, 4–5, 8.

100. NA T 160/197/6, Schuster, "Testimony," July 3, 1924, 9.

101. NA T 160/197/6, Schuster, "Testimony," July 3, 1924, 10.

102. NA T 160/197/6, Schuster, "Testimony," July 3, 1924, 10.

103. The day that Schuster testified, sterling traded at $4.32. Six months prior, it was as low as $4.20. Across the subsequent six months, it rose to $4.75—just eleven cents from parity. GFD Finaeon, "British Pound to US Dollar Exchange Rate (GBPUSD)." What is a knowable 8 percent Bank rate compared to an unknowable 10 percent exchange rate shift? For those who would rather not stake their fortunes in the speculative "gamble" of sterling instability: everything.

104. NA T 160/197/3, Schuster, "Currencies: Foreign and Our Own", April 30, 1924. Cf. Keynes, *Collected Writings*, 17:178–79.

105. NA T 160/197/6, Schuster, "Testimony," July 3, 1924, 11.

106. NA T 160/197/6, Schuster, "Testimony," July 3, 1924, 33.

107. NA T 160/197/6, Schuster, "Testimony," July 3, 1924, 21–22.

108. NA T 160/197/6, Schuster, "Testimony," July 3, 1924, 22–23.

109. Unfortunately, Pigou was not present on the day of this interview.

110. Keynes, *Collected Writings*, 17:12–13, 179–86. The Treasury's reactions and internal discussions are available in NA T 172/1384.

111. Keynes, *Collected Writings*, 19:238.

112. Keynes, *Collected Writings*, 19:238–39. Professor Edwin Cannan, who appeared on the same day, had better understood the committee's purpose. He submitted a memorandum that "[took it] for granted that an eventual return to the gold standard at the old rate of 113 fine grains to the pound sterling is to be aimed at." NA T 160/197/3, Cannan, Memorandum, July 11, 1924.

113. It did not attract the attention of the Chamberlain-Bradbury Committee or further discussion in Parliament.

114. Keynes, *Collected Writings*, 19:240–47.

115. Parliamentary Debates, House of Commons, February 18, 1924, vol. 169, columns 1309–10.

116. Keynes, *Collected Writings*, 19:242.

117. Keynes, *Collected Writings*, 19:248–49.

118. Keynes, *Collected Writings*, 19:249–50.

119. Bank of England, ADM 34/8, 1.

120. Keynes, *Collected Writings*, 19:250.

121. Keynes, *Collected Writings*, 19:250–51.

122. Keynes, *Collected Writings*, 19:252.

123. NA T 185/2, Bradbury, "Future Dimensions of the Fiduciary Issue," March 9, 1918.

124. Keynes, *Collected Writings*, 19:252–53.

125. Keynes, *Collected Writings*, 19:252–53.

126. Keynes, *Collected Writings*, 19:253.

127. Keynes, *Collected Writings*, 19:254.

128. Keynes, *Collected Writings*, 19:255.

129. Locke made this point repeatedly in published books and in memoranda drafted for policymakers. See his Further Considerations (415–18, 438), "Propositions Sent to the Lords Justices" (375–76), and *Short Observations on a Printed Paper entitled "For encouraging the coining Silver Money in England, and after for keeping it here"* (352), in *Locke on Money*, (Oxford, UK: Clarendon Press, 1991). It is of a piece with his arguments in chapter 5 of the *Second Treatise* on the connection between the invention of money and the creation of political society. John Locke, *Two Treatises of Government*, ed. Peter Laslett, 2nd ed. (Cambridge: Cambridge University Press, 1967).

130. Keynes might have replied to Locke that the sanctity of contract required preserving the purchasing power of the currency. He came close to making his argument in his interchanges with Addis in the summer of 1924. Keynes, *Collected Writings*, 19:270–72.

131. Keynes, *Collected Writings*, 19:255–57.

132. Adam Smith, *The Theory of Moral Sentiments* (Indianapolis: Liberty Fund, 1984), VI.ii.2.17–18; Friedrich Hayek, "The Use of Knowledge in Society," *American Economic Review* 35, no. 4 (1945): 519–30.

133. Keynes, *Collected Writings*, 19:260.

134. Roberts, *Saving the City*, 54–61.

135. Keynes, *Collected Writings*, 19:259–60.

## 13. Indulgence

1. NA T 160/197/6, Leaf, "Testimony," July 4, 1924, 2.

2. NA T 160/197/6, Currie, "Testimony," July 4, 1924, 8–9.

3. NA T 160/197/8, Horne, "Testimony," July 30, 1924, 2.

4. NA T 160/197/7, Paish, "Testimony," July 10, 1924, 1.

5. NA T 160/197/7, Paish, "Testimony," July 10, 1924, 15.

6. NA T 160/197/7, Cannan, "Testimony," July 11, 1924, 4.

7. NA T 160/197/3, Bradbury to Farrer, July 24, 1924.

8. Cunliffe Committee, *First Interim Report*, 3; NA CAB 27/71, appendix: 2.

9. NA T 160/197/8, FBI, Memorandum, July 29, 1924, 2.

10. NA T 160/197/8, FBI, Memorandum, July 29, 1924, 4.

11. NA T 160/197/8, FBI, Memorandum, July 29, 1924, 1–2.

12. NA T 160/197/8, FBI, "Testimony," July 30, 1924, 1.

13. NA T 160/197/8, FBI, "Testimony," July 30, 1924, 5.

14. NA T 160/197/8, FBI, "Testimony," July 30, 1924, 2.

15. NA T 160/197/8, FBI, "Testimony," July 30, 1924, 4.

16. NA T160/197/8, FBI, "Testimony," July 30, 1924, 4.

17. Bradbury's misspeaking in suggesting that US prices needed to fall rather than to rise might have followed from this being a new perspective for him. Or it might have been a simple slip of the tongue. NA T 160/197/8, FBI, "Testimony," July 30, 1924, 6.

18. Locke, *Some Considerations*, 263.

19. Smith, *Wealth of Nations*, 216.

20. NA T 160/197/7, McKenna, "Testimony," July 10, 1924, 20–21.

21. NA T 160/197/8, FBI, "Testimony," July 30, 1924, 11. Cf. Skidelsky, *Economist as Saviour*, 190. Boyce writes, "Chisholm agreed that industrialists wished to see stability of both prices and foreign exchanges," "but *under questioning*" "eventually *conceded* that they considered exchange stability the more important of the two." Boyce, "Creating the Myth of Consensus," 190; emphasis added. Boyce interprets this as key proof that the gold standard consensus was a "myth." But this is like saying that there was heresy before the Inquisition. The emergence of consensus was not a myth but a fact—one that was constructed in just this manner by this currency committee curia.

22. When the Labour government tried to save the gold standard in 1931, Snowden and others defended against the charge that they had fallen for a "bankers' ramp." The term "ramp" was slang for a swindle. Philip Williamson, "A 'Bankers' Ramp'? Financiers and the British Political Crisis of August 1931," *English Historical Review* 99, no. 393 (1984): 770–806.

23. It is worth remembering that the committee was originally created without public notification. As Norman wrote to Strong, "You know how secretly [the subject] must be treated; so much so that not a word can be breathed until some decision has been reached." FRBNY 1116.4, Norman to Strong, October 16, 1924. Niemeyer emphasized this to Schuster, lest he mention it in one of his famous speeches. NA T 160/197/3, Niemeyer to Schuster, June 30, 1924. During his testimony, Chisholm himself asked to confirm that "the proceedings of this Committee are confidential." Chamberlain replied, "We will not publish anything that you do not desire to be published." NA T 160/197/8, FBI, "Testimony," July 30, 1924, 2.

24. Young was the committee's secretary, but the transcriptions indicated, "Note taken by Treasury Reporter." Thus, there *may* have been one woman or person of color in the room. And such actors did shape the course of events in more ways than we realize. But, regrettably, there is no extant evidence with which to analyze this influence in this context.

25. NA T 160/197/4, Pigou, "Report," Second Draft, 1924, 1–2.

26. Keynes, *Collected Writings*, 4:138.

27. NA T 160/197/4, Pigou, "Report," Second Draft, 1924, 2.

28. NA T 160/197/4, Pigou, "Report," Second Draft, 1924, 2–3.

29. NA T 160/197/4, Pigou, "Report," Second Draft, 1924, 4, 7.

30. NA T 185/1, Pigou, Memorandum on Fiduciary Note Issue.

31. NA T 160/197/4, Pigou, "Report," Second Draft, 1924, 7.

32. NA T 160/197/4, Pigou, "Report," Second Draft, 1924, 6.

33. NA T 185/1, Pigou, Memorandum on Fiduciary Note Issue.

34. An aside in one of Pigou's 1918 memoranda suggests that he *did* imagine the possibility that the United States would follow the United Kingdom in debasing the real value of its currency relative to gold. NA T 185/1, Pigou, Memorandum on Fiduciary Note Issue. In this scenario, the US dollar and the pound sterling could trade in the market at their prewar exchange rate, but then *both* would fail to achieve the prewar gold values of their currencies. This admission underscores the significance of the shift from the gold value of the pound to the dollar value of the pound. As Pigou admitted, the two need not move in lockstep.

35. Keynes, *Collected Writings*, 4:155.

36. Keynes, *Collected Writings*, 4:153.

37. NA T 160/197/4, Pigou, "Report," Second Draft, 1924, 8.

38. FRBNY 1116.4, Strong to Norman, January 4, 1924.

39. NA T 160/197/4, Pigou, "Report," Second Draft, 1924, 8.

40. NA T 160/197/4, Pigou, "Report," Second Draft, 1924, 9; emphasis added.

41. NA T 160/197/4, Pigou, "Report," Second Draft, 1924, 10.

42. NA T 160/197/4, Chamberlain to Young, September 11, 1924.

43. NA T 160/197/4, Bradbury to Young, September 11, 1924.

44. NA T 160/197/4, Bradbury to Young, September 11, 1924.

45. T 160/197/4, Bradbury Revisions to Second Draft of "Report," September 11, 1924.

46. T 160/197/4, Bradbury Revisions to Second Draft of "Report," September 11, 1924.

47. T 160/197/4, Bradbury Revisions to Second Draft of "Report," September 11, 1924.

48. NA T 160/197/4, Chamberlain to Young, September 13, 1924.

49. NA T 160/197/4, Young to Norman, September 15, 16, and 18, 1924. Citing one of Young's invitations, Moggridge writes that the third draft "was sent to the Governor and discussed with him early in October." Moggridge, *Return to Gold*, 34. But if there were a meeting, there is no record of it in the committee's papers. Nor does it appear among Norman's detailed diary entries for this period. Bank of England, ADM 34/13.

50. FRBNY 1116.4, Norman to Strong, October 16, 1924.

51. FRBNY 1116.4, Norman to Strong, October 16, 1924.

52. FRBNY 1116.4, Strong to Norman, November 4, 1924.

53. Bank of England, G8/56, November 5, 1924, and November 12, 1924. Strong wrote with congratulations—and encouragement. This would grant Norman "another year within which to complete a splendid work." He continued: "Probably you are the one person in the world who knows better than anyone else how anxious I am that you shall succeed in everything that you set out to accomplish, not the least important being to leave the Bank of England with the pound sterling and the gold dollar firmly established as before the war." FRBNY 1116.4, Strong to Norman, November 18, 1924.

54. NA T 172/1500A, Norman to Niemeyer, December 4, 1924.

55. NA T 172/1500A, Niemeyer to Norman, December 8, 1924.

56. These discussions are cataloged quite well by Moggridge. Moggridge, *Return to Gold*, 38–41.

57. Moggridge, *Return to Gold*, 42.

58. FRBNY C261.1, Lubbock to Norman, January 10, 1925. Additional telegrams on January 10 and 12 affirmed that the sentiments were broadly shared by Addis, Lubbock, Revelstoke, and Sir Robert Kindersley. They also confirmed that Deputy Governor Lubbock had passed on the proposals to Niemeyer in the Treasury.

59. NA T 160/197/4, Young to Pigou, December 2, 1924.

60. Keynes, *Collected Writings*, 4:134.

61. NA T 160/197/5, "Report," Fourth Draft, January 26, 1925.

62. There are few surviving papers related to revisions made during December, but a letter from Farrer to Young expressed concern about "enter[ing] into a dissertation on comparative index prices." In the fourth draft, this did become an extended discussion. Farrer also resisted the Treasury's taking control of the timeline: "It is on the Bank of England that the responsibility will rest for finding the gold . . . and it is for the Bank therefore to say the word go." NA T 160/197/4, Farrer to Young, December 20, 1924. This objection was also overruled as Bradbury and Pigou pressed for an accelerated timeline.

63. The sequence is important because it cuts against the oft-repeated line that the committee "echoed" Norman's views and "modell[ed] its Report closely on his latest recommendations." Clarke, *Central Bank Cooperation*, 72–73; Sayers, *Bank of England*, 1:144.

64. Keynes, *Collected Writings*, 19:378.

65. Moggridge, *Return to Gold*, 66–67.

66. Chamberlain-Bradbury Committee, *Report*, 4.

67. Chamberlain-Bradbury Committee, *Report*, 5.

68. NA T 160/197/5, "Report," Fourth Draft, January 26, 1925.

69. NA T 160/197/5, "Report," Fourth Draft, January 26, 1925.

70. NA T 160/197/5, Pigou to Young (undated), Amendments to Fourth Draft Report.

71. NA T 160/197/6, Norman, "Testimony," June 27, 1924, 19.

72. NA T 160/197/5, "Report," Fourth Draft, January 26, 1925; emphasis added.

73. Moggridge, *Return to Gold*, 75.

74. NA T 172/1499B, Bradbury, "The Gold Standard," February 5, 1925.

75. George Orwell, *Nineteen Eighty-Four* (New York: New American Library, 1961), 26, 258–60. The process of steering Churchill is discussed at length below.

76. NA T 160/197/5, "Report," Fourth Draft, January 26, 1925.

77. The report was clear that even if the credit were to be used, it should be treated as "equivalent to the loss of an equal amount from its own reserves." NA T 160/197/5, "Report," Fourth Draft, January 26, 1925.

78. This was a rather different line than these men had taken on the Cunliffe Committee, where they had insisted that credit policy dictates the exchange rate. But now they seemed to believe that speculation plays such a large role that market psychology trumps some portion of the material determinants of exchange rates.

79. NA T 160/197/5, "Report," Fourth Draft, January 26, 1925.

80. In December, Niemeyer had mouthed the possibility of expending £100 million of reserves. NA T 172-1500A, Niemeyer to Norman, December 8, 1924. It is not clear if he meant that hypothetically or as a serious possibility.

81. Chamberlain-Bradbury Committee, *Report*, 7–8.

82. Chamberlain-Bradbury Committee, *Report*, 9.

83. Chamberlain-Bradbury Committee, *Report*, 8.

84. Chamberlain-Bradbury Committee, *Report*, 8–10. Some historians have misunderstood this key point, conflating the fixing of the fiduciary issue with the return to the gold standard. See Ahamed, *Lords of Finance*, 220.

85. NA T 160/197/5, "Report," Fourth Draft, January 26, 1925.

86. NA T 160/197/5, "Report," Fourth Draft, January 26, 1925.


## 14. Deposition and Coronation

1. Bank of England, ADM 34/14, January 20, 1925, to January 28, 1925.

2. Bank of England, G8/56, January 26, 1925. The previous summer, Addis had appeared before the Chamberlain-Bradbury Committee in his own right. NA T 160/197/6, Addis Testimony, June 27, 1924.

3. NA T 160/197/6, Norman and Addis, "Testimony," January 28, 1925, 1–4. If only Cunliffe had lived to see the day when countries felt "encumbered" by their gold reserves and sought to "[get] rid of [their] surplus gold," there might never have been the problems of war debts and reparations.

4. NA T 160/197/6, Norman and Addis, "Testimony," January 28, 1925, 3–4, 7.

5. NA T 160/197/6, Norman and Addis, "Testimony," January 28, 1925, 12.

6. NA T 160/197/6, Norman and Addis, "Testimony," January 28, 1925, 14. In fact, Churchill's announcement required the Bank to sell gold at the prewar fixed price (£3.89 per troy ounce) in quantities of 400 troy ounces or more. This was considerably lower than the bar suggested by Norman. But with a minimum purchase of £1556 (roughly half a million pounds at 2020 prices), it was still beyond the reach of virtually every Briton.

7. NA T 160/197/6, Norman and Addis, "Testimony," January 28, 1925, 14.

8. NA T 160/197/6, Norman and Addis, "Testimony," January 28, 1925, 15–16.

9. NA T 160/197/6, Norman and Addis, "Testimony," January 28, 1925, 16.

10. NA T 185/2, Cokayne, "Testimony," July 8, 1918, 5.

11. NA T 160/197/6, Norman and Addis, "Testimony," January 28, 1925, 16.

12. This was not a case of judging a method by its findings so much as changing the method, the finding, and the conclusions all at once.

13. NA T 160/197/6, Norman and Addis, "Testimony," January 28, 1925, 16–18.

14. NA T 160/197/6, Norman and Addis, "Testimony," January 28, 1925, 21, 26.

15. NA T 160/197/6, Norman and Addis, "Testimony," January 28, 1925, 19–20.

16. NA T 160/197/6, Norman and Addis, "Testimony," January 28, 1925, 20–21.

17. NA T 160/197/6, Norman and Addis, "Testimony," January 28, 1925, 22–24.

18. NA T 160/197/6, Norman and Addis, "Testimony," January 28, 1925, 24.

19. NA T 160/197/6, Norman and Addis, "Testimony," January 28, 1925, 27.

20. NA T 160/197/6, Norman and Addis, "Testimony," January 28, 1925, 28–30.

21. NA T 160/197/6, Norman and Addis, "Testimony," January 28, 1925, 33.

22. NA T 160/197/6, Norman and Addis, "Testimony," January 28, 1925, 33.

23. NA T 160/197/6, Norman and Addis, "Testimony," January 28, 1925, 34.

24. NA T 160/197/6, Norman and Addis, "Testimony," January 28, 1925, 34.

25. Sayers, *Bank of England*, 1:151.

26. NA T 160/197/6, Norman and Addis, "Testimony," January 28, 1925, 34.

27. NA T 160/197/6, Norman and Addis, "Testimony," January 28, 1925, 35–36.

28. NA T 160/197/6, Norman and Addis, "Testimony," January 28, 1925, 36. The Cunliffe Committee had indeed discussed this numerous times. Everyone knew that this would make it easier to leverage the UK's total gold holdings to defend the gold standard. But it was deemed unviable. In part there was exceptionally strong opposition on principled grounds from Norman's own predecessor: Cokayne. But there was also the practical issue: How could a country "on the gold standard" forbid private actors from holding the gold to which they were entitled?

29. NA T 160/197/6, Norman and Addis, "Testimony," January 28, 1925, 36–37.

30. NA T 160/197/6, Norman and Addis, "Testimony," January 28, 1925, 38.

31. NA T 160/197/6, Norman and Addis, "Testimony," January 28, 1925, 40.

32. Daniel W. Drezner, *The System Worked: How the World Stopped Another Great Depression* (New York: Oxford University Press, 2014).

## 15. The Sanhedrin

1. Moggridge, *Return to Gold*, 39–40; Boyle, *Montagu Norman*, 179; Frederick Leith-Ross, *Money Talks: Fifty Years of International Finance: The Autobiography of Sir Frederick Leith-Ross* (London: Hutchinson, 1968), 88. Sayers is slightly more forgiving, casting Churchill as a "highly efficient gadfly." Sayers, *Bank of England*, 1:144n. Others emphasize the Conservatives' comparative callousness. Barry Eichengreen and Olivier Jeanne, "Currency Crisis and Unemployment: Sterling in 1931," in *Currency Crises* (Chicago: University of Chicago Press, 2000), 18.

2. Leith-Ross, *Money Talks*, 118.

3. Even while challenging the "myth of consensus," Boyce concedes, "The only major daily strenuously to resist the return to gold was Lord Beaverbrook's *Daily Express*, which occasionally gave the question front-page coverage." Boyce, "Creating the Myth of Consensus," 187.

4. CHAR 18/2, Churchill to Baldwin, December 13, 1924.

5. NA T 172/1499B presents this material in a peculiar way, splitting it into different portions of the folio. They are also undated. However, T 175/9 presents these materials together. Part I is a broad view. Part II has specific responses to Churchill's queries in "the exercise." NA T 172/1499B has much marginalia that is not reflected in the version in NA T 175/9. These appear to be corrections rather than annotations. Moggridge dates this as February 2, 1925. Moggridge, *British Monetary Policy*, 267. The date is noted on the version in NA T 175/9 as "Mr. Churchill's Exercise," January 29, 1925.

6. NA T 172/1499B, "Mr. Churchill's Exercise," January 29, 1925.

7. Keynes, *Collected Writings*, 4:138.

8. NA T 172/1499B, "Mr. Churchill's Exercise," January 29, 1925.

9. NA T 172/1499B, "Mr. Churchill's Exercise," January 29, 1925.

10. NA T 172/1499B, "Mr. Churchill's Exercise," January 29, 1925.

11. NA T 172/1499B, "Mr. Churchill's Exercise," January 29, 1925.

12. NA T 172/1499B, "Mr. Churchill's Exercise," January 29, 1925.

13. NA T 172/1499B, "Mr. Churchill's Exercise," January 29, 1925.

14. NA T 172/1499B, Bradbury to Niemeyer, February 5, 1925.

15. NA T 172/1499B, "Mr. Churchill's Exercise," January 29, 1925. This rendering is the direct inverse of that offered in retrospect by Sir Frederick Leith-Ross. Leith-Ross explained Churchill's decision on the grounds that "[Churchill] knew that if he adopted this course Niemeyer would give him irrefutable arguments to support it, whereas if he refused to adopt it he would be faced with criticisms from the City authorities against which he would not have any effective answer." Instead, Churchill sought these arguments to defend this position rather than chose this position because it brought the easiest defense. Leith-Ross, *Money Talks*, 92.

16. Keynes, *Collected Writings*, 4:138.

17. NA T 172/1499B, Niemeyer, "The Gold Export Prohibition," February 2, 1925.

18. NA T 172/1499B, Niemeyer, "The Gold Export Prohibition," February 2, 1925.

19. NA T 172/1499B, Niemeyer, "The Gold Export Prohibition," February 2, 1925; Chamberlain-Bradbury Committee, *Report*, 7.

20. NA T 172/1499B, Niemeyer, "The Gold Export Prohibition," February 2, 1925.

21. NA T 172/1499B, Niemeyer, "The Gold Export Prohibition," February 2, 1925.

22. NA T 172/1499B, Niemeyer, "The Gold Export Prohibition," February 2, 1925.

23. NA T 172/1499B, Bradbury, "The Gold Standard," February 5, 1925.

24. NA T 172/1499B, Bradbury, "The Gold Standard," February 5, 1925.

25. NA T 172/1499B, Bradbury, "The Gold Standard," February 5, 1925.

26. NA T 172/1499B, Hawtrey, "The Gold Standard," February 2, 1925.

27. NA T 172/1499B, Hawtrey, "The Gold Standard," February 2, 1925; emphasis in original.

28. NA T 172/1499B, Norman, "Commentary by the Governor," February 2, 1925.

29. NA T 172/1499B, Norman, "Commentary by the Governor," February 2, 1925.

30. NA T 172/1499B, Norman, "Commentary by the Governor," February 2, 1925; emphasis in original.

31. NA T 172/1499B, Norman, "Commentary by the Governor," February 2, 1925.

32. NA T 172/1499B, Norman, "Commentary by the Governor," February 2, 1925.

33. NA T 172/1499B, Churchill to Niemeyer, February 6, 1925.

34. NA T 172/1499B, Churchill to Niemeyer, February 6, 1925.

35. NA T 172/1499B, Churchill to Chamberlain, February 6, 1925.

36. NA T 172/1499B, Chamberlain to Churchill, February 8, 1925.

37. NA T 172/1499B, Niemeyer Response to Goodenough's Proposals, [February] 1925.

38. Snowden, "Return to Gold."

39. Keynes, *Collected Writings*, 9:192–93. See also Morrison, "Shocking Intellectual Austerity," 197–202.

40. Keynes, *Collected Writings*, 9:194–97.

41. Keynes, Collected Writings, 9:194.

42. Keynes, *Collected Writings*, 9:195.

43. Keynes, *Collected Writings*, 9:196–98.

44. Keynes, *Collected Writings*, 9:193–94, 197.

45. Keynes, *Collected Writings*, 9:196.

46. Keynes, *Collected Writings*, 9:198–200.

47. Keynes, *Collected Writings*, 9:194.

48. NA T 160/197/6, Norman and Addis, "Testimony," January 28, 1925, 28.

49. At one point, Niemeyer complained to a colleague, "Gold is excessively active and very troublesome. None of the witch-doctors see eye to eye, and Winston cannot make up his mind from day to day whether he is a gold bug or a pure inflationist." Leith-Ross, *Money Talks*, 92.

50. NA T 172/1499B, "Note by Sir O. E. Niemeyer," February 21, 1925.

51. NA T 172/1499B, "Criticism by Mr. Churchill," February 22, 1925.

52. NA T 172/1499B, "Criticism by Mr. Churchill," February 22, 1925.

53. NA T 172/1499B, "Note by Sir O. E. Niemeyer," undated.

54. NA T 172/1499B, "Note by Sir O. E. Niemeyer," undated.

55. NA T 172/1499B, "Note by Sir O. E. Niemeyer," undated.

56. It did not help that Snowden explicitly linked the two in an editorial criticizing Churchill for moving too quickly. He did still agree, however, "that it is desirable to . . . reestablish the gold standard." Philip Snowden, "Mr. Churchill's Responsibility," *Evening Standard*, March 27, 1925.

57. NA T 172/1499B, London Chamber of Commerce to Churchill, March 16, 1925.

58. Boyce minimizes the significance of this letter. Citing this piece, among others, in passing, he writes, "How many of these warnings Niemeyer allowed to cross Churchill's desk is not clear." Boyce, *British Capitalism at the Crossroads*, 75. But it is clear that Churchill received this crucial letter and offered a serious response to it. See chapter 16 for his reply and his comments directed to industry in his announcement to Parliament.

59. NA T 172/1499B, Nugent to Churchill, March 17, 1925.

60. Using Keynes's appointments diary, Moggridge has pinned down the date of the meeting. Moggridge, *Return to Gold*, 109. The memoirs of Churchill's private secretary, P. J. Grigg, furnish the only surviving account of the evening. Grigg, *Prejudice and Judgment*, 182.

61. Nicholas Mayhew, *Sterling: The History of a Currency* (New York: John Wiley & Sons, 2000), 214; George C. Peden, *Keynes and His Critics: Treasury Responses to the Keynesian Revolution, 1925–1946* (Oxford: Oxford University Press, 2004), 44.

62. This might be corroborated by Churchill's approach to the handful of letters sent to him subsequently that expressed misgivings about moving too quickly. He generally pressed his subordinates to draft specific refutations, but he does not seem to have sent many replies himself.

63. Grigg, *Prejudice and Judgment*, 182–83.

64. Grigg, *Prejudice and Judgment*, 183.

65. Grigg, *Prejudice and Judgment*, 183–84. Ahamed ascribes this kind of thinking to Strong: "He was acutely aware that British prices were still 10 percent too high," but jumping now would be a kind of "shock therapy" that would "forc[e] Britain to compete in world markets" and "bring about the necessary realignment in prices more efficiently than a long drawn-out policy of protracted tight credit." Ahamed, *Lords of Finance*, 227. Ahamed does not cite the source; and the letter to Norman to which he appears to be referring (dated November 4, 1924, and discussed in chapter 13) does not advance this argument. Instead, Bradbury (and perhaps McKenna) made a version

of this argument in response to Keynes at Churchill's dinner. But this was a departure for Bradbury, who had just assured Churchill that the difference between British and American price levels was "not more than 2% or 3%." NA T 172/1499B, Bradbury, "The Gold Standard," February 5, 1925. As we have seen, Norman deprecated all such thinking, repeatedly arguing that the exchange rate depended more on the psychological factor (confidence) than on the economic factors (fundamentals). He refused to assess the state of the UK economy based on the market exchange rate at a given time. This is an important point because generalizing from McKenna's remark and Bradbury's one polemic has led to the conventional interpretation that the orthodoxy saw the return as a kind of "shock therapy" being administered to a damaged patient rather than as the fulfillment of years of planning and preparation. The restoration proved to be unwise, but it was not embarked upon as a desperate, last-ditch gamble.

## 16. Judgment

1. NA T 172/1499B, Draft of Chancellor's Reply to Nugent, March 19, 1925.

2. NA T 172/1499B, Niemeyer to Churchill, March 20, 1925; NA T 172/1499B, Niemeyer's Revised Draft of Chancellor's Reply to Nugent, March 20, 1925.

3. In this way, possible heretics were hewn to the path of righteousness. But the new "luminous certainty" that was cultivated would less "[fill] up a patch of emptiness" than crowd out the doubts. Orwell, *Nineteen Eighty-Four*, 258. Similarly, these were Foucault's "techniques of knowledge and strategies of power" in action. Foucault, *History of Sexuality*, 98.

4. NA T 172/1499B, Grigg to Nugent, March 26, 1925.

5. NA T 172/1500A, Niemeyer's Notes on Meeting, March 20, 1925; NA T 172/1500A, Norman to Strong, Telegram 91, March 26, 1925.

6. NA T 172/1499B, Norman to Niemeyer, April 8, 1925.

7. NA T 172/1499B, Norman to Niemeyer, April 8, 1925; emphasis added.

8. Sayers, *Bank of England*, 3:12.

9. NA T 160/197/6, Norman and Addis, "Testimony," January 28, 1925, 14.

10. One assumes that Norman was describing fine (pure) gold rather than standard (22 carat) gold, as the bullion bought and sold by the Bank was pure gold. From September 1919, the quotations of the London gold price were also switched from describing standard to fine gold.

11. Roberts, *Saving the City*, 73–77.

12. NA T 160/197/3, Schuster, "Currencies: Foreign and Our Own", April 30, 1924.

13. NA T 172/1499B, Norman to Niemeyer, April 8, 1925.

14. NA T 172/1499B, Niemeyer to Norman, April 15, 1925. The next day, one of Niemeyer's memoranda for Churchill made reference to the fact that "notes are at present a 100% claim to gold. After April 28th, they will remain legal tender and a claim to gold bullion." An undated, unsigned memorandum in the Treasury papers (NA T 172/1499B) entitled "Internal Gold Circulation" makes the case for Norman's two proposals: "There is general agreement, that in the event of a return to the gold standard, gold should not be put into circulation, gold being centered in the hands of the Bank of England to be used for export."

15. NA T 160/197/4, Farrer to Young, December 20, 1924.

16. NA T 172/1499B, Niemeyer to Norman, April 15, 1925; NA T 172/1499B, Niemeyer Memorandum on Gold and Currency Notes, April 16, 1925. This might explain the somewhat peculiar way in which Churchill describes the transfer to Parliament.

17. Not all of the suggestions and drafts survive. There is one noteworthy interchange on the framing of the US credit. Norman offered some technical discussion concerning the terms of the loan, and Niemeyer supported deploying a defense of those terms. But Churchill overruled them, eliding both elements. NA T 172/1499B, "Mr. Norman's Proposed Addition to Budget Speech," undated; NA T 172/1499B, Niemeyer to Norman, April 16, 1925; NA T 172/1499B, Niemeyer to Churchill, April 17, 1925.

18. When he declared, "I am quite ready to argue the important currency controversies which are naturally associated with a decision of that kind," this was not a bluff but a threat. Parliamentary Debates, House of Commons, April 28, 1925, vol. 183, column 53.

19. Parliamentary Debates, House of Commons, April 28, 1925, vol. 183, columns 52–54.

20. Parliamentary Debates, House of Commons, April 28, 1925, vol. 183, column 53.

21. Parliamentary Debates, House of Commons, April 28, 1925, vol. 183, column 53–54.

22. NA T 172/1499B, Nugent to Churchill, March 17, 1925.

23. Parliamentary Debates, House of Commons, April 28, 1925, vol. 183, column 54.

24. Parliamentary Debates, House of Commons, April 28, 1925, vol. 183, column 54.

25. Churchill said, "The Bank of England will be put under obligations to sell gold bullion in amounts of not less than 400 fine ounces in exchange for legal tender at the fixed price of £3 17s. 10½d. per standard ounce." Parliamentary Debates, House of Commons, April 28, 1925, vol. 183, column 55. This was slightly ambiguous. The Gold Standard Act clarified that it would sell 400 troy ounces of fine (24 carat) gold bullion but with a price specified for "standard" (22 carat) gold. Gold Standard Act, 1925 (15 & 16 Geo. 5, c. 29).

26. Capie and Webber, *Monetary History*, chapter 7.

27. Parliamentary Debates, House of Commons, April 28, 1925, vol. 183, column 55.

28. Parliamentary Debates, House of Commons, April 28, 1925, vol. 183, column 55.

29. Parliamentary Debates, House of Commons, April 28, 1925, vol. 183, column 56.

30. Chamberlain-Bradbury Committee, *Report*, 9.

31. Parliamentary Debates, House of Commons, April 28, 1925, vol. 183, column 56.

32. Parliamentary Debates, House of Commons, April 28, 1925, vol. 183, column 56.

33. Parliamentary Debates, House of Commons, April 28, 1925, vol. 183, column 56.

34. Parliamentary Debates, House of Commons, April 28, 1925, vol. 183, column 57.

35. Parliamentary Debates, House of Commons, April 28, 1925, vol. 183, column 57.

36. GFD Finaeon, "British Pound to US Dollar Exchange Rate (GBPUSD)."

37. Lawrence H. Officer, *Between the Sterling-Dollar Gold Points: Exchange Rates, Parity, and Market Behavior* (Cambridge: Cambridge University Press, 1996): 36.

38. Before the war, the total monetary base was £237 million. There were more than £136 million of gold coins in the UK. Some portion of this was held in reserve by the Bank of England and the Scottish and Irish banks, but this is a fraction of those

banks' £9.5 million of gold, silver, and bronze specie reserves, the rest being comprised of bullion. All told, the £55 million of Bank of England notes made up less than a quarter of the monetary base. Local banknotes were more prevalent in Scotland and Ireland, totaling £16 million. There was another roughly £38 million of silver and bronze coin. Capie and Webber, *Monetary History*, chapter 7, table I.(1), table III.(1). At £137.4 million, the Bank's internal estimates provide a slightly higher figure for the prewar sum of gold coin. Bank of England, *Summary of Statistics for the United Kingdom: January, 1927* (London: Bank of England, 1927).

39. NA T 160/197/6, Norman and Addis, "Testimony," January 28, 1925, 14.

40. NA T 172/1499B, Notes on the Bill, 3, 7.

41. I am grateful to Harold James and Michael Bordo for discussion on this point.

42. The Bank lost £11 million of gold across 1925 with the combined reserve falling from £154 million to £143 million. But Norman was able to rebuild these reserves and keep them around £150 million until the 1931 re-suspension. US Federal Reserve, *Banking and Monetary Statistics*, 544–55. Bank rate was at 5 percent when Churchill resumed gold exports. Norman kept it at or below this rate for most of the period. He took it as high as 6.5 percent—its highest rate—for one month in the autumn of 1929. "On a quarterly average basis," Cairncross and Eichengreen calculate, "Bank rate ranged from 4.3 to 5.6% during the years of the interwar gold standard. Over the first part of this period, from 1925 to 1927, Bank rate in London consistently exceeded the Federal Reserve's discount rate by 0.5 to 1.5 percentage points. Only in the final two quarters of 1928 did the American rate exceed the British rate, and then by a mere half a percentage point." Cairncross and Eichengreen, *Sterling in Decline*, 38. Niemeyer closely followed these metrics, and the national unemployment rate, at the time. NA T 176/13, Restoration of Gold Standard 28th April 1925.

43. Keynes, *Collected Writings*, 9:207–11.

44. Keynes, *Collected Writings*, 9:207–8.

45. Keynes, *Collected Writings*, 9:212.

46. Keynes, *Collected Writings*, 9:212.

47. Keynes, *Collected Writings*, 9:212.

48. Keynes, *Collected Writings*, 9:213–14.

49. Keynes, *Collected Writings*, 9:220–24.

50. Keynes, *Collected Writings*, 9:213–20.

51. Keynes, *Collected Writings*, 9:224.

52. D. H. Robertson, "A Narrative of the General Strike of 1926," *Economic Journal* 36, no. 143 (1926).

53. GFD Finaeon, "Great Britain Unemployment Rate (UNGBRM)." Global Financial Data, November 20, 2020, https://globalfinancialdata.com.

54. Grigg, *Prejudice and Judgment*, 180. Grigg, however, provides no source to ground this claim. All told, Churchill's abortive Gallipoli campaign inflicted half a million casualties.

55. Moggridge, *Return to Gold*, 71–76; Eichengreen, *Globalizing Capital*, 59–60.

56. Keynes, *Collected Writings*, 9:223.

57. Bertrand Russell cast "Keynes's intellect" as "the sharpest and clearest that I have ever known. When I argued with him, I felt that I took my life in my hands, and I seldom emerged without feeling something of a fool." Bertrand Russell, *Autobiography* (London: Routledge, 1998), 69.

58. Cheryl Schonhardt-Bailey, *From the Corn Laws to Free Trade: Interests, Ideas, and Institutions in Historical Perspective* (Cambridge, MA: MIT Press, 2006), 42.

## 17. Faith in History

1. Polanyi, *Great Transformation*, 26.

2. Moggridge, *British Monetary Policy*; Moggridge, *Return to Gold*; Eichengreen, *Golden Fetters*, 51; Simmons, *Who Adjusts*, 36–37; Ahamed, *Lords of Finance*, 220.

3. Kitson, *Bankers' Conspiracy*, 25.

4. Simmons, *Who Adjusts*, 11–12.

5. Brendan Chilton, "Trading on WTO Rules Will Be a Liberation for the UK—and the Labour Leadership Needs to Embrace It" (Brexit Central, 2019), https://brexit-central.com/trading-wto-rules-will-liberation-uk-labour-leadership-needs-embrace/.

6. Since becoming prime minister, Johnson's language has softened; but distrust prevails on both sides. George Parker and Daniel Thomas, "Boris Johnson Steps Up Campaign against Business Lobby," *Financial Times*, February 3, 2020.

7. Edmund Burke, "Speech to the Electors of Bristol [November 3, 1774]," in *The Political Tracts and Speeches of Edmund Burke* (Dublin, n.p.: 1777), 354.

8. Shakespeare, *Hamlet*, act 3, scene 2.

9. Keynes, *Collected Writings*, 6:274.

10. Due to contemporaries' own mangling of the timeline, this point has often been misunderstood.

11. Milton Friedman and Anna Jacobson Schwartz, *A Monetary History of the United States, 1867–1960* (Princeton, NJ: Princeton University Press, 2008), chapter 7.

12. Peter Walker, "Jacob Rees-Mogg: Hard Brexit Would Boost UK by £135bn over Five Years," *The Guardian*, November 14, 2017.

13. Parliamentary Debates, House of Commons, April 28, 1925, vol. 183, column 55.

14. The reference is to Churchill's "Finest Hour" speech. Parliamentary Debates, House of Commons, June 18, 1940, vol. 362, column 60.

15. Edmund Burke, *Reflections on the Revolution in France* (Buffalo, NY: Prometheus, 1987), 35; emphasis in original.

16. Cf. Herbert Butterfield, *The Whig Interpretation of History* (London: W. W. Norton & Co., 1965).

17. Thomas Jefferson, "Notes on Coinage," in *The Papers of Thomas Jefferson*, ed. Julian P. Boyd, vol. 7 (Princeton, NJ: Princeton University Press, 1953), 176.

18. Czar Peter the Great had decimalized the ruble a century before. But the trend gained international momentum following the American and then the French Revolutionary reforms.

19. Christopher Hope, "Return of Pounds and Ounces? Britain Might Allow Firms to Use Imperial Measures after Brexit," *The Telegraph*, February 18, 2017, https://www.telegraph.co.uk/news/2017/02/17/return-pounds-ounces-britain-might-allow-firms-use-imperial.

20. "The G20 Must Look beyond Bretton Woods II," *Financial Times*, November 7, 2020.

21. Patience Akumu and Annie Kelly, "Silence Far from Golden for Child Labourers in the Mines of Uganda," *The Guardian*, May 20, 2016.

22. Alfred Marshall, *Money, Credit, and Commerce* (London: Macmillan, 1923), 52.

23. Keynes, *Collected Writings*, 25:22.

24. Locke, *Further Considerations*, 458–63; Lowndes, *Report containing an Essay*, 56–57.

25. Kelly shows that Locke and Newton clashed over both the question of devaluation and the opportunity to serve as master of the mint. Locke prevailed on the former, but Newton secured the latter, with Locke left to take up a position on the Board of Trade. Patrick Hyde Kelly, "General Introduction," in *Locke on Money*, 23–29. In 1698, Locke used this position to stop the mint from continuing to overvalue gold (relative to silver). NA CO 389/16 September 20, 1698, to September 22, 1698. Locke resigned from the board in 1700 and died in 1704. Peter Laslett, "John Locke, the Great Recoinage, and the Origins of the Board of Trade: 1695–1698," *William and Mary Quarterly* 14, no. 3 (1957): 402.

26. This was true even three centuries ago: "Public securities are with us become a kind of money, and pass as readily at the current price as gold or silver. . . . No merchant thinks it necessary to keep by him any considerable cash. Bank-stock, or India-bonds, especially the latter, serve all the same purposes." David Hume, "Of Public Credit," in *Essays: Moral, Political, Literary*, ed. Eugene F. Miller (London: Liberty Fund, 1987), 353.

27. It is manifestly not true that "the market has always chosen gold." Llewellyn H. Rockwell Jr., Introduction to *The Gold Standard: Perspectives in the Austrian School*, ed. Llewellyn H. Rockwell Jr. (Auburn, AL: Ludwig von Mises Institute, 1992), x.

28. Jean-Jacques Rousseau, *Of the Social Contract or Principles of Political Right*, in *The Social Contract and Later Political Writings*, ed. Victor Gourevitch (Cambridge: Cambridge University Press, 1997), 53.

29. NA T 160/197/3, Schuster, "Currencies: Foreign and Our Own", April 30, 1924.

30. Grigg, *Prejudice and Judgment*, 183.

31. Skidelsky, *Economist as Saviour*, 192.

32. Schumpeter added some nuance to this position in a footnote. Schumpeter, *History of Economic Analysis*, 405–6.

33. Rockwell, introduction to *The Gold Standard*, xi.

34. Judy Shelton, *Money Meltdown* (New York: Free Press, 1994), 344. During her recent (February 2020) Senate nomination hearing, Shelton refused to defend her earlier views on the gold standard. Instead, she simply said multiple times, "It is important to acknowledge that the power to regulate the value of US money is granted to Congress by the Constitution, not to the Fed." Senate Committee on Banking, Housing, and Urban Affairs, *Nomination Hearing*, 116th Cong., 2nd Sess., February 13, 2020.

35. See Michael D. Bordo and Finn E. Kydland, "The Gold Standard As a Rule: An Essay in Exploration," *Explorations in Economic History* 32, no. 4 (1995): 423–64.

36. Keynes, *Collected Writings*, 4:65.

37. Since then, we have had a century's worth of advancement and refinement in this mode.

38. This might cast some doubt onto theoretical models that private banks efficiently optimize their note issuance. Lawrence Henry White, *Free Banking in Britain: Theory, Experience, and Debate, 1800–1845*, 2nd ed. (London: Institute of Economic Affairs, 1995). Of course, the Bank of England had effectively monopolized the issue of notes in England. But does not the theory predict that the monopolist central bank will tend to overissue its notes? Lawrence H. White, "Free Banking and the Gold

Standard," in *The Gold Standard: Perspectives in the Austrian School*, ed. Llewellyn H. Rockwell Jr. (Auburn, AL: Ludwig von Mises Institute, 1992), 122.

39. This is the same critique issued by Keynes of the Federal Reserve in 1923.

40. Holmes and Green, *Midland*, chapter 5.

41. If it had not been Norman at the Bank of England, it might have been Holden at Midland or perhaps Schuster at the National Provincial and Union Bank. Such bankers had long held that the Bank of England was in danger of being eclipsed by the increasingly large and powerful private banks. Roberts, *Saving the City*, 73–78.

42. Georg Simmel, *The Philosophy of Money*, 3rd ed., ed. David Frisby, trans. Tom Bottomore, David Frisby, and Kaethe Mengelberg (London: Routledge, 2004).

43. Simmel, *Philosophy of Money*, 296–97, 345, 347.

44. Locke, *Two Treatises of Government*, §§47–51.

45. Keynes, *Collected Writings*, 4:xvi–xvii. After a decade of failing to persuade policymakers and the public with his economic facts, he famously argued for the enduring power of old ideas against material interests at the end of the *General Theory*. Keynes, *Collected Writings*, 7:383–84. Had Keynes grappled with this innate racism, he might have seen this truth that much sooner. But those who are "modern" believe that they have transcended belief.

46. Hayek, *Counter-Revolution of Science*.

47. These shifts were pushed to their *reductio ad absurdum* in the form of the simple Phillips Curve and the Phillips Machine, the latter of which had economists working quite a bit like plumbers.

48. Given his particular role in the creation of the metallic standard, it needs to be said that Locke was not responsible for this. Richard Boyd, "The Calvinist Origins of Lockean Political Economy," *History of Political Thought* 23, no. 1 (2002): 31–60.

49. Marx, "On the Jewish Question," in *Karl Marx*, 57.

50. Marx, "Economic and Philosophical Manuscripts," in *Karl Marx*, 98; Marx, *The German Ideology*, 180.

51. Marx, "Towards a Critique of Hegel's *Philosophy of Right*," 72.

52. Karl Marx and Friedrich Engels, "The Communist Manifesto," in *Karl Marx*, 248. Perhaps the 1926 General Strike finally did force this reconciliation. Geographically, it did outgain the Paris Commune. But whatever lessons were learned were quickly forgotten by a population that, in 1931, returned the largest electoral mandate in British history to the government promising to restore the gold standard then as well.

53. In his 1924 memoir of Alfred Marshall, Keynes noted the extensive influence of religion and religious thinking on Cambridge in the nineteenth century. But of Marshall, Keynes noted that his "Cambridge career came just at the date which will . . . be regarded by the historians of opinion as the critical moment at which Christian dogma fell away from the serious philosophical world of England, or at any rate of Cambridge." Keynes, *Collected Writings*, 10:168. In an intellectual autobiography, Keynes later (in 1939) recanted the "superficiality" and "thin rationality" of "[His] Early Beliefs." Keynes, *Collected Writings*, vol. 10, chapter 39.

54. Marc Flandreau, *Money Doctors: The Experience of International Financial Advising 1850–2000* (New York: Routledge, 2003).

55. Keynes, *Collected Writings*, 2:24.

56. Consider Addis's formulation in January 1925 regarding the return to gold: "God willing." Likely, Addis did not expect that the conditions turned on divine inter-

vention of the sort that fills the Torah. But he did not believe that the ability to return was entirely within any human's control. NA T160/197/6, Norman and Addis, "Testimony," January 28, 1925.

57. Michel Foucault, "Governmentality," in *The Foucault Effect: Studies in Governmentality*, ed. Graham Burchell, Colin Gordon, and Peter Miller (Chicago: University of Chicago Press, 1991), 87–104.

58. As one country after another left the gold standard in the 1930s, Simons explained the task to his fellow economists in proto-Foucauldian terms: "To put our present problem as a paradox we need to design and establish with the greatest intelligence a monetary system good enough so that, hereafter, we may hold to it unrationally—on faith—as a religion, if you please. The utter inadequacy of the old gold standard, either as a definite system of rules or as the basis of a monetary religion, seems beyond intelligent dispute." Simons, "Rules versus Authorities in Monetary Policy," 14.

59. David Hume, *The Natural History of Religion* (London: A. H. Bradlaugh Bonner, 1899), 72–73.

60. Even Orwell's Winston recanted his "stubborn self-willed exile from the loving breast" in the end. Orwell, *Nineteen Eighty-Four*, 297.

61. Martin Feldstein, "An Interview with Paul Volcker," *Journal of Economic Perspectives* 27, no. 4 (2013): 107–8.

62. Cf. Karl Marx, "On the Jewish Question," 67–68.

# SOURCES AND BIBLIOGRAPHY

## Contemporary Published Reports

Bank of England. *Summary of Statistics for the United Kingdom: January, 1927*. London: Bank of England, 1927.

Committee on Currency and Foreign Exchanges after the War [Cunliffe Committee]. *First Interim Report*. Cd. 9182. London: His Majesty's Stationery Office. 1918.

Committee on Currency and Foreign Exchanges after the War [Cunliffe Committee]. *Final Report*. Cmd. 464. London: His Majesty's Stationery Office. 1919.

Committee on the Currency and Bank of England Note Issues [Chamberlain-Bradbury Committee]. *Report*. Cmd. 2393. London: His Majesty's Stationery Office. 1925.

Committee on Financial Facilities. *Report*. Cd. 9227. London: His Majesty's Stationery Office, 1918.

Cook, Charles, ed. *Defence of the Realm Manual, Revised to March 31st, 1919*. 7th ed. London: His Majesty's Stationery Office, 1919.

Trades Union Congress (TUC). *Annual Report*. London: Co-operative Printing Society, 1920–1925.

Trades Union Congress (TUC): Joint Committee on the Cost of Living. *Final Report on the Cost of Living*. London: Co-operative Printing Society, 1921.

Trades Union Congress (TUC): Joint Committee on the Cost of Living. *Interim Report on Money and Prices*. London: Co-operative Printing Society, 1920.

Trades Union Congress (TUC): Joint Committee on the Cost of Living. *Wages and Prices: A Reply to the Federation of British Industries*. London: Co-operative Printing Society, 1920.

## Newspapers and Periodicals

*British Gazette*
*Chicago Tribune*
*The Daily Telegraph*
*The Economist*
*Evening Standard*
*Financial Times*
*The Manchester Guardian / The Guardian*
*Nation and Athenaeum*
*New Statesman*

*The Observer*
*Saturday Review*
*Time*
*The Times [of London]*
*The Wall Street Journal*
*The Washington Herald*
*The Western Journal*


## Related Legislation

Act for the Encouragement of Trade, 1663 (15 Car. 2, c. 7).
Bank Charter Act, 1844 (7 & 8 Vict., c. 32).
Bank of England Act, 1694 (5 & 6 W. & M., c. 20).
Bank Notes (Scotland) Act, 1845 (8 & 9 Vict., c. 38).
Bankers (Ireland) Act, 1845 (8 & 9 Vict., c. 37).
Currency and Bank Notes Act, 1914 (4 & 5 Geo. 5, c. 14).
Currency and Bank Notes (Amendment) Act, 1914 (4 & 5 Geo. 5, c. 72).
Currency and Bank Notes Act, 1928 (18 & 19 Geo. 5, c. 13).
Defence of the Realm Act, 1914 (4 & 5 Geo. 5, c. 29).
Gold and Silver (Export Control, &c.) Act, 1920 (10 & 11 Geo. 5, c. 70).
Gold Standard Act, 1925 (15 & 16 Geo. 5, c. 29).
Government of Ireland Act, 1920 (10 & 11 Geo. 5, c. 67).
Termination of the Present War (Definition) Act, 1918 (8 & 9 Geo. 5, c. 59).


## Archival Sources

*Bank of England*

ADM 34/5. Diary of Montagu Collet Norman. 1917.
ADM 34/6. Diary of Montagu Collet Norman. 1918.
ADM 34/8. Diary of Montagu Collet Norman. 1919.
ADM 34/9. Diary of Montagu Collet Norman. 1920.
ADM 34/13. Diary of Montagu Collet Norman. 1924.
ADM 34/14. Diary of Montagu Collet Norman. 1925.
G4/140. Court of Directors: Minutes. March 29, 1917–March 21, 1918.
G4/141. Court of Directors: Minutes. March 28, 1918–March 20, 1919.
G4/142. Court of Directors: Minutes. March 27, 1919–March 25, 1920.
G4/146. Court of Directors: Minutes. April 26, 1923–March 20, 1924.
G8/53. Committee of Treasury: Minutes. July 29, 1914–May 3, 1918.
G8/54. Committee of Treasury: Minutes. May 8, 1918–February 15, 1922.
G8/55. Committee of Treasury: Minutes. February 22, 1922–July 30, 1924.
G8/56. Committee of Treasury: Minutes. August 6, 1924–April 21, 1926.
M7/156–159. *The Bank of England, 1914–1921*, by John Arundel Caulfeild Osborne
    (unpublished war history). 4 vols.

*Federal Reserve Bank of New York*

FRBNY 1116.4. Strong Papers. Correspondence with Montagu Norman, 1923–1924.
FRBNY C261.1. Foreign Files. Box 4, Folder 1: Bank of England Credit, 1925–1947.

*Papers of Sir Winston Churchill, Churchill College (Cambridge)*

CHAR 18/2. Chartwell Papers. Treasury. Correspondence from Churchill. November 9, 1924–December 30, 1924.
CHAR 22/143/10–12. Chartwell Papers. Cabinet. *British Gazette.* May 5, 1926–July 22, 1927.

*UK National Archives (NA)*

CAB 24/5/37. Cabinet Office. "Unemployment and the State of Trade. An Enquiry into the Question of Rehabilitating Trade and Providing Employment, Undertaken by the Minister of Reconstruction and National Service at the Request of the Prime Minister." March 14, 1919.
CAB 24/5/38. Cabinet Office. "Unemployment and the State of Trade." April 22, 1919.
CAB 24/75/20. Cabinet Office. "Unemployment and the State of Trade. Notes of a Conference Held at Downing Street on Monday, February 17, 1919."
CAB 24/75/87. Cabinet Office. "Unemployment and the State of Trade. Shorthand Notes of a Conference of Ministers at Downing Street on Tuesday, February 25, 1919."
CAB 27/71. Cabinet Office. "Finance: Minutes." 1919–1922.
CO 389/16. Colonial Office. "Board of Trade: Petitions, Correspondence, Reports, Orders in Council, etc." 1698–1700.
RECO 1/860. Ministry of Reconstruction. "Financial Facilities Committee: Minutes of Meetings, Memoranda, Notes on Foreign Banking Systems." 1917–1918.
T 160/197/2. Treasury. "Committee to Consider Currency, Note Issues and the Gold Standard." April 16, 1924–April 24, 1924.
T 160/197/3. Treasury. "Proceedings of Chamberlain-Bradbury Committee on Gold Standard and Amalgamation of Treasury Note Issue with Bank of England Issue." June 26, 1924–August 23, 1924.
T 160/197/4. Treasury. "Proceedings of Chamberlain-Bradbury Committee on Gold Standard and Amalgamation of Treasury Note Issue with Bank of England Issue." August 28, 1924–January 29, 1925.
T 160/197/5. Treasury. "Proceedings of Chamberlain-Bradbury Committee on Gold Standard and Amalgamation of Treasury Note Issue with Bank of England Issue." January 30, 1925–February 5, 1925.
T 160/197/6. Treasury. "Proceedings of Chamberlain-Bradbury Committee on Gold Standard and Amalgamation of Treasury Note Issue with Bank of England Issue; Evidence." June 27, 1924–July 1924.
T 160/197/7. Treasury. "Proceedings of Chamberlain-Bradbury Committee on Gold Standard and Amalgamation of Treasury Note Issue with Bank of England Issue; Evidence." July 1924.
T 160/197/8. Treasury. "Proceedings of Chamberlain-Bradbury Committee on Gold Standard and Amalgamation of Treasury Note Issue with Bank of England Issue; Evidence." July 1924–January 1925.
T 172/1384. Treasury. "Memorandum on 'Dear Money.'" 1919–1920.
T 172/1499B. Treasury. Chancellor of the Exchequer's Office: Miscellaneous papers. "Gold Standard; Treasury Memoranda." 1925–1927.

T 172/1500A. Treasury. "Gold Standard, 1925; American Credits." 1924–1929.

T 175/9. Treasury. Papers of Sir Richard Hopkins. "Proposed Return to the Gold Standard." 1925.

T 176/13. Treasury. Papers of Sir Otto Niemeyer. "Bank Rate." 1923–1930.

T 185/1. Treasury. Committee on Currency and Foreign Exchange (Cunliffe Committee): Minutes and Reports. "Minutes of meetings Numbers 1 to 19." 1918.

T 185/2. Treasury. Committee on Currency and Foreign Exchange (Cunliffe Committee): Minutes and Reports. "Minutes of meetings Numbers 20 to 34." 1918–1919.

T 185/3. Treasury. Committee on Currency and Foreign Exchange (Cunliffe Committee): Minutes and Reports. "Sub-Committee on Silver: Report and Evidence." November 6, 1919–December 3, 1919.

## Edited Collections

Keynes, John Maynard. *The Collected Writings of John Maynard Keynes*. Edited by Elizabeth Johnson and Donald Moggridge. London: Macmillan, 1971–1989.

Locke, John. *Locke on Money*. Edited by Patrick Hyde Kelly. Oxford: Clarendon Press, 1991.

Marx, Karl. *Karl Marx: Selected Writings*, 2nd ed. Edited by David McLellan. Oxford: Oxford University Press, 2000.

## General Bibliography

Adolph, Christopher. *Bankers, Bureaucrats, and Central Bank Politics: The Myth of Neutrality*. Cambridge: Cambridge University Press, 2013.

Ahamed, Liaquat. *Lords of Finance: The Bankers Who Broke the World*. London: Windmill Books, 2010.

Akerlof, George A., and Robert J. Shiller. *Animal Spirits: How Human Psychology Drives the Economy, and Why It Matters for Global Capitalism*. Princeton, NJ: Princeton University Press, 2010.

Alesina, Alberto, Vittorio Grilli, and Gian Maria Milesi-Ferrett. "The Political Economy of Capital Controls." National Bureau of Economic Research, Working Paper 4353, 1993. https://www.nber.org/papers/w4353.

Atkin, John. *The Foreign Exchange Market of London: Development since 1900*. New York: Routledge, 2004.

Bagehot, Walter. *Lombard Street: A Description of the Money Market*. New York: Scribner, Armstrong, 1873.

Bayoumi, Tamim and Michael Bordo. "Getting Pegged: Comparing the 1879 and 1925 Gold Resumptions." *Oxford Economic Papers* 50, no. 1 (1998): 122–149.

Beckert, Jens. *Imagined Futures: Fictional Expectations and Capitalist Dynamics*. Cambridge, MA: Harvard University Press, 2016.

Beckert, Jens, and Richard Bronk. *Uncertain Futures: Imaginaries, Narratives, and Calculation in the Economy*. Oxford: Oxford University Press, 2018.

——. "Uncertain Futures: Imaginaries, Narratives, and Calculation in the Economy." Watson Institute for International and Public Affairs, Brown University. October 24, 2019. https://youtu.be/FseT_EU-EbI.

Binder, Sarah, and Mark Spindel. *The Myth of Independence: How Congress Governs the Federal Reserve*. Princeton, NJ: Princeton University Press, 2017.

Blyth, Mark. *Austerity: The History of a Dangerous Idea*. New York: Oxford University Press, 2013.

——. *Great Transformations: Economic Ideas and Institutional Change in the Twentieth Century*. New York: Cambridge University Press, 2002.

——. "Structures Do Not Come with an Instruction Sheet: Interests, Ideas, and Progress in Political Science." *Perspective on Politics* 1, no. 4 (2003): 695–706.

Bordo, Michael D. "The Gold Standard: The Traditional Approach." In *A Retrospective on the Classical Gold Standard, 1821–1931*, edited by Michael D. Bordo and Anna J. Schwartz, 23–119. Chicago: University of Chicago Press, 1984.

Bordo, Michael D., and Finn E. Kydland. "The Gold Standard As a Rule: An Essay in Exploration." *Explorations in Economic History* 32, no. 4 (1995): 423–464.

Bordo, Michael D., and Hugh Rockoff. "The Gold Standard as a 'Good Housekeeping Seal of Approval.'" *Journal of Economic History* 56, no. 2 (1996): 389–428.

Boyce, Robert. *British Capitalism at the Crossroads, 1919–1932: A Study in Politics, Economics, and International Relations*. Cambridge: Cambridge University Press, 1987.

——. "Creating the Myth of Consensus: Public Opinion and Britain's Return to the Gold Standard in 1925." In *Money and Power: Essays in Honour of L. S. Pressnell*, edited by P. L. Cottrell and Donald Moggridge, 173–97. London: Palgrave Macmillan UK, 1988.

——. *The Great Interwar Crisis and the Collapse of Globalization*. New York: Palgrave Macmillan, 2009.

Boyd, Richard. "The Calvinist Origins of Lockean Political Economy." *History of Political Thought* 23, no. 1 (2002): 31–60.

Boyle, Andrew. *Montagu Norman: A Biography*. London: Cassell, 1967.

Bronk, Richard. *The Romantic Economist: Imagination in Economics*. Cambridge: Cambridge University Press, 2009.

Broz, Lawrence. "The Domestic Politics of International Monetary Order: The Gold Standard." In *Contested Social Orders and International Politics*, edited by David Skidmore, 53–84. Nashville: Vanderbilt University Press, 1997.

Burke, Edmund. *Reflections on the Revolution in France*. Buffalo, NY: Prometheus, 1987.

——. "Speech to the Electors of Bristol [November 3, 1774]." In *The Political Tracts and Speeches of Edmund Burke*, 347–55. Dublin: n.p., 1777.

Butterfield, Herbert. *The Whig Interpretation of History*. London: W. W. Norton & Co., 1965.

Byman, Daniel L., and Kenneth M. Pollack. "Let Us Now Praise Great Men: Bringing the Statesman Back In." *International Security* 25, no. 4 (2001): 107–46.

Cairncross, Sir Alec, and Barry Eichengreen. *Sterling in Decline: The Devaluations of 1931, 1949, and 1967*. Oxford, UK: Basil Blackwell, 1983.

Capie, Forrest, and Alan Webber. *A Monetary History of the United Kingdom: 1870–1982*. London: George Allen and Unwin, 1985.

Capoccia, Giovanni, and R. Daniel Kelemen. "The Study of Critical Junctures: Theory, Narrative, and Counterfactuals in Historical Institutionalism." *World Politics* 59, no. 3 (2007): 341–69.

Cartwright, Alan Patrick. *Gold Paved the Way: The Story of the Gold Fields Group of Companies*. London: Macmillan, 1967.

Chilton, Brendan. "Trading on WTO Rules Will Be a Liberation for the UK—and the Labour Leadership Needs to Embrace It." Brexit Central, 2019. https://brexitcentral.com/trading-wto-rules-will-liberation-uk-labour-leadership-needs-embrace/.

Chwieroth, Jeffrey M. *Capital Ideas: The IMF and the Rise of Financial Liberalization*. Princeton, NJ: Princeton University Press, 2009.

Clarke, Stephen V. O. *Central Bank Cooperation: 1924–31*. New York: Federal Reserve Bank of New York, 1967.

Clay, Henry. *Norman*. New York: Macmillan, 1957.

Costigliola, Frank C. "Anglo-American Financial Rivalry in the 1920s." *Journal of Economic History* 37, no. 4 (1977): 911–34.

Davenport-Hines, Richard. "Felix Otto Schuster." *Oxford Dictionary of National Biography*. Online. Oxford: Oxford University Press, 2010.

Desan, Christine. *Making Money: Coin, Currency, and the Coming of Capitalism*. Oxford: Oxford University Press, 2014.

Dickson, P. G. M. *The Financial Revolution in England: A Study in the Development of Public Credit, 1688–1756*. London: Macmillan, 1967.

Drezner, Daniel W. *The System Worked: How the World Stopped Another Great Depression*. New York: Oxford University Press, 2014.

Eichengreen, Barry. *Globalizing Capital: A History of the International Monetary System*. Princeton, NJ: Princeton University Press, 1998.

——. *Golden Fetters: The Gold Standard and the Great Depression, 1919–1939*. New York: Oxford University Press, 1992.

Eichengreen, Barry, and Marc Flandreau. Introduction to *The Gold Standard in Theory and History*. Edited by Barry Eichengreen and Marc Flandreau, 1–30. 2nd ed. London: Routledge, 1997.

Eichengreen, Barry, and Ricardo Hausmann. "Exchange Rates and Financial Fragility." National Bureau of Economic Research, Working Paper 7418, 1999. http://www.nber.org/papers/w7418.

Eichengreen, Barry, and Douglas Irwin. "The Slide to Protectionism in the Great Depression: Who Succumbed and Why?" *Journal of Economic History* 70, no. 4 (November 2010): 871–97.

Eichengreen, Barry, and Olivier Jeanne. "Currency Crisis and Unemployment: Sterling in 1931." In *Currency Crises*, edited by Paul Krugman, 7–43. Chicago: University of Chicago Press, 2000.

Eichengreen, Barry and Peter Temin. "Fetters of Gold and Paper." *Oxford Review of Economic Policy* 26, no. 3 (Autumn 2010): 370–384.

Einzig, Paul. *Montagu Norman: A Study in Financial Statesmanship*. London: Kegan Paul, Trench, Trubner and Company, 1932.

Feavearyear, Albert. *The Pound Sterling: A History of English Money*. 2nd ed. Oxford: Clarendon Press, 1963.

Feldstein, Martin. "An Interview with Paul Volcker." *Journal of Economic Perspectives* 27, no. 4 (2013): 105–20.

Ferguson, Niall. *The House of Rothschild: The World's Banker, 1849–1999*. London: Penguin, 2000.

"Finding Aid for 'Bank of Liverpool, 1831–1919.'" Archives Hub. November 20, 2020. https://archiveshub.jisc.ac.uk/data/gb2044-bb25/2.

Finnemore, Martha, and Kathryn Sikkink. "International Norm Dynamics and Political Change." *International Organization* 52, no. 4 (1998): 887–917.

Flanders, M. June. "A Model of Discretion: The Gold Standard in Fact and in Fiction." *World Economy* 16, no. 2 (1993): 213–35.

Flandreau, Marc. *Money Doctors: The Experience of International Financial Advising 1850–2000*. New York: Routledge, 2003.

Foucault, Michel. *Discipline and Punish: The Birth of the Prison*. 2nd ed. New York: Vintage, 1995.

——. "Governmentality." In *The Foucault Effect: Studies in Governmentality*, edited by Graham Burchell, Colin Gordon, and Peter Miller, 87–104. Chicago: University of Chicago Press, 1991.

——. *The History of Sexuality, Vol. 1: An Introduction*. New York: Vintage, 1990.

Frieden, Jeffry. "Exchange Rate Politics: Contemporary Lessons from American History." *Review of International Political Economy* 1, no. 1 (1994): 81–103.

——. *Global Capitalism: Its Fall and Rise in the Twentieth Century*. New York: W. W. Norton & Co., 2007.

Friedman, Milton. *Capitalism and Freedom*. Chicago: University of Chicago Press, 2002.

——. "The Case for Flexible Exchange Rates." In *Essays in Positive Economics*, 157–203. Chicago: University of Chicago Press, 1953.

Friedman, Milton, and Anna Jacobson Schwartz. *A Monetary History of the United States, 1867–1960*. Princeton, NJ: Princeton University Press, 2008.

GFD Finaeon. "British Pound to US Dollar Exchange Rate (GBPUSD)." Global Financial Data. November 20, 2020. https://globalfinancialdata.com.

——. "Great Britain Unemployment Rate (UNGBRM)." Global Financial Data. November 20, 2020. https://globalfinancialdata.com.

Ginzburg, Carlo. *The Cheese and the Worms: The Cosmos of a Sixteenth-Century Miller*. Baltimore: Johns Hopkins University Press, 1992.

Goldstein, Judith, and Robert O. Keohane. "Ideas and Foreign Policy: An Analytical Framework." In *Ideas and Foreign Policy: Beliefs, Institutions, and Political Change*, edited by Judith Goldstein and Robert O. Keohane, 3–30. Ithaca, NY: Cornell University Press, 1993.

Gowa, Joanne, and Raymond Hicks. "Commerce and Conflict: New Data about the Great War." *British Journal of Political Science* 47 (2017): 653–74.

Gray, Julia. *The Company States Keep: International Economic Organizations and Investor Perceptions*. Cambridge: Cambridge University Press, 2013.

Green, Edwin. "Edward Hopkinson Holden." *Oxford Dictionary of National Biography*. Online. Oxford: Oxford University Press, 2004.

Grieves, Keith. "James Lyle Mackay, First Earl of Inchcape." *Oxford Dictionary of National Biography*. Online. Oxford: Oxford University Press, 2008.

Grigg, P. J. *Prejudice and Judgment*. London: Jonathan Cape, 1948.

Haas, Peter M. "Introduction: Epistemic Communities and International Policy Coordination." *International Organization* 46, no. 1 (1992): 1–35.

Hall, Peter A. *The Political Power of Economic Ideas: Keynesianism across Nations*. Princeton, NJ: Princeton University Press, 1989.

Hamilton, Alexander. *The Works of Alexander Hamilton*. Edited by Henry Cabot Lodge. New York: G. P. Putnam's Sons, 1904.

Hargrave, John Gordon. *Professor Skinner, Alias Montagu Norman*. London: Wells Gardner, Darton & Co., 1939.

Hayek, Friedrich. "A Commodity Reserve Currency." *Economic Journal* 53, no. 210/211 (1943): 176–84.

——. *The Counter-Revolution of Science: Studies on the Abuse of Reason*. Glencoe, IL: Free Press, 1952.

——. "Interview with Leo Rosten, November 15, 1978." In *Nobel Prize-Winning Economist: Friedrich A. von Hayek*, 108–142. Los Angeles: Oral History Program, University of California, Los Angeles, 1983.

——. "The Use of Knowledge in Society." *American Economic Review* 35, no. 4 (1945): 519–30.

Helleiner, Eric. *The Making of National Money: Territorial Currencies in Historical Perspective*. Ithaca, NY: Cornell University Press, 2003.

Holmes, Anthony Ralph, and Edwin Green. *Midland: 150 Years of Banking Business*. London: BT Batsford, 1986.

Howson, Susan. *Domestic Monetary Management in Britain, 1919–1938*. Cambridge: Cambridge University Press, 1975.

Hume, David. *The Natural History of Religion*. London: A. H. Bradlaugh Bonner, 1899.

——. "Of the Balance of Trade." In *Essays: Moral, Political, Literary*, edited by Eugene F. Miller, 308–26. London: Liberty Fund, 1987.

——. "Of Money." In *Essays: Moral, Political, Literary*, edited by Eugene F. Miller, 281–94. London: Liberty Fund, 1987.

——. "Of Public Credit." In *Essays: Moral, Political, Literary*, edited by Eugene F. Miller, 349–65. London: Liberty Fund, 1987.

Ikenberry, G. John. *After Victory*. Princeton, NJ: Princeton University Press, 2001.

——. "Creating Yesterday's New World Order: Keynesian 'New Thinking' and the Anglo-American Postwar Settlement." In *Ideas and Foreign Policy: Beliefs, Institutions, and Political Change*, edited by Judith Goldstein and Robert O. Keohane, 57–86. Ithaca, NY: Cornell University Press, 1993.

James, Robert Rhodes. *Churchill: A Study in Failure, 1900–1939*. London: Weidenfeld & Nicolson, 1970.

Jefferson, Thomas. "Notes on Coinage." In *The Papers of Thomas Jefferson*, vol. 7, edited by Julian P. Boyd, 175–88. Princeton, NJ: Princeton University Press, 1953.

Kennedy, David M. *Freedom from Fear: The American People in Depression and War, 1929–1945*. Oxford: Oxford University Press, 1999.

Kindleberger, Charles P. *The World in Depression, 1929–1939*. Berkeley: University of California Press, 1986.

Kitson, Arthur. *The Bankers' Conspiracy! Which Started the World Crisis*. London: Elliot Stock, 1933.

Knight, Frank. *Risk, Uncertainty, and Profit*. Boston: Houghton Mifflin, 1921.

Krasner, Stephen D. "State Power and the Structure of International Trade." *World Politics* 28, no. 3 (1976): 317–47.

Kunz, Diane. *The Battle for Britain's Gold Standard in 1931*. Sydney: Croom Helm, 1987.

Kynaston, David. *The City of London*. Vol. 3, *Illusions of Gold, 1914–1945*. London: Pimlico, 2000.

———. *Till Time's Last Sand: A History of the Bank of England, 1694–2013*. London: Bloomsbury, 2017.

Laslett, Peter. "John Locke, the Great Recoinage, and the Origins of the Board of Trade: 1695–1698." *William and Mary Quarterly* 14, no. 3 (1957): 370–402.

Leith-Ross, Frederick. *Money Talks: Fifty Years of International Finance: The Autobiography of Sir Frederick Leith-Ross*. London: Hutchinson, 1968.

Lentin, Antony. "Lord Cunliffe, Lloyd George, Reparations, and Reputations at the Paris Peace Conference, 1919." *Diplomacy and Statecraft* 10, no. 1 (1999): 50–86.

Locke, John. *Two Treatises of Government*. Edited by Peter Laslett. 2nd ed. Cambridge: Cambridge University Press, 1967.

Lowndes, William. *A Report containing an Essay for the Amendment of the Silver Coins*. London, 1695.

Lubenow, William C. "Walter Leaf." *Oxford Dictionary of National Biography*. Online. Oxford: Oxford University Press, 2010.

Manchester, William. *The Last Lion: Winston Spencer Churchill: Visions of Glory, 1874–1932*. Boston: Little, Brown, and Company, 1983.

Marshall, Alfred. *Money, Credit, and Commerce*. London: Macmillan, 1923.

———. *Principles of Economics: An Introductory Volume*. 8th ed. London: Macmillan, 1920.

Mayhew, Nicholas. *Sterling: The History of a Currency*. New York: John Wiley & Sons, 2000.

Middlemas, Keith and John Barnes. *Baldwin: A Biography*. London: Weidenfeld & Nicolson, 1969.

McNamara, Kathleen R. *Currency of Ideas*. Ithaca, NY: Cornell University Press, 1998.

Moggridge, Donald. *British Monetary Policy 1924–1931: The Norman Conquest of $4.86*. New York: Cambridge University Press, 1972.

———. *Maynard Keynes: An Economist's Biography*. New York: Routledge, 1992.

———. "The 1931 Financial Crisis: A New View." *The Banker* 120, no. 534 (1970): 832–39.

———. *The Return to Gold, 1925: The Formulation of Economic Policy and Its Critics*. New York: Cambridge University Press, 1969.

Morgan, Mary S. *The World in the Model: How Economists Work And Think*. Cambridge: Cambridge University Press, 2012.

Morrison, James Ashley. "Before Hegemony: Adam Smith, American Independence, and the Origins of the First Era of Globalization." *International Organization* 66, no. 3 (July 2012): 395–428.

———. "Shocking Intellectual Austerity: The Role of Ideas in the Demise of the Gold Standard in Britain." *International Organization* 70, no. 1 (2016): 175–207.

Nelson, Stephen C. *The Currency of Confidence: How Economic Beliefs Shape the IMF's Relationship with its Borrowers*. Ithaca, NY: Cornell University Press, 2017.

Nelson, Stephen C., and Peter J. Katzenstein. "Uncertainty, Risk, and the Financial Crisis of 2008." *International Organization* 68, no. 2 (2014): 361–92.

Newman, Omarosa Manigault. *Unhinged: An Insider's Account of the Trump White House*. New York: Simon & Schuster, 2018.

Novak, William J. *The People's Welfare: Law and Regulation in Nineteenth-Century America*. Chapel Hill: University of North Carolina Press, 1996.

Oatley, Thomas. "How Constraining Is Capital Mobility? The Partisan Hypothesis in an Open Economy." *American Journal of Political Science* 43, no. 4 (1999): 1003–27.

Officer, Lawrence H. *Between the Sterling-Dollar Gold Points: Exchange Rates, Parity, and Market Behavior*. Cambridge: Cambridge University Press, 1996.

Orwell, George. *Animal Farm: A Fairy Story*. New York: Signet Classic, 1996.

——. *Nineteen Eighty-Four*. New York: Signet Classic, 1961.

——. *The Road to Wigan Pier*. London: Penguin, 2001.

Peden, G. C. *Keynes and His Critics: Treasury Responses to the Keynesian Revolution, 1925–1946*. Oxford: Oxford University Press, 2004.

——. *The Treasury and British Public Policy, 1906–1959*. Oxford: Oxford University Press, 2000.

Perkins, Anne. *A Very British Strike: 3 May–12 May 1926*. London: Macmillan, 2006.

Pigou, Arthur Cecil. "The Foreign Exchanges." *Quarterly Journal of Economics* 37, no. 1 (1922): 52–74.

——. "Some Problems of Foreign Exchange." *Economic Journal* 30, no. 120 (1920): 460–72.

Polanyi, Karl. *The Great Transformation*. Boston: Beacon Press, 2001.

Pollard, Sidney. Introduction to *The Gold Standard and Employment Policies between the Wars*, edited by Sidney Pollard, 1–26. London: Methuen, 1970.

Prior, Katherine. "Harris, George Robert Canning, Fourth Baron Harris." *Oxford Dictionary of National Biography*. Online. Oxford: Oxford University Press, 2006.

Roberts, Richard. *Saving the City: The Great Financial Crisis of 1914*. Oxford: Oxford University Press, 2013.

Robertson, D. H. "A Narrative of the General Strike of 1926." *Economic Journal* 36, no. 143 (1926): 375–393.

Rockwell Jr., Llewellyn H. Introduction to *The Gold Standard: Perspectives in the Austrian School*, edited by Llewellyn H. Rockwell Jr. Auburn, AL: Ludwig von Mises Institute, 1992.

Rogowski, Ronald. *Commerce and Coalitions: How Trade Affects Domestic Political Alignment*. Princeton, NJ: Princeton University Press, 1989.

Rousseau, Jean-Jacques. *Of the Social Contract or Principles of Political Right*. In *The Social Contract and Later Political Writings*, edited by Victor Gourevitch, 39–120. Cambridge: Cambridge University Press, 1997.

Ruggie, John Gerard. "International Regimes, Transactions, and Change: Embedded Liberalism in the Postwar Economic Order." *International Organization* 36, no. 2 (1982): 379–415.

Russell, Bertrand. *Autobiography*. London: Routledge, 1998.

Salerno, Joseph T. "Gold and the International Monetary System: The Contribution of Michael A. Heilperin." In *The Gold Standard: Perspectives in the Austrian School*, edited by Llewellyn H. Rockwell Jr., 81–112. Auburn, AL: Ludwig von Mises Institute, 1992.

Sargent, Thomas J., and François R. Velde. *The Big Problem of Small Change*. Princeton, NJ: Princeton University Press, 2003.

Saunders, Elizabeth N. *Leaders at War: How Presidents Shape Military Interventions*. Ithaca, NY: Cornell University Press, 2011.

Sayers, Richard. *The Bank of England, 1891–1944*. Cambridge: Cambridge University Press, 1976.

Scaramucci, Anthony. *Trump, the Blue-Collar President*. New York: Center Street, 2018.

Schacht, Hjalmar Horace Greeley. *My First Seventy-Six Years*. Translated by Diana Pyke. London: Allen Wingate, 1955.

Schmoller, Gustav. *The Mercantile System and Its Historical Significance Illustrated Chiefly from Prussian History*. New York: Macmillan, 1896.

Schonhardt-Bailey, Cheryl. *From the Corn Laws to Free Trade: Interests, Ideas, and Institutions in Historical Perspective*. Cambridge, MA: MIT Press, 2006.

Schumpeter, Joseph A. *History of Economic Analysis*. London: Routledge, 1954.

Scott, W. R., and John Maloney. "Nicholson, Joseph Shield." *Oxford Dictionary of National Biography*. Online. Oxford: Oxford University Press, 2004.

Seabrooke, Leonard. "The Everyday Social Sources of Economic Crises: From 'Great Frustrations' to 'Great Revelations' in Interwar Britain." *International Studies Quarterly* 1, no. 51 (2007): 795–810.

Semmel, Bernard. *The Rise of Free Trade Imperialism*. Cambridge: Cambridge University Press, 1970.

Shefftz, Melvin C. "The Trade Disputes and Trade Unions Act of 1927: The Aftermath of the General Strike." *Review of Politics* 29, no. 3 (1967): 387–406.

Shelton, Judy. *Money Meltdown*. New York: Free Press, 1994.

Shiller, Robert J. *Narrative Economics: How Stories Go Viral and Drive Major Economic Events*. Princeton, NJ: Princeton University Press, 2019.

Shrigley, Irene. *The Price of Gold: Documents Illustrating the Statutory Control through the Bank of England of the Market Price of Gold, 1694–1931*. London: P. S. King & Son, 1935.

Simmel, Georg. *The Philosophy of Money*. 3rd ed. Edited by David Frisby. Translated by Tom Bottomore, David Frisby, and Kaethe Mengelberg. London: Routledge, 2004.

Simmons, Beth A. *Who Adjusts? Domestic Sources of Foreign Economic Policy during the Interwar Years*. Princeton, NJ: Princeton University Press, 1994.

Simons, Henry C. "Rules versus Authorities in Monetary Policy." *Journal of Political Economy* 44, no. 1 (1936): 1–30.

Skidelsky, Robert. *John Maynard Keynes*. Vol. 1, *Hopes Betrayed, 1883–1920*. London: Macmillan, 1983.

——. *John Maynard Keynes*. Vol. 2, *The Economist as Saviour, 1920–1937*. London: Macmillan, 1992.

Smith, Adam. *An Inquiry into the Nature and Causes of the Wealth of Nations*. Edited by R. H. Campbell, Andrew S. Skinner, and W. B. Todd. Indianapolis: Liberty Classics, 1981.

——. *The Theory of Moral Sentiments*. Indianapolis: Liberty Fund, 1984.

Stearn, Roger T. "Simpson, Sir John Hope." *Oxford Dictionary of National Biography*. Online. Oxford: Oxford University Press, 2012.

Steil, Benn. *The Battle of Bretton Woods: John Maynard Keynes, Harry Dexter White, and the Making of a New World Order*. Princeton, NJ: Princeton University Press, 2013.

Steinberg, David A. *Demanding Devaluation: Exchange Rate Politics in the Developing World*. Ithaca, NY: Cornell University Press, 2015.

Tilly, Charles. *Coercion, Capital, and European States, AD 990–1990*. Cambridge: Basil Blackwell, 1992.

Tucker, Paul. *Unelected Power: The Quest for Legitimacy in Central Banking and the Regulatory State*. Princeton, NJ: Princeton University Press, 2018.

US Congress. Senate. Committee on Banking, Housing, and Urban Affairs. *Nomination Hearing*. 116th Cong., 2nd Sess., February 13, 2020.

US Federal Reserve. *Banking and Monetary Statistics: 1914–1941*. Washington: Board of Governors of the Federal Reserve System, 1976.

White, Lawrence H. "Free Banking and the Gold Standard." In *The Gold Standard: Perspectives in the Austrian School*, edited by Llewellyn H. Rockwell Jr., 113–128. Auburn, AL: Ludwig von Mises Institute, 1992.

——. *Free Banking in Britain: Theory, Experience, and Debate, 1800–1845*. 2nd ed. London: Institute of Economic Affairs, 1995.

Widmaier, Wesley W., Mark Blyth, and Leonard Seabrooke. "Exogenous Shocks or Endogenous Constructions? The Meanings of Wars and Crises." *International Studies Quarterly* 51, no. 4 (November 2007): 747–59.

Williamson, Philip. "A 'Bankers' Ramp'? Financiers and the British Political Crisis of August 1931." *English Historical Review* 99, no. 393 (1984): 770–806.

——. *National Crisis and National Government: British Politics, the Economy, and Empire, 1926–1932*. Cambridge: Cambridge University Press, 2003.

——. *Stanley Baldwin: Conservative Leadership and National Values*. Cambridge: Cambridge University Press, 1999.

Wolff, Michael. *Fire and Fury*. London: Hachette UK, 2018.

Zarakol, Ayşe. *After Defeat: How the East Learned to Live with the West*. Cambridge: Cambridge University Press, 2011.

# INDEX

Page numbers in *italics* refer to tables.